Modern Applied Economics

260 - 264 , 423 - 24 · The multiplier

264 - 268 - Demand Management

Policy.

Modern Applied Economics

A Problem-oriented Approach to Economic Theory

Ken Heather
University of Portsmouth

HARVESTER
WHEATSHEAF

New York London Toronto Sydney Tokyo Singapore

First published 1994 by
Harvester Wheatsheaf
Campus 400, Maylands Avenue
Hemel Hempstead
Hertfordshire, HP2 7EZ
A division of
Simon & Schuster International Group

Typeset in 10/12pt Meridien
by P&R Typesetters Ltd, Salisbury

Printed and bound in Great Britain by
Redwood Books, Trowbridge, Wiltshire

British Library Cataloguing in Publication Data

A catalogue record for this book is available from
The British Library

ISBN 0-7450-1465-8

1 2 3 4 5   98 97 96 95 94

To Sally, James, Simon and Catherine

Contents

3 Traffic jams: could Britain import a solution from Singapore? 44

4 The National Health Service: is radical treatment needed? 65

10 Government spending: do we get value for money? (with David Bibby) *189*

Efficiency
Public goods

11 Trade unions: labour market manipulators? (with Rob Thomas) *209*

The demand for labour
Wage rate determination

Preface

Economics is a fascinating area of study. Since it deals with important issues that have such an effect upon all of us, it is of immediate interest. Nevertheless, it is not an easy subject. The economic problems that confront society require analysis, not simply description, and that means getting to grips with economic theory.

Now it is possible to confront the world of economic theory and to lose sight of how that theory can be used to tackle issues that appear to confront society, traffic jams, the state of the National Health Service, recessions and so on. As a result, several books have become available in recent years which consider current issues using economic analysis.

However, this book is not simply a list of topics of applied economic analysis. It sets out to address a series of issues of current concern, but in a particular order. The great majority of economics courses and textbooks follows a particular order in building up an understanding of economic analysis. The choice of applied topics in this text follows that development. It is therefore possible to study economic theory and to find in this book how each of these main areas of theory can be used to shed immediate light on real world issues. In studying this book, then, the student will not learn everything there is to know about economic theory nor about every economic issue facing society. What the student will do is gain a good grasp of all the major analytical tools of introductory economic analysis and see how they can be used. It should then be possible to approach other topics of interest and analyse them because the student has begun to think like an economist, and has learned to apply economic analysis to real problems.

This book, then, not only explains the tools of economic analysis, it teaches the *use* of that analysis.

A word to the student

Welcome to economics! I hope you feel excited about embarking on your studies. But you may be feeling nervous too. This book is for you. You can learn much, but at a pace to calm your nerves. Before you tackle the book I want to offer you four pieces of advice. The advice applies to studying economics in general, but it relates particularly to the use of this book.

1 *Read each chapter in the correct order.* It is best not to find and immediately read about an issue in which you are particularly interested. Each chapter not only introduces ideas in economic theory but also uses concepts already met. You will be able to build up your understanding by tackling the topics in the set order. If you read the chapters out of sequence you are likely to find the topics more difficult.

2 *Read each chapter slowly and actively.* No chapter is very long. You should not feel the need to rush. Have a pen and paper with you. Make brief notes on what you read and draw the diagrams for yourself as you come to them. It will fix things in your mind so much better if you do that. When you are referred to tables of data, take time to absorb the information they convey. If there is anything you do not understand, you need to do something about it in one of two ways. First, you can refer to the Further Reading section given at the end of each chapter. This includes reading on the theoretical topics covered and further reading on the particular issue that the chapter is examining.

   The second way in which you can help yourself, if you have a difficulty, is to ask someone else. Try talking to a fellow student. If that does not resolve the problem, raise the matter with your tutor, but do not leave it unresolved. The next concept will be understandable if you have grasped the previous one. It probably will not be if you have not made sure of what has gone before.

3 *Give time to the questions for discussion at the end of each chapter.* They are a vital part of the learning process. You may be studying on a course where the classes will revolve around these questions. It is vital that you prepare! Then take part in the discussion. It will be enormously beneficial. You may be nervous to hear the sound of your own voice in a classroom context, but you will be well rewarded if you can overcome that fear. If your contribution is correct and valid, it will give you confidence. If it is wrong because you have

misunderstood something, then that will be put right and you will have gained by improving your understanding. One way or another, if you contribute orally, you must gain.

If you are on a course where these questions will not be the basis of class discussion, then form your own study group and go through them together. The time will not be wasted.

4 *Do not imagine that, when you have studied a topic, you know all there is to know about it.* However much you study, there are always further insights to be gained. In this book you are being introduced to real world problems very early on. So remember that ideas that come later in the course will throw additional light on topics met previously. It will be valuable if you can apply the ideas you meet, not only to the question in hand, but also to topics encountered earlier.

By taking a sensible approach to the use of this book, you are sure to come to the end of it having made a substantial beginning to the process of thinking like an economist.

Outline of contents

Economics is often divided into two, micro-economics and macro-economics. Micro-economics is the basis of the first half of the book. It deals with individual markets. Macro-economics, the second half of the book, deals with the broad aggregates of the economy. So micro will examine the establishment of the price of a particular good or service, for example shares in Chapter 2. Macro deals with the overall economy, for example the general price level in Chapter 17. Micro analyses a particular market, for example the coal industry in Chapter 7. Macro will consider a whole sector, for example the manufacturing sector and its relationship to the balance of payments in Chapter 19.

The contents pages will tell you what topics are covered and what concepts are introduced to examine them. But it is important to realise that these are only the new concepts introduced. Later chapters will pick up and utilise concepts met in earlier chapters. In particular, when dealing with macro-economic topics, much use is made of the micro principles already analysed.

By the time you come to the end of the book, you will not have all the answers to all economic problems. However, you should know what the major problems are, and you should be in a position to engage in intelligent debate about any of them.

Further reading

At the end of each chapter there is suggested further reading. There are many books to which the student could usefully refer, but for illustrative purposes reference is made to three widely used introductory economics texts. They are:

J. Sloman (1994) *Economics*, 2nd edn, Harvester Wheatsheaf, (referred to as 'Sloman').

D. Begg, S. Fischer and R. Dornbusch (1994) *Economics*, 4th edn, McGraw-Hill, (referred to as 'Begg').

M. Parkin and D. King (1992) *Economics*, Addison Wesley (referred to as 'Parkin and King').

Additional reading on the particular topic discussed in each chapter is also given.

Appendix 1 also gives a list of readily available sources of applied economics material. Again many sources could be listed, but the appendix is confined to what are the most helpful for the study of the subject at an introductory level.

Self-help disk

Each chapter of the book introduces the student to economic concepts in the context of one or two specific real world problems. However, the ideas have wide applicability. The purpose of the self-testing disk is to enable the student to test that he/she has a clear grasp of these principles by tackling multiple choice questions. There are 300 questions, 15 to cover the material from each of the 20 chapters of the book. They are designed to help the student use the concepts in other contexts. Instructions on how to use the questions are provided on the disk. No knowledge of computing skills is needed, but a PC-compatible machine with a hard drive and a monitor with VGA graphics capabilities is required to run the software. $3\frac{1}{2}''$ disk is available to purchasers of the book for £9.95, including post and packing. Alternatively, a disk and a site licence is available to institutions for £300. Send a cheque for £9.95 for each disk required (or £300 for the disk plus site licence), made payable to J. Heather, and the form provided at the back of the book to: Economics disk offer, J. Heather, 2 Airlie Road, Winchester, Hants, SO22 4NQ.

A word to the instructor

This text has been designed to offer maximum flexibility. It can be used in many different ways.

1 The questions for discussion are designed to be the basis of a seminar programme. Each week the student can read the material, prepare answers to the questions and bring them to the seminar/class. Students will be enthusiastic. Although much of the discussion will revolve around formal concepts they will be related to a topic of current interest. The chapter they have read will have given them ideas on how to apply principles to such topics – the very thing which students find hardest.

   The questions for discussion can be covered in a class in around one hour. One chapter per week will probably be about right. You may well have slightly more than twenty weeks available but you will probably need these for other purposes as well – going over essays, working on multiple choice exercises, dealing with problems raised by students, and so on. But for most weeks the book will serve as a ready-made seminar programme. This may be of particular value on large courses where different people are involved as leaders of different classes. The book will serve as an integrating device ensuring similar coverage for all class groups.

   If classes/seminars meet less often, you could go through some material in formal class groups and encourage the formation of self-help study groups to work through the rest of it.

2 The book is designed to be used as the main textbook, particularly if the instructor wishes to concentrate his/her lecturing/teaching on theoretical issues. The theory can then be expanded upon as necessary. The main elements of the theory and its relationship to the real world can be left to this book, preferably with discussion groups as suggested above. This may well be a particularly suitable approach to introductory economics courses on professional/business type courses.

3 The book could be used, perhaps with a more theoretical text, on non-specialist courses, over a period of either one or even two years. At the end of each section of theoretical analysis a chapter could be used as a point of reference to revise the main elements covered as well as to see its application in the world.

A chapter would then be read less often than once per week, but would be a high point of the course every two or three weeks.

4 In addition to the above, the questions for discussion can be used as the basis of written assessed work. One could select a question as an essay title. Often the last one will be the best for this purpose. Alternatively, short answers to all the questions can be requested. It can work well if students bring their answers for submission at the end of class, knowing that they can use what they have written as notes when they are called upon to contribute in the class.

In whatever way you choose to use it, the theory supporting the topics follows a standard traditional order so it can be used as a stand-alone text or in conjunction with other books if required. It can also be used without alteration to your existing economics course.

Solutions manual

An increasing problem for instructors is shortage of time. In using this book there will be costs involved in finding time to work through the questions. To save this time, a solutions manual is available from the publishers free to adopters. The solutions manual gives suggested outline answers to the questions raised in the Questions for Discussion sections. The result is that a complete tutorial package is now available – reading material, discussion material and material for instructors to guide discussion, although, of course, some instructors may prefer to work through the questions and prepare their own answers. The self-help disk will also prove invaluable since it enables the student to work through a set of exercises without reference to a tutor.

Acknowledgements

I have received much help in writing this book and I wish to record my sincere thanks to those involved.

First, I must thank, Dave Bibby and Rob Thomas, each of whom co-authored a chapter with me, and Michael Asteris who shared in the writing of two chapters. Others kindly commented most helpfully on earlier drafts. To John Thomson and John Craven, who made many constructive criticisms of the whole script, and to Pat Cooper, Sandy Smith and Dave Bibby, who commented on parts of it, I am most grateful. Pat and Dave in particular spent time with me, helping me sort out my thinking on several issues. It is a better book because of this help, but I take full responsibility for any errors and ambiguities that remain.

Since this is an applied text, I have used many sources of data. I would like to offer my thanks to those who gave permission to reproduce material for use in this book. My thanks are also due to the office staff of the Portsmouth Business School, particularly for help with some of the typing. My handwriting is not of the very best. I would particularly like to thank Jane Marchant for the high quality of her skills in deciphering my handwriting. Writing a book consumes a great deal of time and energy. Pradeep Jethi of Harvester Wheatsheaf has done a splendid job, encouraging me to keep going, and showing patience with my many frailties.

I am conscious that I owe a great debt to my delightful family in many ways. In the production of this book James has been a tremendous help to me through his computing and word processing skills. Simon wrote Appendix 3 for me and made many suggestions for improvement in several chapters. Sally and Catherine listened to me trying to explain ideas and supplied me with endless snacks and cups of coffee.

Finally, I wish to record my great gratitude to generations of my ex-students, who helped to sharpen my thinking on many issues. I have fond memories of so many of them, especially the few who still write to me. We discovered that learning economics together can be, at the same time, hard work and a lot of fun.

Further editions

I hope it will be possible to produce further editions of this text. To that end I would be glad to receive any written correspondence at the University of

Portsmouth with constructive criticisms or suggestions for improvements. Meanwhile, enjoy your studies!

University of Portsmouth, Spring 1994

CHAPTER 1

Eastern European economic reforms: *the road to freedom?*

During the 1990s the old USSR and its now independent satellite states have tried to move their economic system to a Western 'market-based' economy – so far with limited success. The transition has proved costly and difficult.

In this chapter we explain why this is so, introducing the following concepts:
- Economic models
- Resources and opportunity cost
- Market and planned economies

1 Introduction

When the old Soviet Union fell apart in the late 1980s and early 1990s, the way was open for its former communities to form independent governments. Most of the leaders of these newly independent countries wasted no time in declaring that they wished to transform their economic systems into Western-style ones. It was clear that the bureaucratic centralised approach in which they had been obliged to operate had failed. Average incomes were only a fraction of those enjoyed in the West. The intention, therefore, was to introduce a Western-style market economy. This would give far greater efficiency in production and lead rapidly to improvements in living standards.

Despite some significant changes in former Soviet controlled states, this simply has not happened. Take, for example, Romania. The communist regime of President Ceausescu disappeared in December 1989. The elected government of May 1990 began quickly to change the direction of its economic policies and by the end of that year it had ended price controls on half its prices. But Table 1.1 below gives a depressing picture of the state of the economy thereafter.

Let us make sure that we understand the meaning of the terms given in Table 1.1. Real *gross domestic product* (GDP) means essentially the amount of output of goods and services the country is producing. The change is negative – output was falling! This is typical of such countries, as we will see shortly. Consumer prices give us a measure of what is happening to the general level of prices faced by consumers. Clearly these prices were rising sharply. In other words there has been inflation. More than that, the rate at which those prices were rising accelerated remarkably. Average real wages measure what is happening to peoples' wages relative to the price level. Since 1990 the average Romanian wage has bought *less*

Table 1.1 Selected economic indicators in Romania

	Percentage changes		
	1989	*1990*	*1991*
Real gross domestic product	−5.8	−7.6	−13.7
Consumer prices	0.9	4.7	161.1
Average real wages	3.1	5.6	−14.2
Gross external debt	0.8	0.9	1.8

Source: International Monetary Fund (IMF) *Survey.*

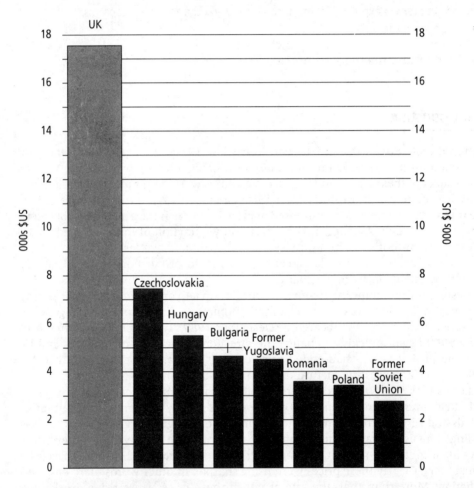

Source : Mintel Report, The Eastern European Consumer.

Figure 1.1 Comparative living standards in Eastern Europe, 1991 (estimated GDP per capita)

than it did during the communist regime. *Gross external debt* is a measure of the extent to which a community owes money to foreigners. The Romania debt is rising.[1] In other words, after the period of reforms had started, all these indicators of economic activity were moving in the direction opposite to what might have been hoped. Other economies of this kind present a similar picture. Figure 1.1 gives a clear indication of the low living standards in many of these economies in the early post-communist era.

One obvious explanation of the fall in living standards and output is seen in Table 1.1. Unemployment has been rising rapidly, and you may be surprised by the data relating to it. Why was it so low in 1989? Why did it increase so rapidly after that time?

Why has such a depressing picture emerged? By the end of this chapter you should have gained some insights into the reasons. However, it is necessary that you first understand the approach economists usually take in examining such problems. Indeed, you will find this approach often in this book, so you will need to be clear about it at the outset. Economists deal with problems by constructing economic 'models'. Let us see what is meant by this.

2 The use of economic models

When economists wish to examine a problem, they have difficulties not faced by physical scientists. One such difficulty is that they cannot make experiments under controlled laboratory conditions. It is not possible to shake people and prices around in a test tube to see how they react.

It is, however, possible to gain an insight into the main economic relationships that exist by the construction of an 'economic model'. Suppose we make a model railway engine. It may not be the real thing, but by concentrating on the main features of the real thing we can reproduce something which is clearly recognisable as such. We can also play around with the model, increasing our understanding of how the real one works, and we can experiment by altering certain parts inside and seeing what effect it produces. This may enable us to discover what would happen without having to experiment on the real thing. The same is true in principle of constructing an *economic* model. By making certain simplifying assumptions about the world we can concentrate on the essential features of economic relationships to see how they interact.

It may seem at first to be unrealistic to ignore features of the world which are really there, but we are not trying to explain every detail, merely to establish the major relationships, such that what we have is recognisable as an explanation of the way in which economic society can be ordered. We can also then predict what will happen if we make certain changes. Just as we can change the size of piston in a model railway engine to see whether it goes faster or slower, so we can use our economic model to see what effect there will be on the economy because of, say, changes in taxation. Unlike the railway engine, though, our model of the economy is not something tangible. It exists only in the mind or on paper. Furthermore, people are not machines. This makes them less predictable. Nevertheless, a model can be a useful and powerful tool to analyse the real world of economic relationships.

When we have worked through our conclusions from the model, we can test whether we have got it right by looking at available economic data. Thus, we have an interaction between observing data and formulating hypotheses. In terms of Table 1.1 we should be able to construct a model that can offer an explanation of the data. However, it will be a very simple one at the moment given our, as yet, limited understanding of economics. If the model 'fits' it will give us confidence to use the model to make predictions about the future. This process of constructing models is something you will observe often as you study economics. Sometimes a model appears to fit very well, but at a later time not so well. Other models are then put forward. Sometimes different economists come to different conclusions about the way an economy operates. This is because they arc using different models as tools for explaining data. You will find, as you progress in your studies, that some economic models are widely accepted by most economists. Others are the subject of considerable controversy.

Let us now begin to construct a model to show how an economy can find itself in the kind of difficulties described in Table 1.1.

3 Beginning to construct a model

a Resources in economics

Micro-economics is all about choice. The essence of choice is that in the selection of one thing we have decided to go without another. This is sometimes called the 'economic problem'. Man's wants are unlimited. There are basic needs of food, clothing, shelter, health, and so on, but there are also desires for education, travel, entertainment, books – a seemingly endless list of possibilities presents itself to the mind. The discontent of a population with far less of these things than many Western economies was a driving force for reform in Eastern Europe.

But resources necessary for the production of these goods and services are limited. Hence there is no possibility of a level of output that is anything but finite, whereas needs and wants are infinite. Clearly, then, society must make choices about which kinds of output it wants to use its resources to produce. The resources, or factors of production, available to society can conveniently be divided into four main categories.

First, there is *labour*. Some people have the ability to make things; others have the mental ability to work out how to make them. So, for example, one person may think of how to design a machine for making knitting needles, while another may make the machine itself from instructions. But both are involved in making output. They are therefore a 'resource' and since the population is limited, a finite resource. Over time this resource that we call labour may increase. For example, if the birth rate is sufficiently high and the death rate sufficiently low, or if there is immigration, the labour supply will increase. However, at any moment in time labour supply is finite. Hence the amount of output that labour can produce for satisfying society's wants is similarly finite.

Second, there is *capital*. Capital is a manufactured resource. Factories, machinery, office buildings are all examples of capital. At first this may not seem to be a finite resource. One could always build more buses or police stations! While this is true, at any moment in time there is a limit to the amount available. Even if a society chooses to have more of such capital goods, it must then have less of something else. If we increase the capital stock over time, we call this act investment. But at any given moment the volume of capital is limited. This is particularly noticeable in Eastern Europe where so many machines are antiquated and buildings are in poor condition. The extent to which Eastern European economies were investing during the late 1980s and early 1990s can be seen in Table 1.2. It shows how the proportion of their output set aside for additions to the capital stock was actually declining. These figures are 'gross'. This means all additions to capital, whether replacing what was worn out, or adding to the stock. Since much of the capital was wearing out, it suggests that these societies were not creating a great deal of new capital. However, even in Western economies, where the capital stock is much higher, the supply of capital is still not infinite.

Third, there is *land*. This is most obviously the resource that is limited. Apart from small land reclamation schemes, notably in Holland, the amount of land available is clearly limited, though for what was previously the USSR the amount of land is vast.

Finally, there are other natural resources. These include, for example, fish stocks, coal seams and oil deposits. Siberia, for example, has enormous oil and mineral wealth, as yet largely unused. Increasingly, media attention has been focused on the view that many of these resources are non-renewable. When oil

Table 1.2 Investment in Eastern European economies

| Countries | Gross fixed investment | | | | |
| | As a percentage of GDP | | | | |
	1988	1989	1990	1991[1]	1992[2]
Bulgaria	26.1	25.2	20.4	11.3	13
Czechoslovakia	25.2	25.1	25.0	18.2	20
Hungary	21.0	19.9	17.8	17.8	18
Poland	22.5	16.4	19.1	19.6	19
Romania	28.0	29.6	20.0	13.1	13
Slovenia	20.1[2]	19.1[2]	18.0	18.9	17

Notes: [1] partly estimated; [2] estimated.
Source: Bank for International Settlements (BIS) *Annual Report*, 1993.

has been burned for heating, it cannot be used again, although presumably there are, as yet, undiscovered oil reserves. The same is true of other resources. Even though there are resources as yet untapped, such as wave power and deep-sea mineral deposits, there is a limited amount available since we live in a finite world. Furthermore, they are only exploitable with investment. Certainly there is a limited amount of such resources which society can use at any given moment.[2]

Now, whatever the society – whether it is the wealthiest nation on earth, or a relatively poor one such as Romania, or a desperately poor one such as Ethiopia – each has resources; none has an infinite amount of them. They all have to make choices.

b The concept of opportunity cost

Clearly, then, the finite value of resources means that one must make choices. We may like more accountants and more doctors but one person cannot be both at the same time. Romania might like more orphanages and more hospitals, but any one building can be used for only one of these purposes. Society must choose how it wishes to use that capital. Similarly we might like more food and more roads but we shall have to choose to which use we wish to put a given piece of land. The same choice confronts us with natural resources. Oil, for example, is something we can use to heat people's homes or to lubricate motor engines but the same barrel of oil cannot do both tasks.

The economist expresses this idea in terms of a concept called 'opportunity cost'. Since to make some given output we must commit some limited resources that have an alternative use, the next best alternative that has to be foregone is called the opportunity cost of its production. Suppose a man is an economist and he then changes his job and becomes a policeman. The services of protection of people and property that he produces are only provided at the opportunity cost of the services of an economist. The economist's services must be foregone in order to have the services of the policeman. The principle of opportunity cost applies to all factors of production, not just labour.[3]

c An opportunity cost curve

The concept of opportunity cost curve can be illustrated in a diagram. Figure 1.2 below shows the position for the economy of Anyland. We shall use this name as a reminder that although different economies have different resources and different *amounts* of resources, the principles of opportunity cost will apply to *any* economy. Only two goods can be produced each year – here guns and butter.[4] Given that the resources available to the nation are limited, it must decide how best to employ its resources. For example, it could decide to use all its resources to produce guns. Society would then have all guns and no butter, a position described by point X. Alternatively, all the economy's resources could be devoted to the production of butter. It would then have a certain output of butter per

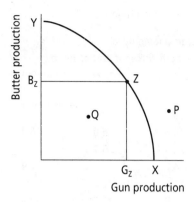

Figure 1.2   Production possibility curve: Anyland

annum but zero guns; a position described by point Y. Suppose, however, Anyland wanted both guns and butter. By devoting some of its resources to each of these goods, it could produce at say, point Z, where it could enjoy, per annum, G_z guns and B_z butter. The line between X and Y would then describe all the different combinations of guns and butter that could be available to Anyland at any given time. Our society would have to decide which of these combinations it would prefer. In other words, it must choose which point on the curve it would most like to be. Since the curve describes the possibilities open to an economy during the course of a year, we sometimes call the line a 'production-possibility frontier'. A point outside the frontier such as P is unavailable to Anyland given its limited volume of resources. It is unable to produce such a level of output. Position Q, on the other hand, would indicate that some resources are not being used efficiently. It would be possible to have more of both goods. The problem then is either one of unemployment or that all resources are being used but some are being used inefficiently. Where this is the case, the opportunity cost of increasing output is nil.

Now look at Table 1.3. You will see how the unemployment situation appeared to worsen markedly as Eastern Europe changed its economic system. Why were unemployment rates so low in the days before Eastern Europe began moving to a market economy? A significant part of the answer is this: everyone had a job. However, much of it was what we might call disguised unemployment. Several people were employed to do a job which one could do. The shift to a market economy uncovered this disguised unemployment. These societies were inside the opportunity cost curve in 1989, although the data showed virtually no unemployment.

d Resources and increasing opportunity cost

Why is the line between X and Y not straight? Why does it curve outwards from the origin? The answer is to be found in the nature of resources. Suppose Anyland

Table 1.3 Unemployment in selected East European countries (percentages)

Countries	Unemployment rate (officially registered unemployed) As a percentage of the labour force, at end of period				
	1989	1990	1991	1992	1993 Q1[1]
Albania	1.9	2.1	5.1	12.5[2]	–
Bulgaria	0.0	1.5	10.8	15.6	16.0
Czechoslovakia	0.0	1.0	6.6	5.1	–
Czech Republic	0.0	0.6	4.1	2.6	2.9
Slovak Republic	0.0	1.6	11.8	10.4	12.0
Hungary	0.4	1.9	7.5	12.3	13.4
Poland	0.1	6.3	11.8	13.6	14.2
Romania	0.0	0.4	3.0	8.4	9.6
Russia	0.0	0.0	0.1	1.4	–
Slovenia	2.9	4.7	10.1	13.4	13.5

Note: [1] Q1 = first quarter; [2] Estimated.
Source: Bank for International Settlements (BIS), *Annual Report*, 1993.

is now producing all guns and no butter – it is at point X. Its citizens then decide they would like some butter for next year. Clearly, there is an opportunity cost involved. Since all its factors of production are already being used, resources must be transferred from gun production to butter production. Therefore the butter output will only be achieved at the sacrifice of some gun output. However, since all Anyland's resources are at present engaged in gun making, only some resources need to be transferred. Obviously, the best resources to be transferred are resources least suited to producing guns and most suited to producing butter. So, for instance, if we take cows out of gun making, the loss of gun output to Anyland is likely to be small. This is because cows are not renowned for their gun-making capacity! But putting them into butter production may well achieve the output of a significant amount of butter. Figure 1.3 below will serve to show this. Anyland has moved from X to X'. Butter output has risen from nothing to B' and gun output has declined from its maximum possible amount at X only to G'. However, it should be clear that increasing butter output further will be possible only at a higher and higher opportunity cost. This is partly because resources transferred are less and less ideally suited to butter production and partly because those same resources are more and more suitable for gun production.

Suppose Anyland at some stage were to be producing on the curve somewhere near Y, with only a small volume of gun output and a large amount of butter being produced. Now a further increase in butter output could only be possible through the transference of resources highly suited to gun production, for example, gunsmiths. The curve suggests that increased output of a good, then, is only possible at an increasing opportunity cost.

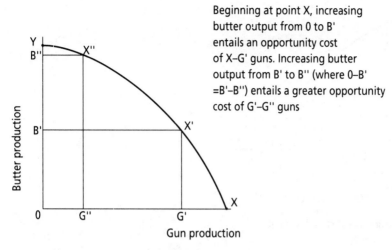

Beginning at point X, increasing butter output from 0 to B' entails an opportunity cost of X–G' guns. Increasing butter output from B' to B'' (where 0–B' =B'–B'') entails a greater opportunity cost of G'–G'' guns

Figure 1.3 Increasing opportunity cost in Anyland

It should be clear that the curve does not, nor is it supposed to, make any comment on what society's preferences are for various kinds of output. It only indicates what possibilities are open to an economy. Two nations, one butter loving and the other gun loving, might well be faced with the same possibilities for output if its resources are the same, even though its choice about where on the curve it wishes to be will be different.

e The opportunity cost of investment

The same principle of opportunity cost will apply in choices that the community must make concerning consumption now or in the future. Some resources could be put either to present consumption or future consumption. A piece of steel could be used to make a machine this year to produce something next year or it could be used to make a washing machine for someone to use immediately. Thus, our society faces a choice. How much current consumption do we wish to have? The more we consume the less is available for investment and therefore the less consumption there will be next year. For Anyland the choices would be described by Figure 1.4 below. Suppose Anyland chose point Z where its citizens would enjoy OC'_t current consumption. They would be foregoing present consumption of $X–C'_t$, a volume of goods which they could have enjoyed in addition to the output C'_t. This was foregone so that some resources could be used for investment purposes. This investment in machinery, etc., will enable consumption next year of C'_{t+1}. If the process is to be worthwhile, this year's foregone consumption will generally have to be less than the consumption it will make available for next year. You can see from Figure 1.4 that this is so.

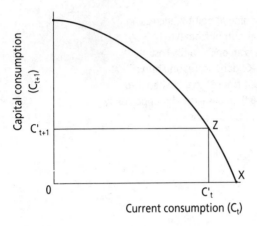

Figure 1.4 Opportunity cost of investment

Now, what should be clear is that the 'economic problem' which the opportunity cost curve displays, is not a problem faced by some societies because of their particular economic or political systems. It is a problem faced by all societies whatever system they use. Different economic and political systems can be viewed as different ways of attempting to solve the problem. Two such systems are the planned economy once used in such societies as Romania, and the market economy to which they are trying to change.

4 Developing the model: two types of economy

a Opportunity cost and planned economies

Let us first think briefly about the nature of a planned economy. In section 2 above we showed how society must make choices. But a key question for any society is this: how are society's preferences going to be articulated so that those who control the resources allocate them such that what society wishes is produced?

In a planned economy resources are owned by the government. The government decides what society needs and then issues instructions about what output to make. The prices to be charged for the output are also set by government.[5] These prices can be set at a level that is fair and reasonable to purchasers. However, it is this system that has been rejected by many states, such as Romania, in recent years. There are four main reasons for this, each of which can be related back to Figure 1.2.

First, if decisions are taken by government for its citizens, there is no reason to suppose that their needs and preferences will be correctly anticipated. People might prefer, for example, more food and less clothing, more cars and less heating than government decides. That is why, by contrast, in market economies decisions are made by households themselves. The communist authorities discovered how strongly people wished to be free to make their own decisions. In terms of Figure 1.2, society might prefer to be on a different point of the opportunity cost curve than that which is selected by government. There is also the distinct possibility that those who make the decisions will reflect their *own* preferences rather than reflect the preferences of the people. A significant feature of these societies has been the continued mistrust of politicians, though you may not think that is very different in market economies!

Second, the planned system raises enormous coordination problems. The goods that people purchase are called 'final' goods. In order to produce them many 'intermediate' goods are produced, that is goods made by one industry to be used by another. For example, one may buy a car, a final good. To make this possible rubber, steel and electric wiring has been made by intermediate industries for the car producer. Now, if in a planned economy, a decision is taken that one million loaves of bread are needed per day, there is implied in that one decision hundreds of other decisions that must be consistent. This amount of bread requires an adequate amount of wheat to be grown, a sufficient number of combine harvesters, sufficient steel, enough coal, and so on. Now the coordination of these decisions has proved increasingly difficult. If the production of one intermediate good fails, it has enormous knock-on effects for the whole system. Output is lower than it might be. We are inside the opportunity cost curve of Figure 1.2.

Third, the selection of an appropriate price at which to sell the final output creates difficulties. Often the price of a good is one at which the quantity people wish to buy is greater than the amount that is available for sale. The result is long queues for basic commodities. Shortages of this kind are one aspect of inefficiency that we saw puts a society inside the opportunity cost curve.

Fourth, there is the problem of incentive. If wages are also administered, there is no reward for producing beyond a specified target. There is thus no reason to try very hard. The inevitable inefficiency means that again society is inside the opportunity cost curve. But it has a further cost. There is no incentive to learn how to do things better so that over time the economy can grow and output can be increased. The opportunity cost curve is not going to move out from the origin over time as far and as fast as it could.

b Opportunity cost and prices in market economies

Many Eastern European economies, then, aspire to a Western type market economy. How do these Western economies solve the economic problem? The basic means of dealing with the economic problem in a market system is by establishing a link between prices and opportunity cost. Resources are not owned by the state but are privately owned. People are free to use the resources they own in whatever way they wish. You probably have a resource, labour, capable of producing output. When you finish studying economics you may well choose to use it to produce output. You are free to allocate your resource in any way you like. The government will not command you to produce output that it feels others in the community need. How does this lead us to a link between prices and opportunity cost?

Why do you expect to pay more for a new pair of jeans than for an ice cream? In essence the answer is that to produce these goods resources have to be committed to their production. Since more resources are needed to produce the jeans than the ice cream, those involved in jeans production will not invest the greater resources unless they are persuaded that this is worth doing. The price you pay for a good, then, should reflect the opportunity cost of the resources allocated to its production. Take this book you are reading. You would have appreciated the chance to buy it for less. But many people – author, publisher and printer – had to give time to its production, time they could have used for something else. Owners of the capital, printing presses, and so on, could have allocated their resources elsewhere. The price reflected what you had to pay to draw resources into this area of activity – the resources' opportunity cost. Only by the end of the book will you have fully realised what an excellent choice from your limited income you have made!

Now, the publisher would like to have charged a much higher price than the modest sum for which you were asked. The problem was that you have a limited income. By purchasing the book you denied yourself the choice to buy something else, for example, a different textbook or a compact disc. You were not prepared to pay more than the opportunity cost to you of the foregone goods. In a market system, it is this principle of opportunity cost that underlines how the economic problem is dealt with. All this will be developed as you increase your understanding of economics.

c Relative price changes in market economies

Armed with this understanding we can see why, over time, prices of goods and services in a market system change dramatically. We illustrate this with some prices taken from *The Economist* at the end of 1990. They are shown in Table 1.4. First, though, we must be clear what the numbers are that we are looking at. The first row gives the actual price of that item in each year quoted. However, over time, the price level has risen dramatically. The average good was *40 times* more expensive in 1990 than in 1900 (although average incomes have increased by far more than that). So the second row revalues each good to show what the price would have been in each year had the 1990 price level obtained throughout the period. Clearly, what is happening to the general level of prices is of great interest; indeed it is the subject matter of Chapter 15. But what we are interested in here is *relative* price. How much does one good cost in terms of another? The second row enables us to see whether prices have fallen or risen *relative* to other goods over that period. So while a rail fare has gone up and up in price since 1930 its relative price has fallen quite significantly.

Table 1.4 Relative prices in Britain since 1900

Actual and (in bold) revalued to 1990 prices, £	1900	1930	1960	1990
Railway fare	1.66	5.00	8.40	59.00
London to Glasgow 2nd class, return	**66.40**	**156.25**	**84.00**	**59.00**
Atlantic crossing, by ship	12.33(a)	16.00(b)	67.00	970.00
(to New York) cheapest Cunard ticket available	**674.00**	**516.80**	**670.00**	**970.00**
Atlantic crossing, by air	n/a	n/a	154.35	323.00
London to New York (return) cheapest ticket available			**1,543.50**	**323.00**
London to Nairobi by air (return)	n/a	178.20	199.30	642.00
cheapest ticket available		**5,562.50**	**1,993.00**	**642.00**
Bottle of whiskey	0.18(c)	0.71(d)	1.95(e)	8.80
including tax	**6.74**	**20.31**	**19.31**	**8.80**
Car	225(f)	170	494	6,180
Ford, cheapest model	**10,238**	**5,313**	**4,940**	**6,180**
Monet painting of Waterloo Bridge,	793(g)	1.744(h)	20,000	4,000,000
'Effet de soleil' (oil on canvas, 1903)	**34,496**	**67,144**	**200,000**	**4,000,000**
English dinner at The Savoy	0.38(i)	0.78	2.38	28.75
Soup, main course, pudding, coffee	**15.20**	**24.38**	**23.80**	**28.75**
Top of the range camera	20.0	18.60	145.00	1,200
Sanderson, Leica, Nikon	**800.00**	**581.25**	**1,450**	**1,200**
Telephone call, 3 minutes	0.25(j)	0.33	1.30	0.41
London to Glasgow	**8.93**	**10.31**	**1.30**	**0.41**
Telephone call, 3 minutes	n/a	15.00	3.00	2.33
London to New York		**468.75**	**30.00**	**2.33**
Opera ticket	0.13	0.33	0.18	3.00
at Covent Garden, least expensive	**5.20**	**10.31**	**1.80**	**3.00**
Opera ticket	1.50	1.40	2.10	101.00
at Covent Garden, most expensive	**60.00**	**43.75**	**21.00**	**101.00**
Household coal,	1.18	1.24	4.22	120.66
per short ton	**47.20**	**38.75**	**42.20**	**120.66**
The Economist	0.03	0.05	0.08	1.60
	1.20	**1.56**	**0.75**	**1.60**
Theatre ticket	0.08(k)	0.08(l)	0.30	7.50
at Theatre Royal, least expensive	**1.86**	**2.58**	**3.00**	**7.50**
Theatre ticket	0.60(k)	0.75(l)	1.50	25.00
at Theatre Royal, most expensive	**13.98**	**24.23**	**15.00**	**25.00**
Gold,	4.24	4.25	12.56	209.16(m)
per oz	**169.60**	**132.81**	**125.60**	**209.16**
Hotel room, single	n/a	1.50	6.00	189.00
at Hyde Park Hotel		**46.88**	**60.00**	**189.00**

Undergraduate fee for one year	48.88	36.75	70.10	1,675.00
at King's College, London University	**1,955.20**	**1,148.44**	**701.00**	**1,675.00**
Most expensive Jaguar,	n/a	310(h)	2,197	43,200
two-seater		**11,935**	**21,970**	**43,200**
Pair of men's handmade shoes	0.84(n)	1.99	4.98(g)	125.00
	30.00	**62.19**	**72.21**	**125.00**
Standard Dunhill pipe	0.38(p)	1.25	8.38	108.00
	14.63	**39.13**	**83.80**	**108.00**
Men's suit	n/a	4.20(q)	30.00	269.00
Daks 2-piece		**99.62**	**300.00**	**269.00**
Taxi ride	0.03	0.11	0.11	1.60
one mile	**1.20**	**1.25**	**1.13**	**1.60**
Lighter,	1.75(r)	2.25	7.25	185.00
gold-plated	**41.66**	**70.31**	**72.50**	**185.00**
Potatoes	0.02	0.02	0.08	0.91
per 7 lbs	**0.71**	**0.77**	**0.80**	**0.91**

Actual and (in bold) revalued to 1990 prices, pence

Bread, unsliced loaf	0.5	0.7	2.4	42
per 400g	**18**	**27**	**24**	**42**
Milk	0.7	1.2	3.3	30
per pint	**26**	**38**	**33**	**30**
Postage stamp	0.42	0.42	1.25	22
London to Scotland	**17**	**13**	**12.5**	**22**
Postage stamp	0.01	0.63	1.25	37
London to America	**0.40**	**19.5**	**12.5**	**37**
The Times	0.83(n)	0.83	3.3	35
	33	**25.9**	**33**	**35**
Underground ticket	0.83	0.63	2.08	0.70
Victoria to South Kensington	**33**	**20**	**20.8**	**0.70**
Mars bar	n/a	0.80	2.5	21
		31	**25**	**21**

Note: All food prices are July 1914 average instead of 1900, and 1933 instead of 1930. (a) 1895; (b) 1934; (c) 1906; (d) 1939; (e) 1961; (f) 1904; (g) 1905; (h) 1932; (i) 1900 price includes fourth course of fish; (j) 1912; (k) 1922; (l) 1935; (m) average for third quarter; (n) 1913; (o) 1949; (p) 1910; (q) 1938; (r) 1926; (s) 1933
Sources: National Railway Museum; Cunard; Liverpool University; British Airways; Scotch Whisky Association; Ford Motor Co.; Sotheby's; Savoy Hotel; National Museum of Photography, Film and Television; British Telecom; Royal Opera House; British Coal; *The Economist*; Theatre Royal, Drury Lane; Bank of England; Hyde Park Hotel; King's College; Jaguar Cars; Church's Shoes; Dunhill; Simpson (Picadilly); Metropolitan Police; Dunhill; Central Statistical Office; Post Office; *The Times*; London Regional Transport; Mars (UK).

Source: The Economist, 22 December 1990.

Why is a phone call to New York so cheap now? As technology has improved, the volume of resources needed to produce a call has fallen. Fewer resources mean a lower opportunity cost. Prices reflect opportunity cost in a market system.

Why has the price of an expensive opera ticket at Covent Garden risen much more sharply than a cheaper one? One possible explanation is a change in tastes by consumers. People are prepared to pay more for a better seat. They must bid those seats away from others who will also be willing to pay more. Again the explanation is opportunity cost.

You might study Table 1.4 and speculate upon the reason for the significant changes in the relative prices of other goods.

So we now understand a key idea of how a market system uses prices to deal with the problem of resource allocation.

d Planned versus market economies

Now let us think back through what we saw earlier were the problems of using a planned economy. In doing so we shall see how a market system, which allows changes in relative prices, can overcome these problems.

First, planned economies require a central authority to decide what to produce to meet people's needs. In a market system people express their own preferences by how they use their incomes. When you buy something in the shops because it reflects your preferences, since the price you pay reflects the resources used in its production, you are determining how those resources are allocated. Thus resources in a market system follow consumers' wishes, so that we move towards the best spot around the opportunity cost curve.

Second, governments do not need to coordinate decisions between intermediate and final buyers. Markets operate in intermediate industries too. The market not only determines the price of a car, but the price the car industry pays for the component parts also.

Third, governments do not have to administer prices. Prices are determined by the market. They move to a level at which the available output matches people's preferences. It is rare to see people in the West queue for hours to buy food or clothes. The price acts as a rationing device. You may feel that shopping in Sainsbury's on Christmas Eve is an exception to that rule. If so, you are beginning to think like an economist. Before reading on you might ask yourself why Sainsbury's doesn't raise prices on Christmas Eve!

Fourth, the problem of an absence of incentives is solved by a market system. Since people are paid a price for their output which reflects what buyers are prepared to pay, they have an incentive to produce what society actually wants.

Of course a market system is not without its problems. It is not perfectly efficient. It has not always produced full employment. Many people feel that it gives an unfair distribution of income – too much for the rich, too little for the poor.[6] These and other problems we shall consider in detail in later chapters, but there are several things we can say about our market model now.

One needs to appreciate that it is only a model. Its conclusions are only as good as its assumptions. We shall see during our studies that given the right conditions a market system is the best that can be done with the economic problem. To use the jargon, it represents the optimal solution. But, of course, the assumptions rarely hold in practice. We must also bear in mind that we can increase the validity of the model – and we shall do so. However, the cost is its increasing complexity. So we shall start with something simple and, as confidence grows, make it more realistic.

One can say, furthermore, that the market system must have a great deal to commend it. The enthusiasm of almost the whole of Eastern Europe for rejecting in the late 1980s and early 1990s the planned economy and embracing the market is a powerful testimony to its advantages. But one must also be aware that no society has ever seen fit to embrace a market system wholly. Some output is always in the hands of government. For example, in Britain that output includes much of health care, much of education, national defence, and more besides.[7] In practice then, Western societies are 'mixed' economies. The degree of mix varies, as Table 1.5 shows. One can see how in Western societies the proportion of national output in the hands of government varies. Well over half of what Sweden produces is taken by its government in taxes. This is a measure of the extent to which households do not make their own decisions about spending. Decisions are made for them by government. In the United States that figure is under one-third.

Table 1.5 shows something else of interest. Although Western-type market orientated economies have produced much more output per head than planned economies, as Figure 1.1 makes clear, there is within Western-type advanced economies no close correlation between the extent of government intervention and output per head or growth of output per head. Japan has a relatively small

Table 1.5 Government tax income and growth of output in selected OECD countries

Country	Tax and social security payments, as percentage of national output 1989	Average growth of output 1976–91
Switzerland	32	1.8
USA	32	2.6
Japan	33	4.4
United Kingdom	43	2.1
Germany*	45	2.6
Norway	55	3.1
Sweden	66	1.5

Note: * Excluding East Germany.
Source: Economic Trends, OECD.

government sector and a high growth rate. Sweden has a very large state sector and a very low growth rate. On the other hand, the United States with a very similar sized government sector to Japan has a much poorer growth rate. Norway, with a substantial state sector, has a growth record which is quite impressive.

5 From planned to market economies: some problems

We have seen why Eastern European states have attempted to shift their economic systems towards a more market orientated one. We have also seen that they still have substantial problems. Investment rates are low. Unemployment rates are high and if you look at Table 1.6 you will see that output has continued to fall in virtually all of these countries for virtually all of the late 1980s and early 1990s. Finally, we use our model to see three reasons why they have not met with the kind of economic success that many Western countries take for granted.

Table 1.6 Developments in Eastern European real GDP[1]

| | Developments in real GDP[1] | | | | |
| | Percentage changes | | | | |
Countries	1988	1989	1990	1991	1992[2]
Albania	−1.4	9.8	−10.0	−27.7	− 8
Bulgaria	2.6	−0.3	− 9.1	−16.7	− 8
Croatia	−0.9	−1.9	− 9.3	−28.7	−25
Czechoslovakia	2.6	1.4	− 1.4	−14.7	− 7
Czech Republic	−	−	− 0.4	−14.2	− 7
Slovak Republic	−	−	− 2.7	−15.8	− 6
Hungary	3.2	−0.2	− 4.0	−11.9	− 5
Poland	4.1	0.2	−11.6	− 7.6	1
Romania	−0.5	−5.8	− 7.6	−13.7	−15
Slovenia	−1.9	−2.7	− 4.7	− 9.3	− 7
Yugoslavia	−1.3	−1.9	− 8.4	−12.2	−25
Average[3]	1.6	−1.0	− 7.6	−13.0	− 9
Former Soviet Union	4.4	2.5	− 2.2	− 9.0	−19
Russia	4.5	1.9	− 2.0	− 9.0	−19
Baltic states	8.0	4.9	− 3.0	−11.2	−34
Overall average[3]	3.5	1.3	− 3.9	−10.3	−16

Notes: [1] For Croatia, gross social product; for the Czec and Slovak Republics, GNP; for Yugoslavia, gross material product and, from 1990, Serbia and Montenegro only; for the former Soviet Union (including Russia and the Baltic states) prior to 1990, net material product (NMP). [2] Preliminary and partly estimated. [3] Weighted average, based on 1990–91 GDP/NMP and exchange rates.
Source: BIS Annual Report, 1993.

a Immobile resources

Consider Figure 1.5 below. We might think of the Romanian economy in 1990 as represented by point S. There were few consumer goods, and large volumes of resources committed to military uses. But given the inefficiencies outlined earlier point S is inside the opportunity cost curve. Suppose now this society wishes to move to a market economy. People want fewer guns and more butter. They wish to be at point W. This entails a switch of resources. There is an opportunity cost of more butter, or other consumer goods, namely fewer guns. However, this is a sacrifice they are prepared to make. Less output of a military nature is now produced and the labour and capital are supposed to make consumer goods instead. But the men have no training and the machines are not convertible. Given this resource immobility the economy shifts to point T – and there is *less* national output not more.

Perhaps this will be a short-term problem. Labour can be retrained for example. But it is easier to see the problem in a text on economics than for a Romanian to accept that his low income is going to get lower before it gets higher.

b Low capital stock

Inefficient and outdated methods of production have left Eastern European economies with old and worn out capital equipment that needs replacing. For example, many of their nuclear power stations are unsafe and need rebuilding. This requires large volumes of resources committed to producing new equipment for future power production. In terms of Figure 1.4, C_{t+1} can be increased but only by a reduction in C_t. Again the effect of moving towards a market economy is a reduction in living standards in the short run. Given the immobility of resources problem the short-term effects of improving the capital stock could be severe.

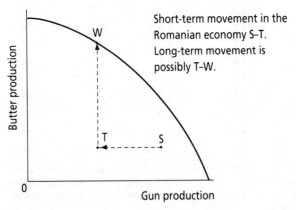

Short-term movement in the Romanian economy S–T. Long-term movement is possibly T–W.

Figure 1.5 The problem of resource immobility

Some Eastern European economies have persuaded Western governments to give some aid to alleviate the worst effects of this problem. If the aid is in the form of loans rather than outright gifts this simply shifts the problem into the future. It will appear in such data as Table 1.1 (Gross external debt).

If things do improve, private investors will be willing to invest in such countries. Then such ventures as a McDonald's in Moscow will seem less remarkable.

c Inflation

Our focus in this chapter has been upon relative prices, that is, the price of one good compared with the price of others. But societies can find themselves in difficulties if prices in general are rising. In other words, there are difficulties if they are experiencing inflation. In Britain, inflation has been problematic in that the price level has tended to rise every year since the Second World War. At its peak it was rising at over 20 per cent per year. However, for Eastern European countries in recent years, prices have been rising far faster than that.

The reasons why societies experience inflation and the problems created by it will be considered in Chapter 15.

6 Conclusion

We began by observing how former communist countries are finding real problems in their transition to a market-type economy. We approached the problem, as economists usually do, by constructing a model of economy. Our model ignored some elements of reality; for example, we did not focus on the political elements of the problem. Nevertheless, our model sufficiently reflected reality to enable us to explain and predict certain features of such societies.

We then considered the nature of resources, especially the fact that they have an opportunity cost. We found that one great advantage of market economies is that relative prices can reflect the opportunity cost of resources used in production.

But the transition from planned to market economies is not an easy one. Resources are often immobile so changes in society's preferences affect resource reallocation slowly. Increasing the capital stock has an opportunity cost in terms of foregone consumption lowering already low living standards in the short run. Furthermore, inflation has now become a serious difficulty for these economies. If the process continues, other problems of market economies will appear, problems which we will consider in later chapters.

The 1990s, then, are likely to prove an uncomfortable period for these societies if they press on with reform. The adjustment process will continue to be painful.

7 Questions for discussion

1 One famous American economist, Milton Friedman, says that the value of an economic model lies in its power to predict, not in the realism of its assumptions. What do you think he means? Is he right?

2 Suppose that a government in its desire for re-election stimulates economic activity as the end of its term of office approaches. This results in a drop in the unemployment figures and a rise in output. It therefore can claim that the economy is growing. After all, output is now rising. Clearly, the electorate should not miss the opportunity to give the government a chance to continue this good work. But can this growth be sustained? (HINT: Where, before the election, was the economy in terms of Figure 1.1?)

3 Why might we be reluctant to compare the Romanians standards of living on the basis of, say, the number of GPs per head of population or the output of clothing per head? Can you think of more suitable measures of comparison?

4 A point inside an opportunity cost curve is 'inefficient'. What do you understand by the term 'efficiency'?

5 How well does the market system overcome each problem of a planned economy mentioned in the text in section 5(a)?

6 In the text we considered the reasons for significant changes in the relative prices of some of the goods and services in Table 1.4. What explanations would you offer for the changes in some of the other goods and services? Particularly consider (a) undergraduate fees, (b) coal, (c) cameras.

7 Examine the data in Table 1.7. What trends do you discern? What is the likely reason for the trends? What effects might you expect these changes to have on the Western European steel industry?

8 In this chapter we have examined the difficulties of a planned economy *and* the difficulties of transition from a planned to a market economy. What problems do you see for a society which uses a market system?

8 Further reading

Economic models
Sloman, pp. 26–30; Begg, pp. 20–24; Parkin and King, pp. 16–22

Resources and opportunity cost
Sloman, pp. 8, 11–14; Begg, pp. 5–9; Parkin and King, pp. 8–10, 46–53

Market and planned economies
Sloman, pp. 16–26; pp. 8–10

The road to freedom
1 E. Borensztein and P. Montiel (1992) 'When will Eastern Europe catch up with the West?', *Finance and Development*, September.

Table 1.7 Crude steel consumption and production in Eastern Europe (all measurements in '000,000 metric tonnes)

	Capacity 1992	Production			Apparent consumption		Capacity utilisation 1992 (%)
		1990	1991	1992	1990	1992	
Poland	14.8	13.6	10.3	9.3	10.7	7.3	63
CSFR	16.7	14.9	12.3	10.8	10.3	7.1	65
Romania	19.1	9.8	7.1	5.1	8.1	4.4	27
Hungary	4.3	2.9	1.9	1.4	2.4	1.1	34
Bulgaria	4.7	2.4	1.7	1.3	3.7	2.0	27
Albania	0.4	0.1	0.1	0.1	0.3	0.2	19
Latvia	0.6	0.3	0.3	0.2	0.2	0.1	38
Total Eastern Europe	60.6	44.0	33.7	28.2	35.7	22.2	47
Total CIS*	174.0	154.1	133.3	113.3	156.2	117.0	65
Total Eastern Europe and CIS	234.6	198.1	167.0	141.5	191.9	139.2	60

Note: CSFR = Czech and Slovak Federal Republic (the old Czechoslovakia). CIS = Confederation of Independent States (part of the old Soviet Union).
Source: Eurofer.

2 J. Fleming (1993) 'Price and trade reform: the economic consequences of shock therapy and possible mitigating measures or why liberalisation is not enough', *National Westminster Bank Quarterly Review*, May.

9 End Notes

1 We have indicated the meaning of the items in Table 1.1 very briefly. During your studies these concepts will be examined more fully. Gross domestic product (GDP) is explained in Chapter 12. Inflation is dealt with particularly in Chapter 15. Wage rates form an important part of Chapter 11. International economic relationships are considered in Chapters 19 and 20.
2 There are difficulties in defining the term 'non-renewable'. Fish stocks are a good illustration of the point. In one sense a fish is non-renewable. Once it is eaten, it is gone for ever. In another sense it is renewable in that it can have young. The question of oil in this context raises issues discussed in Chapter 12.
3 Some economists draw a distinction between 'relative' and 'absolute' scarcity. An absolutely scarce item is Van Gogh's painting 'Sunflowers'. *It* is unique. Its supply cannot be increased. Most resources are relatively scarce. They are scarce relative to the demands made upon them, but they can be increased, albeit at an opportunity cost.
4 The choice of these two commodities, as an illustration of a principle, is a deliberate one. 'Guns' will stand for national defence, tanks, soldiers, etc. 'Butter' will represent consumer goods, food, clothing, housing, etc. Therefore in these two headings we have covered all different kinds of output.
5 In principle the question of ownership of resources is separate from the setting of prices. A state could own resources but set prices that were based on what households were prepared to pay. In practice, in countries where governments have owned resources, government has usually also administered prices.
6 All these and other issues will be considered in later chapters. In particular the question of efficiency is examined in many places, especially Chapter 10. The question of unemployment is the focus of Chapter 13 and the distribution of income will be dealt with in Chapter 16.
7 In the first half of the book we shall devote considerable thought to why markets are used for allocating resources. We shall also explore, in some detail, why some output is *not* allocated through markets.

CHAPTER 2

The stock market: a quick way to riches?

Why do share prices fluctuate so much? Are large fortunes made as a result? Does it make any difference to the firms concerned? Does it matter for the economy generally?

As we analyse these things, we *introduce* the concept of:
- Supply and demand
- Price elasticity of demand
- Speculation

1 Introduction: what is the stock market for?

Although most people are aware of the existence of The Stock Exchange, and aware that some people make and lose large sums, many people are unaware of what actually happens there, why the price of shares fluctuates so much, and what this has to do with the real economy. Do events in the stock market really make any difference to the lives of most people? The answer is that they most certainly do.

Firms need capital, buildings and machinery to produce output; in the case of large firms many million of pounds worth. What sources are available to them if they wish to invest? The main options are, first, internal funds from profits that they have made in the past; second, banks and other financial institutions who will lend at a rate of interest; third, the floating of shares. Shares, or equities are pieces of paper that show that the holder owns part of the company. Some people will be willing to hold the shares in the expectation of sharing in the profits that the company hopes to make. The shareholder receives this payment as a 'dividend'. This dividend, paid out to all shareholders, will represent only part of the company's profit. Some profit will be retained.

Large companies never concentrate exclusively on just one source but will use a variety of sources to raise funds for investment. At first it might seem that the ideal is to fund all its capital needs out of past profits since it will then not need to pay out interest or dividends. But we must remember two things. First, large companies' capital needs will be too great for this to be possible. Second, even the use of internal funds has costs. There are opportunity costs in terms of the interest foregone by using the funds for capital investment rather than, say, lending to a bank. So large firms use a variety of sources for funds, including equity finance.

When a company wishes to raise finance through a share issue, it usually gets a merchant bank to offer the shares for sale. Often the merchant bank will be paid a fee by the company to 'underwrite' the issue, that is, to guarantee that all the shares offered will be sold. If people do not offer to buy all the shares, the underwriter has to buy all the excess whether he wishes to or not! After all, taking that risk is part of what he has been paid for. The company then uses the finance raised for investment and those holding the shares will be rewarded according to the degree of success the company has in making profits.

But suppose you bought some new shares in BP so that they can build a new oil rig, but you then decide that you do not wish to tie your savings up in BP anymore. It is clearly not possible for BP to sell a leg of an oil rig so that they can pay you your money back! However, they do not need to. The Stock Exchange will enable you to sell your shares to someone else who wishes to buy them. In other words, it acts as a market for the dealing in secondhand shares, which is vital for firms, otherwise they would find it harder to persuade people to buy new issues of their shares. The harder firms find it to float new shares the less investment society gets. As we saw in Chapter 1, capital is a manufactured resource. Less investment means less capital stock. This results in less growth of output, and therefore lower future living standards. Most Stock Exchange dealings on a day to day basis are trades in the 'secondary market', so we shall begin here. Table 2.1 shows a selection of share price movements for a number of companies during the last few years. You can see that the movement can be very substantial. These movements are not at all uncommon. Neither are they the very largest. They are simply representative of a common occurrence.

We are going to see how the share price of such company shares is determined in the secondary market, and, in doing so, see why such fluctuations can occur. We shall do this by using a crucial tool of economists – supply and demand analysis. Supply and demand analysis helps us to see how the price of many things is determined in a market economy. By the end of this chapter you should understand the elements of the analysis. This will help you, not only to understand the market for shares, but the determination of many other prices also. First, we shall concentrate on the concept of demand.

Table 2.1 Share price movements of selected companies

Company	Time period	Price movement	Percentage change
Harland Simon	Feb. 92–Jul. 92	655p–37p	−94.4
Tanjong	Dec. 91–Dec. 92	10p–40.5p	+30.5
LIG	16 Sep. 1993	203p–140p	−31

Source: Financial press.

2 Prices in the secondary market: supply and demand

a The demand for shares

What factors influence people's plans to buy goods and services? Many things influence the demand for a good; the price of the good, the price of other goods, incomes, sometimes interest rates, sometimes expectation about future prices. For different goods different things will be important. The demand for apples might be influenced by the price of pears. The price of pears is unlikely, however, to exert much influence on the demand for cars. But we start by considering a crucial influence on the demand for a good – its price. Here we take the example of the demand for Sainsbury's shares and relate it to the price of those shares. Many individuals would like to buy but the market demand for Sainsbury's shares is the sum of all individuals' demands at each price. We can graph that relationship, as shown in Figure 2.1. The 'demand curve', as it is called, represents a set of plans, plans to buy Sainsbury's shares at different possible prices. As with most goods it is negatively sloped. The lower the price the greater the quantity demanded. The most important reason is that the higher the price the more worthwhile buyers will find it to shift their demand into something else, in this case another share. For example, if Sainsbury's share price rises from P_1 to P_2 some who planned to purchase Sainsbury's shares at P_1 will buy another share, perhaps Tesco's or some quite different company's. There would be fewer people planning to buy Sainsbury's shares at the higher price. The change in price from P_1 to P_2 caused *a change in the quantity demanded*.

Of course, determinants of demand, other than the price itself, can change. If this were to happen, it would cause purchasers to demand different quantities at each price. We call such shifts changes in demand, as shown in Figure 2.2. One thing that might shift demand in the way described is the announcement by Sainsbury's of unexpectedly high profits. This is because expectations are one factor influencing demand. Now *at each price* people will wish to hold more shares

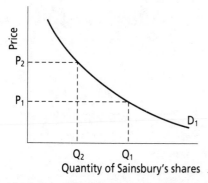

Figure 2.1 The demand for shares

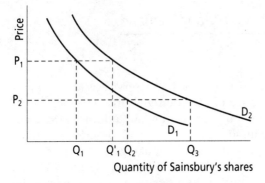

Figure 2.2 A change in demand

than they wished to hold before at that price. Now that the demand curve has shifted to the right, plans to buy at P_1 have increased from Q_1 to Q'_1 and plans to buy at P_2 have increased from Q_2 to Q_3. A similar shift in demand might take place in the market for cars, if it was thought that car prices were likely to rise. Perhaps it is anticipated that car taxes are about to be raised. Demand would increase in expectation of the price change. Of course many other factors can shift the demand curve. We shall consider some of them shortly.

b The supply of shares

The supply of a commodity depends on a variety of things including its own price. If we hold all things constant except the price of the share we can plot a 'supply curve' in Figure 2.3. It represents a set of plans by those who wish to sell Sainsbury's shares. At higher prices, more shares are offered for sale.

The curve, then, is positively sloped. At first this might seem odd. There is a limited number of Sainsbury's shares which have been issued. Surely people cannot offer more for sale than are available? However, what we are interested in is people's willingness to sell them. At a higher price more people will judge that

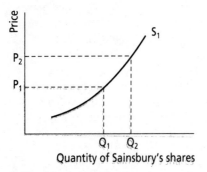

Figure 2.3 A supply curve

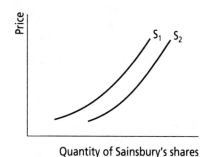

Quantity of Sainsbury's shares

Figure 2.4 A change in supply

they would be better off selling these shares and perhaps switching to some other share. A rise in price, then, will cause an increase in the quantity supplied. In Figure 2.3 a change in price from P_1 to P_2 causes a change in quantity supplied from Q_1 to Q_2. The upward sloping supply curve represents the position in most markets, not just shares. If the price rises, more will be offered for sale by suppliers.

But determinants of supply, other than the price itself, can change. We call such shifts changes in supply. So Figure 2.4 shows a change in supply. Suppose, for example, Sainsbury's wish to raise more funds for expansion and choose to do it through a new share issue. To the plans of holders of shares we must add the plans of the company's board to sell new shares, as we show in Figure 2.4. The supply curve has shifted right from S_1 to S_2.

There are other influences on the supply of shares as we shall consider a little later. Before that, however, we are now in a position to see how the price of a share is established at any given time.

c Establishing a market price

At any moment in time then, there will exist a supply and demand curve for Sainsbury's shares. Figure 2.5 represents the position in the market after close of business on 17 June 1993. We do not have enough information to know exactly what the shapes of the supply and demand curves are, but the diagram will illustrate the basic principle. Dealers were receiving instructions from clients, some wishing to purchase, some wishing to sell. Had the price been set at 500 pence, the price of the share at the end of the previous day, there would have been more planned sales than planned purchases. Dealers would have adjusted the price downwards in order to find purchasers for their clients wishing to sell – that is to say, at 500 pence there would have been excess supply.

On the other hand, at a price of, say, 470 pence there would have been excess demand. Dealers would then be adjusting price upwards to get the best possible price for those wishing to sell. So a price of 487 pence is an equilibrium price. Two million of Sainsbury's shares were traded on that day.

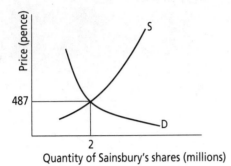

Figure 2.5 Position of market at close of business, 17 June 1993

Sometimes during one day the price of a share is unchanged. Does that imply that nobody is buying or selling that share on that day? That is by no means the case. Thousands of shares can change hands. But the number of willing buyers is equal to the number of willing sellers. If there is a decreased willingness to hold the shares (the demand curve is shifting left) the price will fall.

Notice that this a free market. There is no coercion. People are free to buy or sell as they please. What the market does is to establish a price at which suppliers' and demanders' plans are consistent. That is the only price at which this is possible. At a price below equilibrium suppliers can fulfill their plans. All those who wish to sell at that price can do so, but demanders' plans cannot be fulfilled. That is the nature of excess demand. Similarly at a price above equilibrium demanders' plans can be fulfilled but all who would wish to sell at that price cannot do so. This is the nature of excess supply. The market has ensured that both suppliers' and demanders' plans are consistent by the adjustment of price. What is true for shares will be true in the market for most goods and services also.

d The market 'clearing' price

There are no queues for shares. They are freely available at the equilibrium price. By contrast the queues for food that were a feature of the planned economy could occur because prices were administered. If the price were administered at a level at which quantity demanded exceeded quantity supplied, the excess demand needed to be rationed. Queues became that rationing device. In a market system the rationing device is price. The market price is a clearing price. It clears the market of any excess demand or supply.

In the stock market prices adjust very quickly. Is that true of markets for goods and services? Given that queues for goods are uncommon in market economies, it would appear that they do so.

Do markets for factors such as labour clear quickly? This is a question that we shall consider in more detail later in the book. However, given that some people are unemployed for a considerable time, it would appear that they may not do so.

Unemployment can be viewed as an excess supply of labour services. Our model suggests that a fall in the price of labour services would 'clear' the market of unemployment. So if the price mechanism works for labour services, it would seem that it works much more slowly than for shares.

3 Changes in demand for equities

We have now established that the price of a share, or indeed any good or service, can change because of changes in either demand or supply. We look now at factors most likely to change *demand*.

a Expectations

Demand for shares is a derived demand. They are bought not for themselves but for what they represent in the form of an expected income. This contrasts with the demand for most goods where goods are usually demanded for their own sake. The expected income from shares takes two forms. One is the dividend paid out of the company's profits, the other is the prospect of 'capital growth', which is to say, an increase in the value of the share. However, the capital value of the share can be seen as representing the future expected stream of earnings of dividends from the shares. Therefore profitability of the company is obviously important because it helps to determine the dividend payment. But profitability is not the main thing that decides the share price. Eurotunnel shares were floated in 1987 for £3.50 a share, though a dividend may not be paid until into the next century! The key here is *expectation* of profits. The value of the shares is in the anticipated capital growth. The shares become worth more as the time of the expected dividend payments draws near. Expectations can greatly affect share prices through large and sudden shifts in demand. One such example is the announcement by one firm of a takeover bid for another firm. In order for a takeover bid to succeed the acquiring company has to persuade the owners of over half the 'target' company's shares to accept the price they offer. This will typically involve offering substantially more than the going market price – a bid premium. Therefore a takeover announcement or even a rumour of one can increase demand and hence price considerably. This gives us one reason companies care about their share prices. A high price may deter other companies from launching a takeover bid.

Expectations can affect not only the price of a particular share but also the general level of share prices. In early 1994 company profits were low because of a severe recession but share prices reached record levels as people purchased shares in anticipation of a recovery.

Expectations may be important in shifting the demand curve for commodities. As we saw earlier, the demand for cars may rise if car price increases are expected. However, for many goods expectations will be a minor factor. For shares it is of major significance.

b Risk

A second important element in determining demand for a company's shares is risk. The future earnings stream is more uncertain than the income from, say, a building society deposit account. Therefore, in the long run, buying shares generally gives a higher return than safer forms of savings. Having said that, not all shares will give higher returns. Some companies will go bankrupt! Some company's shares are inherently more risky than others because they are in riskier markets. In pharmaceuticals for example, a company can spend millions of pounds on research for nothing. The high risk requires high compensation. Large companies tend to be safer than small companies. The share price will reflect this. In extreme cases one could be holding shares in a small firm which then goes bankrupt. The shares may then be worthless! Large firms are not immune from the possibility of bankruptcy but, on average, the risk is somewhat smaller.

c Substitutes

Perhaps the other important determinant of the demand for equities is the price of substitutes. As far as the general level of share prices is concerned the substitutes are other forms of saving. So if, for example, building societies were to offer a higher interest rate on savings, some people would decide that the risk of holding shares is unacceptably high. Equity demand might then fall. Equities in other countries are also a substitute. It is perfectly possible to invest in European or Japanese firms. If the return on these financial investments is seen to be rising, demand for British equities might well decline.

What are the substitutes for an individual share? Clearly, the closest substitutes are the shares of other companies – particularly those in the same area of activity. So changes in the prospects of Tesco will not only affect the Tesco share price but Sainsbury's share prices also.

The same principle will apply to goods. At any particular time there is a given demand curve for apples. If the price of bananas falls, people will switch into banana consumption. Therefore, there will be a leftward shift in the demand curve for apples. Remember what we said in Chapter 1: it is relative prices that are important. If the price of bananas falls, the price of apples has become relatively expensive.

See pp 12–15

d Interest rates

The demand curve for some individual companies' shares can shift, but the demand for shares generally can be quite sensitive to interest rate changes. There are two reasons for this. Higher interest rates can affect company profitability, making investment more expensive to undertake by increasing the cost of borrowing. The other reason is that higher interest rates make substitutes more attractive. Higher yields can be made from government debt such as bonds since the holder of the bond gets a higher return on his savings.

Will interest rates affect the demand for goods? It depends upon the particular good in question. Interest rate changes affect the demand for cars. Since most people borrow money to buy cars, higher interest rates make the purchase of the vehicle more expensive. A rise in interest rates shifts the demand for cars leftward. For other goods interest rates are of small significance. The demand for strawberries will be affected little by interest rate changes.

e Income

One most important determinant of the demand for shares, or indeed of almost any good, is income. If income rises, people will feel able to buy more shares. This may happen directly or people may do it indirectly by increasing their savings in, say unit trusts or pension funds. So a rise in income will, all other things being equal, move the demand curve to the right.

This will also be true for most goods. Think of the things that you purchase. You will find that for the great majority of them you would be willing to buy more at any given price, if your income were to be higher.

One exception to this rule is known as an 'inferior' good. This is a good where as incomes rise, the demand curve moves inwards. An example of such a good is a black-and-white television. As incomes rise, people feel able to afford colour sets. Therefore, as income increases, the demand for black-and-white televisions falls.

f Wealth

Wealth can also be an important consideration. Wealth is different from income. Income is a flow of payments received. It is so much per period of time. You may be paid £30 per day for working in Woolworths during the holidays. This is income. Wealth, on the other hand, is a stock. It is an amount that you have. It might be that you have a deposit account at the bank with one thousand pounds in it. This is not a flow. You are not receiving one thousand pounds per week. Your wealth, then, is a stock of assets. Clearly, an increase in wealth will affect demand for shares. It will also affect the demand for some kinds of goods also. One thing that was said to exacerbate the recession in Britain during the early years of the 1990s was the fall in house prices which occurred then. A fall in house prices caused house owners to feel less wealthy. They reduced their spending as a result. The fall in demand for goods generally reinforced the recession.

g Other factors

The factors that affect demand other than the price of the good itself will be many and varied. For some things one will be more important, another less. Tastes can change and shift demand. For fashion goods this can be very rapid. Weather can influence demand for ice cream. The list is almost endless.

What is important is to remember that for anything, a change in its price will be represented by a movement along the demand curve. A change in anything else shifts the whole demand curve.

4 Changes in the supply of equities

You may wonder why a company should care about the price of its secondhand shares. After all, if any are sold, the firm does not get the money! But the company does care a great deal. One reason concerns the threat of a takeover that we have already discussed in section 3 above, but another reason is the funding of future investment plans. The valuation of the secondhand shares influences the price of any new shares the company may choose to issue for any expansion plans. The higher the price the more funds it can raise for any given dividend payment. In other words, the higher the share price the cheaper it is to borrow money via the issue of new shares.

So one might expect more new share issues when stock-market prices are high. This is exactly what happens. So for example, in 1991 and the first part of 1992, during a recession in the economy, equities were surprisingly highly priced. Demand was high since there was increased expectation of a recovery from the recession. Many companies took the opportunity to make 'rights issues' where existing shareholders can purchase additional shares. However, given the depressed nature of the economy much of this money was not used to finance new investment but to reduce company debt to the banks during a period of high interest rates. Later in 1992, when the hoped for recovery had failed to materialise, demand for shares fell and many companies found the process of new share issues a very difficult one.

Figure 2.6 below describes what usually happens when a new share issue takes place. Supply is increased from S_1 to S_2 so the equilibrium price falls from P_1 to P_2. Fewer people are willing to hold the shares now since if there are more shares but

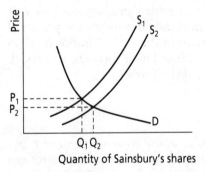

Quantity of Sainsbury's shares

Figure 2.6 Effects of new share issue

the same amount of dividends available, the earnings per share will be diluted and the worth of the shares correspondingly less.

5 Sensitivity of demand for share prices: elasticity of demand

By how much will the share price be depressed by an increase in its supply? This is an important question because it decides the price the company can get for its new share issue. The answer is to be found in the price *elasticity* of demand for the shares.

Price elasticity of demand

Consider Figure 2.7 where we examine assumed supply and demand curves for two companies, Sainsbury's and Euro Disney. In each case a new share issue increases supply from S_1 to S_2. If our diagram correctly shows the nature of the demand curve for these companies' shares, it suggests that Sainsbury's could float shares much closer to the present market price than Euro Disney.

Remembering that these numbers are for illustrative purposes only and may not accurately reflect supply and demand conditions for these companies' shares, let us consider the position as suggested by the diagrams.

First, consider Sainsbury's, shown in Figure 2.7(a). For a 5 per cent increase in the number of shares a 1 per cent fall in price will be required. Elasticity of demand is a measure of the sensitivity of demand with respect to price changes. It is given as

$$\frac{\% \, \Delta \, Q_D}{\% \, \Delta \, \text{price}} \qquad \begin{array}{l} \text{where } Q_D = \text{quantity demanded} \\ \Delta = \text{change in} \end{array}$$

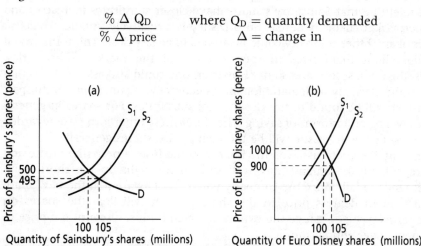

Figure 2.7 Illustrative changes in share prices in response to new issues

In this case, given the current price, a 1 per cent *fall* in price was necessary to produce a 5 per cent *increase* in the number of shares buyers were willing to hold, hence

$$\frac{\% \, \Delta \, Q_D}{\% \, \Delta \, \text{price}} = \frac{5\%}{-1\%} = -5\%$$

For a 1 per cent fall in price, Sainsbury's can issue 5 per cent more shares.

For Euro Disney the position would be represented by Figure 2.7(b). From that diagram we can see how elastic is the demand for Euro Disney shares at that price:

$$\frac{\% \, \Delta \, Q_D}{\% \, \Delta \, \text{price}} = \frac{5\%}{-10\%} = -0.5\%$$

Notice that the elasticity value is negative. A fall in price yields an increase in quantity demanded. A rise in price yields a fall in quantity demanded. For almost any good, since its demand curve is negatively sloped, price elasticity of demand is negative.

So for every 1 per cent fall in share price it could issue only 0.5 per cent more shares. It must be stressed that these are assumed, not known, values. Since Sainsbury's shareholders are assumed to be more sensitive to price changes, we say that demand for their shares is more price elastic. There are various other ways of measuring price elasticity that the interested reader can examine from the reading recommended at the end of the chapter.

What decides the elasticity of demand for shares? The most important consideration is the closeness of substitutes. This is true of shares or indeed of virtually any commodity. The demand for apples tends to be relatively price elastic because there are close substitutes – pears, bananas, and so on. With respect to shares, it might be that Sainsbury's shares have closer substitutes in Tesco's and other supermarket chains, whereas Euro Disney is a relatively unique project so the shares of any other company could be argued to be less close. This is the case if shareholders limit themselves to specific areas of the market – breweries, chemicals, the retail sector, and so on. However, one could also ask what it is that determines the elasticity of demand for shares generally. Again an important part of the answer will be found in the closeness of substitutes. For shares in general substitutes will be other forms of saving. The closer these other forms are regarded as substitutes, the more elastic will be the demand for shares generally.

If a company is seen to use well the finance raised from a new share issue and profits are enhanced, demand may well shift to the right. In the short term, though, it tends to fall. Since the company will be well aware that the new share issue will tend to depress price in the short term, it will float the shares on attractive terms trying to gauge the extent to which it must discount the price to find the new lower equilibrium level.

It would like to know exactly the elasticity of demand for its shares but it cannot do so. It must estimate it. Since it is difficult to gauge what this price will be and many companies will wish to play safe, the offer price is often pitched low enough that a profit can be made by those who purchase new shares and then resell them. This is called speculation, to which we turn shortly.

The most extreme example of this problem of estimating share price demand elasticity is when the government privatises an industry and issues new shares for the first time. This has been done recently with, for example, water and electricity. Government has no equilibrium market price of secondhand shares by which to be guided. In order to avoid the political embarrassment of a share issue flop, it has generally set the price rather low. Large profits have been made as people have purchased and then later resold these shares at much higher prices. Sometimes privatisation has been done in parts. So, for example, only about half of British Telecom (BT) was sold in 1984 and immediate profits of about 80 per cent were made. When a further sale of shares was made in December 1991 the profits that could be made were much smaller. This was largely because the government then had a market price in BT shares to guide it in pitching the price of the new shares. We shall return to the privatisation issue in Chapter 17.

See pp 330–46

If the equity market works efficiently, then, it performs a valuable function in allocating resources where they are most needed. If consumers value a product the price of the product will be high. Profits to the companies producing the product will also be high. The share price will thus be high. These companies will be able to increase investment and output in just those industries where consumers want the resources to go.

6 Changes in share prices: speculation

People are inclined to think of speculation as people who upset markets and cause damage to the economy. Many economists would take a much more benign view. The reason for a more kindly view of speculation is that it can be argued that it brings *stability* to markets.

Suppose a company's share price is in equilibrium. It reflects people's views about the company's performance and is giving correct signals to the market about the company's assets. Now suppose for some reason people begin to sell the shares. This makes them, in some sense, too cheap. This is shown in Figure 2.8(a) as a rightward shift in supply depressing price from P_1 to P_2. Speculators will anticipate that this temporary low price cannot last and will buy, speculating on the price rise. Demand will shift from D_1 to D_2 and price will return to P_1.

Some argue, however, that what will happen is described by Figure 2.8(b). As price begins to fall, speculators may fear that it will fall further. They sell in anticipation of the fall. The supply curve shifts again to S_3. This may be reinforced by a fall in demand to D_2, further depressing price and destabilising the market.

Which of the above scenarios is more likely to be the case? The answer is that eventually speculation will stabilise the market as in (a). At some point those who

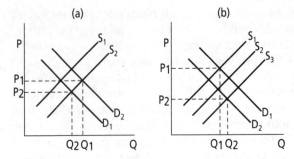

Figure 2.8 Effects on price of speculation

believe price is set to rise will outweigh those who believe it will fall. But this may take some time. In the meantime the share price may be volatile. Its effects on the real economy may be harmful in making people fear to save via share ownership, thus making it harder for the company to raise funds for investment.

Note that equilibrium is not the same as stability. Equilibrium is a state of rest. A market is in equilibrium where the price is that which causes the plans of those wishing to sell to be equated with the plans of those wishing to buy. If something disturbs that equilibrium, and market reaction causes the equilibrium to be restored, then we have a stable equilibrium. If, when equilibrium is disturbed, forces push the market price further away from equilibrium, the market is unstable.

A marble in the bottom of a cup represents a stable equilibrium. If a finger moves the marble and pushes it out of its state of rest, it will tend eventually to return to its original equilibrium. A marble resting on an upturned cup is an example of an unstable equilibrium. The marble will stay there if left alone, so it is in equilibrium. But if a finger pushes it off the cup, it will not roll back to where it came from. Figure 2.8(a) shows a stable market; Figure 2.8(b) shows an unstable market.

Fortunately for the market system the vast majority of markets are stable. A market with an upward sloping supply curve and a downward sloping demand curve will in the long run give a stable equilibrium. Only in very unusual circumstances, then, will the market for a commodity not be stable in the long run. In the short run, as Figure 2.8(b) demonstrates, speculation might be destabilising.

Speculation is not unique to stock markets. It happens in the market for foreign currency, as we shall see in Chapter 20. It also happens in markets for agricultural commodities, metals and housing.

The same principles of supply and demand analysis can be used to examine any speculative act.

7 Share price changes: a Wellcome company illustration

We turn now to illustrate some of the principles of share price determination via supply and demand analysis by observing the share price of one particular company, Wellcome, over a period of eighteen months from January 1991 to August 1992. The movement in its share price is charted in Figure 2.9 below. Clearly one could illustrate these principles from many share prices during many periods. This is just one example of a company and a time period when price changes were substantial.

Until 1986 all the shares were held in a charitable trust. Then just over 20 per cent of the shares were sold on the stock exchange to raise funds for further medical research. A further 38 per cent were sold for the same purpose in July 1992.

It is not surprising that the share price is volatile. Drug companies are a high risk. They spend millions of pounds on research with no certainty that it will lead to anything profitable. In Wellcome's case its income is derived from a limited range of drugs. Probably the most profitable earner is the anti-AIDS drug known either as AZT or Retrovir.

The five letters (a)–(e) in Figure 2.10 correspond to significant share price movements for Wellcome. We now use supply and demand analysis to suggest reasons for the price change. Notice that the price does not always follow the average of all share prices, although it sometimes does. Shares are substitutes for one another, but they are not perfect substitutes.

a American medical opinion expresses doubts over the effectiveness of Retrovir. There is an increased supply of Wellcome stock. Price falls from P_1 to P_2.

b A major AIDS conference makes favourable comments on Retrovir. Demand for Wellcome's shares increases. Price rises from P_1 to P_2.

c Enthusiasm for pharmaceutical stocks had been growing; Wellcome is one of the major drugs companies. Demand had risen. Now American investors decide they are over-priced. Supply of Wellcome shares increase. Price falls from P_1 to P_2.

d Speculation that the shares have been 'oversold'. Demand increases and supply is reduced as people speculate on a further rise in price. Price rises from P_1 to P_2.

e The Wellcome trust announces its decision to sell 38 per cent of its shares. The market is taken by surprise. The supply curve shifts right at a time when share prices are generally depressed with Britain expected to remain in a recession. Wellcome's share prices fall from P_1 to P_2.

You should now be able to see that supply and demand curves can be a useful tool for explaining price movements in the stock market.

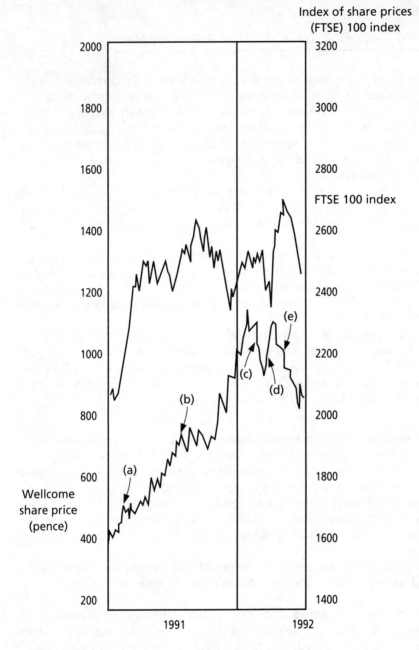

Index of share prices
(FTSE) 100 index

FTSE 100 index

Wellcome
share price
(pence)

Source : Extel

Figure 2.9 Wellcome's share price movement

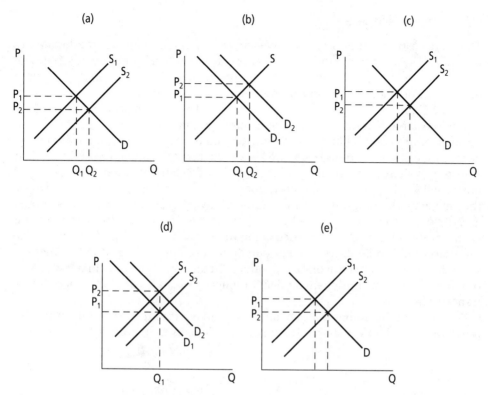

Figure 2.10 Using supply and demand analysis: Wellcome's share price.

8 Conclusion: limits to the model

Is our supply and demand model a very accurate model of stock market behaviour? For a perfect market a number of conditions need to hold. There are perhaps three which are particularly important.

a Identical product

A supply and demand curve assumes that we are talking about supply and demand for one product. All units of that product must be identical. Shares fit this condition very well. Each share of a given type will have the same rights and benefits attached to it as all the others. In this respect the model very closely resembles reality.

b Many buyers and sellers

The model assumes that no large buyer or seller can dominate the market. Many buyers and sellers meet anonymously through a middleman to buy and sell. The price is derived impersonally. But who are the people who engage in the purchase of shares? The main purchasers are not, in fact, individuals. Indeed, as can be seen from the Figure 2.11 below the significance of individual buyers of shares is small relative to large institutions, such as insurance companies and unit trusts. The reasons for this are not hard to fathom. They can be found largely in terms of what economist call 'transactions costs'. Go back to Figure 2.5, which we used to look at Sainsbury's shares. The implication here is that on that particular day you could buy or sell for that price. In fact this is not so. The dealers require an income which they make by charging a fee for the selling or buying of shares. If a share is quoted at £10.00 they actually sell shares for their clients at, say, £9.70 or buy for the clients at say £10.30, the difference being their own income. The fees for buying the shares tend to be much smaller per share if one is dealing in large amounts since the volume of paperwork is the same whether one is dealing in a few shares or many. Hence, institutions who deal in millions of shares at a time incur lower transactions costs.

The result of this is that many people invest in equities through unit trusts who purchase large blocks of shares at a time. It also means that individuals can reduce

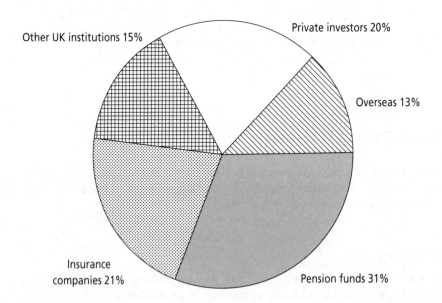

Source: CSO

Figure 2.11 Share ownership in Britain, 1992

their risks, for by investing in unit trusts one is effectively buying a few shares each from a number of companies – a prohibitively expensive thing to do as an individual. However, the number of buyers and sellers is still quite large.

c Adequate information

Markets work best in the presence of sufficient information for all buyers and sellers to make informed decisions. At first sight the stock market seems a good example of adequate information. Company accounts are published giving available information. Up to the minute share prices are available through television screens. The *Financial Times* publishes a wealth of information daily, some of the key points of which are explained in Appendix 2.

However, all do not have the same level of information. Sometimes people make large sums by 'insider trading'. This is where, for example, a member of a Board of Directors knows about an imminent takeover bid before it becomes public knowledge. Dealing in shares with such privileged information is illegal but tempting since it can be very lucrative. Under such circumstances the market is far from the perfect one described by our model.

However, despite these reservations, supply and demand analysis can be seen to be a very powerful tool with which to analyse the stock market. We have seen that it can be used to understand many other markets too. Try to think through the value of these tools of analysis for other markets. The questions for discussion will help you begin to do this. Just remember that the extent to which one can use these tools for a given market is the extent to which the assumptions outlined above are valid.

Returning to the question which we posed in the title of the chapter, is the stock market the place to make a fortune? By now you should realise that one key is information. You need to know what others do not. Once the information is known, the market reacts very quickly. You may discover that a company is the target of a takeover bid. If you find this out thirty minutes later than others, the price may already have risen by 20 per cent! The second key is the ability to forecast. If you can correctly foresee changes in key indicators you will quickly make a great deal of money. The third key is luck. Sometimes people buy or sell shares just before the announcement of some economic news and discover they have made a capital gain entirely fortuitously. But be warned; the dealing costs are high. You may easily find that to cover your costs and break even your chosen shares need to rise by 10 per cent. For most people then, share investment should be thought of as a long-term strategy in which one will probably do better than safer forms of savings. The market will tend to compensate you for the additional risk taken.

Short-term buying and selling of shares to make a fortune is like trying to win the pools. Information, ability to forecast and good luck all play their part – but the odds are greatly against success. On the whole a wiser investment is probably the study of Economics!

9 Questions for discussion

1 (a) Using Figure 2.5. What could you expect to happen to a company's share price under the following circumstances:

(i)   A large rights issue?
(ii) A sustained rise in interest rates in the economy?
(iii) A large balance of payments deficit for the British economy?

(b) Consider part (a) again. Which companies' share prices will be *most* affected?

2 We have seen that large variations can occur in share prices in a short time. Would price fluctuations be larger or smaller in agricultural markets? Use supply and demand curves to explain your answer.

3 Consider Table 2.2. What, in terms of supply and demand curves, caused the price changes shown?

Table 2.2   Changes in selected share prices, 1st, 2nd December 1993

Company	Share price day one (pence)	Share price day two (pence)	Price change (+ or −)	Quantity of shares traded (vol. '000s) Day one	Quantity of shares traded (vol. '000s) Day two	Quantity change (+ or −)
Wessex Water	660	677	+	265	965	+
Eastern Electric	614.5	620	+	1900	735	−
BT	477.5	469	−	11,000	10,000	−
Racal	189	160	−	2,100	20,000	+

4 (a) Given the present level of prices, rank the following categories of goods from most to least elastic in demand: housing, pork, strawberries, rail travel. Explain your answer.
(b) Why is it difficult for companies issuing new shares to estimate the elasticity of demand for those shares?

5 If someone successfully speculates in shares and therefore makes a financial *gain*, who make a loss?

6 One way of deciding which shares to buy is to look at those shares being bought or sold by companies' own directors. What is the logic of this?

7 What effects do you think it has on companies if many of their shares are owned by institutions like unit trusts rather than by individuals?

8 The British government offers subsidies to house buyers by granting tax relief on part of the mortgage costs.
   (a) Use supply and demand curves to show the effect of this policy on the market for housing.
   (b) How might the government's subsidy of house purchases make the task of raising equity finance more difficult?
9 'Insider trading' is illegal in England. Does such a law make sense?

10 Further reading

Supply and demand
Sloman, pp. p 48–65; Parkin and King, pp. 62–86; Begg, pp. 32–46

Price elasticity of demand
Sloman, pp. 67–81; Parkin and King, pp. 93–101; Begg, pp. 60–69

Speculation
Sloman, pp. 89–92

The market for shares
P. Howells (1990) 'The UK Equity Market', *British Economy Survey*, Spring.
K. Bain and P. Howells (1988) *Understanding Markets* (London: Harvester Wheatsheaf).

CHAPTER 3

Traffic jams:
could Britain import a solution from
Singapore?

All over the world roads, especially in cities, are becoming blocked with too much traffic causing frustration to people, industry and government. Is there a way out of the problem? One solution is that used by Singapore city.

In this chapter we review the following concepts:
- Opportunity cost
- Supply and demand

We introduce the following:
- Marginal utility
- Consumer surplus
- Income elasticity of demand
- Cross elasticity of demand

1 Introduction

There are few of us who have not, at some time or other, sat fuming in a traffic jam. It might have been on a motorway where the expectation was that we would be travelling at 70 mph (or more), or perhaps in a town, particularly driving during what we refer to, ironically, as the rush hour. Whenever there is a problem that involves the demand for a scarce resource – in this case road space – we can anticipate that economists will have something to say about it. In this chapter we shall examine part of the theoretical basis for tackling the problem of road congestion. Then we shall look at how one place – Singapore city – has attempted a solution to its rush hour problems in recent years. We shall then conclude by asking whether one could regard this kind of approach as valid for dealing with road congestion.

Let us first get some idea of the extent of the difficulty regarding transport. We shall be referring to the situation in Britain, but the general picture we present will be familiar for most parts of the world. The volume of road space available in Britain has been growing over time. Between 1990 and 2000 government plans are to increase road space by around 12 per cent. But the demand for road space has been increasing more rapidly than its supply and is forecast to go on doing so.

Table 3.1 gives an idea of the growth in private road transport demand and supply over recent years. Such a rapid growth in demand clearly implies an increasing pressure on the more slowly growing supply of road space.

Furthermore, all the projections for future demand for road space suggest such real difficulties ahead. If incomes continue to grow through the 1990s and into the next century at the kind of rate we have seen in the last twenty years, the proportion of Britons owning cars will continue to rise. As economists say, the income elasticity of demand with respect to cars is high. You will recall from Chapter 2 that we considered price elasticity of demand. We asked how sensitive consumers' demand would be to a change in the price of a good. Looking into the future, there is not much likelihood of an increase in the quantity of cars demanded because of car prices falling. Car prices are likely to rise as environmental considerations make necessary the addition of such things as catalytic convertors.

But the demand for cars is also a function of income. If we assume that people's living standards continue to rise, as they have tended to do in most parts of the world in recent decades, what will this do to car demand?

We can use our demand curve analysis of Chapter 2 to see the answer. Look at the diagram in Figure 3.1. The rise in income increases demand. The demand curve moves to the right.

However, we could show the same effect in terms of an *income demand curve*. An income demand curve depicts the relationship between income and the quality of a good demanded, holding everything constant (including the prices of cars). This is shown in Figure 3.2 below. As we said in Chapter 2, for most goods a rise in incomes will create an increase in willingness to purchase. Since this seems to

See pp 33–5

Table 3.1   Road space supply and demand in Britain

	Index of vehicle kms travelled – all traffic (1977 = 100)	Index of road space available (1977 = 100)
1984	123	103.85
1985	125	104.18
1986	132	104.59
1987	142	105.37
1988	152	105.86
1989	165	106.54
1990	166	106.96
1991	163	107.61
1992	165	108.29

Source: Adapted from Transport Statistics, 1993.

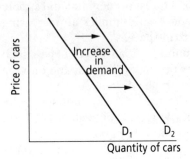

Figure 3.1 Effect of income increases on the demand for cars

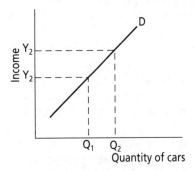

Figure 3.2 An income demand curve for cars

apply to cars we show the income demand curve as upward sloping. So, for example, if incomes increase from Y_1 to Y_2, the quantity of cars demanded will increase from Q_1 to Q_2, assuming that no other things affecting the demand for cars has altered.

But *how much* will a rise in incomes affect the quantity of cars demanded? How sensitive is demand to income changes? This question can be expressed in the following way. How income elastic is the demand for cars? As mentioned above, in the previous chapter we considered price elasticity. We asked by how much will quantity demanded change when the price of a good alters. Here we use the concept of income elasticity. Income elasticity of demand for cars is found by the formula

$$\frac{\% \Delta \text{ Quantity of cars demanded}}{\% \Delta \text{ in income}}$$

where all other things including car prices remain constant. In this case, the proportionate change is quite large relative to the income change. When considering cars, we say that the income elasticity of demand for cars is high. Notice also that it is a positive value. As income increases, the quantity demanded increases. This is typical of most goods.

Table 3.2(a) Car ownership by socio-economic group of head of household: 1992 (in percentages)

| Number of cars or vans available to household | Socio-economic group of head of household* | | | | | | | | |
| | Economically active heads | | | | | | | Economically inactive heads | Total |
	Professional	Employers and managers	Intermediate non-manual	Junior non-manual	Skilled manual and own account non-professional	Semi-skilled manual and personal service	Unskilled manual		
None	6	4	13	28	14	30	48	55	31
1	43	40	54	51	53	52	41	38	44
2 or more	51	56	32	21	32	18	12	7	24

Note: *Excluding members of the Armed Forces, and economically active full-time students and those who were unemployed and had never worked.
Source: General Household Survey, 1993.

Table 3.2(b) Forecast increases in UK roadspace demand

	Actuals, index 1992 = 100			Lower and upper forecasts 1992 = 100						
	1982	1987	1992	1995	2000	2005	2010	2015	2020	2025
Vehicle kilometres:										
Cars and taxis	68	85	100	106	116	126	136	145	154	164
				110	126	142	158	172	186	199
Goods vehicles	75	92	100	104	112	120	128	138	148	159
				107	121	136	154	173	196	222
Light goods vehicles	64	79	100	106	116	127	140	153	168	185
				110	128	149	174	203	237	276
Buses and coaches	76	89	100	100	100	100	100	100	100	100
All motor traffic (except two wheelers)	68	85	100	106	116	125	135	145	154	165
				110	126	142	159	174	190	206
Car ownership:										
Cars per person	77	91	100	106	114	121	128	135	140	146
				108	120	131	141	149	156	163
Number of cars	75	90	100	106	115	124	131	138	145	152
				109	122	134	144	153	162	169
Tonne-kilometres of road freight carried by goods vehicles	75	90	100	106	116	127	140	153	168	185
				110	128	149	174	203	237	276

Source: Transport Statistics, 1993.

Not only is the income elasticity of demand for cars high but, surprisingly perhaps, car ownership is still relatively low. Table 3.2(a) suggests that if incomes across all income groups continue to rise, there is much scope for an increase in the demand for cars and therefore road space. Even among high income professional groups there is much scope for an increase in the number of cars per household. So given a continued rise in incomes and the limited projected increase in the supply of road space the problem is set to get worse and worse. Indeed the Department of Transport's own estimates, given in Table 3.2(b), suggest a growing problem over time. Of course, what is true for Britain is true to a greater or lesser extent for most other countries, as we have already suggested.

But we are trying to think like economists. The next time we are stuck in traffic, let us use our time profitably and reflect on our understanding of the nature of demand to think through to some feasible solutions.

2 The demand for road space

a Marginal utility and demand[1]

Why do people wish to consume road space? Clearly, it is because they want to get from A to B. The consumption gives them something they value, or as economists tend to say, it gives them utility. The same principles about the relationship between utility and demand are true for roads as for any other good. The more we consume, the greater our utility up to some point at which additional units of consumption produce no increased satisfaction. However, although utility increases with consumption, it increases at a decreasing rate. Figure 3.3 shows this.

Since total utility rises more slowly as more is consumed, marginal utility, the change in total utility must be falling. At Q an additional unit consumed adds nothing to the individual consumer's total welfare. His total utility does not change. His marginal utility is zero.

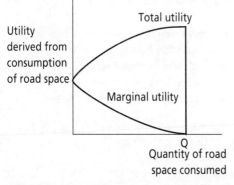

Figure 3.3 The relationship between utility and road space consumed

But how much will our consumer demand if this is the utility he derives from road space consumption? The answer, of course, is that the consumption of any good also depends upon the price of the good in question, the price of other goods and the level of the consumer's income. But he will certainly wish to arrange his consumption to maximise his welfare. This means consuming goods such that the last pound spent on each good gives him the same utility as the last pound spent on any other good. Formally, this means arranging expenditure such that, where MU is marginal utility, P is price and A, B ... N are the various goods the consumer purchases, then

$$\frac{MU_A}{P_A} = \frac{MU_B}{P_B} = \ldots \frac{MU_N}{P_N}$$

This explains why the demand curve slopes downwards. If the price of a good falls, the consumer will no longer be maximising welfare if he continues with this present consumption pattern. He will rearrange his expenditure. If P_A falls, MU must fall to restore his equilibrium. But what brings a fall in MU? As Figure 3.1 shows, MU will fall when consumption increases. So as price falls consumption increases. The demand curve has a negative slope because marginal utility declines with increased consumption.

Now, of course, if we know what any individual consumer will demand at different prices, we can sum all consumers' demands at each price to obtain the market demand curve. Suppose that Figure 3.4 shows the market demand for French motorway space. What is the value to consumers of that space? Given that the French set a toll on most motorways, there is a price, the price P_1. Then we know that Q_1 space is demanded. At present the price in France is a little over four pence per kilometre. The price is similar in Italy. In Greece it is far less, in Spain, considerably more.

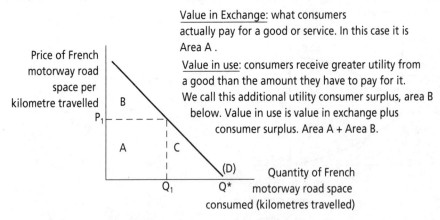

Figure 3.4 The value to consumers of French motorways

b Demand and value

If Q_1 space is being consumed, can we now see what that space is worth to consumers? The value in exchange is area A, the number of kilometres demanded, multiplied by its price. Area A in this case represents the revenue received by the government, but it can also be seen, of course, as representing the amount that consumers pay in exchange for the space.

What is area B? It represents the utility consumers receive in excess of what they have to pay for it. Each person except the last marginal consumer at Q thought the utility of the road usage was greater than he or she had to pay for it. This is consumer surplus. If we want to know the value in use of the road space, it will be areas A + B. In other words, value in use is value in exchange plus the consumer surplus so value in use will, except under very unusual circumstances, be greater than the value in exchange.

What is area C? It represents utility to consumers of road space that they have decided to forego because the price they are charged is greater than the value they feel they will receive. Since they do not consume the space, either by not travelling or by going on a different unpriced road, they will not enjoy that utility.

c Cross elasticity of demand

One matter to take into account when considering a change in motorway tolls is the burden it imposes on non-toll roads. This question needs to be considered in Britain as the British government has put the idea of motorway pricing on the political agenda. An increase in the price of road space will have an effect in increasing the demand for non-motorway (non-toll) roads.

The extent to which the switch to non-toll roads occurs can be examined by elasticity concepts. This time we use the concept of *cross elasticity of demand*. Figure 3.5 shows a cross-price demand curve. It shows the quantity of one good

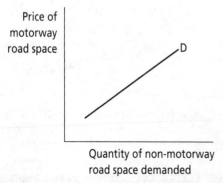

Figure 3.5 A cross price demand curve: substitutes

demanded as the price of another good changes, all other things remaining equal. In this case, motorway road space price is changing and we are observing the change in the quantity of other road space demanded. As you might expect we have a positive relationship. As motorway tolls increase, the quantity demanded of the now relatively cheap substitute good rises. Goods that are regarded as substitutes for one another will always exhibit this relationship.

How sensitive will demand for non-motorway roads be to changes in motorway tolls? We can express this in terms of cross elasticity. Formally,

$$\text{Cross elasticity of demand for X with respect to the price of Y} = \frac{\% \ \Delta \text{ in Q of x demanded}}{\% \ \Delta \text{ in price of Y}}$$

where in this case X is non-motorway space and Y is motorway space. Notice that the value of this cross price elasticity will give a positive number. As the price of good Y increases, the quantity of good X demanded also rises.

Not all pairs of goods exhibit this positive relationship. Figure 3.6 shows a possible negative relationship. As the price of motorway space increases, some may decide not to travel by car at all. Fewer cars will therefore be bought. This is what Figure 3.6 depicts. As motorway space price rises, the quantity of cars demanded will fall. Such pairs of goods are called complements. The two goods complement one another. The cross price elasticity of demand for such complements will be negative.

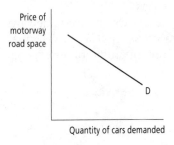

Figure 3.6 A cross price demand curve: complements

By now you should be asking yourself some questions. Have the French got it wrong in charging a price at all? Would it not be better, as is done in Britain, to set a zero price? Consumption would then be Q* in Figure 3.4, so that although the value in exchange is now zero, the value in use has increased by area C. Doesn't that increase welfare? Before we can answer such a question we need to give some thought to the question of the cost of providing the road space.

3 The supply of road space

There are two important considerations here. One is, how much of our scarce resources should we invest in road building? The production of road space has an opportunity cost. We could produce other things with those resources. So what is the best, the optimal, volume of investment in roads? It is an important question but one to which we shall give little attention here in this chapter. You will be in a better position to think about this question after you have worked through Chapter 10.

The other question that is of direct relevance to us now is this: What is the opportunity cost of the road space that we already have? The answer, of course, is very little, since the roads have already been built. They are what economists call sunken costs, and are, in that sense, irrecoverable. Hence if we ignore the wear and tear of the road surface caused by vehicles travelling on it, a question we shall return to later in this chapter, we can represent the position in Figure 3.7. Until the roads have become clogged, say at Q, an increase in the quantity of road space demanded imposes no cost on society. The road is there already. One journey is costless in terms of the use of the road space. Beyond Q this is not so. The supply curve, for that essentially is what it is, is vertical. Suppose the demand for that road space is D_1. It is an inefficient use of society's scarce resources to charge consumers for its use. Any price other than zero reduces consumer surplus. Since that surplus is achievable at a zero opportunity cost there is no logic in taking that surplus away from consumers. Consider Figure 3.4 again. The charge for road space redistributes income from road space consumers to the government but at the cost of reducing welfare by area C.

Perhaps you feel that those who use roads are the ones who should pay for their provision. If it is felt that road users should contribute to the cost of road building, a case could be made for saying that there are more efficient ways of doing it. For example, consider a road fund licence in which one makes an annual payment to

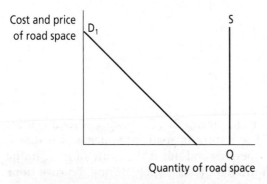

Figure 3.7 Supply and demand for uncongested road space

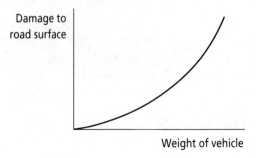

Figure 3.8 The relationship between vehicle weight and road space damage

the government of a given sum *regardless of the demand for road space*. Such a licence will transfer income with fewer effects on efficiency because a rational consumer will still consume road space until MU is zero.

However, as we shall see, there will still be some effect. It will deter marginal consumers of motor cars from purchasing at all. If the demand for cars is reduced, the whole demand curve for road space will shift inwards, which will itself reduce consumer surplus.

One reason governments make fixed charges such as the road fund licence is that there are in reality costs at the margin. Travelling along a road does impose wear and tear costs and roads do need repairing. But collecting it at the point of consumption imposes transaction costs. That is to say there are costs involved in making the transaction of a payment for the road – toll booths, toll booth operators' wages, and so on. These would be substantially higher than the issuing of an annual licence fee. Fees for large lorries are often thought of as very high in relation to the car licence. One justification for such large fees is seen in Figure 3.8 above. The damage done to a road surface does not just increase with the weight of a vehicle but with the square of the weight.

The sliding scale of the licence fee is, in part, an attempt to charge for that marginal damage.

4 Peak use pricing

a Variations in demand

Does the efficiency consideration lead us to suggest that the pricing of road space is a mistaken policy? Not necessarily! The nature of road space demand is that it varies considerably between different periods and this is the cause of most traffic jams. The demand curve will shift to the right considerably during the rush hour or during summer holiday periods in tourist areas.

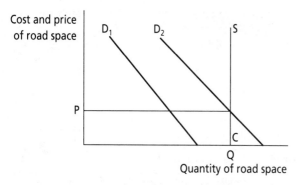

Figure 3.9 Increasing demand for read space

Consider Figure 3.9 above. It shows the demand for road space in a large city during most of the day (D_1) and demand during the rush hour period (D_2). Is there a case for pricing on efficiency grounds? There is not during the off-peak period for reasons we have already considered. But look again at the situation during the peak period when D_2 is relevant. There is now a strong case for introducing a pricing scheme on efficiency grounds.

The area C of consumer surplus is simply not available. Road space is not sufficient for that amount to be consumed. A price at P will still enable all of the possible surplus to be gained. Some of it goes to the consumer, some is transferred from the consumer to the government in revenue that can be used elsewhere.

b Pricing at the peak: efficiency considerations

But why the price and the transfer of income? Why not still a zero price? The answer is that now a zero price is not efficient. We want those who gain the greatest utility from consumption to be the ones to use it.[2] We can be sure that will be the case if a price is charged which will act as a rationing device. But if price does not ration the output and some other measure is used this will almost certainly not be the case. Some space will be consumed by those who gain little benefit from it. Let us illustrate. Remember, people will attempt to consume any good until its marginal utility is equal to the cost of the alternative. Now who are the people who will least mind traffic jams? One group is those with little better to do with their time. In other words, it will be those with a low opportunity cost of time. But some caught in the queues will be those with a high opportunity cost. Efficiency considerations require that these are the ones who avoid the congestion. They will do so if given the opportunity to buy that avoidance.

We have some estimates of the size of inefficiency. Table 3.3 below is the Confederation of British Industry (CBI) estimate published in 1989, of the costs to industry and ultimately to consumers, of congestion of roads in South East England. It gives the percentage increase in various kinds of cost over costs outside

Table 3.3 Averaged additional costs incurred in London and the South East (percentage)

Productivity lost due to lateness of staff	1
Delivery time and cost penalties within M25	30
Additional staff/drivers needed to beat congestion	20
Additional vehicles needed	20
Additional vehicle service/repair costs	20
Additional fuel costs	10
Estimated total additional	20
transportation costs in the London area	

Notes: Statistics were compiled from information provided by national organisations that could compare distribution costs in London and the South East with other areas.
Source: CBI, *The Capital at Risk* (1989).

the South East. The estimates were gathered from national organisations operating in the South East and elsewhere. The total cost of congestion there is about £15 billion at 1989 prices.

Clearly, some firm's costs are affected far more than others. A road pricing scheme would cause those firms with most to gain from reduced congestion costs to be willing to pay for congestion avoidance.

Of course, even with a peak demand situation as in Figure 3.5 we will need to consider the efficiency gains in the light of the transactions costs. But if transactions costs are low the case for road pricing is strong.

c The value of the model

You can now see what a powerful tool for analysis is the concept of marginal utility and consumer surplus. Before we turn to look at the way these ideas are used in Singapore a word of warning is in order. You may be tempted to reject the basis of the case we are constructing on one of two grounds, the first being the realism of the marginal utility assumption. You may feel that consumers simply do not behave in the way we have described. You do not hear someone shopping in Sainsbury's saying to himself or herself 'Is my marginal utility on that pound of sausages divided by its price equal to my marginal utility on that box of cornflakes divided by its price?' In other words, it is tempting to dismiss the arguments about road pricing on the grounds that the theory that underpins it is not true to life.

To argue thus is to show that you have, temporarily we hope, stopped thinking like an economist. Of course, people do not think in terms of the language of the law of diminishing marginal utility. Most people have never heard of consumer surplus. These are formal constructs that help us formulate people's behaviour. But people do behave like this even if they do not think in these terms. Before you started your economics course you still purchased more of a good if the price fell. It is just that you can now describe that behaviour in different terminology.

Maybe a great snooker player like Stephen Hendry has never heard of kinetic energy, conservation of linear momentum and coefficients of restitution, but his behaviour nevertheless conforms to these principles, or the balls would not go into the pockets so often. Exactly the same principle applies when we describe people's economic behaviour. If it enables us to predict their actions, the theory can still be valid.

The second ground on which you might be tempted to reject our analysis is that although consumer surplus is an accurate description of a real world phenomenon, it is of little use because it is not measurable. What is the money value of consumer surplus in the demand for road space? But as you have now seen some of these concepts are measurable. We *can* measure congestion costs and we can find an equilibrium price as we are about to see from the illustration of Singapore. But for now let us return to the problem of congestion pricing and see how it is approached in that city.

5 An example of road pricing

a Singapore city's scheme

Singapore is a city state of about 2.75 million inhabitants. About 70 per cent of its population live within 8 kilometres of the city centre. Back in 1974 the government looked at the problem of excess demand for road space during the rush hour, forecast that the increase in car demand by 1992 would be over 350 per cent and concluded that something had to be done.

After careful study it decided that some increase in road space was possible. But the opportunity cost of providing sufficient road space to meet the expected increase in demand was considerable. So it was the demand side that would need to be dealt with primarily. However, on the supply side there was some *reduction* in road space for cars by the provision of bus only lanes. The economic rationale is simple. Travelling by car imposes costs on oneself but also on others by increasing congestion. The provision of bus only lanes recognises that divergence between private and social benefits.

On the demand side several possibilities suggested themselves. One was an advertising campaign arguing the advantages of staggered working hours. This shifts the demand curve left at the peak but rightward off peak. Provided that the off peak increase in demand did not create an excess quantity demanded at a zero price, this would result in a net improvement in welfare. There would also be an opportunity cost of the resources allocated to the advertising.

Another measure for shifting the demand curve to the left is to increase the price of complementary goods via increased taxes on cars or petrol. The problem is that it does not affect demand at peak times relative to off-peak demand and was therefore rejected. A complete ban on cars fails to recognise that car travel is a benefit and should not be controlled unless the benefit of control exceeds its cost.

The obvious solution, however, was to use the price mechanism for space. This was the option taken. It took two forms: the pricing of road space and the pricing of parking space. Road space pricing was done via area licences. These required a payment if a car were to be used within a delineated restricted zone at peak times. The use of a toll was rejected because it was felt that this would impose too high a transaction cost in terms of collection of payment and in slowing traffic still further.

Not all vehicles paid since commercial vehicles and public transport vehicles were exempt. The other major exception was particularly interesting. A car with at least four occupants was also exempt. This, of course, was to encourage pooling of cars since the additional demand for road space is nil if a driver carries extra passengers. Nevertheless, in an attempt to restrain growing demand further, car pooling was no longer exempted after 1989. In fact, all vehicles including motorcycles were included. Only ambulances, fire engines, police vehicles and public buses are now excluded.

A further problem for the authorities was to decide what constituted peak time. The original choice was 7.15–9.30 am. Excess demand was soon apparent immediately after 9.30 am so the restricted time was extended to 10.15 am.

No restrictions were placed on travel during the evening rush hour. The argument was that the evening is a mirror image of the morning. If morning excess demand is eliminated, the evening problem automatically disappears.

The second form of price mechanism was the pricing of parking space. Parking charges in the publicly owned car parks were increased steeply. Since parking space is a close complement this further shifts demand for road space left. It is not a perfect complement because, for example, it does not affect through traffic. Private car park operators were not able to enjoy a windfall increase in profits because a levy was introduced on them.

A park and ride scheme was also introduced but was not judged to be very successful.

b Assessing the scheme

The view of the authorities was that prior to 1974 the excess demand for road space at the peak was 25–30 per cent. That is to say, the estimate was that this was the kind of reduction that would enable traffic to flow freely. The problem was that there were no known studies as to how motorists would react to large increases in the price of road space. In other words it was not known how 'price elastic' demand would be. The equilibrium price was to a large extent guesswork. The area licence was set at 60 Singapore dollars per month or 3 Singapore dollars per day. In fact, with the other measures taken demand was reduced at the peak by 40 per cent. Diagrammatically it would suggest what we have in Figure 3.10. Car parking fees, etc., shifted the demand curve left.

Car parking and road space are complementary goods. A rise in the price of car parking fees reduces the quantity of road space demanded. The price that was set

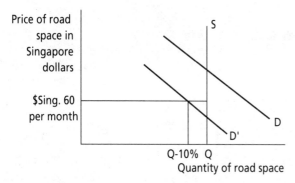

Figure 3.10 Influencing the demand for road space in Singapore

moved motorists along the lower demand curve to 10 per cent or so less than road space supply. The authority's decision was to leave the price unchanged anticipating that over time increased incomes would move the demand curve back to the right until the optimum was reached.

How has the scheme affected the distribution of benefits within Singapore? There are several things to be thought through. First, the external effects of consumption on those walking or using public transport have been reduced – those responsible for creating the effects having to bear the costs. Second, the speed of traffic is now much greater, albeit at considerable expense to those gaining the benefit. Third, government revenue is sufficient to cover all the transaction costs involved so that no cost falls on the general taxpayer.

6 Singapore today

a Pricing private transport

Present fees for the area licences are now as below in Table 3.4. Notice that the main change from the 1970s, apart from the reduction in exemptions and the inclusion of motorcycles as previously mentioned, is the differential pricing between private and company cars.

Table 3.4 Prices of area licence fee (in Singapore dollars)

Type of vehicle	Daily area licence fee	Monthly area licence fee
Motorcycle	1	20
Company car	6	120
Any other vehicle	3	60

Table 3.5 Singapore motor vehicle population, 1982–92

End of year	Total	Cars[1]	Rental cars	Taxis	Buses	Goods vehicles	Motor cycles and scooters	Others
1982	440,276	179,635	4,515	10,283	7,585	94,632	136,899	6,727
1983	476,288	202,092	4,168	10,673	7,985	102,533	141,569	7,268
1984	491,322	217,119	4,159	11,062	8,283	108,631	134,693	7,375
1985	486,760	221,279	4,030	10,941	8,717	107,146	127,564	7,083
1986	473,659	220,566	3,314	10,677	8,638	103,429	120,387	6,648
1987	471,124	222,487	3,081	10,552	8,733	102,643	116,544	7,084
1988	491,808	237,801	3,140	10,473	8,924	106,843	117,570	7,057
1989	520,537	257,371	3,135	10,652	9,126	111,940	120,996	7,317
1990	542,352	271,174	3,343	12,239	9,448	115,536	122,525	8,087
1991	559,304	283,746	3,665	12,705	9,478	118,209	122,410	9,091
1992	557,584	285,500	3,879	13,445	9,658	119,335	116,532	9,235

Note: [1] Include private cars and company cars.
Source: Singapore Year Book, 1993.

In recent years the price of purchasing a car has also risen significantly. The rise in incomes has shifted the demand curve to the right as the authorities in the 1970s predicted. Table 3.5 shows the scale of the increase in demand through the 1980s and into the 1990s. So in addition to the area licence scheme demand for road space outside the peak times is being restrained.

How is this being done? Again it is through price, this time by raising the price of cars – a complementary good to road space. There are two main forms of pricing. One form is the use of taxes and fees on the registration of new cars, the other, introduced in May 1990 is the certificate of entitlement scheme (COE).

The taxes and fees payable on registration of a car are as follows (amounts are in Singapore dollars):

1 Import duty of 45 per cent of market value.
2 Registration fee of $1000 for a private car, $5000 for a company car.
3 Additional registration fee of 150 per cent of market value.
4 In addition there is an annual road tax based on engine capacity. A medium-sized saloon would be around $2000 for a private vehicle, $4000 for a company car.

b The certificate of entitlement (COE) scheme

The COE scheme is particularly interesting. We have seen how it can be difficult to gauge the appropriate price for restricting demand to a given amount. The authorities have decided that a way of overcoming this difficulty is by a bidding system.

Each month a predetermined number of COEs valid for ten years are issued for various sizes of car, goods vehicles and motorcycles. People are then free to bid for a COE. All successful bidders pay the lowest single successful bid price for the appropriate category of vehicle. Notice that some will pay less than they bid. The authorities do not remove all the consumer surplus.

As an illustration of the point imagine there are five people wishing to purchase a COE. One of them values a COE at $10,000 (Singapore), one at $9000, one at $8000, one at $7000 and one at $6000. This is shown in the demand curve for COEs. Each will bid what he or she is willing to pay. That is what the demand curve tells us.

Assume now that there are only four COEs to be issued at this time. The lowest successful bid will be $7000. Government Revenue will be 4 × $7,000 = $28,000 since all four successful bidders pay the lowest successful bid price.

By charging all bidders the maximum they were prepared to pay, government revenue could have been $34,000, value in exchange plus value in use. The other $6000 is the consumer surplus that the government chose not to take.

7 Conclusion

If incomes continue to grow, the present problems of urban congestion can only become worse. There is still enormous potential for an increase in private vehicle ownership. It is widely recognised that something has to be done. The problems of a low average traffic speed in some British cities are repeated in large towns and cities in many parts of the world. Efficiency considerations suggest that, since road space is a scarce commodity the supply of which cannot be rapidly expanded, it is demand growth that must be tackled.

To a large extent the problem is one of peak demand. On theoretical grounds marginal utility analysis suggests that this peak can be controlled via an increase in the relative price of road space from zero to whatever is necessary for equilibrium at those particular times.

Singapore city gives an excellent illustration of an attempt to deal with the problem and provides some idea of the likely size of price increase which this solution to the problem would require. Although every city has its own particular characteristics, the change in relative price needed to achieve equilibrium would, if the example of Singapore were typical, be very considerable.

8 Questions for discussion

1 Using the concept of value in exchange and value in use, why is the price of diamonds so high relative to the price of bread, if bread is so much more useful as a commodity?

2 If the French government were to raise the toll charged on its motorways would the value of the consumed road space be higher or lower than before? (HINT: What two different ideas did we say that we had for 'value'?)

3 Can you think of other instances where queues are used as a rationing device rather than price? Why, in the instances you have thought of, do you think pricing is rejected as a solution? Is this the correct decision?

4 College canteens are crowded at lunch time. What would you think of a scheme to solve the problem whereby prices were reduced by, say, 30 per cent from 11.30–12.15 and 1.30–2.30 and increased by 20 per cent from 12.15–1.30, thus spreading the peak and eliminating the need to queue?

5 Consider Table 3.6. Which goods would appear to be those with the highest income elasticity of demand? Which have the lowest? Are there any which appear to be inferior goods? What does the table tell you about the price elasticity of demand for all of these goods?

6 Why will all of the costs of purchasing area licences not fall on private commuters? (HINT: What happens to businesses if the effect is to reduce the supply of labour to those in the centre?)

Table 3.6 Consumer durables by economic activity status of head of household, Great Britain 1992

| Percentage of households with: | Socio-economic group of head of household* | | | | | | | | |
| | Economically active heads | | | | | | | Total | Economically inactive heads |
	Professional	Employers and managers	Intermediate non-manual	Junior non-manual	Skilled manual and own account non-professional	Semi-skilled manual and personal service	Unskilled manual		
Television:									
colour	97	98	96	97	98	94	93	97	94
black and white	1	1	2	2	2	5	5	2	5
Video recorder	87	91	84	84	90	82	73	87	48
CD player	54	53	49	40	40	39	29	44	15
Home computer	52	41	38	26	29	22	21	33	7
Microwave oven	68	77	69	64	74	63	55	70	41
Deep freezer/ fridge freezer	94	94	87	88	93	87	87	91	76
Washing machine	96	96	93	93	94	90	88	94	79
Tumble drier	66	71	59	51	60	51	44	60	32
Dishwasher	41	38	23	13	14	7	4	21	7
Telephone	98	98	95	90	90	81	73	91	86
Central heating	95	93	87	84	83	77	72	86	78
Car or van – more than one	51	56	32	21	32	18	12	35	7

Note: * Excluding members of the Armed Forces, and economically active full-time students and those who were unemployed and had never worked.
Source: General Household Survey, 1993.

7 Why will all of the costs of purchasing area licences for company cars not fall entirely on business profits?
8 What advantages and disadvantages are there in removing all the consumer surplus under the COE scheme?
9 What problems and benefits do you see in introducing a scheme similar to Singapore in your own city?

9 Further reading

Marginal utility
Sloman, pp. 123–33; Parkin and King, pp. 147–55

Consumer surplus
Sloman, pp. 126–8; Parkin and King, pp. 156–7

Income elasticity of demand
Sloman, p. 84; Begg, pp. 70–2; Parkin and King, pp. 103–4

Traffic jams
Some of the data regarding the original introduction of road pricing in Singapore city can be found in P. Watson and E. Holland (1976) 'Congestion Pricing – The example of Singapore', *Finance and Development*, March.

A general introduction to the problem of road congestion, but without reference to Singapore is given in S. Ison, 'The Economics of Road Transport Congestion', *Economics*, Autumn 1990.

10 End notes

1 Some of the concern about the use of cars relates not so much to the problems of congestion but to damage to the environment. There is very little in this chapter on this aspect of the problem of transport. However, the problems raised by such matters are dealt with at various points in later chapters, especially in Chapter 12.
2 You may feel that this is unfair! The rich can afford to consume the road space. In fact there are two factors governing the demand for road space, or indeed for any good. One is willingness to pay; the other is ability to pay. We are concentrating here on willingness to pay. We want those who are most willing to pay to consume the product. In other words, we want, *for any given distribution of income*, those who are most willing to pay to be consumers. The question of ability to pay and the distribution of income is examined in Chapter 16.

CHAPTER 4

The National Health Service:
is radical treatment needed?

In recent years the provision of many services widely regarded as essential has been moved from the state to the private sector. Would we have a more efficient health care system if we transferred the NHS to the private sector? Would most people gain? How would it affect the poor? Would we have greater resources devoted to health and a healthier population?

In this chapter we review:
- Supply and demand

We introduce:
- Indifference theory
- Merit goods
- External benefits
- The distribution of income
- Pareto optimality

1 Introduction

Most people accept without question the fact that the great majority of things they wish to have are provided on a market basis. Whether it be relatively unimportant items, such as balloons and ice cream, or things essential to survival such as clothing and food, people expect to pay for these things at the point of consumption. One notable exception to the rule is that of health care. The majority of people in this country favour the provision of 'free' health care through the National Health Service (NHS). Most appreciate, of course, that such treatment cannot be provided at a zero cost. But they believe that those costs should be borne by the government through general taxation so that the care is given free at the point at which it is consumed. To pay to go into hospital for an operation or to pay for a visit to the GP would be regarded as unacceptable.

Let us examine Table 4.1. One striking factor of expenditure on health care is how much importance is attached to it. In established market economies, over 9 per cent of total output is consumed by health care. Notice, too, that health care appears to be highly income elastic. Per capita, health expenditure in established market economies is nearly eighty times as great as in sub-Saharan Africa and 160 times as great as it is in China. Yet even in established market economies, as can be seen from column four, 60 per cent of all this expenditure is incurred by the

Table 4.1 Health expenditure in all countries, 1990

Demographic region	Percentage of world population	Total health expenditure (billion dollars)	Health expenditure as percentage of world total	Public sector health expenditure as percentage of regional total	Percentage of GNP spent on health	Per capita health expenditure (dollars)	Ratio of per capita spending (SSA = 1)[1]
Established market economies	15	1,483	87	60	9.2	1,860	78.9
Formerly socialist economies of Europe	7	49	3	71	3.6	142	6.0
Latin America	8	47	3	60	4.0	105	4.5
Middle Eastern crescent	10	39	2	58	4.1	77	3.3
Other Asia and islands	13	42	2	39	4.5	61	2.6
India	16	18	1	22	6.0	21	0.9
China	22	13	1	59	3.5	11	0.5
Sub-Saharan Africa	10	12	1	55	4.5	24	1.0
Demographically developing countries	78	170	10	50	4.7	41	1.7
World	100	1,702	100	60	8.0	323	13.7

Note: SSA = Sub-Saharan Africa.
Source: Finance and Development, September 1993.

public sector. The market mechanism plays a fairly small part in Britain, one of the established market economies, since most health care expenditure is undertaken by government. Furthermore, relatively little of it is charged for at the point of use. In Britain the system commands widespread public support. In the course of this chapter, we shall ask whether such a system makes economic sense.

We want to question whether there is any economic rationale in saying that, say, food should not be free at the point of consumption but should be provided for out of taxation, whereas health care should be distributed on a non-market basis.

What we shall do in this chapter, therefore, is as follows. First, we shall argue the case for treating health care like any other good or service and providing it on a market basis as is largely the case in the USA. Then we shall consider the main objections to this view, concentrating particularly upon the view that a free NHS is the only way of ensuring an adequate level of health care to the poor.

2 The market case

a The demand for health care

The first reason for allocating health care on a market basis is that it gives a solution to the problem of rationing. Allocating health on a non-market basis tends to assume that the demand for health care is a finite one even if there is a zero price. One is either 'healthy' or 'ill'. In fact, this is not the case. There are degrees of illness and health. This has become even more obvious with improved medical techniques, which not only cure illness, but also discover it. Body scanners, for example, have the potential to diagnose conditions which twenty years ago would have gone unnoticed. Furthermore, medical technology has created a demand for hip replacements, heart transplants and many other forms of health care. The demand was previously not there because the treatment was, given the state of technology at the time, impossible.

It is, therefore, probably true that health care is capable of absorbing more than the whole of the gross national product! As economists never tire of pointing out, when resources are scarce choices have to be made. The conclusion is inescapable. Medical care has to be rationed, a point which Figure 4.1 forcefully makes. Notice how there has been a significant increase in resources devoted to health care in Britain in the last 10–15 years. But complaints about hospital waiting lists and overcrowded doctors' surgeries have not abated at all during this period!

Figure 4.1 also shows that the increase in spending is partly due to inflation. The chart shows expenditure at current prices. If we concentrate on the amount of real resources going into the NHS we must remove the effect of inflation. This is shown as 'real growth in spending'. The long-term trend is still upward, but not so markedly as the increase in current spending.

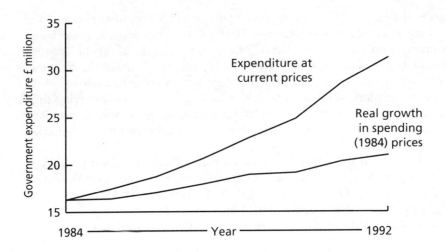

Source: Author's estimates from Department of Health data.

Figure 4.1 Government on health care in Britain

The second, closely related, reason for thinking that health care might be better allocated on a market basis is that the market mechanism can offer a means of distinguishing between wants and needs. Medical care *can* mean the difference between life and death. A man with a heart attack 'needs' medical attention or he will die. However, a relatively small amount of medical care is for life-threatening conditions. Think of your trips to hospital or the doctor in recent years. Most of them have been for the purpose of improving the state of health. In most cases you could have survived without the care. These trips will range from the serious to the trivial. They are 'wants'. How does one distinguish between wants and needs? The economist's answer is willingness to pay. If it is really needed the consumer will demand it. If it is a want he may or may not do so. If one does not use a market system there will be great difficulty making the distinction. An obvious illustration of the difficulty is found in the somewhat abitrary decisions of government over what aspects of health care should be charged for. Hospitalisation is free and medication provided while in hospital is also free. Medication provided by a GP is, to many, partly paid for in the prescription charge. Suntan lotion to protect from melanoma is not regarded as a need. It is clearly an attractive idea, then, to let the consumer decide which he regards as important via the price system.

b Rationing health care by price: efficient resource usage

Let us now see how a price system overcomes these disadvantages of an NHS type system. Consider Figure 4.2. We examine one part of the NHS system for

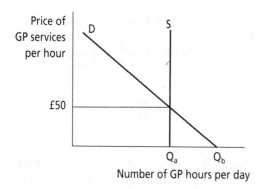

Figure 4.2 Illustrating a market price of GP services

illustrative purposes, the GP system. The government determines the number of GPs it is prepared to fund out of taxation. This gives us a fixed supply of GP services, at least in the short run.

There will clearly be a negatively sloped demand curve for the reasons outlined above. What happens if the price of a visit to the doctor is zero? There is excess demand of $Q_b - Q_a$. This is not simply some textbook problem. It illustrates powerfully what happens all over Britain every day. People who value the visit to the surgery at 20 pence, that is people who would not go if they were charged more than 20 pence, are going and using up scarce resources with a high opportunity cost. In other words they are depriving others who 'need' the GP's services. The benefit of the price system is that only the visits to the surgery where people believe the GP's time to be worth at least £50 are made, that is, they will only go if they value the GP's time at its opportunity cost. This will *not* be so within the NHS where a visit to the doctor is free at the point of use. Non-price rationing will take place. Since there is excess demand at this zero price, the alternative form of rationing, queues, will not efficiently see to it that those who most value the visits are the ones found in the doctor's surgery. In essence the problem is similar to that of the excess demand for road space we encountered in Chapter 3.

There are other ways in which this inefficiency displays itself. It is not simply that some who value the doctor's time will not get to see him. Further problems occur. The average time spent with the GP is also reduced. Whereas in the USA fifteen minutes is an average consulting time per patient, five minutes or less is typical in England. This is probably *not* a reflection of the greater number of GPs per head in USA than England. It is rather a reflection of the huge demand for GP services in England due to the absence of a price mechanism. However, the nature of medical care in the USA tends to mean more specialists and fewer general practitioners than in England, so that comparisons are very difficult to make.

Non-price rationing also reduces the array of services provided by a GP. Except for the elderly and chronically sick it is not always easy to get a check-up on the NHS. Tests to detect breast cancer, for example, are also less common than in the

USA. There is simply not time to provide such services if price does not ration output. GPs now have to meet 'targets' in terms of numbers given check-ups, etc. These have been introduced in recent years specifically to try to deal with this excess demand situation.

Another inefficiency which non-price rationing creates is, alas, by its nature virtually impossible to measure. Excess demand where there is an effective price ceiling usually results in the creation of some form of discrimination. Doctors and surgeons can on occasion allow someone to 'jump the queue'.

Finally, one must not underestimate the degree of inefficiency associated with transferring decisions about health care from the economic sphere to the political one. Most people who have a relatively minor complaint can get treatment quickly. A throat infection requiring a GP to prescribe antibiotics usually can be treated within a few days. More serious conditions will be treated far more slowly. Waiting times for surgical treatment of a heart condition may take months or even years. In a market system this would not be so likely to happen. Since the heart condition treatment would be valued more, it will be treated relatively quickly. So why in an NHS-type system is the reverse the case? One explanation is that when resources are allocated by politicians, they are primarily interested in buying votes. There are more votes in providing resources to treat large numbers of people for minor complaints than there are in allocating large volumes of resources to treat relatively few. This may or may not be the best way to use limited health care resources.

3 Private medical care in Britain: using indifference theory

So far the discussion has been conducted as though there were no private health care market in Britain. Such is not, in fact, the case. It is possible to insure through organisations such as BUPA against the need for many forms of medical care. Growing numbers of people have chosen to do so, as Table 4.2 below indicates. Preliminary estimates for the early 1990s suggest that this process is continuing, although the recession in Britain slowed the trend somewhat.

Table 4.2 Subscriptions to private health insurance, 1986–90

	1986	1987	1988	1989	1990
Subscribers (000)	2,450	2,540	2,742	3,430	3,613*
Covered (000)	5,250	5,340	5,784	7,241	7,552*
Subscriptions earned (£m)	614	615	801	959	1,113*
Claims incurred (£m)	513	587	680	821	980*

Note: *preliminary ABI estimates.
Source: Key Note Compilation, Private Health Care, 1992.

One advantage of having a state health care service *plus* a private service would appear to be that *more* resources are thus devoted to health care. Careful thought, however, will lead us to the conclusion that this may not be so. In order to follow the argument we need to acquaint ourselves with the elements of indifference theory, or what is sometimes called indifference curve analysis.

When we looked at consumer behaviour in Chapter 3 we used the concept of marginal utility analysis. An alternative approach to explaining how consumers behave is indifference theory. There is more to indifference theory than we shall consider now[1], but understanding the elements of this approach will shed light on choices people make with respect to consuming many goods and services, including health.

Consider first people's preferences for health and all other goods, which we shall do from Figure 4.3. We are particularly interested in people's preferences about health but the principles we are developing apply for most consumers with any good or service.

Figure 4.3 shows Jessica's preferences. Each spot represents a level of utility she receives from consuming the given quantities. So spot X gives some level of utility, or satisfaction, received by consuming, $O\text{-}H_1$ of health care and $O\text{-}O_1$ of other services. Other combinations which lie along IC_1, indifference curve 1, are assumed to give the same level of satisfaction. She would regard herself as 'indifferent' between any such combinations, including spots Y and Z. Notice the slope of the curve. It is negative. This shows that in order to retain a given level of utility, Jessica requires more health care in order to compensate for a reduction in the amount of other goods and services she consumes. But the shape of the curve is also significant. It is what one would expect for most consumers and most goods and services. She is indifferent between X and Y. Yet she gets only a little more health care at Y for a large sacrifice of other goods and services. This is reasonable. The loss of some goods of which Jessica has a great deal is not too serious. The gain of a little more health care when she has so little is worth quite a lot to her. But the less of other goods she has and the more health care she has, the less

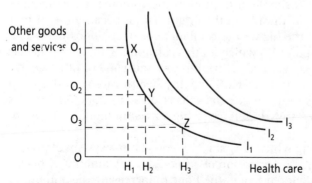

Figure 4.3 Indifference curves for health care and other goods and services

enthusiasm she has for switching into even more health care. So moving from Y to Z will keep her equally happy, but she will need greater amounts of health care to compensate for the loss of other goods. This is the principle which underlies the shape of the indifference curve as being convex to the origin.

We assume, of course, that consumers would prefer more of both goods if it were possible. So combinations along IC_2 are preferred to combinations along IC_1 since these show greater combinations of both goods and hence greater welfare.

But can our consumer afford all these combinations? Clearly that depends upon her income and upon the prices of the goods and services in question. We can use Figure 4.4 to show the constraint income places on the ability to meet preferences. Assume her income is £1000 per month.

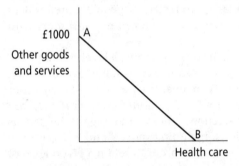

Figure 4.4 Relative price of health care to other goods and services

She could consume at point A, spend all her income on other goods and none of it on health care. She could be at point B spending her entire income on health care. It is much more likely that she will choose one of the combinations of health care and other goods and services which her £1000 income will purchase. These combinations are represented by the straight line AB called a budget line. Which combination will she actually choose? Figure 4.5 shows both her preferences and the budget line. The solution is simple. She chooses the combination which gets her on the indifference curve furthest from the origin. This is because the further from the origin the curve lies the higher the combinations of all goods she is able to enjoy. For Jessica this is at point W, which for this consumer with her particular preferences means she buys £400 worth of health care and £600 of other goods.

Now all this assumes that there is no NHS and any health care she consumed must be purchased. We turn now to see the effects on consumer preferences towards health if we introduce an NHS service giving a free but limited amount of health care.

There is one interesting thing which may surprise you about a system of private health care existing alongside state provision of a free statutory amount of health care. If a statutory amount is offered free in the hope of increasing the amount of health care everyone receives, it is unlikely to achieve that for all. In fact it may

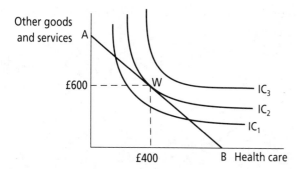

Figure 4.5 Consumer equilibrium in health care preference

actually reduce the amount some receive. If you find this surprising look at Figure 4.6 below.

The budget line AB represents the options open to a consumer with a given income with respect to health care where there is no state scheme. The consumer can choose any combination of health and other goods and services along that budget line. But now the government introduces an NHS scheme. There is a limited amount of health care offered, OH. However, since it is free at the point of consumption, the consumer is being offered the combination at point C in addition to all combinations along AB. Note that if this consumer chooses point C he or she can have OA of all other goods because he or she does not have to pay for the volume of health care OH offered by the government. Now, suppose that one could either choose NHS provision or private health, but not a combination of both. Will a rational consumer always choose point C? Indeed not! It will depend upon his or her preferences. The volume of health care one may wish to consume may exceed what is on offer free by the NHS. Let us look at three different consumers and impose their preferences on the budget line from Figure 4.6. We do this in Figure 4.7(a), (b) and (c).

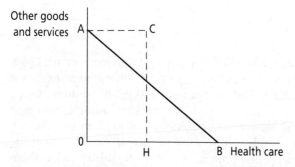

Figure 4.6 Free government provision of health care: effects on consumer choice

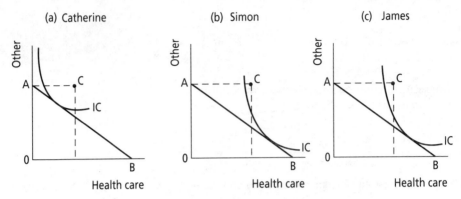

Figure 4.7 Possible consumer reactions to government free health care provision

Catherine, the consumer in (a) does not value health care very highly and would choose little of it in the absence of an NHS. Point C is on a higher indifference curve for this particular consumer. So, given an NHS system, Catherine will choose point C and be healthier. The consumer in Figure 4.7(b), Simon, is much more health conscious. He is willing to devote a high proportion of his income to health care. So how does NHS provision affect him? Not at all! Point C puts him on a lower level of welfare because he values so highly the additional health care which he will continue to purchase from the private sector.

Now consider James, whose preferences are shown in (c). He has some concern for health care but not a passionate one. Does such a person seem most typical? Now look again at his preferences. Point C puts him on a higher indifference curve. When the NHS is provided he will opt out of private health care into the state provision of the statutory amount. Notice that this means he is consuming less health care than he would have done without that provision. It is distinctly possible that the government's provision of health care of the kind offered by the NHS would reduce the volume of health care which society consumes if those choosing private health care are excluded from the consumption of free state care.

4 The case for the NHS

As we saw earlier on the NHS system is politically popular. During the late 1980s and early 1990s in Britain it was rumoured that the Conservative government was considering abandonment of the NHS. The government was left in no doubt that it would be highly unpopular for doing so and the present administration is adamant that although it will seek to reform the NHS by making it more efficient, it will not seek to abandon the principle of universal health care free for all at the point of consumption. On what grounds might one seek to justify the present system? There are four areas where a case can be made. We shall briefly examine each one in turn.

a Merit goods

First, health care is a 'merit good'. Unfortunately the textbooks do not agree as to what a merit good is. Some say that they are goods (or services) provided on the basis of need such that those with a particularly low level of income are able to consume them. Defined thus health care is often seen as a merit good since some would not be able to afford health care without government subsidy. This is clearly a matter of some importance to which we shall return shortly. However, others see merit goods as those which people will choose to under-consume because they will fail correctly to see the benefit to themselves of the consumption of the good. It is not that consumers lack income, or even information but they are unable to make the judgements on the basis of that information which would maximise their welfare. If we accept this as a definition of a merit good, we can illustrate the merit good case for an NHS via the debate about payment for eye tests. Eye tests were provided free in Britain until the late 1980s. At that time it was decided that a contribution should be made to the cost of providing the test. All must now pay £10 for the test. Those unhappy with the charge protest on three grounds. First some cannot afford it even though they need it. On some definitions in the textbook this makes it a merit good. We shall not examine the point here since we return to it below.

Second, some feel that the eye test charge is wrong since people will be put off taking it even though it is well worth it given the potential benefit of early treatment for eye conditions such as glaucoma. Again, this is a point we shall examine below but it does not constitute a 'merit good' case. It is simply a problem of inadequate information. Some argue that the charge for the eye test is wrong because some will not be capable of evaluating the information even if it is available and will therefore make a free choice which will reduce their own welfare. On some definitions of a merit good this is the key point. Merit goods should be provided free to protect people from themselves.

Let us stay specifically with this argument for government provision of health care. Several points should be thought through as you consider the strength of this view. Clearly it is essentially paternalistic. The argument amounts to saying that other people, in this case the government, can make decisions for you better than you are able to make them yourself. Perhaps the British are more enthusiastic about such an argument than the Americans. It is interesting to note that virtually all British introductory economics textbooks make reference to the question of merit goods – and virtually no American text does so.

One other thing needs to be thought through with respect to merit goods. There is no obvious distinction between what is and what is not a merit good. Health care certainly has a strong claim to be one, however one defines a merit good. Other goods have a less strong claim. It will not be easy to decide which things people should decide for themselves and which things should be decided for them. The use of the market mechanism is built, of course, on the belief that people can act in their own interests better than others can act for them.

b External benefits

The second area where a case can be made for the provision of state health care centres around the concept of 'external benefits'. An external benefit occurs where an action confers benefits on parties not directly involved in an exchange. If you purchase a good or service you will gain some benefit from it. This benefit is internal to you. Sometimes, however, your purchase brings benefits to others as well. This is an external benefit. One illustration of such an external benefit in the context of health care is innoculations against communicable diseases. If you choose to be innoculated against diphtheria it increases the chances of your not catching it. That is a private internal benefit. It is a benefit to you. But your innoculation also decreases the risk of my catching it. Clearly, this presents a powerful case for government intervention, in that the benefits to society as a whole, the external benefits plus the internal ones are greater than the benefits accruing to those purchasing the benefits in a market.[2]

However, we must be careful in our thinking at this point. The consumption of most health care has no such external effects. If you break your leg, whether or not it is mended properly does not affect the chances of my 'catching' your broken leg. Most health care confers private benefits only. Powerful though the externalities argument is, then, its power embraces only a limited amount of health care provision.

c Imperfect information

The third area of thought in which NHS provision is often justified is in relation to the lack of information on which decisions by consumers are taken. The argument is as follows. When consumers make decisions to purchase any commodity it is because they believe the purchase will improve their welfare. Markets are efficient, therefore, only if consumers have sufficient information to make informed choices. This is not the case in the doctor–patient relationship. The patient has come because he lacks knowledge. Markets, therefore, are not efficient because the necessary conditions for efficient exchange are not present. This justifies the removal of a price mechanism such that the doctor/surgeon has no incentive to cheat on the basis of his superior knowledge, undertaking expensive medical treatment of little value to his patient.

As you think through you own views on this matter let us see how a market economist might argue when faced with this point of view. He would probably say something like this. We are inclined to think that information is something costless to acquire. But, of course, it is not. If we want to buy a car which represents the best value for money, we need to spend time acquiring information about fuel consumption, prices, etc. Each of us decides how much information we think it is worth acquiring before taking a decision. In other words, as with any other area of life, we proceed until the expected marginal benefit of acquiring more information equals its additional cost. Since information is not costless, there is an optimal volume of information, which the market will itself provide at a price which reflects its cost. For example, in the case of cars, one does not have perfect information but it can be bought from such sources as the Consumer Association magazine *Which*? Such a journal is, in essence, part of the market in information.

In the case of health there is nothing to stop us asking for advice from a number of different medically able people. We do not have to put ourselves at the mercy of one doctor only, unless the additional cost of acquiring the additional information from others is high relative to the benefits. On this basis there is no case for providing health care on a non-market basis. It does not matter that consumers do not have perfect information. They need only to be aware that the information they have is not perfect.

Even if the above argument is thought to be unconvincing it would still not be clear that NHS provision is a good use of resources. In other areas of essential services, food for example, there are laws requiring producers to give some kind of information on the content of packets, and so on. It is not felt that imperfect information provides an argument for government provision of food on a non-market basis, merely some control of the market.

But we have still not examined the major concern of most people about leaving health care to market forces. The major concern is surely this. Could the poor afford to buy health care? In other words we should think not only about questions of efficiency but also about equity. It is to this important matter that we now turn.

d Equity

If we want to know how many people in Britain are poor, we have an obvious problem. What constitutes poverty? One definition is to say that someone is poor if he or she lives at or below the level of income support set by the government. For a married couple with two children this is not much over £90 per week. On that basis over 10 million people in England are poor. It is obvious why it is so difficult to find an unambiguous definition of poverty. If the government were significantly to raise income support so that lower income groups were made substantially better off just as many people would still be poor on the above definition!

Another aspect of the problem of measurement is that we may not agree whether poverty is an absolute or a relative concept. An income of £90–£100 per week is large compared with that received by a family in Bangladesh. It is pretty minimal compared with average incomes in the UK!

Before we look at the question of health care provision in the light of the problem of poverty, it is worth getting some idea of the distribution of income in Britain and how it has changed in recent years. We do that in the three diagrams below labelled Figure 4.8(a), (b) and (c).

Consider first Figure 4.8(a). The device we are using to represent the distribution of income is known as a Lorenz curve. It shows on the vertical axes

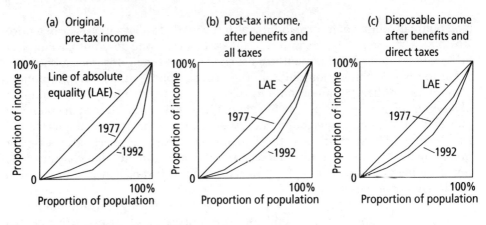

Source : Economic Trends, January 1994.

Figure 4.8 Shares of UK household income

the proportion of income available to British citizens and on the horizontal axes the proportion of the population cumulated from the poorest. Consider first what this means in terms of the line of absolute equality. Suppose that everyone in society had the same level of income. Then 10 per cent of the population would have 10 per cent of the income, and 80 per cent of the population would have 80 per cent of the income and so on. The line representing this distribution is indeed the line of absolute equality. Any other distribution can be represented by a Lorenz curve. So considering the 'original' distribution of income, the income before tax, for the year 1977, it can be seen that the poorest 20 per cent of the population had only 2 per cent of income before tax and social security payments were taken into account. Since the next poorest 20 per cent had 7 per cent of the income, the poorest 40 per cent had 9 per cent. Notice how the top 20 per cent had 50 per cent of income before tax.[3]

The numbers on which the above diagrams are based have been 'equivalised'. That is to say, allowance has been made for the numbers of people in each household. Clearly, a larger household with more children needs more income to support it. These figures take account of this.

The above statistics show a number of important things. First, the distribution of income before tax is widening. Clearly, the more even the distribution of income is, the closer to the line of absolute equality the Lorenz curve would be. The curve bulges further from the origin for 1992 than for 1977. The post-tax distribution of income has also widened. Figure 4.8(b) largely reflects the cuts in higher rate taxes made during the 1980s. Cuts in higher rates of taxes paid by higher income groups have moved the 1992 Lorenz curve further from the line of absolute equality. Whether it should be more even we consider in due course.

Finally, remember that when comparing the distribution of income over time, the total income is over the long run tending to rise. A constant proportion of increasing national income will still mean that a group is getting absolutely better

Table 4.3 Adults claiming to have private medical insurance by age and social grade (%), 1991

	Have private medical insurance	Paid by self	Paid by employer
AB	32.3	17.5	12.2
C1	17.9	8.0	7.9
C2	11.2	6.6	3.7
D	7.7	4.2	2.8
E	2.7	1.6	0.2

Source: Key Note. Compilation, Private Health Care, 1992.

off. The diagrams do not take account of this. It therefore disguises the fact that for some even at the lower end of the scale, they have become better off absolutely while becoming worse off relatively. For others they are worse off both relatively and absolutely.

It is this equity consideration which presents the problem of using a market for health care. It is felt by many that the distribution of income is simply too uneven for such a policy. Notice how closely the proportion of people having private medical insurance is related to social grade. These figures are given in Table 4.3. The letters A–E represent a standard grading of socio-economic status, with AB representing 'professional', relatively well paid groups, and E representing unskilled manual workers on relatively low incomes. Given the uneven distribution of income in society, one could argue that it is more just to distribute health care on a non-market basis, even if efficiency considerations suggest otherwise. A market for health would bear heavily on lower income groups.

As we think through this key issue there are some areas of thought of which we need, as economists, to be aware. The first area concerns what is usually referred to as Pareto optimality.

5 Developing the equity argument: Pareto optimality

Pareto optimality is a state in which it is not possible to improve one person's welfare without reducing someone else's. It, therefore, follows that freely negotiated trades are regarded as good because they offer a Pareto improvement. If you buy my CD player, presumably you regard yourself as benefitting from the trade, or you would not have bought it from me. Similarly, I will also have improved my welfare or I would not have sold it. As a result of the exchange we are both better off and nobody is worse off (assuming you do not produce an external effect by the noise!). If, of course, the government taxes me and increases your student grant, it has increased your welfare and reduced mine. This is not considered a Pareto improvement because it is not a voluntary exchange.

Now this is the main reason why economists tend to approve of free markets. It maximises the number of mutually beneficial exchanges. But then how do they regard enforced exchanges, as for example when higher income groups are made to pay taxes which are used for income support for lower income groups or for the provision of more medical care than lower income groups would choose to buy? Are these bad? The answer is that most economists feel that as economists they cannot pronounce upon such matters. Since one cannot measure the extent to which one person has lost welfare and the extent to which another has gained, there is no objective way of deciding whether the enforced exchange improves community welfare. It is not, therefore, Pareto-optimal. It is a subjective matter to which we are all entitled to a view. But economists, as economists, are not able to make such value judgements.

Does this leave us in a position where economists as economists have nothing to say about equity considerations? Indeed it does not! Economists have much to say, particularly about the form of redistribution.

If you are impressed by the view that the NHS is a good system on equity grounds you might return to Figure 4.1 and think it through a little further. An argument for an NHS system could be made along the following lines. Given the NHS, what will determine who visits the GP? One factor is clearly the assessment one has of the benefit of receiving medical care, the other is the opportunity cost of receiving it. In a market system, when the price of £30 per hour is payable, that would be largely the alternative goods and services one had to sacrifice in order to pay the GP. In an NHS system there is no price, so the opportunity cost is largely in terms of the time spent waiting. During that time one could, for example, have been working and earning an income.

Now who are the people with the lowest opportunity cost? The answer is those with lower incomes who foresake fewer pounds of income to queue! Hence lower income groups will receive more of the scarce resources available. On equity grounds this is what we are looking for.

Not everyone is an enthusiastic supporter of this view. Some who are concerned about the equity issue fear that in practice those with high incomes from high socio-economic groups are better able to overcome the administrative hurdles imposed by a rationing system. For example, many GPs use an appointments system which may mean several days wait for an appointment except in urgent cases. Those from higher income groups may be more persuasive in arguing that their own case is urgent.

Thus, of those who believe that low income people need free health care, many would still prefer to see some kind of market system in which only low income groups are exempted from payment.

One other interesting aspect of the equity argument concerns the question of whether lower income groups would benefit more from free health care provision

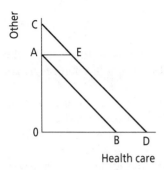

Figure 4.9 Free health care provision or income transfers to the poor?

or from an equivalent increase in income via a direct transfer while still having to pay the market price for health care. There is an argument that says that such groups would gain more from an income increase than from free health care provision. We use Figure 4.9 to demonstrate this view.

The budget line AB shows the combinations of medical care and other goods which our low income consumer can choose if no redistribution of income and no free provision of health care is offered. Suppose now this consumer is offered free health care. The budget line becomes AED. He can have more care but not more of other goods. This improves his welfare and enables him to be on a higher indifference curve. Suppose now this consumer is offered instead additional income, equivalent in value to the health care. What options are open now?

His budget line is now CD. Notice that by offering free health care the low income consumer cannot choose greater levels of other goods and services. The options in triangle ACE are denied him. This may or may not lead him to increase his demand for health care but it can further improve his utility by offering combinations of health care and other goods which the subsidy did not make possible. Hence, there is a case for saying that an increase in disposable income is a better policy than a distorted relative price of health care, if one wishes to help lower income groups. There is, however, an important qualification to this. If one feels that the externalities or merit goods argument is valid, one may not *want* the low income consumer to choose combinations of health care and other goods which leads him to higher utility but lower health care consumption. In this case the restricted options offered by free health care provision may be a better option.

One other issue of some importance may have occurred to you. Couldn't the transfer of income via tax increases on higher income groups affect their incentives to work? Could we not therefore find that a cost of helping lower income groups in *whatever* form might be less output and lower average living standards? This is clearly an important question. We have not attempted to analyse it here because it forms the basis of Chapter 16.

6 Conclusion

Overall, how good is the NHS? One way of answering this is to try to make international comparisons. This is fraught with difficulties but a few figures might be instructive. Look at Table 4.4.

The first thing which is immediately apparent is that, despite the increases in demand over time for private health insurance which we observed earlier, Britain spends relatively little on health care. France and Germany, for example, spend a higher proportion of their national income on health, but these countries have a higher national income. So the difference in total health spending is very marked. In and of itself this proves little. It could be argued that it is a measure of how efficient the NHS is that we need so few resources to achieve health care for British consumers. Alternatively, it could be argued that it shows how in the absence of market mechanism a fixed amount of medical care means that people are unable to get the amount of health care resources they wish for!

Eurostat has published figures for the level of some specific health inputs in the EU (European Union)[4] countries which are given in Table 4.5. On these measures also Britain is seen to put relatively little into health care.

Perhaps therefore we need to look, not so much at inputs but at outputs. Are Britons as healthy as the citizens of other countries which do not have an NHS-type system? Clearly this is very difficult to measure. Two rather crude measures are given below, namely life expectancy and mortality rates, both infant and maternal. Take the data given in Table 4.6. There appears to be little difference in

Table 4.4 Health expenditure in Europe

Country	$US per capita (1990)	Health spending as per cent of GDP
France	17,431	9.1
Germany	16,309	8.5
Luxembourg	19,340	7.2
Netherlands	15,766	8.3
Italy	16,021	8.3
Belgium	16,407	7.9
Denmark	16,765	6.5
UK	15,730	6.6
Ireland	10,669	7.3
Spain	11,792	6.7
Portugal	8,389	6.8
Greece	7,349	5.2

Source: OECD.

Table 4.5 Selected health inputs in EC countries (per 100 inhabitants)

	Doctors	Dentists	Hospital beds
Belgium	2.4	0.5	6.8
Denmark	2.6	0.9	6.9
Germany	2.7	0.6	11.0
Greece	3.1	0.9	5.3
Eire	3.4	0.1	4.7
France	2.3	0.6	8.9
Northern Ireland	1.5	0.3	8.5
Italy	1.5	—	7.8
Luxembourg	1.9	0.5	12.4
Netherlands	2.3	0.5	11.4
Portugal	2.5	—	3.8
UK	1.4	0.4	7.2

Source: Eurostat (1992).

Table 4.6 Life expectancy in years in European countries, 1987

Country	Life expectancy (years)
Austria	74.1
Belgium	74.6
Denmark	75.2
Finland	74.8
France	75.5
Germany	74.8
Ireland	73.9
Italy	75.4
Luxembourg	74.2
Netherlands	76.7
Norway	76.6
Portugal	73.2
Spain	76.5
Sweden	76.9
Switzerland	76.9
UK	75.0

Source: World Health Statistics.

life expectancy rates despite large differences in health care spending. But the French and Germans do live a little longer. Would this be true of Britain if we increased health expenditure? Above all, who should take such a decision?

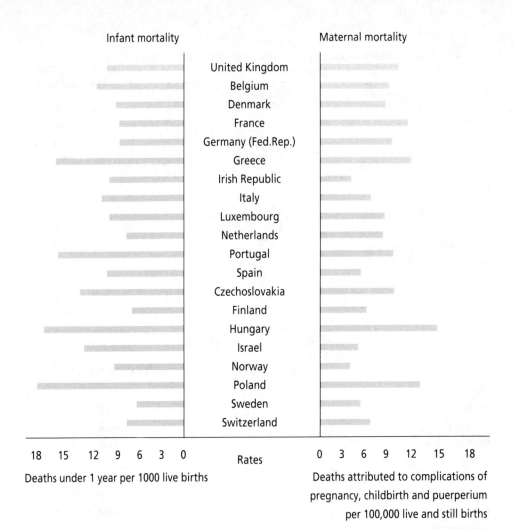

Infant mortality		Maternal mortality

United Kingdom
Belgium
Denmark
France
Germany (Fed.Rep.)
Greece
Irish Republic
Italy
Luxembourg
Netherlands
Portugal
Spain
Czechoslovakia
Finland
Hungary
Israel
Norway
Poland
Sweden
Switzerland

18 15 12 9 6 3 0   Rates   0 3 6 9 12 15 18

Deaths under 1 year per 1000 live births

Deaths attributed to complications of
pregnancy, childbirth and puerperium
per 100,000 live and still births

Source: *Social Trends*, 1993.

Figure 4.10 International infant and maternal mortality rates, averages 1987–9

Should it be governments or households? What the data do not tell is whether people are in general in more pain and discomfort in Britain compared with countries which devote more to health care.

Consider now the question of infant and maternal mortality rates in Figure 4.10. Again we must remember that this is only one aspect of health care. Nevertheless, there is clearly a relationship between such rates and national income.

But it may well be that the relationship is with income rather than health expenditure as such. There is a strong relationship between income and infant mortality rates. Infant mortality rates decline as the social class of the father rises, and there is a close correlation between income and social class.

In the last few years the British government has made great efforts to make the health service more efficient with the introduction of an 'internal market'. The move is designed to make health care resource usage more efficient. One possible problem is that costs associated with markets – advertising, distribution costs, etc. are bound to rise. The allocation of resources within the NHS must improve sufficiently to outweigh these costs. It remains to be seen whether this will be so.

One possible benefit of trying to bring market considerations into the NHS is that it forces those involved to consider the resource allocation questions we have been examining in this chapter. In order to examine the problem we considered health care as one good. One can also see it as a group of products meeting a great variety of needs. The scarcity of resources forces society to face unpleasant choices. We have to decide whether to have more health care and fewer television sets. But should we have more dialysis machines and less maternity care? How do we decide between the competing requirements of lung cancer patients and road accident victims? It is rather too early to judge how successful or otherwise the internal market will prove. But the issues the internal market was devised to address will not go away.

We have not resolved the question of whether an NHS scheme improves welfare in Britain, but the most important areas of debate should now be in sharper focus.

7 Questions for discussion

1 Consider Figure 4.1 in the text. What does this suggest about the extent to which there has been a real increase in resources allocated to health care in Britain?
2 In the USA many people pay insurance to cover unforeseen medical care needs. To what extent can one argue that it is virtually the same in Britain with the NHS? Isn't the only difference the fact that the insurance payment in Britain is compulsory?
3 Examine Figure 4.11. This is an indifference curve map which is of the kind described in Figure 4.3. But this time two of the curves cross. What would such a picture say about the consumer's preference? (HINT: Think about how contented you would be at points P, Q and R.)
4 On the definitions of merit good used in the text, would you rate the following as merit goods? Vaccinations against tropical diseases for those travelling overseas? Education? Fluoride? Cornflakes?
5 Suppose Fred goes to a private doctor with stomach pains and is provided with pills costing him £200 with a guarantee that Fred's stomach pains will disappear in three days if he takes all the tablets. Three days and £200 later Fred's pains have gone. As it happens he had indigestion. The pain would

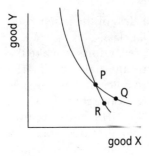

Figure 4.11

have gone anyway as the doctor knew very well but Fred did not. Doesn't this represent a Pareto improvement in welfare? No? Really? Fred is happy. £200 was well worth it to be rid of quite horrid pains. The doctor is happy too. Both parties are better off. No one is worse off. Doesn't that define Pareto efficient welfare improvement?

6 Should people be made to wear seat belts in cars ? (HINT: Who pays if they don't and they have an accident?) Do compulsory MOT certificates raise the same issues?

7 Should the provision of all private health care be made illegal?

8 In a Gallup opinion poll survey in late 1991, 77 per cent of those interviewed agreed with the statement that 'everyone should have all the health care they need no matter how much it costs'. Comment.

9 To what extent are the health reforms in Britain of the last few years a smokescreen for the refusal by the government to commit adequate resources to the NHS?

8 Further reading

Indifference theory
Sloman, pp. 139–57; Begg, pp. 75–91; Parkin and King, pp. 162–77

Merit goods
Sloman, p. 419; Begg, pp. 52–3, pp. 283–4; Parkin and King, p. 465

The distribution of income
Sloman, pp. 354–69; Begg, pp. 230–3; Parkin and King, pp. 429–37

Pareto optimality
Sloman, pp. 400–1; Begg, pp. 256–63

National Health Service (NHS)
D. Green (1992) 'The NHS reforms: from ration-book collectivism to market socialism', *Economic Affairs*, April.

Articles from *World Development Report* (1993) various authors, 'Finance and Development', September.

9 End notes

1 When studying indifference curves in other texts you will be introduced to what are referred to as 'income effects' and 'substitution effects'. This distinction is a useful one but we shall use these concepts a little later in the book rather than stop to examine them now.

2 More frequently actions taken by one person or group can impose *costs* on others not party to an exchange. A factory may emit pollutants which damage forests. This is an external cost. We shall consider the problem of external costs in Chapters 10 and 12.

3 An explanation of how the distribution of income can be calculated is given in Appendix 3.

4 The European Union (EU) was previously referred to as the European Community (EC). Since some of the data in this book was collected when the term EC was widely used, we shall use the two terms interchangeably.

CHAPTER 5

The regional problem:
why is it so depressing?

In this chapter we examine the problem of regional imbalance. Can market forces deal with it? If not, what is the most appropriate action for government to take? We look first at the British regional problem, then at the problem from a European perspective.

In order to do this we review the following concepts:
- Opportunity cost
- Supply and demand

We introduce the following concepts:
- Arbitrage
- Short and long run
- Diminishing returns
- Isoquants and isocosts

1 Introduction

In most economies we find that there are significant differences in living standards in different geographical areas. For example, in Britain it is well known that generally speaking people in Northern Ireland and parts of the North enjoy a lower living standard than do people in the South East. This is an average. The south east has its poor and Northern Ireland its rich. It is also well known that some areas of Europe are much better off than others. What is true of living standards is also true of levels of unemployment. Areas of relatively low living standards are generally areas with a high level of unemployment. As we shall see, these two measures of regional disparities are not unconnected. In this chapter we shall consider the size of these regional disparities within Britain and examine government views on what is the appropriate action to deal with the problem. We shall then consider the problem from a wider EU perspective and ask what the future holds for Europe with respect to regional aid.

This is a topic that is dealt with rather later in most introductory courses. However, there is a great advantage in thinking through this problem now. It is a problem that, as we shall see, we can look at within a framework of supply and demand analysis which makes for good revision and extension of ground already covered. We shall then develop some ideas of how firms make decisions about employing people, which will throw further light on this problem. After that we shall be in a good position to understand the micro-economic aspects of the regional problem. There are certain macro-economic aspects of this matter, to which we shall return in a later chapter.

See pp 406–9

2 The size of the problem in Britain

The most commonly used indicator of the problem of uneven regional development is unemployment. The level of unemployment in Britain has varied considerably over time including the level in the more prosperous regions. So we usually consider the level of unemployment in relation to the national average. Table 5.1 below shows unemployment for the different regions of the UK economy as at January 1993. The economy was still in a recession and output was flat. However, firms had not sufficient confidence that a recovery was imminent so unemployment was still increasing. This explains the high level of average UK unemployment, compared with its average over the previous ten years.

It also shows the same data for the second quarter of 1990. There is a particular reason for choosing this time as a comparison. Britain was experiencing rapid growth then. Demand was strong and unemployment low. But notice that at both periods unemployment rates in certain parts of the country, though lower during the 'boom', were still well above the national average.

These figures are clearly a cause for concern. Unemployment represents a considerable cost to society, socially and in terms of the economic cost.

Table 5.1 Regional unemployment in the UK

Region	June 1990* % unemployed	January 1993 % unemployed
Northern Ireland	13.5	14.3
North	8.5	12.1
North West	7.5	11.2
West Midlands	5.7	11.4
Wales	6.3	10.6
Yorkshire & Humberside	6.5	10.7
Scotland	8.2	9.8
South West	4.0	10.2
East Midlands	4.8	9.9
South East	3.7	10.4
East Anglia	3.4	8.7
UK average	5.6	9.2

Note: *Figures are for the second quarter of 1990.
Source: *Economic Trends,* various issues.

Unemployment is a social problem in that people feel a loss of self-worth and over a longer period, despair. The economic cost is also high. It represents an enormous waste of resources in terms of foregone output. You will recall from Chapter 1 that if an economy is producing a level of output that is inside its opportunity cost curve, this means that the opportunity cost of increased output is zero. Yet as we shall see later the problem viewed from a European perspective is much worse. Unemployment rates vary more from region to region in some other EU countries. We shall also see that if one thinks of each EU country as a European 'region', regional disparities in Britain are comparatively minor.

We must also recognise that the delineating of a geographical area as a 'region' is to some extent arbitrary and the numbers quoted in Table 5.1 can to that extent be misleading. For example, in some areas of the Lake District average unemployment can be lower and average disposable incomes higher than the South East. Since property is cheaper there, and mortgage burdens are smaller, some of these sub-regions can be highly prosperous. That said, there is clearly a problem for large areas of the country. Let us analyse some possible solutions to it.

3 A possible solution: the market case

One approach to the problem outlined above needs to be thought about very carefully. Some economists believe that the appropriate response to the problem is

Table 5.2 Government expenditure on regional aid (£million)

	1983–4	1984–5	1985–6	1986–7	1987–8	1988–9	1989–90	1990–1
Great Britain	648.9	636.8	584.1	746.2	556.2	615.7	540.1	497.2
North	130.2	125.5	96.6	137.3	109.3	134.1	117.0	85.0
Yorkshire & Humberside	36.3	44.3	36.4	41.9	38.8	50.2	32.4	29.4
East Midlands	17.5	11.4	8.8	10.7	9.4	8.8	9.5	5.5
East Anglia	0.0	0.0	0.0	0.0	0.0	0.0	0.0	0.0
South East	0.0	0.0	0.0	0.0	0.0	0.0	0.0	0.0
South West	12.1	14.6	12.3	23.0	14.8	14.7	10.7	9.0
West Midlands[1]	0.0	0.0	7.1	10.6	19.3	26.2	19.9	18.0
North West	104.2	106.4	87.5	129.6	79.0	82.3	74.3	57.5
England	300.3	302.2	248.7	353.1	270.6	316.3	263.8	204.4
Wales	120.0	147.5	138.4	150.7	132.4	148.2	131.7	133.7
Scotland	228.6	187.1	197.0	242.4	153.2	151.2	144.6	159.1

Note: [1]Certain Travel to Work Areas in the West Midlands attained assisted area status on 29 November 1984.
Source: Department of Trade and Industry.

to do nothing! The case is based on the view that market forces will do a better job of correcting regional imbalance than governments will do with interventionist policies. The case needs to be examined with care, because, to a considerable extent, it reflects the thinking of the present government. Table 5.2 shows very clearly how much less interventionist government has become over recent years. Remember too that the data quoted is at current prices. If we deflated this series by an appropriate price index, as we did for health expenditure in Chapter 4, we would find the decline in government spending on regions in real terms. This would show the fall to be even more marked. The large drop in assistance on regional expenditure must be treated with care, however. The figures represent the decline in expenditure by the British government. But expenditure provided by the EU's regional fund is, to some extent, making up that reduction in more recent years. Nevertheless, it was clear during the 1980s and early 1990s that the regional problem was moving down the government's list of priorities.

a Market disequilibrium

So what is the market case for non-intervention in regional unemployment? In essence it amounts to the view that firms and individuals will make better decisions than governments. There are two main strands to the argument. The first strand revolves around the concept of market disequilibrium, the second strand around the concept of arbitrage. Let us first examine the idea of equilibrium.

We have already seen that goods are traded in a market where a clearing price will tend to be established, if the market is free. That is, a price will be found at which plans to supply a good are consistent with plans to consume. In most markets this equilibrium price is a stable equilibrium. If the price moves from equilibrium, excess supply or excess demand will develop. Plans will be adjusted and the equilibrium price will be restored. Now one model of the labour market

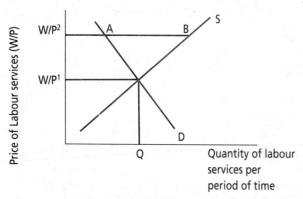

Figure 5.1 Market supply and demand for labour services

suggests that what is true of goods and services will be true of resources such as labour. Resources in a free market will also have a price which will be established in much the same way. Consider the diagram, Figure 5.1.

It shows the market for labour services, let us say in Wales, with the usual variables on the axes. The vertical axis requires a word of explanation. The price of labour services is, of course, the wage rate. This is expressed as W/P in Figure 5.1 to show 'real wages' that is to say the money value of the wage rate divided by the price level. In other words it shows what the price of the labour services will buy for the one who receives the wages. If the wage rate is W/P^1, all those who wish to work will have a job – supply plans are equal to demand plans. So how can Wales have unemployment? Clearly, if the wage rate is too high, say at W/P^2, not all those wanting a job can find one. AB represents that excess supply of labour we call unemployment. You can see now how some economists argue that the problem of unemployment will solve itself. In a free market the price will fall – employers can get all the labour they wish to employ at the lower wage rate. Therefore equilibrium will be found at W/P_1 and there will be no unemployment except for those who chose *not* to work. We have found an equilibrium wage rate for Welsh workers and an equilibrium quantity of labour.

b Arbitrage

But it could be argued that we still have a problem. Consider Figure 5.2. We may feel that it is unfair that Welsh workers receive lower wage rates than those in the South East. Those differences may be quite considerable.

Market economists argue that even this problem will be dealt with in a free market via a process called arbitrage. If significant wage differentials exist, two things are likely to happen. One is that employers, those who demand labour and

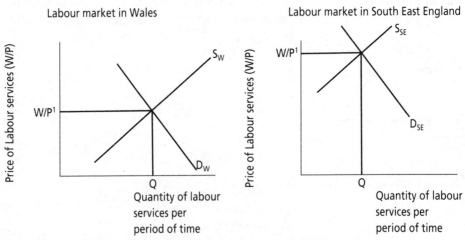

Figure 5.2 Equilibrium wage rates in different parts of the country

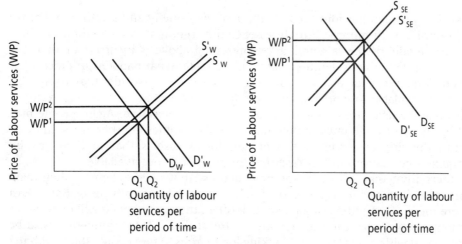

Figure 5.3 Arbitrage in the market for labour services

who are always seeking to minimise production costs, will wish to take advantage of the relatively low wage rates in Wales. It will be worthwhile if they relocate. How will this affect the markets? As firms leave the South East and move to Wales D_{SE} moves left and D_W moves right. Note how in Figure 5.3 this begins to reduce differential wage rates. But at the same time Welsh workers will have an incentive to move to the South East to take advantage of the higher wage rates there. We can see from Figure 5.3 how this also reduces wage differentials, since S_W will shift left, reflecting the willingness of fewer people to supply labour in Wales. S_{SE} shifts to the right, reflecting the increase in the number of willing workers in the South East. The process of arbitrage evens out wage differentials in different parts of the country.

So why does Figure 5.3 not show this process of 'arbitrage' continuing until all labour receives the same wage rate? The answer is that there are costs in moving but Welsh workers will move if they think the gains exceed the benefits. Since some will choose not to, the remaining difference in the wage rate reflects the non-pecuniary value they place on staying where they are. In other words there are non-wage benefits of remaining near one's family for example. Welsh workers and English workers finish with wage rates reflecting an equal net advantage, although the pecuniary rewards are higher in the South East.

4 The interventionist case

Needless to say not everyone would agree with the above reasoning! There are many objections to the view outlined above, some of which the 'questions for discussion' will encourage you to think through. For now we concentrate on objections to the strand of argument we have considered which deals with arbitrage. We mention four areas of thought very briefly and a fifth one that we will examine with more leisure. In essence the arguments are based on the view that the model of the labour market presented above is incorrect or that it is incomplete. Other considerations alter substantially what happens in practice.

Some argue that the above model is invalid because it assumes that knowledge is readily available to workers and firms. This may well be untrue. For example, firms may be unaware of potential cost savings of relocation. Again people may not be aware of wage rates or potential job opportunities in other areas. In other words, the first objection to the market forces case is that markets require adequate information. In this case that information is not available.

Others argue that firms will not move because they need to be near their main markets to minimise transport costs. If these markets are mostly in the South East where the greatest purchasing power is located, they may not be willing to move for lower wage rates even if they are aware of them. This argument has to be approached with care. One is not looking for all firms to move, only those with the greatest advantage in doing so. Some firms are far too market-orientated but others are relatively footloose and may be able to reduce costs by a relocation decision. For example, modern information technology makes it possible for firms to move away from high wage areas such as London because communication costs with input suppliers, who may still choose to remain, are much lower.

Others argue that given time market forces may work but that the process is too slow. If intervention can reduce unemployment more quickly, the benefits of higher output may exceed the costs of money spent on a pro-active regional policy.

The fourth interventionist argument that we will examine in more detail is based on the law of diminishing returns.

This argument is particularly interesting, because it suggests that government intervention is a benefit not only to the regions of high unemployment but to areas of relatively high prosperity too. First we examine the law of diminishing returns, then we relate it specifically to the problem of uneven regional development.

5 The law of diminishing returns

The law of diminishing returns is the law that says that if we go on adding more of one factor such as labour on to a fixed quantity of another factor, say land or capital, the additional output received from each additional unit of the variable factor must eventually diminish.

Let us take an example of a farmer who wants to vary the output of his parsnips for which he requires labour and land. He has one field which he rents and he has a contract to rent the field for a year. Alternatively, if he owns the field, the cost of the capital is the opportunity cost of the funds tied up in the field, and we assume he would take a year to negotiate the sale of it. The farmer therefore has to work

Table 5.3 Short-run product

No. of man days	TP	MP	AP
0	0	–	–
1	10	10	10
2	24	14	12
3	42	18	14
4	56	14	14
5	65	11	13
6	72	7	12
7	77	5	11
8	80	3	10
9	81	1	9
10	81	0	8.1
11	77	−4	7

Notes: TP = Total product
MP = Marginal product
AP = Average product (TP ÷ no. of man days)

with a fixed volume of land. But he can change parsnip output by changing the number of people he employs to work the field. Table 5.3 below shows how many parsnips per week he can get from the field with different amounts of man days of Labour. Note how if at present he is only employing a few man days, adding a few extra men seems a good idea. For example, they may cooperate and do jobs better when there are few men, so the extra man day produces a lot of extra parsnips. That is to say, there are increasing returns to labour. If the farmer goes on employing more men, however, the inevitable occurs. Additions to parsnip output get less since each extra man employed has less land to work on. That is, there are *diminishing returns* to each additional man employed. Indeed, there comes a point where an additional man day employed would result in a fall in total production. That is, the extra men will add a negative amount of output (though no rational farmer would employ that much labour). The *additional* output from one more man day is called marginal product (MP) (or sometimes marginal physical product (MPP) to emphasise that without knowing the *price* of parsnips we do not know what the value of the parsnips is worth to the farmer). We can also work out average product (AP) and find out how many parsnips per man day the farmer gets at differing levels of labour employment. To find this, simply divide the total parsnip output by the number of man days employed.

Now we can plot a graph of the information as we have done in Figure 5.4. Keep it firmly in your mind that all the time we have kept the farmer with the same amount of land – the size of the field is a fixed factor. He cannot invest in the short run; he can simply make optimal use of previous investment decisions.

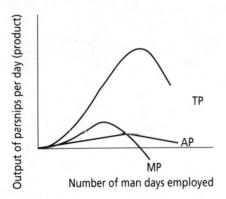

Figure 5.4 Relationship between total average and marginal product

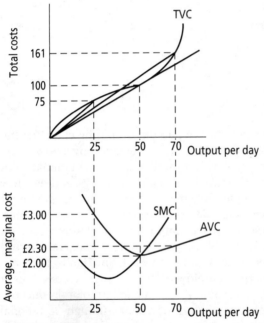

Figure 5.5 Short-run production and cost

What does this suggest about (short-run) production costs? If we ignore the fixed costs associated with the rent of the field and assume that the farmer can employ labour at some given wage rate, we can see the following. While total product (TP) is rising rapidly, total variable costs will be rising relatively slowly, since for the cost of one extra unit of labour large numbers of extra parsnips are being produced. But at some point diminishing returns must set in. Extra units of labour can produce only small additions to output so variable costs rise rapidly.

The principle can easily be extended to average variable and marginal cost as we show in Figure 5.5. Average variable cost (AVC) is the variable cost per parsnip, or whatever unit of output we are considering. It is found by dividing total variable cost (TVC) by the number of units of output. Short-run marginal cost (SMC) is simply the extra cost of producing one more unit of output. We plot these relationships on the lower diagram of Figure 5.5.

Consider first AVC. Suppose twenty-five parsnips per day are being produced. TVC is, we shall assume, £75. AVC is then £75/25 = £3. This can also be seen by referring to the ray that comes from the origin to the appropriate point on the TVC curve. It is the third side of a right-angled triangle, the other two sides being output and TVC.

At 50 units of output per day TVC is £100. AVC is thus only £2. The fall in AVC as output is increased can be seen drawn on the lower diagram. It can also be observed from the fact that the ray from the origin to that point on TVC is less steep than it is at 25 units. If output were to be any higher than 50, however, say at 70 parsnips per day, the ray from the origin would steepen again. TVC is £161 here and AVC has risen to £2.30.

Now look at the marginal cost curve (SMC). For any level of output, how much extra would it cost to increase output by a further unit? To put this another way, how fast does total variable cost rise when output rises by one unit? The rate at which TVC rises is given by the slope of TVC at any point. At low levels of output the slope becomes less steep as output increases. SMC falls. At higher levels of output the law of diminishing returns causes SMC to rise. So we have now explained the shape of SMC.

Notice one other thing. We have drawn MC such that it equals AVC when AVC is at its minimum. This is bound to be true. Take this case where AVC is at 50 units. This is the level of output where the ray from the origin (AVC) is least steep. But MC is given by the slope of TVC. At this level of output the slope of TVC is the same as the slope of the ray from the origin. In our case, at 50 units of output, SMC and AVC are both £2.

There is a way that you might check that you have understood things so far. You might work out for yourself how to add fixed costs onto the top diagram to give total costs and how to add average fixed costs to the lower diagram to give average total costs, but you will not need to do this to follow the argument developed below.

6 Diminishing returns and the optimum population

Now let us see how this relates to the problem of the regional imbalance. Consider the diagram below labelled Figure 5.6. As population increases, income per head rises. There are increasing returns as more of the variable resource is added to the fixed resource, land. But this income per head will rise at a diminishing rate as the proportions of labour to land changes.

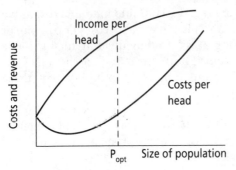

Figure 5.6 Optimum population for a region ·

Now what of costs per head? At first, if population expands, they will decrease. The provision of schools, hospitals and roads, what we refer to as social capital, becomes more economic in areas of higher population. A village school of 10 children may seem to some to be idyllic but costs per head are very high. So a larger population reduces costs per head. But beyond a certain point land becomes relatively scarce and costs per head rise. Transport costs increase significantly, for example, as we saw in Chapter 3. Hence the socially optimum population is at P_{opt}.

However, the increased social capital costs fall on government, not on private producers. There is, therefore, no reason why private citizens will, left to themselves, produce a socially optimal level of population. For example, suppose there is a strong movement of population from Wales to the South East. This might have social costs for Wales in that social capital is underutilised, and for the South East where congestion costs are increasing rapidly. It can, therefore, be argued that it is of benefit to the whole country for the government to intervene in location decisions.

7 The form of state intervention

a Present government policy

Most governments are not convinced by the market based arguments we considered earlier. In most economies intervention on a large scale is typical, although, as we have seen, it has been less so in recent years in Britain. However, one basic principle stands out. For most countries the basic form of intervention is to try to influence the location of firms by inducements to firms to locate in areas of high unemployment. This is usually done by offering a subsidy to firms who will go there. The subsidy is usually given as a proportion of the costs of building, or of capital equipment, or both. The logic is obvious. If these firms can be persuaded to set up in areas of high unemployment, they will need labour. The demand for labour will thus be increased and unemployment reduced.

This is the principle employed throughout Europe. A few examples will illustrate the point. In parts of Belgium 25–30 per cent of investment costs are recoverable by firms locating in depressed areas. In Holland total expenditure on regional assistance is smaller than in most European countries but is again on investment. France has a large regional scheme. Some areas have a range of incentives for firms including 25 per cent subsidies on new buildings, and low interest rates on loans. In Britain automatic investment subsidies for depressed regions have been replaced since 1988 with selective assistance. Since this relatively recent form of assistance is discretionary it is harder to say definitively that it amounts to an investment subsidy.

b Firms' investment decisions – isoquants and isocosts

Let us examine the principles governing long-run production and cost. We shall see if this kind of subsidy, widely available throughout Europe, is likely to be a successful policy in terms of reducing unemployment in disadvantaged regions.

We shall build a model of how companies make decisions to minimise costs. How does a producer choose the best combination of capital and labour when he has the freedom to change his capital as well as labour in the long run? Consider Table 5.4 below, which shows several possible technically efficient ways of making 100 blips, each one involving a different combination of labour and capital.

As you would expect the firm can save on labour (L) by using more capital (K) or vice versa. Now let us plot these combinations on the diagram below and join them together to form a smooth curve as in Figure 5.7. Plotting a smooth curve implies, of course, that there are other processes available which we have not specified.

What we have drawn is called an *isoquant*. We have also drawn other isoquants showing combinations of capital and labour needed to produce larger levels of output.

Now suppose you are going to produce 100 units of output using one of the above four combinations of K and L. Which will you choose? That is, what is the optimal volume of investment in K?

Table 5.4 Assumed possible combinations of capital and labour for blip production

Process	No. of labour hours	No. of machine hours
P	5	10
Q	10	7
R	15	5
S	20	4

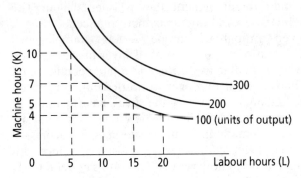

Figure 5.7 Isoquants showing the ouputs for varying combinations of inputs

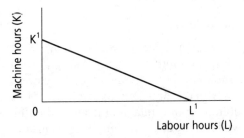

Figure 5.8 The relative price of capital and labour services

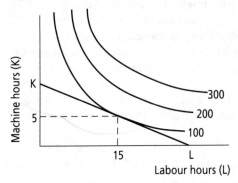

Figure 5.9 Equilibrium combination of capital and labour services

The answer is that you can not decide unless you know how much capital costs and how much labour costs. In other words you have to know the relative price of K and L. Consider the line K^1L^1 in the Figure 5.8 below. It is called an isocost curve. It tells you all the combinations of K and L that you could purchase for some given amount of expenditure. If you choose all investment expenditure you can buy OK^1 capital. If you choose no investment and all labour, you can buy OL^1 labour services. Different combinations costing say £1000 can be represented by points on a straight line between K^1 and L^1. So the isocost curve tells you how expensive capital is relative to labour (like the budget line for consumers).

Now look at Figure 5.9 where the isoquant and isocost curves are together. Which production process minimises costs to the producer of producing 100 blips?

Only the combination of five machine hours and 15 man hours keeps cost down to £100. You have found the optimal volume of investment for a blip producer wishing to produce 100 blips per hour. If the producer were to pick any other combination of K and L that could produce 100 units per week, the isocost curve going through that point on the diagram would be further from the origin, implying a higher cost.

It should not be difficult to see that the minimum cost of producing 200 units of output will be found by an isocost curve drawn parallel to the one drawn in Figure 5.9 touching the 200 unit isocost curve. Given the relative price of capital and labour we now can find the minimum cost of producing any level of output for the long run. From that information the firm's long-run cost curve could be found.

c The effect of investment grants

Let us now see if we can use the concepts we have studied to examine this problem faced by successive British postwar governments – the high level of unemployment in certain regions of the country. We can also consider most governments' preferred solution – investment grants.

In terms of our isoquant diagrams, how is the firm's optimal investment decision affected by government investment grants? Think it through first, then look at our blip producer in Figure 5.10 below.

Isocost X was the original isocost curve. Now the government has made capital investment cheaper, so the producer faces isocost Y. Has it encouraged him to produce more? Yes, there is an *'output effect'*. He can produce more output for the same cost now. To produce more output he will increase investment and increase

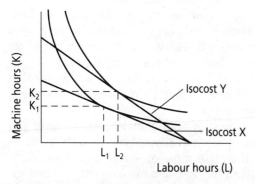

Figure 5.10 Lower capital prices may increase demand for labour services

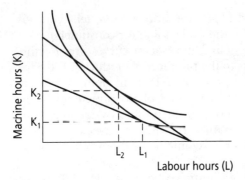

Figure 5.11 Lower capital prices may decrease demand for labour services

his demand for labour from L_1 to L_2. This should help reduce regional unemployment.

Now consider another firm depicted in Figure 5.11. It has the same isocost curves but slightly differently sloped isoquants. Compare the firm's output levels before and after the subsidy. Now compare its investment plans, and look at the amount of labour they wish to employ. Can you suggest any reasons for what may seem a curious result? The firm is using *less* labour because of the government's subsidy! There is more output and more investment but less demand for labour.

The answer to the problem lies in the fact that the investment grant has two effects on the firm. First, there is an output effect – the lower costs of production encourage the firm to expand output, which requires more investment *and* more labour. However, since the grant makes capital cheaper, there is also a second effect, a substitution effect. That is, the grant on capital encourages the firm to substitute what is now relatively cheap capital for what has become relatively dear labour thus reducing the demand for labour. So one effect, the output effect, is encouraging the firm in the area of high unemployment to *increase* its demand for labour. The other effect, the substitution effect, is encouraging it to *reduce* its demand for labour. Which of these two effects is stronger decides whether the grant increases or decreases the demand for labour in the area of high unemployment. Which is the stronger effect will depend upon the ease with which the firm can substitute capital for labour if relative prices change. The effect on some firms is described by Figure 5.10, and on others by Figure 5.11.

We summarise the outcome in Table 5.5 below. In each box we put a plus sign (+) for more demand for the factor, a minus sign (−) for a reduced demand and a question mark (?) if its change is indeterminate.

At best, then, we would predict that most governments' policy towards the regions will narrow output differentials more than it will narrow differences in unemployment rates. It seems strange, then that most governments are reluctant to subsidise labour so that output and substitution effect increase the demand for labour. At worst it would exacerbate the problem of high regional unemployment.

Table 5.5 The effect of a government capital grant on investment demand and labour demand in areas of high unemployment

Effect	Change in investment	Change in labour
Output effect	+	+
Substitution effect	+	−
Total effect	+	?

Table 5.6 Variations in income and employment in UK regions, 1990

Region	Unemployment Rates %	GDP per head 1990 (UK = 100)
UK	5.8	100
North	8.7	88.2
Yorkshire & Humberside	6.7	92.2
East Midlands	5.0	98.2
East Anglia	3.6	102.5
South East	3.9	120
South West	4.2	94.9
West Midlands	5.8	92.8
North West	7.6	90.5
Wales	6.5	84.9
Scotland	8.2	92.6
Northern Ireland	13.5	75.4

Source: Adapted from *Employment Gazette*, January 1992 and Annual Abstract.

There is one piece of evidence which suggests that our predictions may be correct. Consider Table 5.6 below. GDP per head measures the output of the region divided by its population. Observe that there is a high correlation between unemployment rates and GDP per head. But observe also that the variations between regions are greater for unemployment than for output. For example, while unemployment in Northern Ireland is over two-and-a-half times the UK average, average GDP per head is only one-third higher for the UK than for Northern Ireland.

8 European regional policy

Regional policy is being seen more and more in Europe as a problem of the community rather than as a series of individual problems faced by its members. There are, perhaps, three important reasons why this should be so.

Table 5.7 Unemployment and income in EU countries

Country	Income per head 1990 (US$)	Unemployment rate 1990 (%)
Belgium	16,407	8.8
Denmark	16,765	9.5
France	17,431	8.9
Germany	16,309	5.1
Greece	7,349	7.2
Ireland	10,699	13.7
Italy	16,021	11.2
Luxembourg	19,340	n/a
Netherlands	15,766	6.5
Portugal	8,389	4.6
Spain	11,792	16.3
UK	15,720	5.9

Source: OECD, *Economic Outlook.*

a Existing disparities

First, there are enormous differences in regional incomes that are regarded as socially and politically unacceptable. With the accession of more countries into the European Union (EU) during the 1980s, some relatively poor, the disparities between countries are so great as to make those between regions within Britain seem minor. Table 5.7 gives an impression of this. Notice too that it is not simply income per head which shows considerable disparities, but unemployment rates also. What is true of regions in the UK is true of the countries which make up the 'regions' of the European Union.

b European integration: widening disparities?

Second, the erosion of barriers to trade within the EU is generally thought to accentuate the differences in average incomes between countries. As a rule incomes per head are higher close to the centre of the EU. This is partly because firms locating here have an advantage in that their market is potentially nearer. Transport costs limit the area over which firms can hope to sell. The area they can cover reaching out from the centre is obviously greater than if they are reaching inwards from the fringe. The fewer the barriers to trade the more this is so. So, although greater trade in Europe may raise output, it probably widens relative incomes.

Market economists would argue that unemployment would still not result in the long run since wage rates would fall until some firms found it worthwhile to

Table 5.8 European Community budget allocation 1993

	Revenue (%)
1 VAT	56
2 Custom duties and agricultural levies	23
3 Payments based on countries' GNP	21

	Expenditure (%)
1 Agriculture support	49
2 Structural funds	31
3 External action	6
4 Other	14

Source: European Commission.

relocate to the fringes and some workers relocated to the centre. In other words, the process described in section 3 in the context of Britain would work equally well on a Europe-wide basis if barriers to resource movements are eliminated. Others believe that the relative wages that would make this possible are too low on the fringes to be politically and socially acceptable.

c Labour immobility

Third, there are great problems with labour mobility. It is often thought that labour immobility makes reductions in regional wage rates and unemployment levels difficult for areas within a country. Significant language and cultural barriers would be much greater between countries. Therefore, however effective the market mechanism we described earlier, it is likely to be less effective across countries in the EU. It must be said, though, that some economists feel that labour immobility may be lessened over time through, for example, mutual recognition of diplomas, degrees and other qualifications.

Because of these factors the 'Structural Funds' of the EU have been increasing rapidly during the 1990s. Disadvantaged areas can apply to the fund for assistance. General guidelines are laid down about what applications are likely to be successful but the fund administrators make the final decision within those guidelines. The sums going to regional assistance have been increasing rapidly. This is partly because the proportion of the budget used to support regions has increased. Table 5.8 shows that agricultural support and regional assistance have dominated community spending. But comparative figures for the mid-1980s would show agricultural spending around 68–70 per cent of the budget and regional support at around 10 per cent. However, regional assistance spending has

Table 5.9 Percentage of population 'enthusiastic' for European Union

Country	GDP per head (US$)	1962	1973	1980	1985	1990	1991
Luxembourg	19,340	—	47	46	41	34	26
France	17,431	28	23	19	28	24	24
Denmark	16,765	—	17	12	13	23	22
Belgium	16,407	31	22	25	19	23	26
Germany	16,309	50	49	36	37	37	32
Italy	16,021	36	34	39	32	43	43
Netherlands	15,766	62	34	35	28	24	23
UK	15,720	—	14	23	24	26	27
Spain	11,792	—	—	36	36	38	42
Ireland	10,669	—	21	19	18	37	44
Portugal	8,389	—	—	22	28	50	54
Greece	7,349	—	—	33	34	48	47

Source: *Financial Times*, 6 and 7 June 1992.

also increased because the size of the budget has risen so sharply. The size of the total budget, 69 billion ECUs, represents a per capita spending of 195 ECUs in 1993. The comparable figure for 1970 was about 19 ECUs.

The Structural Funds can be paid to any country in the EU. Even the richest have some areas of relatively high unemployment. But clearly the poorer countries benefit most. Now, however, from 1993 there is a new fund for regional support, the cohesion fund. This is specifically aimed at help for the low income countries in order to limit the degree of variation in regional income with the community. Any country with less than 90 per cent of the European average income may qualify but in practice this will mean that for the foreseeable future, significant funds will be transferred to Portugal, Greece, Spain and Ireland.

The main income sources for the European Union budget are income from duties imposed on a wide range of items imported from outside of the EU, plus a contribution paid by member governments, much of it from part of value added tax (VAT) receipts. In general richer countries pay more into the fund than poorer members.

Table 5.9 makes fascinating reading. As significant transfers of income are made from richer to poorer EU members, enthusiasm grows for European union among poor countries but not among people in the more affluent. Richer countries clearly do not believe that the benefits of EU membership will be allocated to them.

The probability must be that European Regional Policy will reduce regional incomes to less than they would otherwise have been. It is doubtful whether the capital bias so prevalent in regional policy in recent decades will do so much for the reduction of regional unemployment diferentials in Europe in the 1990s.

9 Conclusion

Disparities within regions, whether measured by income per head or by unemployment rates are very significant within Britain and between member countries of the EU.

Supply and demand analysis suggests that over time these differences will narrow but the model requires several assumptions that may be unrealistic. For example, significant unemployment levels over a long period in Britain and much of Europe suggest that markets may not clear quickly. This is an issue to which we will return in later chapters. The law of diminishing returns can be argued to show that government intervention would be worthwhile.

Given that firms make investment decisions based on profit maximisation there is a strong case for suggesting that regional subsidies are misdirected and should be altered.

Increased emphasis on European Regional Policy can be argued to be worthwhile but the form it takes will need to be thought through carefully during the 1990s.

10 Questions for discussion

1 The size of the regional problem in Britain was examined in the text by considering regional unemployment figures and output per head. What other indications of regional welfare might be used? What problems arise with using your suggested variables?

2 The British economy since the 1945 has gone through periods of relatively rapid growth followed by periods of slowdown. What would you expect would happen to regional disparities during these 'trade cyles'? Why?

3 How impressive do you find the case for intervention in regional location decisions? Consider especially the arguments mentioned in the text based on knowledge, the nature of firms' location decisions, the speed of adjustment arguments and the optimum population argument.

4 The British government once attempted to influence regional location by insisting that all firms undertaking large development schemes in heavily populated areas obtain an Industrial Development Certificate from the government. It could then refuse a certificate in the hope that the firm would expand in the areas of high unemployment. The scheme was abandoned in 1982. What do you think were its main advantages and disadvantages?

5 Why do you think that if you were producing 100 blips at point P (Table 5.4 in the text) and you decided to use a *more labour-intensive* method it would require five extra man hours to replace three machines but if you were at Q and you decided to be more labour intensive still, another extra five man hours would enable you to save on the investment of only two machine

hours? What does this suggest about a government policy to subsidise labour in order to stimulate regional employment?

6 What counter arguments might be made to defend regional policy's capital bias?

7 How would transport improvements within Europe affect regional location?

8 On balance, should regional policy be more or less interventionist?

11 Further reading

Arbitrage
Parkin and King, pp. 757–8

Short and long run
Sloman, pp. 162–4; Parkin and King, p. 218

Diminishing Returns
Sloman, pp. 164–71, pp. 164–71; Begg, pp. 122–7; Parkin and King, pp. 218–35

Isoquants and isocosts
Sloman, pp. 177–85, pp. 193–99; Begg, pp. 112–15; Parkin and King, pp. 243–54

The regional problem
H. Armstrong and J. Taylor (1993) *Regional Economics* (London: Harvester Wheatsheaf).
'North and South Divided', *Lloyds Bank Economic Bulletin*, August 1992.

CHAPTER 6

Small firms:
on being small and beautiful

Every year, whether the economy is in recession or not, many small firms go out of business. Is this a reflection of the market allocating resources efficiently? Or are the large and powerful ruthlessly exploiting the small and weak? Is it true that small is beautiful and that therefore governments must protect small firms? If so, how should they do it?

In this chapter we review the following concepts:

- Supply and demand
- Long and short-run costs

We introduce the following:

- Perfect competition
- Normal profits
- Minimum efficient scale

1 Introduction

Many people, especially those who study economics and business subjects have a desire to run their own business. Some hope that it will grow into a large organisation, but most want it to remain small. Now, there are around 2.5 million firms employing less than twenty people each in Britain. What that figure does not show is that many who begin their own business are rapidly disappointed. A great deal of them do not survive for more than six months.

In some industries this is readily apparent. Small grocers have not survived the growth of the large supermarket chains. Many independent estate agents have disappeared so that now most estate agencies are part of a large national organisation. Does such a trend matter very much? If Tesco provides cheaper food, is there any reason for bewailing the loss of the grocery outlets whose costs are too high? This is an important question that we shall examine in this chapter. We shall also offer explanations about why many firms *do* survive and consider why the government provides encouragement to them through various schemes.

2 The presence of small firms in Britain

a Defining the small firm

Defining the 'small firm' is no easy matter. We might think of it as one that has no market power. The small firm in the model of 'perfect competition', which we shall examine shortly, has to be small enough so as to have no control over its price. Furthermore, it is assumed to produce a product identical to all other firms in the market. Why can we not find examples of exactly this in the real world? One main reason is that if a firm is too small to have much control over price, it probably survives by differentiating its product – providing a better or more personal service or whatever. So, although we can find many firms whose market power is very limited, we cannot have a precise measure of that limit. Thus, the size of firm which we call small is somewhat arbitrary.

If we choose to define it in terms of size we can avoid the arbitrary nature of what constitutes power but the choice of size variable is also arbitrary. Should we define size in terms of the number of employees? An alternative possibility is to use turnover or the value of sales. A further possibility is to look at the value of the firms' capital, but this is especially arbitrary since it creates problems with respect to the valuation of capital. How much is a firm's two-year-old machinery really worth? Finally, one might use value added, the difference between the value of a firm's output and its purchases from firms in other industries. This gives a good idea of the importance of the firm in terms of its contribution to the economy's output. In practice, turnover and employment size are the two most commonly used criteria. On any definition, we can say that while there are no perfectly competitive firms, there are many small firms who survive in an atmosphere of intense competition. Their position, we can argue, can usefully be analysed in terms of the perfectly competitive model that we shall shortly consider.

b The importance of small firms

Table 6.1 enables us to consider firms or enterprises by numbers of employees. The figures relate to manufacturing. The government produces no equivalent data for services. Notice that while over 96 per cent of manufacturing enterprises are small, employing less than 100 people, they produce under 20 per cent of the output.

The information in this table relates to *establishments* not enterprises. An establishment refers to a location, a site, a plant, where output is produced. An enterprise is an ownership concept. If the firm or enterprise owns say four factories operating in different areas we would say that there is one enterprise but four establishments. So there are more establishments than firms in the UK.

c The durability of the small firm sector

Despite all the problems of the small firms sector, it seems to be quite robust.

Table 6.1 Size of enterprises by employment and output 1991

Number of employees	Total units		Total employment		Total net output	
	Number	% of total	Millions	% of total	£ millions	% of total
1–99	129,790	94.3	1.36	29.9	32,341	23.8
100–499	6,384	4.6	1.35	29.7	38,288	28.2
500–1499	1,112	0.8	0.88	19.4	29,584	21.8
1500+	280	0.2	0.95	21.0	35,622	26.2
Total	137,566	100	4.54	100	135,835	100

Source: Business Monitor.

Table 6.2 Importance of small firms in UK, 1979–86

Employment size band	Changes in size distributions of firms, 1979–86		United Kingdom (%)	
	Cumulative share of total firms		Cumulative share of total employment	
	1979	1986	1979	1986
1–2	61.4	63.9	6.6	9.7
3–5	79.2	83.1	12.4	18.6
6–10	89.1	90.7	19.1	25.8
11–19	95.2	96.4	26.7	35.9
20–49	97.8	98.2	33.6	42.6
50–99	98.7	99.0	38.9	49.5
100–199	99.5	99.5	49.1	59.4
200–499	99.8	99.8	57.3	71.3
500–999	99.9	100.0	64.7	81.8
1000+	100.0	100.0	100.0	100.0

Source: Employment Gazette.

There is some evidence to suggest that small firms are important and that they have been increasing in importance, at least during the first half of the 1980s. Table 6.2 above is from the *Employment Gazette*, May 1990. As can be seen, over 96 per cent of the 2.5 million firms in Britain employ less than twenty people and account for 36 per cent of non-government employment. But notice that the latter figure has risen from 26.7 per cent in 1979.

To some extent it could be argued that the figures overstate the resilience of the small firm sector in that there have been some significant changes to the data. For example, many building firms used to employ painters or plasterers. Later, they

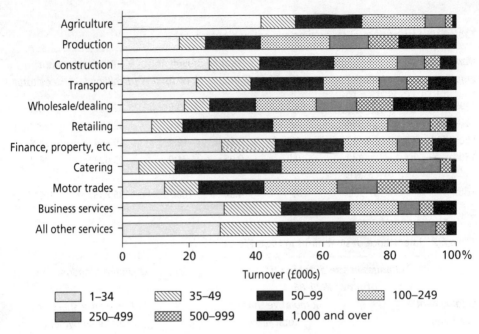

Agriculture
Production
Construction
Transport
Wholesale/dealing
Retailing
Finance, property, etc.
Catering
Motor trades
Business services
All other services

| 0 | 20 | 40 | 60 | 80 | 100% |

Turnover (£000s)

☐ 1–34   ⧄ 35–49   ■ 50–99   ▦ 100–249
■ 250–499   ▨ 500–999   ■ 1,000 and over

Source : Business Monitor.

Figure 6.1 Relative contribution by small and large businesses, 1993

found it cheaper not to employ them, but to buy in their services as required. So many plasterers are now not employees of a large firm but are rather small firms selling their services to the building industry.

d The distribution of small firms between sectors

As one might expect the importance of small firms varies considerably from sector to sector, as can be seen from Figure 6.1. So, for example, small builders have a very significant presence in the construction industry, but small retailers play a relatively small part in the retailing industry.

So do small firms need government help? Or are they best left to help themselves? There is a case for saying that they should not be given assistance. It is to this argument that we turn first.

3 The case for non-protection

a Perfect competition: a model for analysing small firms

In Chapter 1 we explained the value of an economic model. Our model of perfect competition will throw much light on the behaviour of small firms. The essence of perfect competition is that firms in the market are too small to have any control over price. Price is determined by supply and demand. The small firm has to accept that price to sell its output. It will not be able to sell if it tries to charge more. It has no need to charge less since it can sell all the output it chooses at the ruling market price. Notice that smallness in this sense is not simply an absolute concept, but firms must be small in relation to the total size of the market. For further elaboration of the assumptions of perfect competition you could refer back to section 8 of Chapter 2. Note, though, we did not use the term 'perfect competition' there.

See pp 39–41

Now what does the model suggest about firm behaviour and the need for government assistance? Recall from Chapter 5 that we make a distinction between the long run and the short run. The long run is the time in which all factors of production are variable. The short run is the period in which one factor of production, usually capital, is fixed and other factors are variable.

See p 95

We look first to see the case for saying that no government protection of firms is needed in the short run. We first see what our model predicts about short-run behaviour and then consider why we can argue that no government intervention is needed.

b Small firms: the short run

You will recall from Chapter 5 that the short-run cost conditions of the firm are determined by the law of diminishing returns. Figure 6.2 shows the position. Section 5 of Chapter 5 derived the short-run marginal cost (SMC) curve and the average variable cost curve (AVC).

But variable costs are not the only short-run costs which a firm must meet. There are also fixed costs. In terms of our example of the farmer in Chapter 5, he had to pay the rent on the field. This is a fixed cost – fixed in the sense that it is a charge to be met whatever the amount of output he chooses to make. Let us

See pp 94–7

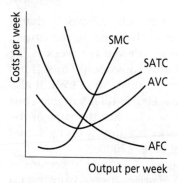

Figure 6.2 Short-run costs of production.

suppose that rent per week is £48. This is the fixed cost. What is the average fixed cost (AFC)? This will depend on the chosen level of output. If the farmer chooses to produce one unit of output per week the AFC will be £48. The total fixed cost (TFC) will be spread over just the one unit. Formally, AFC = TFC/Q, where Q is the level of output. At this output AFC = 48/1 = £48. Suppose he makes two units per week. AFC = 48/2 = £24. Fixed costs remain the same, but as output increases average fixed costs will fall. If he makes 48 units, then AFC = 48/48 = £1 per week. Figure 6.1 shows AFC at all levels of output.

Now let us consider average total cost (ATC). ATC is simply AFC + AVC. This is shown in Figure 6.2. To AVC at each level of output is added the vertical distance of AFC.

We have figured out the short-run cost structure. What of the price the firm can get for its output? Since this is a perfectly competitive market the price is decided by supply and demand. Figure 6.3 shows that the firm can sell as much output as it chooses, but only if it is prepared to charge that price, assumed to be £100. The reason for this is contained in the assumptions. The firm is one of many, all of which are selling an identical product, so it has no control over price. If it were to raise its price, people would go to one of the other firms to purchase. A firm can only have control over its price if it can differentiate its product, so that some will be willing to pay more for it than is being charged elsewhere. So, given that its product is identical, it will just have to accept the ruling market price.

How much output would it choose to make if it wanted to do as well as possible?

The answer is to produce 50 units per week since that is the level of output at which marginal cost = marginal revenue (SMC = MR). Why is that the best? Recall that SMC is the extra cost of producing one more unit. MR is the extra revenue received for making an additional unit. Since for each unit made the firm receives £100, the extra revenue achieved by expanding output by one unit must be £100. In other words, MR is the same as price. Now if making an extra unit adds more to revenue than to cost, it is clearly worth making. But, at 50 units addition to revenue (MR) is as high as addition to cost (SMC). There is no logic in expanding output beyond this level.

But will this level of output result in a profit? Clearly, the answer is that it depends upon whether price is high enough to cover all the costs. In the case of the firm in Figure 6.3 it is obviously not. The revenue received per week is the output multiplied by price: 50 × £100 = £5000. But now consider its costs. It has its fixed costs of £2500. (At 50 units of output AFC is £2500 ÷ 50 = £50). It also has to cover variable costs. Average variable costs are £90 so total variable costs are 50 × £90 = £4500. Total weekly costs (output × ATC) are the sum of the variable and fixed costs, which means £7000 per week. The firm is losing £2000 per week since revenue is £5000 per week and total costs £7000.

Is there anything the firm could do to improve its position? Could it increase its revenue by raising price? No, it has no control over price. It could not find a market for its product at more than £100 per unit. Could it lower its costs? No, the

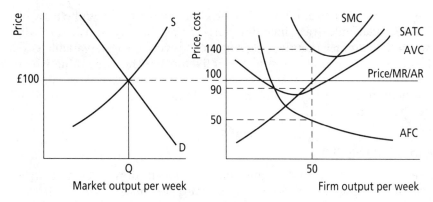

Figure 6.3 The short run in a perfectly competitive industry

assumption we have made about the cost structure is that the cost curve represents the minimum possible costs associated with each level of output.

Could it shut down operations entirely? Indeed it could. It could decide to produce nothing at all. It would then receive no revenue but it would incur costs in the short run – fixed costs. So fixed costs would represent the size of the loss. In this case the costs having shut down down are the £2500 per week of fixed costs. But continuing in production would be a better option, and since this more than covers the variable costs, the firm can make a £500 per week contribution to the fixed costs. This reduces the losses from £2500 to £2000 per week. In general, if a firm is making a loss but can more than cover variable costs, it will pay it to continue in production in the short run.

An illustration of the point could be made from the holiday industry. Figure 6.3 might represent someone letting out flats for holiday accommodation on the coast of Cornwall. Although not perfectly competitive, no one else has exactly the same facilities and view, there is sufficient competition for us to use our model of perfect competition. The situation described in Figure 6.3 might represent the firm in February. Demand and therefore price is low and profit cannot be made. The only option open to the firm is the one we have explored above. It can either let the flats for £100 per week each or close down for the winter if, as in the figure, it cannot cover the wear and tear on the carpet, and the lighting and heating. At least if the £100 per week more than covers such variable costs, it will make a contribution to the fixed costs of rates and insurance, and so on. This explains why, if you buy from W.H. Smiths a book of holiday cottages for let, you will see that only some cottages are available all year, though at much higher rents in the summer. Others are not for let at all off-season – the variable costs are too high relative to the price that can be charged.

It should now be clear that there is a case for saying that no government assistance is required for firms making short-run losses. In the longer run demand may increase, prices will rise and losses will be eliminated. This might be true, for example, of seasonal industries, including large firms such as British Gas who make losses in the summer months. The summer's revenue covers variable costs but is not sufficient to cover all the substantial fixed costs. The same thing would also apply to industries during a recession – in the long run prices will rise. If there is a case for help from government, then, it would have to be found in the long run. It is to that we now turn.

c Small firms in the long run

Free market economists would argue that the small firm does not need government intervention in the long run because the market sees to it that price will be high enough to cover all its costs. To see why this is so, we need to understand the nature of long-run production costs. The long run, remember, is the period long enough for a firm to adjust the amount of its capital as well as its labour.

What happens if a firm increases its output in the long run? It takes on more capital and more labour to produce this output. Clearly this will cost more. But what happens to costs per unit? There is a concept called *economies of scale* which suggests that as output increases unit costs fall. What might these scale economies be?

Some economies are financial. Small firms can appear risky to lenders of money such as banks, who therefore, charge higher interest rates to compensate for that risk. Larger, apparently safer, firms get financial economies. They get lower interest rates for borrowing, so that a larger output will tend to lower their unit costs. Some economies are technical. Larger firms can utilise capital which is impractical for small firms. Robots for operations on a car factory lower unit costs. Such technology is not possible for small producers. These and other scale economies cause average costs to fall as output increases.

But there is an argument for saying that at very large output levels long-run average costs rise. This is the result of *diseconomies of scale*. Diseconomies can occur since very large firms need a large management structure. A large structure of this kind creates coordination problems. The firm becomes difficult to manage, causing unit costs to increase. Figure 6.4 shows an assumed long-run average cost curve (LRAC) falling as output rises and economies of scale are obtained, then rising beyond some point because of diseconomies.[1]

Figure 6.4 also shows the position with respect to costs and revenue. Notice now how the equilibrium price determined by market forces is at a price at which a firm can break even. The firm picks its profit maximising output where marginal cost = marginal revenue labelled on the diagram Q_{pm}. At that output, total revenue, output x price, the shaded area on the diagram, is the same as total cost, output x average cost.

Why should price tend towards P^1? The reason is that in the long run firms can leave or join the industry. If price were higher, new firms would be attracted by

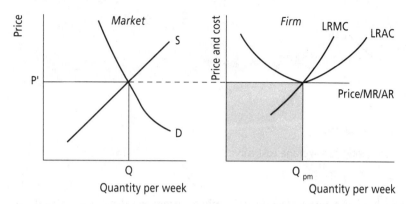

Figure 6.4 Long-run equilibrium in a perfectly competitive industry

the profits available. As they entered, supply would increase, the supply curve would shift right, causing the price to fall. Similarly, if price were lower than P[1] and firms were making losses, some firms would leave the industry. This would shift the supply curve left and the price would rise until firms were covering costs. Therefore, help for such firms can be argued to be unnecessary. The market mechanism protects them by insuring a long-run price high enough to cover costs.

d Normal profit

At this point, however, one might ask why people who can only just break even would stay in an industry. Would they not leave for another industry where profit prospects were better? The answer is no, because of the key concept of *normal profit*. Normal profit is the income an entrepreneur needs to persuade him not to move his resources elsewhere. It is an income representing the opportunity cost of the resources. He must receive this or he will by definition go elsewhere. Economists regard this income as a cost, which is included in the cost of the business. So, for example, suppose a person were to set up his own accountancy firm and leave his present employment where he is paid £30,000 per annum. He would need to make £30,000 per annum to take out of the business for himself, to persuade him not to return to his old job. That £30,000 per annum is the normal profit. It is included in the shaded area of Figure 6.4. So, although he has only just 'broken even', he has no incentive to leave the industry. He has covered all costs including opportunity cost, or normal profit.

4 Competing against large firms: long-run cost curves in practice

a Cost curves in practice

We have now seen how, in perfectly competitive markets, the small firm produces its profit-maximising output where marginal cost is equal to marginal revenue. In

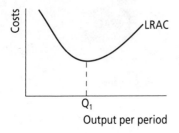

Figure 6.5 A U-shaped long-run average cost curve

the long run this is also a level of output at which average cost is minimised for such firms. The assumption is that the firm must produce a large enough level of output to take advantage of all the internal economies of scale available. If it does not do so, it will be disciplined by the market's competitive pressure and it will die. If it attempts to go beyond the level of output at which average cost (AC) is minimised, it will suffer diseconomies of scale. Again it will be disciplined by the market and will either go out of business or return to its optimum size.

Now one assumption we have been making is that the long-run average cost curve is U-shaped. We have also been assuming that the level of output needed to be at the bottom of the LRAC curve is quite small. Neither of these assumptions is necessarily valid.

Consider Figure 6.5. The firm must produce Q_1 output in order to minimise unit costs, but it may well be that Q_1 represents a large part of the market for the product. For example, estimates are that for some industries one would need to produce about 10 per cent of all European output to reach Q_1. The small firm, then, is going to experience higher unit costs at an output significantly less than Q_1. If it produces at Q_1 it is not going to be a small firm.

In other markets, a different shape of long-run average cost curve is possible. It may be as in Figure 6.6. The market may be one in which there are no significant diseconomies of scale at large levels of output. Smaller firms are inevitably going to have trouble surviving in such markets. This explains why there are no small firms in, for example, aircraft production.

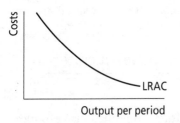

Figure 6.6 A falling long-run average cost curve

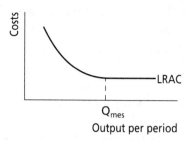

Figure 6.7 An L-shaped long-run average cost curve

Table 6.3 Some estimates of scale economies in selected industries

Industry	MES* as % of output – EC	MES as % of output – UK	% increase in costs as fraction of half MES
Beer	3	12	5
Bricks	0.2	1	25
Cement	1	10	26
Cigarettes	6	24	2.2
Oil refining	2.6	14	4
Paint	2	7	4.4
Washing machines	10	57	7.5

Note: *MES = minimum efficient scale.
Source: Based on C.F. Pratten, *Costs of Non-Europe*, Vol. 2, European Commission, 1989.

In yet other markets, the LRAC may be as in Figure 6.7. Here Q_{mes} represents 'minimum efficient scale'. It is the lowest level of output that a firm can produce and still obtain all the available economies of scale. There are two potential difficulties for the small firm in this kind of market. One is that Q_{mes} might represent a substantial part of the market. The small firm is therefore at a much lower output than Q_{mes}. The other potential difficulty is that the LRAC may fall very sharply from zero output to Q_{mes}. If so, the cost disadvantage of being at a suboptimal output level can be crippling. So it is easy to see why small firms may find it hard to survive.

Table 6.3 gives us some estimates for several industries to see how this might work in practice. A washing machine producer needs to have a plant big enough to produce 57 per cent of all UK machines or 10 per cent of EU output or his unit costs will be higher than optimally sized competitors. That will not be a very small firm.

A firm producing bricks on the other hand, will need to produce only 1 per cent of UK output to be at minimum efficient scale (MES). However, suppose that it is smaller than that, say half that size. Then one can see from column three of Table 6.3 that such a firm's unit costs will be 25 per cent higher.

b Government assistance

Clearly then, in many markets small firms will not survive without government assistance. They will either die because they are uneconomic, grow into larger units or are taken over by larger firms. The forms of possible assistance can be many and varied. In Britain many small firms can get several different kinds of assistance. We shall consider these in section 7.

However, it does not present a case, by itself, for saying that *it is society's interest that they should survive*. After all, if large firms have lower unit costs, they will produce output for fewer resources. To put it another way, large firms' output will be at a lower opportunity cost and society's scarce resources will be better used. Indeed, many small firms will continue to survive without government help. It is to those reasons that we now turn.

5 The survival of small firms

Despite significant scale economies in most markets many small firms continue to survive. Let us look at the major reasons.

a Market dynamics

First, there is the dynamics of the economy. We must not think of the economy as being in equilibrium. The market is always changing in response to changes in technology, changes in demand, changes in international competition and so on. Thus, at any time, there are new young firms who are in the process of developing into much larger ones but have not yet done so. Also, there are industries where low set-up costs have induced would-be new entries who simply will not survive in the longer run, either because they will die, or because they will be taken over by larger more cost-efficient firms. Then again, a rapidly expanding economy can lead to short-term disequilibrium, since larger firms cannot take advantage immediately of all the possible profitable opportunities for expansion. So even if the large firms have a cost advantage over the smaller ones, smaller firms will, at least for some time, have a significant presence. We have argued in earlier chapters that markets tend to have a stable equilibrium. What we are saying here does not contradict this. What is at issue is the speed at which markets move to equilibrium. It may not be rapid.

b Size of market

Second, there is the size of the market. It may be so small that there is only room for one or two firms. This may seem unlikely at first sight. However, to follow the argument, we need to understand the problem that arises in defining a 'market'. Take the example of food. Food retailing is an enormous market. If a consumer in Birmingham wants a loaf of bread, however, he will not buy it from a Sainsbury's store in Plymouth, even if the bread is cheaper than anywhere in Birmingham. The relevant 'market' to him is much smaller. If he does not have a car, then even a large supermarket a mile away may be of no relevance to him. The small corner store, insignificant in the food retailing sector, is the relevant 'market'. In general terms, some kinds of activity are not suited to large firms. Those requiring personal attention or the ability to meet individual customer needs may survive by having a local monopoly of a tiny market.

In other words, the perfect competition model assumes that firms have no control over price because they all produce an identical product. In many markets firms can have some control by differentiating their products.

c Transport costs

Third, there is the question of transport costs. These can be high for certain industries and this makes the presence of small firms highly likely. If transport costs are high, relative to the advantage of production economies, many small local plants will be required rather than a few large ones. If there are high costs to a large firm of coordinating those many small plants, small individual firms will be most efficient.

d Large firm behaviour

Fourth, small firms have public relations benefits for large firms. One may have an industry where there is one large producer, but many smaller ones too. The large firm may have lower costs and thus be capable of driving the smaller firms out of the industry. However, to preserve an aura of competition, perhaps to keep government anti-monopoly bodies happy, the large firm becomes a price leader, dictating whatever price it chooses. Small firms take this as the going price. But the large firm deliberately chooses a high enough price to enable some small firms to survive. In this way the large firm has not eliminated all the apparent competition.

e Changing technology

Fifth, the reduction in information costs associated with modern technology can encourage the existence of small firms. Until a few years ago, the conventional wisdom said that increases in technological development encouraged large-scale production and therefore large firms at the expense of small business. This is now open to question. One reason firms felt the need to be bigger was the need to vertically integrate, that is, to control as much as possible of the manufacturing process from raw material production to the point of sale to the final consumer. One major advantage of vertical integration is that it avoids the costs of acquiring information on which to negotiate prices from input suppliers. The advance of computer technology has reduced those costs and has made more realistic a decision to stay small. The small firm can purchase from a specialist input supplier, who can gain economies of scale in the production of the input.

For all these reasons, even without government aid many small firms do survive.

6 The case for small firm protection

Is there, therefore, no case for government intervention to help the small firm sector? Indeed, there is a case which we shall develop more fully in the next two chapters. But let us very briefly pick out four areas in which one can now see how one might justify state assistance.

a Market power of large firms

First, there is the fear that large firms, though they may have lower unit costs, will have the power to raise prices to consumers in a way in which smaller firms could not. In other words, there is no guarantee that the benefit of lower unit costs will be passed on to consumers in the form of lower prices. On the other hand, it is one attraction for social welfare of small firms that they cannot control prices. The price is impersonally determined by market forces.

b Barriers to entry

Second, new firms will generally need to start at a small size but the barriers to the entry of those firms may be substantial. The most obvious example of an entry barrier is size. Referring back to Table 6.3 there may be significant profits in washing machine production, suggesting that consumers wish to see more resources allocated to this area. A new firm will not be able to survive if it sets up in a small way, yet it is unlikely to be able to find the finance to start up at a size representing 57 per cent of UK output! There may, therefore, be a case for helping small firms to set up in the market.

c 'Unfair competition'

Third, large firms in a market may attempt to use their power to drive smaller competing firms out. For example, they may sell their output below costs in the short term, subsidising their operations by past profits or profits from other markets. Then they can raise prices again when the smaller firms have been driven out. Of course, this may not be a case for helping small firms financially. It may be that they should be protected by law by making it illegal for large firms to behave in this way. In 1991, the European Community (EC) enacted just such laws against unfair competition.

d Government behaviour

One loud complaint heard from small firms is the burden they carry which government itself has imposed. Many laws and regulations bear unfairly on small firms. Preparing accounts for value added tax (VAT) and dealing with planning regulations, for example, create proportionately more problems for a small business than for a large enterprise.

Changes in macro-economic policy during the last ten or fifteen years have had their effects on the small firm sector. Control of the economy has been more through interest rate policy leading to higher real interest rates than in earlier years. This has probably had a detrimental effect on small firms since they are often more heavily reliant upon bank borrowing than larger firms. We consider the reasons for such a change in macro-economic policy in later chapters.

There is, therefore, a case for government helping firms financially to overcome the burden that it has imposed upon those businesses itself.

7 Government aid for small firms

Despite having had a government in Britain during the 1980s and 1990s strongly committed to market forces, the case for intervention in the small firm sector has not gone entirely unheard. The government has introduced changes specifically to assist small firms. The following are probably the most important.

VAT exemption

Firms in most sectors of the economy have to pay VAT – a tax on the difference between their purchases from other industries and the value of the output that they produce. Small firms in all sectors are exempt from the payment of the tax. The size of turnover that is the benchmark for qualification for exemption has increased by more than the rate of inflation at most budgets in recent years. Small firms also pay a lower rate of corporation (profits) tax.

Subsidies on training and research

Small firms can get grants from government to offset costs of training in marketing and management. They can also get help for developing new technologies. This is because small firms have an excellent record for innovation but a poor record for taking ideas through to selling the product. This is often because of the high development costs, which the small firm finds itself unable to afford.

Enterprise investment scheme

The Enterprise Investment Scheme is designed to help small businesses find investment funds. Individuals can invest in new and unquoted companies and receive generous tax incentives on both their income from the shares and from the capital gains if held for a long enough period.

Loan guarantee scheme

Since small firms are often seen as high risk by potential financial investors, this can be a further source of difficulty for them. In recent years, the government has been willing to underwrite part of the original loans made by some institutions. The government thus acts as a kind of cheap insurance company easing the burdens small firms face in raising finance.

Enterprise allowance scheme

The Enterprise Allowance Scheme is a scheme specifically designed to encourage the creation of small firms. An individual who has been unemployed for a qualifying period can receive a weekly allowance in the first year of his setting up a business. Effectively, then, it is a scheme that subsidises high set-up costs.

How successful have all these and many other initiatives been in terms of increasing output and generating employment? Clearly, there have been successes but the number of new businesses that grow rapidly, is quite small. Some will be unsuccessful and die, many will stay small simply because the owners do not wish to grow beyond a size with which they feel comfortable. As a result, much government expenditure is committed for a small number of successes. This leaves the government with two choices if it wishes to improve its use of expenditure. One is to say that it is too expensive to subsidise small businesses and to allow market forces to decide which firms start up and which firms grow. The alternative is to try to identify which factors make small firms successful, so that policy can be better targeted. This would require research to see if certain sectors have a higher success rate, whether certain regions are more successful, or whether certain forms of intervention prove more cost effective than others.

Finally, we turn to one area that has proved of particular concern to small businesses in recent years, namely their relationship to the commercial banks.

8 Small firms and the banking sector

One example of an internal economy of scale mentioned earlier in the chapter is in finance. Larger firms can typically borrow from banks at a lower interest rate than smaller ones. Smaller firms are regarded as more risky and therefore banks argue that they require an 'insurance premium' to cover the additional risk. Typically, the difference in borrowing costs between large and small firms has been of the order of 2–2.5 per cent. During the recession, in the British economy of the late 1980s and early 1990s, interest rates had risen to very high levels and costs of borrowing had risen accordingly. From 1991 onwards interest rates fell sharply and larger firms found that their borrowing costs fell accordingly. Many small firms claimed that *their* borrowing costs did not fall at all. Thus, it was claimed, the disadvantage of smallness was magnified to around 5 per cent.

The banks themselves were under pressure. Increased competition from the building societies in the mid- to late-1980s had reduced their profits. A long and deep recession had hit them hard, particularly since their bad debts had increased as many firms to whom they had lent went out of business. So banking profits fell sharply. But it was the small firms who felt they were bearing the brunt of the banks' problems.

There were at least three areas of disquiet. One was the belief by some that the similarity of charges between the banks reflected the fact that the banks were not in competition but in collusion. The establishment of such a cartel is illegal. The banks denied any such collusion, arguing that the similarity in charges reflected fierce competition and that the higher charges for smaller businesses simply reflected the increased risk of lending to small businesses during a recession. The Treasury examined the banks' lending practices and passed their findings to the Office of Fair Trading (OFT), who made a formal investigation into the matter in 1991. No evidence of collusion was found, although the OFT was critical of the banks' lack of sympathy towards the problems of small firms.

A second area of concern was the belief by some that banks had panicked. During a recession trading conditions for even the most efficient firms are difficult but house prices were falling and houses are the collateral for many small business loans. So house prices were falling as well as firm's profits and some felt that the banks, in desperation, closed down businesses with viable long-term futures. In essence they failed to understand the mechanism that we described earlier in section 3(c) and (d) of this chapter.

The third area of disquiet is the process by which some small businesses go into liquidation. If a bank is concerned about its customer's ability to repay its debt it can send in a team of accountants to examine the firm's books. On the basis of their findings, the bank may foreclose on the business. The source of disquiet is that the receivers generally appointed by the bank will be the same accountants as originally looked at the viability of the business. Since the income received by the accountants for acting as receivers is around ten times the fee for doing the original audit, questions are raised about the impartiality of the accountants' advice.

The banks have little to lose. If the business is wound up and there are not enough assets to pay off the creditors, the banks will still receive loan repayment, since they have a higher priority than almost anyone other than the Inland Revenue.

This whole issue has certainly caused a loss of goodwill with the banks. During the summer of 1991 the Forum for Private Business found that the proportion of its members willing to consider moving banks had increased from around 5 per cent to 50 per cent. However, the practicable alternatives were few.

9 Conclusion

So does small mean beautiful with respect to firms? The economic theory of perfect competition says that it does, and that small firms can survive. Where they cannot do so is in markets where large-scale economies are available. In such markets it is not best that they do so for it would require an inefficient use of scarce resources.

Nevertheless, market imperfections can offer grounds for government assistance to encourage and protect smaller firms. But it must be remembered that wherever such assistance is provided, there are not only potential benefits but costs too. Resources provided for small firm assistance are not available for use elsewhere. Opportunity cost applies even when considering government assistance.

In Britain, government assistance for small firms has been substantial but controversial. Small may mean beautiful – but it may not be always be beneficial to society.

10 Questions for discussion

1 The Conservative party is committed to the operation of free markets. Why, then, do you think that the Conservative government of the 1980s and 1990s introduced so many aids to small firms?
2 Evidence suggests that for much of the postwar period in Britain the share of output of the largest 100 manufacturing enterprises was increasing but the share of output of the largest 100 manufacturing plants was not. What does this suggest:
 (a) about the significance of economies of scale?
 (b) about the climate in which small firms operate?
3 One claimed diseconomy of large-scale production in disaffection of the work force. What do you understand by this? How could you measure it?
4 When economists wish to illustrate the workings of the perfectly competitive system and the place of small firms in an industry, agriculture is the most commonly chosen example. How closely does this industry relate to the perfectly competitive model? Why is it an industry in which government intervention is massive in most countries?

5 Do you see any disadvantages in laws which prevent large firms from eliminating small firm competition by setting prices below average cost?
6 Many small firms find it difficult to change their bank and reduce their borrowing costs if they feel interest charged for their borrowing is too high. Does this suggest the banks are operating a restrictive practice?
7 Building societies have provided very effective competition for the banks in providing banking services for private customers. Could they do the same for small businesses?
8 What economic case might be made for government action against banks charging high interest rates to small firms? What problems do you see with such action?
9 To what extent should governments be willing to aid small firms?

11 Further reading

Perfect competition
Sloman, pp. 214–25; Begg, pp. 133–45; Parkin and King, pp. 264–93

Normal profit
Sloman, pp. 210; Begg, pp. 136

Minimum efficient scale
Sloman, pp. 200–1; Begg, pp. 118–20; Parkin and King, pp. 229–33

On being small and beautiful
K. Keasey and R. Watson (1993) 'Banks and small firms: is conflict inevitable?', *National Westminster Bank Quarterly Review*, May.
Martin Dickson (1992) A little lesson for Big Steel. *Financial Times*, 7 August. This is a fascinating study of the effects of diseconomies of scale on large firms in the US steel industry and the consequent revival of small steel firms' fortunes.

12 End note

1 You will observe that long-run marginal cost is the same as long-run average cost when long-run average cost is at its minimum. This is inevitable for the long run as it was for the short run.

CHAPTER 7

British coal:
why the future is black

Britain has the largest coal reserves in Europe. It produces coal far more cheaply than any other European nation. Yet the last 20 years has seen collieries closing, miners being made redundant, whole communities devastated and imports rising. Does this make sense? What is going on? What should the government be doing? Why is the future for coal so black?

In this chapter we review
- Perfect competition
- External benefits

We introduce
- Taxes and market supply
- External costs
- Monopoly

1 Introduction

In this chapter we shall be examining an industry that has been a vital one in British economic history. It was once the backbone of an industrial structure which made Britain a world power. But what is the position today? Should we now be closing down pits in recognition of a new era of cleaner, more efficient fuel? Or, by putting miners on the dole and closing mines, are we throwing away an opportunity to exploit a precious national asset? We shall begin our study by giving a brief history of the industry to the present day. This will set the scene for an economic analysis of the above issues.

We shall seek to utilise our understanding of the market system to show why many feel that the industry must contract further to have a viable future. But we shall then see why others feel that, in the case of coal, the market forces argument is a false one and that government should play an active role in the industry's future. Finally, in the light of our analysis we shall suggest a suitable way forward for this proud industry. First, we shall put the industry into a historical perspective from postwar Britain to today.

2 Coal: a history of decline

Most of the British coal industry was taken into public ownership in 1947. At the time government policy seemed to be that coal output should be maximised. Relatively little thought was given to the question of the opportunity cost of the resources used in production. The question of whether resources devoted to coal production were best used there rather than elsewhere was not asked. During the 1950s and 1960s the influence of economists was felt as increasing thought was given to the question of the efficiency of industry. This thinking led to the conclusion that the coal industry was too large, a view which coincided with a steady decline in demand for coal as relatively cheap substitute became available, particularly oil. Output continued to fall while productivity continued to rise, so that fewer pits were needed. There were significant redundancies among miners. The speed of decline was arrested in the 1970s when high oil prices, following the re-emergence of the Organisation of Petroleum Exporting Countries' (OPEC's) power, made coal relatively attractive again. The government considered that its longer term future looked reasonably assured, so continuing subsidies kept the industry comparatively buoyant.

The coming to power in 1979 of a Conservative government committed to the concept of market forces as the way to increased efficiency, brought about a more rapid decline for the coal industry. Oil prices were also weakening again. Government macro-economic policy required a tight control of government expenditure. One obvious place to look to achieve such cuts was government subsidies. An obvious target here was the drain on exchequer revenues provided by the National Coal Board (NCB). Accordingly, the NCB was charged with making the industry more cost efficient and therefore less reliant on government subsidies. Essentially this would mean, among other things, accelerating pit closures. The National Union of Mine Workers (NUM) and in particular its president, Arthur Scargill, was not willing to allow its members to be the subjects of such a policy. Matters came to a head over the NCB's insistence that Cortonwood colliery in Yorkshire be closed since it was 'uneconomic'. The year-long strike which followed in 1984–5 left permanent scars on industrial relations in the industry, not least the bitterness caused by many miners leaving the NUM to form a rival union, the Union of Democratic Mineworkers (UDM).

A Conservative government committed to a market mechanism and a weakened union structure provided the background for developments in the industry in the late 1980s and early 1990s. Figure 7.1 illustrates the main trends. Since the miners' strike of 1984–5 output in the industry has continued to fall, as the market for coal has contracted. But labour productivity has risen rapidly. In orther words, the output per employee has increased, almost doubling from 2.72 tonnes per man shift to 5.3 tonnes in just seven years. Employment in the industry has therefore continued to contract markedly, two-thirds of mining jobs having disappeared since 1985.

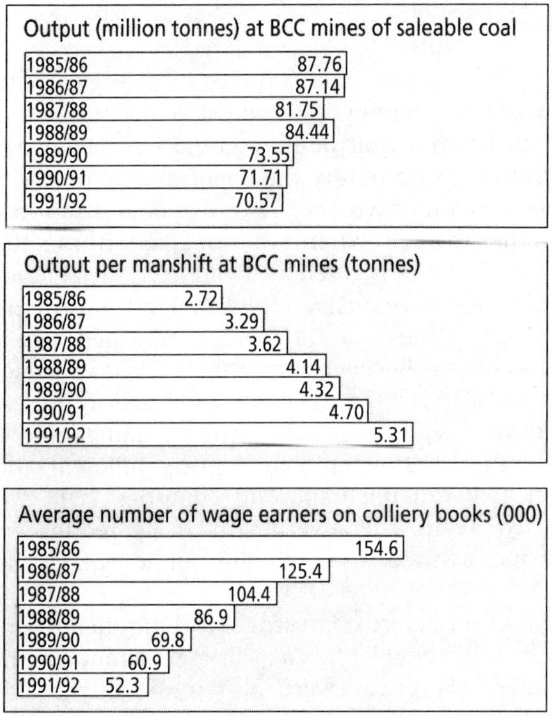

Output (million tonnes) at BCC mines of saleable coal

1985/86	87.76
1986/87	87.14
1987/88	81.75
1988/89	84.44
1989/90	73.55
1990/91	71.71
1991/92	70.57

Output per manshift at BCC mines (tonnes)

1985/86	2.72
1986/87	3.29
1987/88	3.62
1988/89	4.14
1989/90	4.32
1990/91	4.70
1991/92	5.31

Average number of wage earners on colliery books (000)

1985/86	154.6
1986/87	125.4
1987/88	104.4
1988/89	86.9
1989/90	69.8
1990/91	60.9
1991/92	52.3

Figure 7.1 UK coal collieries, employment and output

Two other factors are also of great significance in explaining these trends. First, in 1990 the electricity supply industry (ESI) was privatised. Power generation was placed in the hands of Powergen and National Power, two private companies, and Nuclear Power generation which remained in the hands of the government. Power distribution was to be the responsibility of 12 regional distribution companies who could either buy this electricity from the power generators or produce their own. At the time of the privatisation 80 per cent of British Coal's output was sold to Powergen and National Power. A contract fixed the price of that coal until April 1993. Thereafter Powergen and National Power were to be free to buy whatever they liked in whatever amounts they chose. British Coal lost its guaranteed market and found itself competing against cheaper imported coal and gas-fired electricity. Some gas-fired plant was constructed by National Power and Powergen, some was built by the regional power companies who did not want to rely entirely for their electricity supplies on the big two generators. During 1993 a new five-year contract was signed between British Coal and the power generators, but on terms much less favourable to coal.

The second factor was concern for the environment. Coal burning produces sulphur dioxide, especially British coal which is rich in sulphur. Britain is committed to an international treaty and European Community (EC) directive to reduce by 60 per cent power station emissions of sulphur dioxide between 1980 and 2003. Because expensive equipment must be installed to remove such emissions, coal-burning power stations become more expensive to build. The result is further reductions in the demand for British coal.

Inevitably, unless circumstances change, the industry will continue to contract, and the government believes that it should do so. Others are unconvinced and we shall shortly see why, but first, we look at why the government believes that it is in the best interests of society if the coal industry in Britain continues to decline.

3 Coal decline: 'market forces at work'

a Understanding the supply curve

We have already seen in Chapter 2 that left to itself a market will bring about a situation where supply and demand are equal. Let us look a little more closely at the supply curve to see why that equilibrium can be argued to be an optimum state for society.

See pp 116–7

In Chapter 6 we saw that economies and diseconomies of scale can produce a U-shaped long-run average cost curve and an upward-sloping long-run marginal cost curve. We also saw that in the long run a firm produces output where marginal production costs equal price. One might see this as being a coal mine such as mine (a) represented in Figure 7.2. If the price of coal is P_1 the mine will produce output q_1. If coal prices are lower, for example, at P_2 output will be less at q_2. This assumes that prices are high enough to cover unit costs as we saw in Chapter 6. But there are many such mines; Figure 7.1 shows a sample of three of them.

If we sum the output of each mine at price P_1 we have output Q_1 from the coal industry. This is one spot on the industry supply curve given in Figure 7.2. At a lower price P_2 each mine will, as we have seen, produce less output. The industry

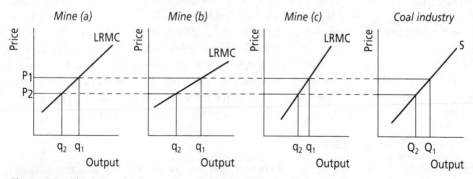

Figure 7.2 Obtaining the long run coal supply curve

output is given as Q_2. In other words, the industry (long-run) supply curve is given as the sum of the individual mines (long-run) marginal cost curves (above long-run average total cost).

But we can go one step further. The long-run supply curve not only shows marginal production costs, it also shows the opportunity cost to society of resources used in producing output. If for one coal mine its marginal production costs are £30 per tonne at some level of output we can ask this question. *Why* is it £30 and not £5 or £100? The answer, of course, is that it needs resources to produce the output. The £30 is being spent on land labour and capital. These resources have an opportunity cost. Other firms in other forms of production are willing to pay something for these resources to make the output they could produce. Thus the coal industry will have to pay £30 to bid these resources away from that use. In other words, the £30 represents the value of output foregone elsewhere. The supply curve shows not only marginal production costs, but marginal opportunity costs.

Now let us consider Figure 7.3. The demand curve for coal is at D_1, the supply curve is at S_1. Equilibrium price is at P_1. Market output is at Q_1. Is the output that the industry produces optimal for society? There is a strong case for saying yes. The demand curve shows us the value society places on the output, the supply curve shows us the opportunity cost of its production. Hence, if Q_1 is produced, all the coal is being mined which society values at its opportunity cost. Society would rather have those resources in coal production than in any other industry. Output Q_1 is socially optimal while demand remains at D_1. Notice that we have concentrated the argument on long-run rather than short-run costs. The significance of this will become apparent later in the chapter.

b Responding to demand changes

As we have seen the demand for coal has not been static. The demand for coal is not only a function of its price but it also depends upon other variables. One most crucial of these is alternative energy sources. As gas has become relatively cheap in recent years the market demand for coal has fallen. Until the 1990s an EC directive prevented the use of gas as a form of electricity production. Freed from that restriction demand for gas increased and the demand for coal fell. This is shown in Figure 7.3. Demand shifts from D_1 to D_2. Marginal pits are no longer profitable at the lower price and must be closed as output contracts to Q_2 at the lower price P_2. Does this make sense from society's viewpoint? Yes. Each unit between Q_2 and Q_1 is valued by society at less than its opportunity cost. The measure of society's welfare loss if the pits are kept open is the shaded triangle in Figure 7.3. The socially optimal output is, given the lower demand, Q_2.

c The problem of externalities

But we have yet to explore other reasons for the projected fall in demand for British coal. A further reason for expecting demand to contract is the presence of

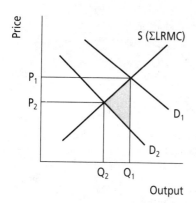

Figure 7.3 Demand and supply for coal

what we call externalities. In Chapter 4 we introduced the idea of an external benefit in the context of innoculations against infectious diseases. An externality can give rise either to an external benefit or an external cost. Furthermore, the externality can be caused by production or, as in the case of innoculations, by consumption. Let us look first at externalities in production. Consider an external cost of production. We have seen that to produce output requires resources. In a market system the amount of resources used in production is equal to the cost that a supplier has to bear. Sometimes, however, a supplier has to bear less than the full costs to society of his actions. He may, by producing output, impose costs on the rest of society. An example of such an action would be a firm producing chemicals that have an unwanted by-product. It then tips the by-product into the nearest river. The firm pays some of the costs of producing output but not all of them. It does not pay the external costs of cleaning up the river, or the loss of fish stocks resulting from its actions. Figure 7.4(a) shows how there is a breakdown in the identity between private costs (costs to the firm) and social costs (costs to society). The difference between the two is the external cost imposed by the externality. The most obvious way to deal with this problem is for a government to assess the size of external cost and impose it on producers as a tax. The effect is to raise the firms marginal private cost upwards to coincide with society's social cost.

Figure 7.4(b) shows an example of how production can lead to benefits to society that the firm itself does not gain. Social costs are lower than private costs. Probably the most significant example of such a situation is where a firm trains its workforce, some of whom then change jobs. The benefit of the training then accrues to the rest of society but not the firm that undertook the training costs. Such a situation suggests a subsidy to reduce marginal private costs to coincide with marginal social costs. Many economists feel that the gap between private and social costs in this area is much greater in Britain than the level of government training subsidy implies.

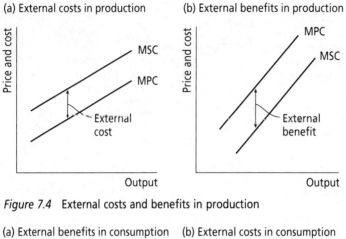

Figure 7.4 External costs and benefits in production

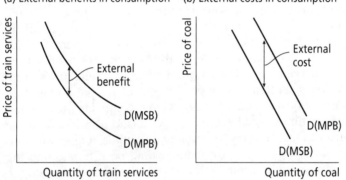

Figure 7.5 External costs and benefits in consumption

Sometimes it is not the act of production that creates such external effects but the act of consumption. Consumption can impose external benefits or external costs on society. Consider Figure 7.5(a). The demand for train services D (MPB) reflects the marginal private benefits derived privately from consumption. But it could be argued that marginal social benefits are greater in that trains free up road space and create less atmospheric pollution. On that basis the demand curve for train services should be shifted outwards until MPB coincides with MSB. But Figure 7.5(b) describes externality effects with coal consumption. One can argue that there are external effects in production of coal in that countryside is spoiled and scarred by the opening up of coal faces. However, the larger problem is that imposed by coal *consumption*. When you burn coal, either directly in the fireplace, or indirectly via the consumption of electricity that has been generated from coal, you impose costs on the rest of society. Sulphur emissions will return as acid rain destroying trees, and CO_2 emissions will encourage the greenhouse effect. D (MPB) is greater than D (MSB). How should government deal with the problem?

d Dealing with externalities in coal production

The obvious answer to the question of dealing with the external effects of coal consumption is to impose taxes to reduce its consumption. Let us see its effects in terms of an example using imaginary data contained in Table 7.1 and represented on a graph in Figure 7.6. Original equilibrium for the coal industry is an annual output of 25 million tonnes at a price of £40 per tonne. This assumes that the government ignores the external consumption effects. It cannot do so for much longer given the EC directive mentioned earlier.

The effect of a £10 per tonne tax is shown in Table 7.1, column 4. At a price of £50 per tonne and no tax, suppliers were willing to supply 50 million tonnes to the market. If the price is £50 per tonne and there is a £10 per tonne tax, how much will the quantity supplied be now? Since the suppliers are left with £40 for themselves we know they will supply 25 million tonnes. By similar reasoning we can find other spots on the new supply curve. When we plot this as S_2 on the diagram in Figure 7.6 we can see the result. We have a higher coal price and less

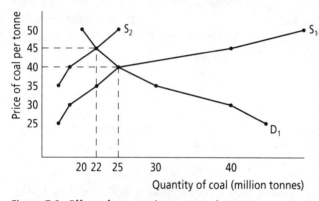

Figure 7.6 Effect of a per unit tax on coal

Table 7.1 Illustrating the effect of a tax by shifting the supply curve

Price of coal (£ per tonne)	Quantity demanded (D_1) (million tonnes)	Quantity supplied (S_1) (million tonnes)	Quantity supplied after tax of £10 per tonne (S_2) (million tonnes)
50	20	50	25
45	22	40	22
40	25	25	18
35	30	22	14
30	40	18	—
25	45	14	—

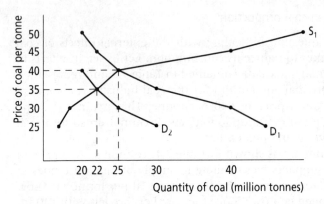

Figure 7.7 Alternative presentation of the effect of tax on coal

Table 7.2 Illustrating the effect of a tax by shifting the demand curve

Price of coal (£ per tonne)	Quantity demanded (D_1) (million tonnes)	Quantity supplied (S_1) (million tonnes)	Quantity demanded after tax of £10 per tonne (S_2) (million tonnes)
50	20	50	—
45	22	40	—
40	25	25	20
35	30	22	22
30	40	18	25
25	45	14	30

output, so fewer resources are needed in the coal industry, and therefore fewer mines, fewer miners and more redundancies are inevitable.

It is possible, however, to see the tax, not as an addition to the cost of suppliers but as a reduction in the demand curve for coal by consumers. We do this in Table 7.2 and Figure 7.7. Beginning from the original data, consider the effect of a tax on the demand for coal. When the price to the supplier was £25 per tonne consumers of coal were willing to purchase 30 million tonnes. What happens now that there is a £10 per tonne tax? With a price to the supplier of £25 per tonne, the consumer must pay the £25 to the supplier plus the £10 tax to the government. Given the total of £35 consumers are prepared to buy 30 million tonnes. This is plotted on Figure 7.7 as a spot on demand curve D_2. We can work out other spots on the demand curve in the same way, giving column 4 in Table 7.2 and demand curve D_2 in Figure 7.7. This gives an equilibrium price to the supplier and consumer net of tax of £35 and a price *with* tax of £45. The effect is the same as before. The equilibrium quantity of coal falls to 22 million tonnes. In principle, then, it does not matter whether a tax is placed on the supplier or the consumer, the outcome in the market on price, output and resources will be the same. Later in the chapter we shall see what the estimates are with respect to the effect of 'greening' British coal.

The *form* which government policy takes is unimportant. A tax on suppliers, a tax on consumers or an imposition on electricity producers that they must fit scrubbers to remove sulphur from coal burning plants, all achieve the same end with respect to the effect on the coal industry. It restores the identity between social and private cost – but further reduces the demand for coal and hence the demand for coal mines and coal miners. 'Going green' is not cheap. Of course, in other respects it is far more efficient to make coal burners fit scrubbers. A tax leaves the problem of redistributing the revenue raised to those affected by the acid rain – a rather tricky exercise.

e The market for coal in an open economy

So far we have assumed that although coal demand will fall and pits must therefore close, all the demand for coal that exists in Britain will be met from British pits. This is not so. Foreign coal is cheaper than coal from some British pits. Given this situation, equilibrium in the coal market can be described by Figure 7.8.

The world price of coal is around £30 per tonne. Demand in Britain is represented by home demand curve D_h and home supply S_h. At £30 per tonne British suppliers competing against such a price can sell only Q_1 coal, British demand for coal is Q_0. The gap is filled by imports. At present Q_0–Q_1 is around 20 million tonnes. Some countries can beat British coal mine prices despite having to pay transport costs over a considerable distance.

World coal prices have been falling relative to British prices. Although British coal prices have fallen, import prices have fallen faster. As a result imports have

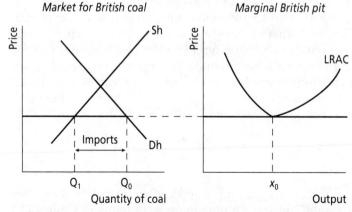

Figure 7.8 Equilibrium in the market for coal in an open economy

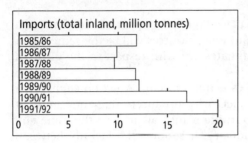

Figure 7.9 The growth of UK coal imports

been growing over time as Figure 7.9 indicates. Figure 7.8 also shows the marginal British pit able to survive against imports. It can cover all costs of production and make a normal profit. Which pits close as demand falls? Clearly there will be those pits with the highest marginal production costs. In Britain, around 17 million tonnes per annum can be produced from low cost opencast mining. Selby coalfield is a cheap cost mine into which £2 billion of investment has been sunk. Since most of these costs are non-recoverable, marginal costs are relatively low. Selby will produce around 10 million tonnes per annum. When one considers that some projections are that demand for British coal may fall to around 30 million tonnes, it suggests that little of the traditional deep mining can survive during the 1990s.

We have now examined the market case for the pit closure programme continuing, and the closure of pits is inevitable. There is no prospect of a market for British coal remaining at the level of the early 1990s, so pits must close and resources must be re-allocated elsewhere where they are needed.

4 Objections to the 'market forces' view

Although it is possible to object to the market forces argument outlined above, not all the arguments one sometimes hears are equally strong. For example, it is sometimes said that the government should protect the coal industry from market forces 'to preserve miners jobs'. There is little logic in taxing people to pay miners a wage to produce output which nobody wishes to buy. A case for protecting the mining industry must be made on other grounds. There are four grounds upon which one *can* make a case for not leaving the mining industry to market forces. They are the problem of resource mobility, the question of a 'level playing field', the uncertainty of future energy supplies and finally the problem of monopoly power.

a Resource mobility

It is often claimed that if miners are put out of work, they do not go into other industries and produce output but remain unemployed. In terms of Figure 7.10 we can express the view like this. If demand for coal falls, society wishes resources

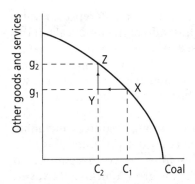

Figure 7.10 Resource immobility in the coal industry

to be shifted out of coal into other goods. As demand falls, the price of coal falls relative to other goods, and the relative price change is a signal to resource owners to relocate resources to other forms of production. Society has signalled that it wants a move from C_1g_1 to C_2g_2, but in a way similar to what we saw in Chapter 1 in planned economies, resources may be unemployed in coal. This moves us from point X to point Y but then the resources may stay unemployed. Then we shall not get the shift from Y to Z, at least not in the short term. The argument can be made, then, that the opportunity cost of producing the coal is zero. Not only this but government is saved the unemployment benefit it would otherwise pay.

See p 18

The famous 'miners' strike' of 1984–5 began over a dispute at Cortonwood Colliery, Yorkshire. The coal board claimed that the pit was 'uneconomic'. Their figures were as follows:

Cost of operations	£326,000 per week
Revenue from coal	£264,000 per week
Loss if remaining open	£ 62,000 per week

The case for keeping it, and other pits like it, open can be seen in the following figures that the NUM supported.

Cost of closure	Dole	£79,000 per week
	Redundancy pay	£67,000 per week
	Lost tax revenue	£101,000 per week
Total cost of closure		£247,000 per week

Translated into cost per employed miner:

Cost to society in keeping the colliery open	£ 74 per week
Cost to society in closing the colliery down	£300 per week

The conclusion is that the pit should have stayed open.

How does one evaluate such an argument? First, a clear difference of view existed between government and unions over the question of the time scale. If the market forces case is a legitimate one, it is based on the idea of a long-run optimum. The miners' argument is, in essence, that one should be concerned with the short run also. One way of looking at the debate, then, is to see it as a disagreement over the relative importance of the short-run costs and the long run benefits of the market forces solution.

Second, there is a powerful case for saying that mining resources including labour, are highly immobile. Most redundant miners do not get other jobs. The problem is that in a dynamic economy resources must move in response to demand and technological change or output will not grow quickly. However, there is a strong case for saying that government can help with that transition by seeing to it that the rate of decline is only as fast as the mobility of resources will allow. Furthermore, on an external benefits argument, considerable resources for retraining should be made available in such areas where mines are being closed.

Third, however, there are costs to society in slowing down the decline of an industry. Either general taxpayers must provide subsidies or government must oblige consumers of coal such as the power generators to take what they regard as non-commercial decisions to use higher cost British coal. The result is that the slowdown is funded by electricity consumers in the form of higher prices. The benefits of slowing resource transfer will be obvious. The costs may well be real though hidden.[1]

b Providing a 'level playing field'

The coal industry has often argued that it believes itself able to compete in a genuinely free market, but the market is not in fact free. One way in which this can be seen is that the competition receives subsidies. This is striking in two areas, the subsidies offered by foreign governments to its coal producers enabling it to undercut British coal, and the subsidies offered by the British government to nuclear power generation. We shall look at these two areas of 'unfair competition' in turn, first subsidised foreign coal.

We saw in Figure 7.9 the increasing degree of import penetration of the British coal market. Table 7.3 shows the origin of these imports. Now the concern is that some of these imports are from countries whose governments heavily subsidise the industry, notably, Germany whose production costs are over twice the average of British coal's costs.

Sometimes there are objections to allowing coal to be imported into Britain from countries such as Columbia and Russia on the grounds that such countries have cheap labour costs. We have to remember, however, that the great advantage of certain imports is that they are cheap. It cannot be in the interests of consumers to raise import prices simply because they are cheap! However, we need to look at the argument that says we should either prevent German imports

Table 7.3 Major sources of coal imports into the UK, 1991–92 (tonnes)

West Germany	3,907,433
Australia	3,183,279
Netherlands	2,582,292
USA	2,108,008
Colombia	1,799,770
Poland	926,878
Canada	907,468
CIS*	733,751
South Africa	455,397

Note: *Commonwealth of Independent States, formerly the Soviet Union.
Source: Trade statistics.

or subsidise British production to the same degree. The case can be made but it is not overwhelming.

Let us consider the question from the German perspective. The market price of an unsubsidised tonne of German coal might be around £120. Thus £120 of resources are used to produce one tonne of coal, resources that have an opportunity cost. When the exported coal sells for £30 because the German government has subsidised it, Germany obtains the right to import £30 worth of goods from Britain. It makes no sense for Germany. The remaining £90 is a grant from the German government to British consumers! It is not at all clear that the appropriate response of the British should be to deny ourselves such largesse or return the compliment by subsidising our goods!

Logically, the only objection to the above reasoning is that coal miners in Britain will produce nothing if we take German coal. This leads us to an important conclusion. The objection to subsidised imports has no validity except in so far as resources are immobile. The 'level playing field' argument cannot stand on its own. It is the resource immobility argument that is really being used.

But now what of the view that British coal should be subsidised because nuclear energy receives a subsidy from the British government? Again the argument is difficult to sustain. The subsidy may represent some external benefit in consumption such as the argument that it is a cleaner fuel. In this case the subsidy is justified. But the main reason is that the government seriously underestimated the decommissioning costs of nuclear plants. These costs have to be met. Nuclear fuel users will not pay so, in part, the coal industry is paying for past poor government decision making. Unfortunately, for coal the government is committed to nuclear energy subsidies until 1998. Even after that it faces a problem. Nuclear energy involves colossal capital costs and low (marginal) running costs. Thus, even after 1998, nuclear energy will be cheap in the short run. British coal will get no help here until into the next century. Nevertheless, it remains true that coal demand is lower than it 'should' be because of the nuclear subsidy.

c Uncertainty in future energy supplies

The view that the government should protect the coal industry because of future uncertainty in energy supplies has two aspects to it. The first is that if there were to be an absence of peacetime conditions at some time in the future, energy imports might be difficult or impossible and home produced energy would then be crucial. But home produced energy might be virtually impossible to obtain if the mines have been flooded.

This, of course, is a political rather than an economic question, but there are two points that need to be made about this view. The first is that to the extent that we would in time of war need to replace coal imports with domestically produced coal, the case is for an explicit subsidy to the coal industry to 'mothball' some pits. In other words, it argues that government should be investing a sum in coal to keep some pits in a state which would enable coal production to be resumed quickly. It does not, by itself, argue that high cost pits produce coal now for which there is no market. The second point is that, to the extent one would wish to substitute indigenous coal supplies for other important energy sources during wartime, it would require a political decision not only to keep mining coal for which there was no (free) market, but to oblige electricity generators to take non-commercial decisions to build new coal-burning stations. Whether such a policy is desirable or not is a political question but there are economic costs associated with such a strategy.

There is, however, a second aspect to the question of future energy supplies. Some argue that while British coal may not be the cheapest fuel available now, it will be in future years. In the very long term, gas supplies will be exhausted more quickly than coal supplies but there is a view that even in the medium term British coal prices will become increasingly attractive. It is argued that there is a danger that sterling depreciation could increase the real cost of imported coal in the medium term. Furthermore, one has to consider that only a limited amount of coal is traded internationally, at present variously estimated at between 5 and 7 per cent of world output. There is at least a serious possibility that a massive switch to coal imports would impose a significant upward pressure on spot prices. It is generally acknowledged that most countries export their surplus coal below cost. It may then be optimistic to assume that a large part of the output at present supplied by British coal is easily substitutable at the present level of import prices.

The above may or may not prove to be correct. However, it is clearly not believed by the power generators or they would modify their generating capacity accordingly. The case really depends upon the view that governments are better speculators in future energy price levels than private decision makers. Whether such an argument can be sustained is, to say the least, dubious.

d Monopoly power

A powerful objection to the arguments we have so far examined is that we have been assuming that energy is a perfectly competitive market. Manifestly it is not. It is often argued that the structure of the market has worked against the interests of British coal.

The structure of the market at present is as follows. There are three producers of power, the nuclear sector, which is government owned, Powergen and National Power. Since 1993 Powergen and National Power have been free to buy any fuel they choose at the best price they can obtain. The generators supply to 12 regional electricity suppliers. The regional suppliers have a monopoly over supply to all customers save the largest. They are also free to produce their own power, rather than take power from the generators, to sell to customers. This in essence has been the arrangement since 1990 when the ESI was sold by government into private ownership. But why does this arrangement adversely affect the demand for coal? To answer this question we need to examine what economic theory suggests is the effect of private monopoly. We shall develop these ideas in the next section and then relate them to the question of electricity supply.

5 Developing the concept of monopoly power

a Monopoly price and output decisions

A monopoly is a single supplier of a good or service. In consequence the industry demand curve is the firm's demand curve. If the firm is a monopolist, the firm is the industry. So a regional electricity company is faced with a downward sloping demand curve as in Figure 7.11.

This has important consequences for the revenue situation of the firm. These can be seen with reference to Table 7.4 and Figure 7.11 where we use some

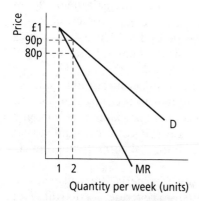

Figure 7.11 Revenue conditions with monopoly power

Table 7.4 Illustrative revenue and cost conditions of a monopolist

Quantity demanded per week	Price	TR	MR	LRAC	LRMC
1	£1.00	£1.00	£1.00	60p	60p
2	90p	£1.80	80p	60p	60p
3	80p	£2.40	60p	60p	60p
4	70p	£2.80	40p	60p	60p
5	60p	£3.00	20p	60p	60p
6	50p	£3.00	0	60p	60p
7	40p	£2.80	-20p	60p	60p
8	30p	£2.40	-40p	60p	60p

Notes: TR = Total revenue
MR = Marginal revenue
LRAC = Long-run average cost
LRMC = Long-run marginal cost

illustrative data for a representative monopolistic firm. Columns one and two in Table 7.4 give us the monopolist's assumed demand curve. The total revenue received at each different level of output, column three, is found by multiplying output by price. As we saw in Chapter 6, marginal revenue is the additional revenue received for selling one more unit of output. Notice how, for a monopolist, this falls with increased output. So, for example, if the firm were making two units of output each week and it then decided to increase output to three units, what would happen to its revenue? To sell three units per week it must drop the price to 80p. If it cannot price discriminate and charge different prices to different customers for the same good or service, it must sell all three units at 80p. Thus to gain the 80p from the extra customer it must forego 10p on each of the two units for which it could have charged 90p. Hence marginal revenue is only 60p. The marginal revenue curve is plotted in Figure 7.11. Notice how this contrasts with the perfectly competitive firm's demand and marginal revenue curves that we examined in Chapter 6.

Before we can see how the monopolist arrives at a price/output decision, we need to consider his cost situation. We shall assume that in the long run his unit costs are constant. Given what we saw in Chapter 6 this is probably true for some but not all monopolistic firms. If long-run average costs (LRAC) is constant so that each unit cost 60p on average then each additional unit must cost 60p to produce. If LRAC is constant LRMC is equal to it.

So how will a profit maximising monopolist price? Clearly, he will want to produce any unit of output that adds less to cost than to revenue. So he will want to produce three units of output per week where marginal cost, addition to total

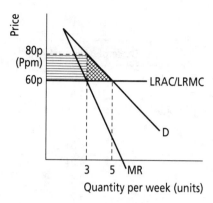

Figure 7.12   The social cost of monopoly power

cost, is equal to marginal revenue, addition to revenue. This is shown in Figure 7.12.

We now have the monopolist's profit maximising level of output. What price would he charge for these units? The answer, of course, is the most he can get for them. The demand curve tells him that. It is clearly 80p per unit, shown on the diagram as 'Ppm'. The striped area shows his profit, namely the difference between LRAC and average revenue multiplied by output. In this case that means 20p × 3 units of output or 60p. Remember that since normal profit is included in the cost structure this represents a profit above the normal. But won't competition erode this away over time? The answer is no since there are substantial barriers to the entry of new firms in monopolistic industries, which prevent this process from taking place.

b The social costs of monopoly power

We are now in a position to see that such behaviour is not socially efficient. It is in society's interests that the monopolist in Figure 7.12 makes five units of output since his marginal cost, and therefore the opportunity cost of the resources used, is less than the value of output to society. Consider the two units per week that he will not make. The opportunity cost of the resources is given by the rectangle under the marginal cost curve. The value of the output if the monopolist were to make it is given by the area under the demand curve between three and five units. So the loss of consumer welfare through the monopolist's behaviour is the shaded triangle. In terms of the coal industry then, the case is as follows. Electricity generators and distributors will charge too high prices to consumers. This will reduce the quantity demanded. The quantity of coal inputs will therefore be less than socially optimal and pits will close which, socially, should stay open.

Is this less than socially optimal demand a sufficient problem to make much impact on the size of the coal industry? The probable answer is no. Electricity

Table 7.5 Power generation costs using different fuels

	Pence per kilowatt hour
British coal at contracted price to Spring 1993, £1.85 per gigajoule	2.4
British coal at post 1993 agreed price £1.51 per gigajoule	1.8
British coal at estimated post 1993 agreed price £1.45 per gigajoule plus estimated cost of emission controll instalation	2.8
Nuclear power without government subsidy	8.0+
Nuclear power with government subsidy agreed to 1997	4.0+
Gas at early 1991 contracted prices	2.4
Gas at price contracted from 1992 onwards	3.2

Source: Various indusry estimates.

suppliers are not free to charge whatever prices they choose. An industry regulator, appointed by the government, controls price, and therefore output decisions, though many believe that profits in electricity generation and distribution suggest the control is not tight enough.

An alternative argument about monopoly power runs as follows. The government price ceiling on electricity set by the industry regulator allows a mark-up on costs so that industry makes a normal profit. It therefore follows that the electricity industry has no incentive to minimise electricity production costs. Whatever costs are incurred can simply be passed on to the consumer as higher electricity prices. Hence although coal may be the cheapest fuel to use, generators are happy to use higher cost gas burning stations.

There are two points about such an argument. One is that it is not immediately apparent why power generators would choose a more expensive fuel even if they could do so, but it certainly represents a major problem for the industry price regulator if this is the case. The second point is that it is extremely difficult to determine which fuel is more cost efficient. Consider Table 7.5 above. On the face of it, coal represents an excellent deal even with the cost of equipment to remove sulphur emissions. However, the figures are disputed. The biggest dispute arises over the question of cost of new coal burning generators. The electricity industry claims that the figures assume that the capital costs of the old coal burning power stations have been written off. Such figures only make sense if one assumes that they will never need replacing. If one adds on the capital costs associated with new generating equipment, gas is a far more cost-efficient fuel.

6 Conclusion

When a coal mine is closed down, the human cost of unemployment with little chance of an alternative job is great. When the repercussions reverberate through a whole community, the cost is multiplied. But the essential point that market economists wish to make is that there are also considerable costs in preventing that unemployment. The costs of higher electricity prices, or higher taxes, or both also imposes costs on others. Simply because the costs tend to be hidden does not mean that they are not real.

If there is an economic case for protecting the coal industry, it is to be found partly in the immobility of resources. This suggests aid to ease the transfer of resources rather than funds to prevent it happening. An economic case is also partly to be found in the monopolistic structure of the ESI.

However, there must be serious doubts about the government's commitment to the power of market forces in this industry. If the government really believed in the market mechanism as a means of determining coal resource allocation, there was an excellent way to prove it. It would have been more consistent if it had stopped shutting pits and allowing them to be flooded. It could then have sold them to pit managers and miners as individual going concerns. Many miners now on unemployment benefit believe that the pits in which they worked were economic. It is difficult to understand why they were never given the opportunity to prove it.

7 Questions for discussion

1   In Table 7.1 in the text, a £10 tax on coal production led to a £5 increase in market price. Why wasn't it £10? What determines the extent to which prices rise when taxes are imposed?
2   Refer to Figure 7.8. How would an import tax help the coal industry? Is such a policy desirable?
3   It is often claimed that although a community, heavily dependent upon one declining form of production, suffers when not protected from market forces, in the long run things do improve. The town of Corby was once heavily dependent on a steel plant which was closed. Unemployment rose significantly. Now its unemployment rate is about the same as the national average. Clearly in the long run resources *do* shift. Assess this argument.
4   Why will a profit maximising monopolist wish to set a price at which demand is elastic? (HINT: What does elastic demand suggest about marginal revenue? How does the profit maximising monopolist's price and output decision relate to marginal revenue?)
5   Consider Figure 7.12 in the text. Now redraw it assuming increased LRMC. Suppose a ceiling of a socially optimum price is set. What price/output results? Will profits be made? What problems will there be in determining a socially optimal price in practice?
6   To what extent should the government intervene in the market for coal?

8 Further reading

Monopoly
Sloman, pp. 204–13; Begg, pp. 145–55; Parkin and King, pp. 294–316

Taxes and market supply
Sloman, pp. 98–100; Begg, pp. 50; Parkin and King, pp. 126–30

External Costs & Benefits
Sloman, pp. 411–14; Begg, pp. 265–72; Parkin and King, pp. 464–70

British Coal: *Why the Future is Black*
D. Charles (1993) 'The future for coal', *New Scientist*, 23, January.
C. Davies (1993) 'Do we really need a coal industry? *Economic Affairs*, 13(2) February.

9 End note

1 You may also have noticed that the redundancy payments are treated as though they are paid continually. In fact, they are one-off payments, which will therefore be a cost only in the first year. Loss of tax and dole money continue as long as the unemployment remains.

CHAPTER 8

Europe's airline prices: the sky's the limit?

(WITH DR MICHAEL ASTERIS)

Europe's airline passengers feel that they pay far too much for the service they receive. Aren't prices much lower in the USA? Why can't it be like that in Europe? In this chapter we consider the possibility of government action to lower airline fares.

We review:
- Economies of scale
- Pareto optimality

We introduce:
- Oligopoly
- Cartels
- Mergers
- Contestable markets

1 Introduction

Europe's airline passengers frequently complain that they have to pay too much for the services provided. Comparisons are often made between prices in Europe and prices for a similar distance travelled within the USA. Table 8.1 indicates that there is evidence that European airline travel is more expensive. Revenue received per route tonne kilometre (RTK) travelled is substantially less for American than for European airlines. What makes for such differences? Can it be that there are greater scale economies for United States airlines which can then be passed to consumers in the form of lower prices? Or has it more to do with the greater competition that exists in the USA?

If the latter, what could the European Commission do to increase competition in Europe? If competition were to be increased would it lower prices? Would there be undesirable side effects? These are the questions we shall address in this chapter. We begin by examining the structure of the European airline industry and what such a structure suggests about the likely level of prices that will obtain in the market-place.

Table 8.1 Revenue received per route tonne kilometre (RTK) by European and US airlines submitting financial data to IATA ($US), 1992

	European	*North American*
Range	0.81–2.55	0.56–1.12
Average	1.11	0.82

Source: IATA, *World Air Transport Statistics*, 1993.

2 The European airline industry: an oligopolistic market

a Defining oligopoly

A market structure is one characterised by oligopoly when there is only a small number of firms in the market. Normally one would expect it to be an industry where there were significant economies of scale available such that, as we saw in Chapter 5, small firms would not survive. However, competition may still remain among the few, indeed it may be very fierce.

How few firms would be needed for us to classify an industry as oligopolistic? There is no specific number. The principle is that there should be few enough for there to be 'interdependence'. In other words, decisions taken by one firm have a direct effect on other firms in that market. If you were a farmer and your neighbour decided to double his output of wheat, his decision would have no direct effect on you, since the effect on total wheat output, and hence prices, would be essentially nil. However, if Shell were to double its output of petrol, the effect on other firms in the oil market would, in terms of price and output, clearly be direct and significant.

It is this feature of interdependence which makes the economic analysis of any oligopolistic market a tricky one. With interdependence comes uncertainty. If British Airways decides to cut its prices to increase market share how will other airlines respond? Will they follow its lead? Leave their fares unchanged? Increase their advertising? Different models of oligopoly make different assumptions as to how firms react to one another in the presence of uncertainty. In this chapter we shall examine two such models. In Chapter 9 we shall examine some other ideas which may throw light on large firm behaviour.

However, oligopoly is not defined simply by the number of firms but also by the nature of the product. In an oligopolistic market what is produced by the various firms is not identical but differentiated. One farmer's wheat is much like another, but by contrast, one journey on an aircraft is not identical with another. Companies may compete, not only on price, but on comfort, width of seats, friendliness of stewardesses, quality of food, timing and frequency of flights and so on. In other words, oligopoly is characterised by what is often referred to as 'non-price competition', since oligopolistic products are not perfect substitutes for one another.

One other feature which characterises oligopoly is that, as with monopoly, there exist substantial barriers to the entry of new firms. That is to say, there are obstacles in the way of new firms joining a market to compete with the existing firms. There are many such barriers. We shall briefly mention a few. Economies of scale can be a barrier as we saw in Chapter 6. A firm cannot effectively compete unless it is very large, but it is not easy to begin business as a large organisation.

See pp 118–19

Product differentiation can be a barrier. An existing firm may have established such brand loyalty that it is difficult for a newcomer to attract sales. Part of the logic of advertising is to build up a group of consumers who are committed to the product. In that way advertising also acts as a barrier to entry in that it is advertising which helps differentiate the product in the mind of consumers.

Finally, governments can create entry barriers. In the case of the airline industry a government may refuse to allow another foreign owned airline the landing rights necessary for it to operate a service. This is important since if existing firms are making substantial profits, new firms cannot easily provide increased competition to push prices downwards. The competition must be largely between the existing firms.

b The structure of the airline industry

Is the airline industry sufficiently concentrated for us legitimately to regard it as an oligopolistic industry? At first sight, one might come to the conclusion that the answer is no. Table 8.2 lists the top 20 airlines in the world by passenger kilometres flown, but even these represent a relatively small proportion of the total number of airlines worldwide.

However, the existence of many airlines tells us less than we might at first think about the degree of competition each company faces, since clearly not all airlines compete on all routes. A more realistic idea of the degree of competition might be given by looking at the European market, but even here the picture the data would present would be somewhat misleading. Often on any particular route a passenger has a very limited choice of perhaps just one or two airlines. Aeroflot's dominance of the former Soviet Union's domestic market, making it the second biggest single provider of domestic airline kilometres flown, was a consequence of the communist government's prevention of competition from other sources. Note that Table 8.2. shows that in 1992 Aeroflot did not appear in the top 20 on international routes.

Table 8.3 gives an impression of the degree of concentration in the UK market. Although British Airways (BA) has very limited competition on international routes apart from Virgin, it has a little more competition on domestic routes. But there are probably few enough 'firms' to describe the UK market as oligopolistic. In this sector of the market fears are often expressed that the competition is limited in that BA is so much larger than any of its competitors.

Table 8.2 UK airlines RTK

	International			Domestic			Total	
Rank	airline	Millions	Rank	airline	Millions	Rank	airline	Millions
1	British Airways	8,859	1	American Airlines	11,315	1	American Airlines	16,281
2	Lufthansa	8,635	2	Aeroflot-Russian Int'l Airlines	10,580	2	United Airlines	15,918
3	Japan Airlines	7,046	3	Delta Air Lines	9,757	3	Delta Air Lines	13,423
4	Air France	6,361	4	United Airlines	9,732	4	Aeroflot-Russian Int'l Airlines	12,107
5	United Airlines	6,185	5	Northwest Airlines	5,910	5	Northwest Airlines	11,635
6	Singapore Airlines	5,904	6	US Air	5,113	6	British Airways	9,143
7	Northwest Airlines	5,725	7	Continental Airlines	4,894	7	Lufthansa	9,135
8	KLM	5,343	8	Federal Express	3,382	8	Japan Airlines	8,327
9	American Airlines	4,967	9	TWA-Trans World Airlines	3,199	9	Air France	7,238
10	Korean Air Lines	4,447	10	All Nipon Airways	2,488	10	Continental Airlines	6,892
11	Qantus	4,168	11	American West Airlines	1,813	11	Singapore Airlines	5,904
12	Cathay Pacific	4,046	12	Japan Airlines	1,281	12	Federal Express	5,872
13	Delta Air Lines	3,666	13	Air Canada	1,118	13	US Air	5,541
14	Alitalia-Linee Aeree Italiano	3,221	14	Air France	877	14	KLM	5,343
15	Swissair	2,646	15	Iberia	856	15	TWA-Trans World Airlines	4,941
16	Federal Express	2,490	16	Canadian Airlines International	819	16	Korean Air Lines	4,801
17	Thai Airways	2,440	17	Air Inter	807	17	Cathy Pacific	4,359
18	Continental Airlines	1,998	18	Alaska Airlines	790	18	Qantas	4,168
19	Varig	1,993	19	Australian Airlines	778	19	Alitalia-Linee Aeree Italiano	3,771
20	Iberia	1,902	20	Japan Air System	700	20	All Nippon Airways	3,736

Source: IATA, *World Air Transport Statistics*, 1993.

Table 8.3 UK airlines RTK's performed 1992

Airlines	Total RTK for 1992	Total international	Total domestic
Air UK	87,620	46,912	40,708
Birmingham European Airways	13,429	10,244	3,185
British Airways	9,142,999	8,659,119	483,880
British Midlands	167,121	77,831	89,290
Bymon Airways	9,265	3,078	6,187
Business Air	1,567	292	1,275
Dan Air	115,879	90,882	24,997
GB Airways	39,564	39,564	
Jersey European	15,733	725	15,008
Loganair	15,927	622	15,305
Manx Airlines	17,010	4,479	12,531
Virgin Atlantic Airways	1,235,644	1,235,644	

Source: IATA, *World Air Transport Statistics*, 1993.

This is a point to which we shall return, briefly, later in the chapter.

Often, when considering the degree of competition in a market the extent of that competition can be even less than appears by reference to a table of data. Market shares in the airline industry are a good illustration of this principle. The smaller the segment of the market, the more market power firms have. On some routes there is only one carrier. On many routes there is only a choice of two. Let us illustrate with a particular example.

When Dan Air ceased operations in late 1992, BA acquired the company with its routes and with its landing and take-off 'slots' at Heathrow and Gatwick. Dan Air had many slots at Gatwick, only a few at Heathrow. At the time Dan Air was the sole carrier out of Gatwick of passengers to many European cities including Brussels, Paris, Rome and Zurich. BA already served these cities from Heathrow. BA's dominance of these routes was thus increased since the 'slots' are allocated rather than open to bidding. Passengers no longer have an option of an alternative carrier from Gatwick on these routes.

In summary, the number of rivals, an important element in oligopoly, is difficult to determine in practice.

c Pricing in oligopoly – kinked demand

In some markets oligopolistic structures are virtually inevitable. If firms find that there are significant economies of scale, they will merge to take advantage of them. Arguably, the acquisition of Dan Air by BA was an example of the point.

Table 8.4 Assumed demand and revenue conditions faced by an oligopolist, firm A

Output of airline journeys	Price firm A can charge (£)	Total revenue (£)	Marginal revenue (£)	Short-run marginal production Costs (£) (SRMC)
1	260	260	260	20
2	240	480	220	20
3	220	660	180	20
4	200	800	140	20
5	180	900	100	20
6	140	840	−60	20
7	100	700	−140	20
8	60	480	−220	20
9	20	180	−300	20

Dan Air was too small to gain economies of scale. It was thus more efficient for society if those resources were in the hands of a large airline, namely BA.

Society may benefit from such mergers in that lower unit costs means less resources used to produce a given volume of output. Of course, the problem pointed out by BA's competitors is that increased firm size means, *ceteris paribus*, increased market power and a potentially non-optimal price/output decision for society. One way of seeing this is via the 'kinked demand model'.

Let us assume that two airlines, A and B, have a given segment of the airline between them and they face no other competition on that route. Further assume that A is at present charging £180 for the journey, then A's demand schedule might be as described in Table 8.4 and its demand curve will be as drawn in Figure 8.1. Why? The argument is that the shape of the curve depends upon the reaction of its rival. In our case the rival is assumed to be firm B.

Why might the demand curve be kinked in this way? The answer is that the model assumes something about the nature of a rival's reactions to a price change. If company A lowers its price in order to increase quantity demanded for its service, company B is assumed to cut its price also out of a fear that it might lose its market share. In consequence it is relatively difficult for company A to increase its output by lowering its price. Demand is relatively price inelastic when price is cut.

What happens if company A attempts to increase its price? The assumption of the model is that the rival is likely to leave its price unchanged in the hope of increasing its market share. Hence, the effect of a price increase by company A is a significant reduction in the quantity demanded. So A's demand curve is relatively elastic for a price increase. This is shown in Figure 8.1 as demand curve D.

Notice now the implications of such a kinked demand curve for firm A's revenue. Table 8.4. shows how marginal revenue falls very steeply if firm A tries

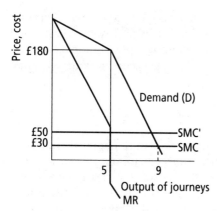

Figure 8.1 Oligopoly: kinked demand conditions

See pp 94–7

to stimulate quantity demanded for its product via a price cut from the present price of £180. The marginal revenue curve is plotted in Figure 8.1 as MR.

To determine the profit maximising price/output decisions of firm A we also need to know about its cost conditions. For reasons we established in Chapter 5, a firms' marginal cost curve may well slope up in the short run as a result of diminishing returns. But in the case of an airline it would be more reasonable to assume a low and constant marginal cost – at least until the plane is full. An extra passenger entails some extra cost, the provision of a ticket, a meal and perhaps a little extra fuel. But most of the costs in the short run are fixed. Once the plane is full, the marginal cost of the next passenger is very high. The low, constant SMC is shown in Figure 8.1. Profit maximisation, as always, requires the firm to choose an output at which marginal cost equals marginal revenue. The price is £180 per ticket.

Two important points follow from the above argument. First, an oligopolist's prices are going to tend to be 'sticky', even in the face of shifts in marginal costs. That is to say, the firm has no wish to change price even if there are changes in marginal cost. For example, if fuel costs rise and marginal costs shift from a constant £20 to a constant £50 per unit of output, the profit maximising price (and output) remains the same. This can be seen in Figure 8.1. SMC has risen to SMC'; profit maximisation is where SMC = MR. This is still at an output level of 5. It needs a substantial increase in marginal costs before SMC = MR at a lower level of output and a higher price.

The second conclusion to be drawn from such a model is that the profit maximising price/output decision is not socially optimal. Recall that social optimality requires an output at which the marginal cost is equal to the marginal value placed by society on the output. In other words, social optimality is where MC = D. Since the ninth passenger values the journey at £20 and marginal production costs are only £20, that journey is socially worthwhile even if it does not pay the airline to provide it.

You may feel that there is a problem here. If the airline had to charge everyone £20 per seat and so set a socially optimal price, its total costs may not cover its total revenue and so it would make a loss. This is a problem for governments wanting to intervene in industries where there is some market power, and we shall examine the problem further in Chapter 17.

See pp 339–40

d Oligopolistic markets: takeovers and cartels

Both price and non-price competition can be very fierce in oligopolistic markets. Clearly there is an attraction to firms in such markets to try to reduce that competition. One way to do so is by takeover. In most countries governments have laws to prevent such an occurrence until they are sure that it is in the public interest to allow the increase in market power which the takeover creates. A further complication for government policy towards takeovers occurs when there is a proposal for a merger between two relatively small firms. Such a merger could be seen as increasing market power by reducing the number of firms in the market. Alternatively, it can be seen as making competition more effective by creating a large company that will reap economies of scale. Thus it is better able to compete with other large companies in that market.

Even mergers which clearly increase concentration can sometimes be argued to be in the public interest. One case in point arose in 1992. The data in Table 8.3 for 1992 shows BA and Dan Air as separate companies. During 1992 it was clear that Dan Air's financial position did not allow it to continue trading. BA was allowed to purchase the company for a nominal sum. Some of Dan Air's employees were able to keep their jobs now working for BA. It was argued that without the merger the unemployment situation for the former Dan Air employees would have been even worse. The competition authorities therefore allowed the takeover on employment grounds, despite the reduction in competition which would result.

An alternative means of reducing competition is by the operation of a cartel. A cartel is an agreement between two or more producers to restrict the degree of competition between them, often by reducing output, raising price and agreeing not to compete on the higher price. One way of seeing how this might benefit the companies is via *games theory*.

Suppose again there are just two airlines on a particular route. When there are just two companies involved in a market, the companies are often referred to as duopolistic. Suppose also that market demand is fairly price inelastic at the present price. It is still likely to be the case that the demand curve faced by either company is very price elastic in that there is a close substitute available – a flight on the rival's airline. Company A might see itself facing the choices outlined in Figure 8.2 below which represent a 'pay-off matrix'. Each square shows the pay-off for the two companies, the 'players' in the 'game', given the strategies adopted and given that there is no collusion between the players. Taking firm A, then, the firm knows the size of its profits given each of its strategies. What strategy will it adopt? The reasoning may well go like this. It may decide that the worst it can do, if it

		Low price	High price
A's Strategy	Low price	A. small profit B. small profit	A. very large profit B. loss
	High price	A. loss B. very large profit	A. large profit B. large profit

Figure 8.2 Possible pricing strategies for two oligopolists

chooses a low price, is make a small profit. The worst it can do, if it chooses a high price, is make a loss. It will therefore choose a low price, and this will be its dominant strategy. By the same reasoning company B will, if it adopts the same strategy, choose a low price. Both airlines finish up making small profits. If both were to collude and to agree a high price, both could do better and make large profits. A cartel is therefore an attractive option for an oligopolist.

Under the laws of most countries such agreements are illegal, though it is not always easy for a government to know that companies are using such cartels. Companies can make secret deals, agreeing not to compete on price, but argue publicly that the similar prices are a reflection of fierce competitive pressures. It would not be easy for the authorities to prove otherwise.

In the case of the European airline industry, some elements of a cartel are present with government approval. The reasons for this and the pressure for change is examined in the next section. It is not intended, of course, to suggest that European airlines operate *illegal* cartels, but to show that such arrangements can be profitable for the participants.

Cartels are not always very stable. Although two companies may agree to raise prices, there is now an incentive for one of them to lower prices a little. Even though their price will now be high, it is low relative to its erstwhile rival. Of course, if the other company becomes aware that this is happening it will lower its price also and the cartel agreement will have collapsed. On the other hand, knowledge that this is a possible outcome may prevent 'cheating' on their cartel partners by the companies concerned.

3 Government attitudes towards the airline industry: state regulation

So far we have assumed that airlines take account of other airlines' pricing and non-price behaviour, but that governments do very little by way of controlling the industry. For some oligopolistic markets, government intervention is relatively limited but with airlines it is substantial.

a The form of airline regulation

Regulation of air transport constitutes a situation where the state tightly controls entry to the industry, services offered, fares to be charged, routes to be flown and the capacity to be provided. For example, it has been the norm for air service agreements between two countries to share out capacity on a 50/50 basis, to grant each nation the power of veto over fare levels, and to specify the number of carriers allowed to operate. Indeed, the US–UK governments' agreement of 1977, known as Bermuda II, went so far as to name the individual carriers allowed to fly between Britain and America.

b The motives for airline regulation

Why have nations felt it necessary to regulate air transport so closely? To answer this question we need to refer back to the early years of the industry. During the 1920s passenger aircraft were characterised by relatively poor performance and high costs. At the same time, intense competition resulted in financial instability and difficulties in establishing route networks. Consequently, governments curbed competition via regulatory bodies such as the Civil Aeronautics Board (CAB) in the USA and the Air Transport Licensing Authority in the UK. These bodies controlled market entry, fares, service frequencies and capacity on routes.

Moreover, nations were anxious to maximise the political and military benefits of civil aviation. Generous subsidies were, therefore, given to selected carriers so that they could operate scheduled services. Ever since, governments have sought to protect the market position of their national airlines. These are often perceived as more than simply a means of conveying passengers and freight; instead they are treated as though they reflect the strength of a nation. In short, national airlines (often state owned) tend to be looked at almost as virility symbols. This view is reflected in the term 'flag carriers' to describe major operators such as British Airways, Air France and KLM. Hence, governments normally adopt a partisan attitude towards the airline industry, seeking to ensure a 'fair' market share for their champions rather than the most efficient service for consumers.

Tight state control has, therefore, continued to be a dominant feature of air transport.

c The problem of safety

Perhaps the greatest concern about unfettered competition in the airline industry is the question of safety. Figure 8.3 demonstrates just how safe airline travel is. Could it be that one reason for this is government policy to limit competition? Would less government regulation lead to such intense price competition that safety considerations were ignored in an attempt to cut costs?

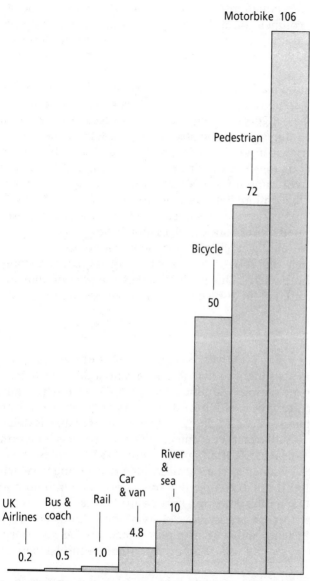

Motorbike 106

Pedestrian
|
72

Bicycle
|
50

River
&
sea
|
10

Car
& van
|
4.8

Rail
|
1.0

Bus &
coach
|
0.5

UK
Airlines
|
0.2

Source : Transport Statistics

Figure 8.3 Average number of deaths in Britain per billion passenger kilometres, 1980–90

An alternative view might be that people are better able to make their own judgements about such matters. Those who wish for greater safety will pay higher fares on airlines which provide the higher standards. We said that oligopoly is characterised by product differentiation, and this could be argued to be an example. Companies could compete on airline safety. If passengers value such safety highly, airlines will find it profitable to provide this, even though it means charging higher fares. On this view, government setting of safety standards would not be needed.

See pp 76–7

A counter argument could be made, following the same line of thought as we saw in the context of health care in Chapter 4. We could reason that the argument above will only be correct if passengers have adequate knowledge of the degree of safety offered. If they do not, they will not be able to make informed choices.

A third view which deserves consideration is that airlines should be free to engage in competition on all matters such as price, routes flown, and so on, but that government will lay down minimum safety standards to which all airlines will comply. This is an attractive option, but is one not free of difficulty. How safe should safety standards be? Increasing safety standards will impose higher costs, and in the long run, increased prices. Society does not believe that safety is paramount. If it did no one would fly at all! A government will not find it easy to determine the point at which the costs of increased safety standards become greater than the value of the benefits. This is what makes the idea of allowing passengers to decide for themselves an attractive one to some economists.

d 'Open skies' a way forward

As part of the move towards a single market, certain members of the European Union (EC) have for some years sought to liberalise its airline industry. Progress has, however, been slow for the reasons examined above. One reason why many economists believe that greater competition and more open skies would be beneficial is that the airline industry, comes close to being what, arguably, is called a 'contestable market'. A contestable market is one in which it is costless for a firm to enter and costless for it to leave. So, if an airline were making profits above normal on a particular route, it would be relatively easy for a rival airline to switch aircraft on to that route and so through competition force prices down to normal profit levels. Hence, an existing airline, knowing how easily another airline could compete, would not attempt to raise prices above costs of production. The very threat of competition is sufficient. Actual competition would not be necessary. Perfect contestability requires, among other things, that there be no barriers to entry.

In practice, the airline industry is not perfectly contestable. A new entrant on a particular route would still have the costs of acquiring landing slots, advertising its presence, and so on. However, there is clearly power in the argument that the more real the threat of a possible new entrant, the more likely it is that the existing airline will set a competitive price.

A further reason for believing that more open skies would be beneficial is the US experience of deregulation. It is to that experience that we now turn.

4 US experience of airline deregulation

a The history of US deregulation

By the 1970s, regulation was being called into question by mounting evidence of the relative efficiency of airlines operating in the least controlled sectors of civil aviation. In particular, United States studies revealed that intrastate operations, which were not subject to Civil Aeronautics Board (CAB) regulation, could offer fares of about half those of CAB regulated carriers and still show a profit. It is not surprising, therefore, that the pressure for change was greatest in the USA.

Following a series of Congressional hearings in the early 1970s, the US passed the Airline Deregulation Act in 1978. This removed the framework of economic controls and the industry became competitive for the first time in 40 years. New carriers entered the market: the number providing scheduled services tripled by 1984. However, the domination of the industry by a limited number of firms continued because the new entrants were small. Hence, while in 1976 the top 12 carriers accounted for about 96 per cent of overall passenger miles, by 1984 they still accounted for 91 per cent.

Nevertheless, faced with the challenge of new efficient companies, the main carriers were compelled to reduce costs and make themselves more competitive or risk the loss of a much larger market share. Consequently, fares were reduced, service frequency improved and traffic rose rapidly – by almost 50 per cent between 1978 and 1985. At that time deregulation appeared to be an unqualified success. Since then, however, competition has diminished.

b Problems for new entrants

Firms faced with increased competition tend to seek to be more cost efficient. They also prefer that potential competition faces high entry barriers. Sometimes these barriers are natural ones. For example, as we mentioned earlier, if there are substantial economies of scale in a market, it will be difficult for a new firm to enter the market at a sufficient size to compete. Some barriers can be raised by the existing firms themselves. For example, in the USA some airlines were able to replace their linear (point-to-point) route systems, with 'hub-and-spoke' networks. This has proved particularly effective in this respect.

See pp 118–9

The latter arrangement allows an airline to concentrate its operations at a central airport to which passengers are flown from surrounding cities so as to connect conveniently with outbound flights. During the early stages of deregulation this type of scheduling involved coordinating deals with local 'feeder' operators, which were later consolidated by means of takeovers. As a result, many of the hub-and-spoke systems are now dominated by a single airline. This is able to feed traffic along one spoke into its hub airport and then out along other spokes. Passengers are thereby encouraged to fly with the same carrier for their entire journey, so reducing interline traffic. It is thus more than coincidental that the most powerful and most profitable airlines, such as United and American, are also those with the strongest hub-and-spoke networks. By contrast, airlines such as Pan Am, which lacked dominant positions at major hubs, have failed to survive as major firms.

In March 1993, BA acquired a stake in US Air. Its main purpose was to build such a system. Without such a purchase BA was unable to do this in the North American market because of government restrictions on the operations of foreign airlines. BA can now link its flights from outside of North America to many destinations within it.

Existing carriers also had the advantage that where airports were congested new firms were often unable to obtain access. The reason for this was that take-off and landing slots were awarded by scheduling committees of incumbent carriers. The allocations were based on 'Grandfather' rights, whereby carriers owned capacity at an airport merely as a consequence of having been there at an early stage in its development. Consequently, while there was no formal restriction on an airline flying a particular route, its ability to do so could be jeopardised by an allocation of slots favouring incumbents. Shortage of airport capacity was also a powerful motive for agreed mergers and takeovers involving scarce take-off and landing options.

Control of an efficient computer reservation system is second only to a dominant position at a major hub as a source of market power because travel agents tend to favour the airline supplying the reservation system. It is, therefore, noteworthy that the reservation systems of two giant airlines – United and American – account for over two-thirds of the terminals used by travel agents in the USA. More broadly, information technology constitutes an important management tool since it provides instant market information. Consequently, those firms which can afford sophisticated systems are able to fine tune their pricing policy, for example, by varying the availability of discount tickets. Large US carriers were able to harness these systems so as to maximise the profit of each aircraft seat in a manner denied to smaller firms. Major airlines were also able to obtain economies of scale of the kind mentioned earlier in the chapter.

c The outcome of US deregulation

The advantages enjoyed by large carriers in the US airline market are such that their share of it is now marginally greater than it was under regulation. In 1977 the five largest airlines accounted for 63 per cent of traffic: today they account for over 70 per cent. To a considerable degree this outcome reflects a highly sympathetic attitude towards takeovers on the part of the Department of Transportation, which scrutinised airline mergers following the abolition of the

Table 8.5 British Airways: recent acquisitions

Airline	Country	Date	Size of stake (%)
Delta Air	Germany	Mar. 92	49
TAT	France	Sep. 92	49.9
Dan Air	UK	Oct. 92	All
Qantas	Australia	Mar. 93	25
US Air	United States	Mar. 93	24.6

Source: Financial press, various editions.

CAB. The refusal to allow foreign airlines 'cabotage rights' – the ability to fly internal US routes – has also played a part, by excluding a very important potential source of competition. That said, the failure to permit freer access to the US market is understandable bearing in mind the reluctance of most governments to deregulate international flights.

While the United States' deregulation of its internal airline industry has been flawed in some respects, it has, nevertheless, proved highly successful. Domestic airlines now have lower real costs than in the mid-1970s, partly as a result of more efficient use of labour. Overall, after allowing for inflation, fares are, on average, some 20 per cent lower. Moreover, there are far more flights and the number of passenger-kilometres travelled have just about doubled. Consumers have thus gained a great deal without the adverse effects on air safety which some critics of liberalisation had predicted.

The financially fragile carriers have, however, found the last few years extremely uncomfortable with a consequent division of the industry between the strong and the weak. The most successful airlines are those such as American and United, which have consolidated their position in the market. Those at the other extreme include Trans World Airlines (TWA) and Eastern which have severe financial problems. In between the strong and the weak are a number of middle-ranking carriers, including Northwest Airlines and US Air. Overall the trend is towards a comparatively small number of strong firms – in the language of economists, a more concentrated industrial structure.

Mergers and takeovers, then, can come about in an oligopolistic industry whatever the level of profitability of the firms concerned. BA has remained profitable and has gained a dominant position in the airline industry. But as Table 8.5 shows it has continued to strengthen its position via a whole series of acquisitions.

On the other hand, loss making firms may well wish to merge if they feel that the resulting economies of scale, or the resulting increase in market power, will lead to improved financial performance.

5 Applying North American lessons to European airlines

a Two crucial lessons

The US experience thus suggests two crucial lessons for Europe. First, that there are huge potential gains from deregulation in the form of increased efficiency, lower fares, improved service frequency and a substantial increase in air travel. By 1985, at 1977 prices, US consumers and producers probably enjoyed total gains of around $8 billion a year as a result of an open skies approach to air travel.

The second principal lesson is that deregulation does not automatically prevent the acquisition of a high degree of monopoly power by certain airlines. Measures directed towards encouraging and sustaining competitive forces are thus highly desirable. In this context, freer access to take-off and landing slots for new entrants at major airports is particularly important. It is also important to use anti-cartel legislation to avoid reductions in competition. Anti-merger legislation is more problematic in that preventing mergers may keep up competition, but at the expense of preventing the gaining of scale economies.

b Differences in the two airline markets

By far the most significant inter-continental difference, however, is the fact that the USA constitutes a single economic entity, while air transport in Europe is still organised as a set of national markets. The political obstacles to change are, therefore, substantial because some governments are fearful of even limited competition.

In attempting to learn from US experience, it is, of course, essential to take account of certain important differences between Europe and America. To begin with, the US civil aviation industry is more than four times larger than its European counterpart, thereby presenting more opportunities for scale economies. For example, the larger US market permits more extensive use of wide bodied jets. Second, unlike the situation in the USA, the various computer reservation systems in Europe are owned by a number of airlines and present information in an unbiased manner. The danger that these systems will become sources of monopoly power is thus minimised. Third, holiday travel in Europe is mainly the preserve of charter airlines, which account for more than 50 per cent of the total market. The relative cheapness of air charter travel goes some way to explaining why there has been less pressure for reform of scheduled services than in the United States.

c Changing European policy

There are, however, considerable benefits to be reaped from freer skies. In 1988 the European Commission estimated the likely gains for member Community states at over $1 billion per annum. The extent to which these gains are realised will be largely determined by the Commission itself since it is a supra-national body which is supposed to be acting in the interests of the Community as a whole. It is, therefore, encouraging that there is now an agreed Community liberalisation strategy. This includes freeing carriers to compete in each others' markets; permitting more competition on fares and the ending of bilateral agreements for sharing revenue and capacity in the case of airlines flying the same routes.

The achievement of a single market in civil aviation is being approached in three stages. The first, agreed in 1987, was mainly symbolic. While providing for some relaxation of controls on fares, capacity and market access, its effect was comparatively modest because the main flag carriers remained largely undisturbed. The second stage came into force in November 1990 and promises to have much greater impact. In essence, the package of measures includes the relaxation of existing capacity rules so that one country can take up to a 75 per cent share, greater freedom in fare setting, and route access for more airlines.

The third and last stage provides for the ending of capacity sharing, multiple designation of carriers on all routes, freedom for airlines to set fare levels, unless there are objections from the governments of both countries at each end of the route, and uniform licensing. This final measure is particularly significant because it implies that any EU airline will be able to fly any route within the Community. Hence, since January 1993 the area within the 12 member states; boundaries are to be perceived as a single 'domestic' market. The reluctance of some nations wholeheartedly to support liberalisation, however, will certainly delay aspects of the third stage well beyond that date.

d Problems for European deregulation

The liberalisation measures clearly herald substantial change in European air transport. Even so, as we noted earlier, US experience suggests that the attempt to generate a far more competitive environment could prove abortive unless two threats are dealt with vigorously.

The first is the method by which take-off and landing slots are awarded at airports especially at peak periods. As in the USA, allocation within the EU is decided by committees of incumbent airlines largely on the grandfather principle. In the presence of capacity constraints at most leading European airports newcomers find it very difficult to acquire slots. A better allocation mechanism is required. In a market economy scarce capacity has a price. Slot auctions could, therefore, be used to solve the congestion problem, with airlines bidding for access to runways. Those wanting peak time slots at congested airports would have to pay a high price for them: conversely, space at less popular airports could be obtained relatively cheaply. A pricing system of this kind would have substantial advantages.

The second obstacle to a freer market is the increasing concentration of the European aviation industry. Even at this comparatively early stage of the deregulation process, major European airlines are following the example of their US counterparts in seeking to protect themselves from competition by means of mergers, cross-shareholding agreements and various kinds of commercial pacts.

The European Commission is concerned that deals of this kind will stifle competition at birth. It has, therefore, examined proposed mergers very closely. On the other hand, in a global context, there is a danger that a highly fragmented EU aviation industry, consisting of small- and medium-sized carriers, might not be able to compete with the mega airlines of the USA and Asia. In addition, the possibility exists that, in an attempt to ensure a competitive environment, the EU could end up introducing a new range of tight regulatory devices.

In an ideal world, the dilemma of size versus competition could be solved by opening the European market to international competition. However, such a liberal policy is unlikely to be adopted unless the rest of the world reciprocates by abandoning a protectionist stance. Unfortunately, at the present time there appears to be little chance of such a fundamental change in attitudes. Even so, once the EU has forged an internal market, it would be possible to achieve much of the benefits of openness if Europe and the United States were to grant each others' airlines reciprocal access.

6 Conclusion

We began by seeing that the European airline industry has an oligopolistic structure. That leads us to draw certain conclusions about the type and degree of competition one might expect. Government attitudes in Europe have restricted that competition, whereas within the USA a much more open skies policy prevails. Europe is under pressure to deregulate also.

United States experiences suggest that the deregulation of civil aviation may prove to be an extremely uncomfortable experience for Europe's airlines while presenting new opportunities for the more efficient. It is also clear from the course of events in the USA that passengers will benefit very greatly from a freer air-travel market: they will enjoy lower fares and far more choice. The potential overall gains from a single internal market probably exceed $1 billion.

However, in order to extract the maximum benefit Europe must be careful not to reproduce two major flaws in the US deregulation process. The first was the failure to ensure that entry barriers were as low as consistent with scale economies. In particular there was a failure to ensure that an airline wishing to start operating on a popular route had a high probability of gaining access to a busy airport. Britain's recent opening up of Heathrow, the home base of BA, to greater competition has set an example to the rest of Europe in this respect. More specifically, the move has demonstrated a willingness to discomfort the national carrier in the interests of an ideology.

With hindsight, the second flaw in the US deregulation process was too relaxed an approach to anti-trust and merger controls. The European Commission is determined not to repeat this error and has made it clear that activities which could pose a threat to competition will not be tolerated. It has also scrutinised proposed airline mergers very closely.

Unfortunately, not to sanction mergers runs the risk of leaving the EU airline industry too fragmented to compete with the world's mega carriers. However, the scale versus competition dilemma could be neatly solved if an open skies policy in the EU proves to be the prelude to a North Atlantic free market in air travel embracing both Europe and America. But at the moment that prospect seems a long way off.

7 Questions for discussion

1 Another oligopolistic market is the market for cigarettes. In Chapter 7, question 4, we saw that profit maximisers operate on the elastic section of the demand curve. But it would appear that cigarette manufacturers are on the inelastic section of their demand curve. Consider what happens to cigarette prices when the Chancellor increases tobacco duty at budget time. Usually prices rise by the full extent of the tax. Hence at the current price demand is inelastic. Can this be profit maximising behaviour?

2 How realistic are the assumptions of the kinked demand model? How far does it aid our understanding of oligopolistic price determination in general, the European airlines in particular?

3 Construct a pay-off matrix similar to Table 8.3. In doing so, assume (a) that the variable which the duopolists are considering is high or low volumes of advertising and (b) that advertising is much more effective in shifting demand between brands than in increasing demand for the product.

4 Why might a cartel agreement between firms be unstable? Would it be easier to stabilise for price or non-price variables?

5 How much government intervention in the airline industry is appropriate to ensure adequate safety standards?

6 Another oligopolistic market is the market for cross-channel journeys. Eurotunnel is a new entrant. P&O European Ferries and Stena Sealink want to run a joint service in competition with Eurotunnel. Would this be beneficial or harmful to consumers?

7 How much does oligopoly theory add to our understanding about how prices are determined in a market system?

8 Further reading

Oligopoly
Sloman, pp. 247–62; Begg, pp. 162–70; Parkin and King, pp. 327–43

Cartels
Sloman, pp. 249–50, 439–47; Begg, pp. 162–6; Parkin and King, pp. 333–7

Mergers
Sloman, pp. 279–88, 472–85; Begg. pp. 305–8

Contestable Markets
Sloman, pp. 234–7; Begg, p. 166

European airline prices
'Airlines: losing their way', *Economist Survey*, 12–18 June, 1993.

CHAPTER 9

Business behaviour
are profits everything?

What is the business community really trying to achieve? Making as much profit as possible? Enjoying a quiet life? Increasing the size of their businesses as quickly as they can? Do the shareholders know what the firms are doing and can they do anything about it? In previous chapters we have assumed that the overriding aim is profit maximisation. But are profits everything?

In this chapter we review
- Monopoly
- Oligopoly
- Normal profit

We introduce
- Full cost pricing
- Sales revenue maximisation
- Growth maximisation
- Managerial utility

1 Introduction

An assumption commonly made by economists when they analyse business behaviour is that firms, in whatever market structure they operate, attempt to maximise profits. For example, in Chapter 6 we assumed small firms aimed to maximise profits. In Chapter 8 we assumed that airline companies do likewise, although they may have sufficient market power to pursue other goals. Whether this is a legitimate assumption or not is an important question. There are, perhaps, two things that make it so important. One is that it is at the heart of the market economist's claim that, given certain conditions, society maximises its welfare by allowing resources to be used by their owners in whichever way they choose. After all, part of profit maximisation is the minimisation of costs for whatever is the firm's chosen level of output. Now, if the firm minimises costs, it keeps to a minimum the amount of resources needed to produce that output and so resources are not wasted. We have already seen in Chapter 7 that a monopolist's chosen level of output may well not be that which maximises welfare for society. But the presumption of profit maximisation is that, having chosen a level of output, the monopolist will seek to minimise the cost of producing that output.

See pp 145–6

This leads us on to a second, related reason. Where markets do not produce an optimum use of resources, for example, in the view of most economists, where there is monopoly power, governments will wish to intervene. The appropriate form of intervention may depend upon the way in which firms are choosing price/output decisions. For example, the logic of price controls in monopolistic industries such as gas, electricity distribution and water depends, among other things, upon an assumption that managers of these industries will behave by attempting to maximise profits, and thus dividends for the shareholders.

Profit maximisation, then, is an important assumption often made by economists. So what does the evidence suggest? Are profits everything?

2 The profit maximisation view

Let us briefly remind ourselves of the normal assumptions made about firm behaviour. In competitive markets there are no barriers to the free movement of resources. Therefore if firms make more than a normal profit, new firms will enter the market, increasing supply and depressing price until only normal profit is made. Since in the long run firms can only make normal profit, that is, just cover all costs including opportunity costs, they *have* to be profit maximisers to survive. We saw this in Chapter 6.

See pp 116-8

In markets where there are barriers to entry, firms may be able to make profits above the normal even in the long run. For example, a profit maximising monopolist's price/output decision would be as shown in Figure 9.1. We first met this in Chapter 7, although here we are assuming that unit costs increase with increased output.

See pp 143-5

Since the firm has some market power, it is shown as having a downward sloping demand curve. If the demand curve is downward sloping, the marginal revenue curve will be as described in Figure 9.1. The relationship of these curves to one another we examined in Chapter 7.

See pp 143-5

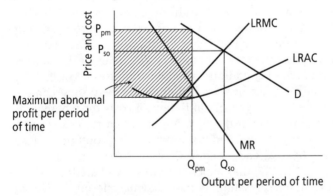

Figure 9.1 Profit maximising monopoly

The profit maximiser chooses an output level Q_{pm}, at which marginal cost = marginal revenue. He sells that output for the highest price he can get. This is P_{pm}. The total profit is then given as QxAR (TR) minus QxAC (TC). If he were to make any more output, and therefore have to lower price, addition to cost, MC, would be greater than addition to revenue, MR. He would therefore make a marginal loss on such units reducing his overall level of profit. Accordingly Q_{pm} is his optimum output.

Management is assumed to produce Q_{pm} output at a price of P_{pm}. But notice two important points. First, costs are still assumed to be at a minimum. By this we do *not* mean that the firm produces at the bottom of LRAC, but that at whatever level of output it chooses to produce, here Q_{pm}, it will produce that output as cheaply as it possibly can. Although it could make some profit if it failed to do so, it will not wish to forego the lost profit that would result. So it will still strive to get down costs of producing Q_{pm} as low as possible.

Second, notice that it is assumed that management under these conditions will seek to restrict output below the social optimum. The socially optimal output is where addition to opportunity cost, LRMC, is equal to the value society places upon that marginal output (D). So management is assumed to produce less output than the level which would maximise social welfare in its drive to maximise profits.

Some economists, notably those of what are generally known as the Austrian school, would not see this a reason for government intervention in firm behaviour. To them the profit above normal is a reward for efficiently meeting society's needs. If it is really in excess of a fair return that is being made others will, in a free society, use their resources to compete.

We saw in Chapter 7 that profit maximisation is an assumed goal in oligopolistic markets too. Firms will have to think carefully about rivals reactions. There is much greater uncertainty but the goal is still the same.

Now, although many economists would regard profit maximisation as a legitimate assumption for analysing firm behaviour, others have real doubts about these assumptions. In general the models that do *not* assume profit maximisation relate to oligopolistic markets.

3 Full cost pricing

One interesting criticism of the profit maximisation assumption is that firms simply do not have enough information to behave as the textbook models suggest. It is accepted that firms wish to maximise profits but they cannot do so because they do not have the information which the textbooks assume. So how do they choose their price and output decision according to this view?

a The problem of inadequate information

We start with the information available to a firm. First look at costs. The firm can get a good idea of its cost structure. Typically, it will have a good idea of what it

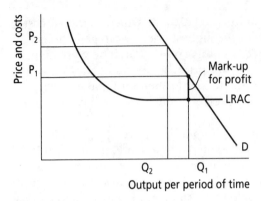

Figure 9.2 Full cost pricing

See pp 118–120

would cost to produce any level of output it chooses. This model assumes that the typical production process gives it a long-run average cost curve of the shape described in Figure 9.2. As output increases from low levels economies of scale are available. At some output these are exhausted but it can avoid diseconomies of scale by decentralising its operations and running a number of largely separate plants. There is some support for this assumption as you will see if you refer back to Chapter 6. There we saw the evidence for cost structures in some industries. Economies of scale are available over a large range of output. It can be argued, though, that there comes a point at which such economies are exhausted.

Now consider the firm's demand conditions. Its demand curve is given in Figure 9.2 as D. The problem is that the firm does not know where its demand curve is. It knows one spot on its demand curve. It knows the output it is selling at the present price. But it does not know what output it would sell at other prices.

You may feel that if the firm wishes to know this it is not too difficult to find out. A way of getting the information would be to raise price for a period and see how much of an effect it had on sales. It could set a price of, say, P_2 and observe the extent of fall in sales to Q_2. Alas this will not do. It may find that it loses a lot of sales and the goodwill of its customers in the experiment that could do lasting damage. In other words, the cost of acquiring the information it needs to establish its demand curve is simply too high. But there is another problem. Recall that demand is a function of price, incomes, the price of other goods and perhaps of other things too. However, when we draw a demand curve we are assuming that all other things affecting demand other than price are held constant. If the firm raises its price to P_2 and observes a fall in its sales to Q_2, it must be sure that the only thing that has changed is its price. If something else has changed, consumer tastes or other prices, for example, the whole demand curve will have shifted. It will not have found two spots on one demand curve at all! It will have found one spot on one demand curve and one spot on the new one.

Table 9.1 Profit maximisation and full cost pricing predictions

Model	Set price or Output ?	Rise in demand	Fall in demand
Profit maximisation with perfect information	Output	Raise price and output	Cut price and output
Full cost pricing model	Price	Raise output	Cut output possibly raise price

The argument, then, is that the firm must make a price/output decision knowing only its cost and very little about the nature of demand for its product. Its decision will then be a simple one. It will take its full average costs, including overheads, add a mark-up for a profit margin to establish its price, and sell whatever it can at its chosen price.

b Predictions of the full cost pricing model

If the firm's mark-up is as in Figure 9.2, it sets a price equal to P_1 and finds that it can sell Q_1 output. Suppose now that demand increases. The firm will not raise the price, but will simply sell more at its chosen price. Suppose the firm's costs increase. It will, of course, increase price in order to restore its profit mark-up. What is the prediction of the model if demand is falling? Provided that it falls over a range where unit costs are constant, there will be no change in price. If demand falls back to the range where the firm begins to lose its scale economies, the price may even rise.

Table 9.1 above compares these predictions with those we would make using the traditional profit maximising model where information is perfect. You could check back to Figure 9.1 and make sure you understand the predictions of the traditional model. Notice also that we show in the table the choice of variable. Our full cost pricing model recognises, as does the traditional model, that a firm cannot choose price and output. It can choose any output it wishes but the demand curve then constrains it with regard to the price it can set. Alternatively, it can choose any price it wishes and the demand curve will constrain the output it can make at that price. The traditional model predicts that the firm will decide its output by establishing the point at which LRMC = MR, and then selling at the highest price it can get for its chosen output level. On the other hand, the full cost pricing model predicts that it will select its price. In fact, most businesspeople, when asked, say that they choose price rather than output.

There is one question to which we gave no attention in the above analysis. What decides the *size* of the mark-up that the full cost pricing model predicts the businessperson chooses? We shall not deal with that question now but you will be asked to think about it as part of the questions for discussion at the end of the chapter.

4 Sales revenue maximisation

a Doubts about the profit maximisation assumption

In the full-cost pricing model firms wish to maximise profit. Their ability to do so is constrained by imperfect information. We turn now to consider several models of business behaviour where the assumption is that management is not even trying to maximise profits. It would be impossible to cover *all* such models in one chapter, but we can review most of the main ideas and pick out some key strands of evidence. Although, as we shall see, these models are very different in what they believe is important to management, they all have one feature in common. They all assume that in the great majority of markets there is significant market power. In other words, they believe that monopolistic or oligopolistic structures are prevalent. They also believe that in these markets there is a separation of ownership from control. This is a very important idea and we need to be clear about what this means. In small firms the owners are the ones who take the decisions. Since their income is determined by the profit they make, they may well attempt to maximise profit in the way in which the perfectly competitive model suggests. Large firms, however, are owned by shareholders. They wish firms to maximise profit since their incomes, in the form of dividends, depend largely on those profits. But the ones who take the decisions, the managers of the companies, do not usually find a close correlation between company profits and their incomes. If managers are given incentives it is often in the form of rewards for increasing sales rather than profit. Salespeople, in particular, are often paid a commission, not on the profits of the company, but on the level of sales achieved. Management has less incentive, therefore, to maximise profits and may well pursue other goals, such as growth or sales revenue.

Now, of course, if shareholders had perfect knowledge they would know if management were not profit maximising and would seek to replace them. They do not have that knowledge. They also have limited power to do much about it, since the distribution of a company's shareholding is so widespread that any individual shareholder is unable to influence things more than marginally. Now, of course, if large numbers of shareholders were to be disenchanted with profit performance, they would sell their shares. This would have the effect of depressing the share price of the company, leaving it in danger from a takeover bid. Clearly, this is something management will wish to avoid. So profit is not irrelevant. An adequate level of profit to keep the shareholders happy is a constraint upon management behaviour. Thus managers are seen as seeking to achieve other goals subject to an adequate level of profit rather than being seen as profit maximisers.

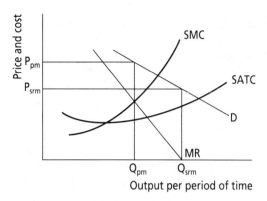

Figure 9.3 Sales revenue maximisation

b The Baumol model

One example of a model not assuming profit maximisation is that associated with William J. Baumol. Baumol suggested that firms seek not to maximise profit but to maximise sales revenue subject to a profit constraint. The size of the profit constraint is, as explained above, whatever is necessary to keep the shareholders happy.

Let us see from Figure 9.3 below what that will mean for the firm's behaviour.

The model, in its most commonly discussed form, concentrates upon short-run management goals. Accordingly, Figure 9.3 shows a firm's short-run cost and revenue conditions.

The short-run cost curves are those which we have met before. The shapes of these cost curves, you will recall, are determined by diminishing returns. However, we need show only SATC. The profit maximiser, of course, produces where SMC = MR at Q_{pm} and price P_{pm}.

On the other hand, the sales revenue maximiser is not trying to achieve maximum profits but maximum sales revenue. So what output and price is appropriate for him? He will always increase output provided that the increased output causes his total revenue to rise. In other words, it is worth making more if marginal revenue (addition to total revenue) is positive. The appropriate level of output for him is therefore Q_{srm}, where marginal revenue is zero. The appropriate price is P_{srm}.

The sales revenue maximiser wants to produce more output than the profit maximiser, since although it reduces profits if output is increased beyond Q_{pm}, it raises sales revenue. His ideal is Q_{srm} where sales revenue maximisation is achieved.

The problem for him, though, is whether the smaller level of profit that he will then make is sufficient to keep the shareholders happy. If the minimum profit felt to be necessary is greater than his profit constraint, he would not be able to achieve his goal. Interestingly, Baumol argued that the profit constraint is *always* effective. That is to say, he will never be in a position where he can ignore the profit constraint when trying to maximise total revenue. His argument for saying this goes as follows.

Suppose the profit constraint were to be quite low. In other words, suppose at Q_{srm}, in Figure 9.3, the level of profit being made is sufficient to keep shareholders happy. Would he not just produce Q_{srm} output and be able to forget the profit constraint? The argument is that since he is a sales revenue maximiser he will simply advertise more if he were faced with this situation. This will shift the demand curve to the right, and cause MR to shift right too. He would then be able to increase output and enable more sales revenue to be earned. But surely advertising will increase his costs? This is true but, even if the advertising adds more to costs than revenue, he will not mind, since he is a sales revenue maximiser, not a profit maximiser. At least he will not mind until the profit constraint bites. He will stop increases in the advertising budget when the effect of diminishing returns on the advertising budget reduces the profit level to the profit constraint. So, according to the Baumol model, a sales revenue maximiser will undertake larger volumes of advertising than profit maximisers because of their concern for sales revenue, even at the expense of some reduction in profit.

What makes this so interesting, of course, is that it offers an alternative explanation for high volumes of advertising prevalent in Western society. It can be argued not simply to be a form of oligopolistic non-price competition, but a reflection of the fact that firms are undertaking more advertising than is consistent with profit maximising behaviour.

You may have watched large amounts of television advertising. You may have wondered whether the enormous costs to the company whose products are being advertised are justified by the increased sales. One view is that it is justified. We could use the games theory idea developed in Chapter 8 to show that, while it would be better for these companies if they all decreased advertising, one company alone cannot afford to do so because of the devastating effects on its profits.

See pp 156–7

We now have an alternative possible explanation. Perhaps the motive is sales revenue maximisation. Provided that the advertising increases sales a little, it will not matter if the increased costs are greater than the increased revenue. This is, of course, subject to the proviso that the advertising does not push profits below the profit constraint.

5 Growth maximisation

a Growth versus security

An alternative view of business behaviour is given by Professor Robin Marris. His view of firms is that its managers concentrate on the *growth* of the company.

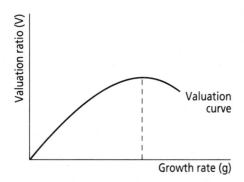

Figure 9.4 Relationship between growth rate and valuation ratio

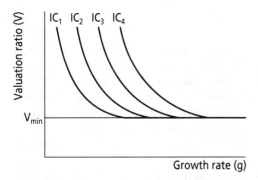

Figure 9.5 Management preferences between growth and valuation ratio

However, they discover that pursuing growth creates problems for the managers in terms of their security. They, therefore, have to trade growth against security. Figures 9.4 and 9.5 above explain the Marris view.

Consider first Figure 9.4. Security is essentially security from the fear of being taken over and hence the possibility of losing position, status and salary. How do we measure security? We can not do so directly, but indirectly we can. The likelihood of a takeover is much reduced if management can gain a high valuation ratio (V). This we figure out by taking the value of the company as measured by the stock market (number of shares issued x price of shares) and dividing it by the 'book' value of the company, that is, the assets as valued by the accountants in the company's balance sheet. So, for example, if the book value of the company is £1 million and the stock market values the company at, say, £$\frac{1}{2}$ million, it becomes an attractive takeover target. On the other hand, a potential takeover may well be deterred if, in order to acquire £1 million worth of assets, the price to be paid via a takeover bid is around £2 million. So, *ceteris paribus*, the higher is V the happier is management.

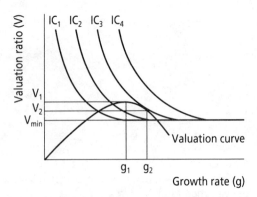

Figure 9.6 Maximising welfare for management

But management also wants growth. Greater growth may mean enhanced status and possibly salary. So what will happen if management decides to undertake more investment and go for a greater rate of growth? As g rises, V rises also. Management is undertaking profitable projects. Even if shareholders receive lower dividend payments they will not sell their shares and depress the valuation ratio. They expect to be compensated by enhanced profits in later periods. At some point, however, increased growth can only be achieved with poorer investment projects. Shareholders do not feel that they are likely to be compensated later for lower dividend payments. The valuation ratio will fall as the growth rate gets beyond g. Clearly profit maximisation requires a growth rate of g, maximising the worth of the company to its shareholders.

b Optimising the trade-off

See pp 71–4

Given that management has a desire for growth and security, what will management choose? Management preferences are found in the indifference curves in Figure 9.5. Just as for a consumer there is a diminishing marginal rate of substitution between goods, so for management there is a diminishing marginal rate of substitution of growth for security. Just as a consumer would always prefer to be on a higher indifference curve where he can obtain more of both goods, so management would prefer more security and more growth. However, fear of being taken over is so strong at V_{min} that when the valuation ratio has fallen this low, no amount of extra growth would compensate for the increased feeling of insecurity.

We can now see what management will actually choose if we combine Figures 9.4 and 9.5 on to one diagram. Clearly, given the constraint of the valuation curve management will choose g_2 and v_2, the highest possible indifference curve it can reach as shown in Figure 9.6 above. Notice this means that there is a higher growth rate than is consistent with profit maximising behaviour. Management is, therefore, assumed to undertake more investment than would be the case if its goal was to be profit maximisation.

The question of the volume of investment and whether it is adequate for the British economy is examined further in Chapter 13.

6 A 'managerial utility' model

If it is accepted that management seeks its own welfare rather than the welfare of its shareholders, then one may find that management does not have *one* goal but a number of goals. In Oliver Williamson's view three such goals stand out. First, managers will wish to pay themselves more than would be necessary to cover the opportunity cost of their services. In recent years there have been frequent complaints that top pay is out of all proportion to the value that management contributes to company profitability. This 'pay' may include staff 'perks' such as company cars and expensive offices. Second, managers will wish to have more staff than is necessary, since a greater staff enhances their status and prestige. Third, they will wish to undertake 'discretionary investment'. Discretionary investment covers projects which may not add to company profitability but gives managers utility in other ways. It may be that buying a newspaper company or a football club gives management utility while not adding to profit.

In the Williamson view profit is of some importance. It is not only a constraint to keep shareholders content but profits provide funds which enable such things as discretionary investment to be pursued. But profit will not be maximised for it is not the only thing that gives managerial utility. Consider the trade-off between staffing and profitability in Figure 9.7. The staffing curve shows the relationship between the number of staff and profits. If no staff are employed no profits are made. As more staff are employed, profits rise until S_1. Beyond that level the usefulness of additional staff as measured by their marginal output is less than the wage paid. Profit, therefore, falls. A profit maximiser employs S_1 staff and makes

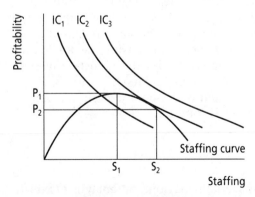

Figure 9.7 Trading off profitability with staffing levels

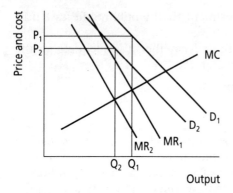

Figure 9.8 Response of a profit maximiser to a fall in demand

P_1 profits. Williamson suggests that management will, given their indifference curves as between profit and staffing, maximise their utility at $S_2 P_2$.

One interesting possibility is that this sheds light upon the behaviour of companies during a recession. They frequently say that conditions are such that they have to become more efficient, which often means laying off staff. If they were profit maximisers, they would already be cost efficient. One could argue that during a recession a reasonable level of profit is harder to earn. Thus, at such times, it reduces scope for employing additional staff beyond the optimum level for profit maximisation. Hence, while the need to be more efficient during a recession is meaningless for a profit maximiser, such statements fit very well with the Williamson view.

The argument needs to be stated with some care. At first sight it may not seem to lead to a different result from a traditional profit maximising assumption. Consider Figure 9.8 above.

The original position is represented by demand curve D_1 and marginal revenue curve MR_1. Profit maximisation requires an output level of Q_1 where $MC = MR_1$. Suppose a recession now causes demand to fall to D_2. The marginal revenue curve will shift to MR_2. Then the profit maximising response is to reduce output to Q_2 (and price to P_2). Less output requires less inputs. So some staff are laid off.

Reducing staff in a recession, then, is not inconsistent with the traditional model. What *is* inconsistent is to say that the reason for the reduction in staff levels is the need to become more efficient. The traditional model assumes, as we have already seen, that whatever level of output is chosen, the profit maximiser will seek to minimise the cost of producing that output.

7 Other models

There are other attempts to explain managerial behaviour, an analysis of which goes beyond the scope of this chapter, but which are worth mentioning. Some view management behaviour not as an attempt to maximise *anything at all*, be it profits, sales, revenue or whatever. They believe that management is essentially 'satisficing'. They argue that managers have a variety of interests and goals, and that they have an idea of what is a 'satisfactory' performance rather than what constitutes maximisation. Frequently, these models examine the process by which management achieves its goals. Unfortunately, it is difficult, using this approach, to get a general model of firm behaviour, which we can use for the purposes of prediction. Even if this is all true the goals of management may vary from firm to firm.

One different view of management behaviour is that presented by the well-known US economist, Professor J. K. Galbraith. Since Galbraith has written a number of books it is hard to summarise his views briefly.

In essence, however, Galbraith's view is that decisions of firms are taken primarily to reduce risk. Firms seek, therefore, to control the environment within which they operate. They do so largely by advertising and manipulating people's preferences. In the Western world the problems of scarcity have long been solved, and incomes are more than adequate to provide for people's basic needs. People therefore need to be persuaded to buy all kinds of things for which they have no use, in order to ensure the continuous flow of production necessary for the survival of the firm. Markets can therefore be seen, not in terms of consumer sovereignty but of producer sovereignty. The teaching of profit maximising models of behaviour in colleges and universities serves business well in that it diverts attention from an analysis of how large businesses really operate and suggests that, apart from a few small problems associated with monopoly power, the market system is a benign one. In reality the resources consumed go into producing largely unwanted products. This means that resources do not flow to those areas of the economy where they are really needed – social services, public goods, and so on. Private oligopolists produce far too much output. Galbraith would therefore regard as ridiculous the idea that large firms do not produce enough output for the social optimum!

8 Some strands of evidence

It is not easy to test which of these differing views best explains firm behaviour. One reason for this is that it is difficult to test for *motives* directly. One is looking for things that one can measure, which will suggest what management motives are. We shall look briefly at four strands of evidence which will help you to decide whether you think management seeks profit maximisation as its goal.

a Ownership and control

First, let us consider the question of the divorce of ownership and control. Remember that a key idea behind some profit-maximising models is that owners,

Table 9.2 Structure of UK shareholding 1963–1992, percentages

Sector of beneficial owner	1963	1969	1975	1981	1989	1990	1992
Individuals and unicorporated businesses	54.0	47.4	37.5	28.2	20.8	20.5	20.0
Non-profit making bodies	2.1	2.1	2.3	2.2	2.1	1.6	2.2
Public sector	1.5	2.6	3.6	3.0	2.0	2.0	1.2
Banks	1.3	1.7	0.7	0.3	0.7	0.7	0.2
Insurance companies	10.0	12.2	15.9	20.5	18.5	20.4	20.7
Pension funds	6.4	9.0	16.8	26.7	30.5	31.4	31.1
Unit trusts	1.3	2.9	4.1	3.6	5.9	6.1	5.7
Other financial institutions	11.3	10.1	10.5	6.8	3.1	2.7	2.8
Industrail & commercial companies	5.1	5.4	3.0	5.1	3.8	2.8	3.3
Overseas	7.0	6.6	5.6	3.6	12.7	11.8	12.8
Total	100.0	100.0	100.0	100.0	100.0	100.0	100.0

Note: The apparent trend in these series, particularly for the overseas sector, is affected by the sampling errors and the
varying methods of identification of nominee holdings.

Source: Economic Trends.

shareholders, do not have enough information about whether management is profit maximising, nor enough power to oblige them to change their behaviour.

In fact, one can argue that this divorce is now less marked than in the past. Concentration of shareholder power has moved more and more into the hands of groups large enough to force changes in management behaviour. This is exactly what the rise of the institutional investors has been causing. As you can see from Table 9.2 opposite, fewer and fewer shares are owned directly by individuals and more and more are held indirectly by individuals in their pension funds, unit trusts, and so on. You will remember that in Chapter 2 we looked at the question of share ownership. What we are emphasising here, however, is not so much the present structure of share ownership but its dramatic change over time.

See pp 40–1

It has also become more common for these institutions to hold larger blocks of shares in fewer companies than was once the case. This further increases institutional power. Moreover, company management is increasingly aware of the decisiveness of the institutions' voting behaviour in takeover battles. This makes management far more receptive to institutional pressure. It can therefore be argued that it is becoming more difficult for the management of large companies to pursue goals other than profit maximisation.

b Owner and manager controlled firms

A second strand of evidence could be found by looking at owner-controlled firms to see if they do better, in terms of profitability, than manager controlled firms. The difficulty here is deciding what constitutes an owner controlled firm. Since many shareholders are passive, never voting or attending shareholder meetings, it has been argued that an 'owner' can be an individual or family which has only perhaps 15–20 per cent of the shares. This gives sufficient power to exercise effective control. Some studies have been made over the last 20 years or so, using this idea of what constitutes owner control, most finding both in Britain and the United States that manager-controlled firms are less profitable.

c Profits: are they inevitable in oligopoly?

Some models suggest that decision takers in oligopolistic markets have considerable control over their economic environment. Galbraith in particular feels that firms can control prices and production so that while profit is not the dominant motive, a reasonable level can be virtually guaranteed. The world recession of the early 1990s makes this difficult to believe. Many companies in oligopolistic markets have made large losses. The airline industry, which we studied in Chapter 8, is just one industry among many where this is so. Figure 9.9 shows the drmatic turnaround in the fortunes of the International Air Transport Association (IATA) members in a short space of time. To be sure not all airlines

See pp 149–68

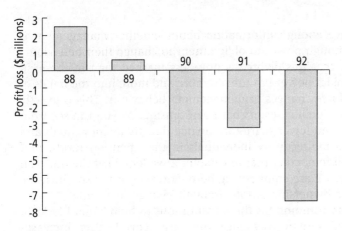

Figure 9.9 Profit figures for IATA airlines, 1988–92

Table 9.3 Selected individual airline profit/losses, 1992 ($ millions)

Airline	Profit/loss ($ millions)
American Airlines	− 935
United Airlines	− 957
Northwest Airlines	−1,064
US Air	−1,229
Singapore Airlines	519
Cathay Pacific	385
British Airways	298

Source: IATA, *World Air Transport Statistics*, 1993.

have made losses in recent years as Table 9.3 indicates. But as the table shows, some, particularly American airlines' losses, have been considerable. Some part of the worsening of their position was attributable to a one-off change in American laws concerning pension requirements. However, the overall picture is still one of an oligopolistic industry unable to control its economic environment in a way which guarantees a reasonable return to its shareholders. The airline industry is by no means unique in this respect.

d Profits and growth: is there a correlation?

A third strand of evidence is any correlation between firms which grow fast and firms which make large profits. This is particularly interesting to those who take the Marris view that firms are willing to sacrifice profit for growth. If the companies who grow fastest are also those who make the largest profits, the Williamson argument is meaningless. It would not matter whether companies

Table 9.4 'Top' 20 European companies

Rank	By profitability	By growth of assets
1	Aegis Group	Pinault
2	Ecco Trav Temp	Fin Agache
3	Bertelsmann	Poliet
4	SK Beecham	Aegis Group
5	Delhaize	Tractebel
6	Reuters	Tomkins
7	Argos	Schmalbach-Lub
8	RWE-DEA	Williams Holdings
9	Glaxo	Cap Gem Sogeti
10	Audi	Adia
11	Ford-Werke	Polygram
12	Polygram	Hanson
13	Pryca	LVMH
14	Kwik Save	Legrand
15	Smurfit	Rank Org.
16	Benetton	Fisons
17	Adia	Ecco Trav Temp
18	Rothmans	Guinness
19	Astra	Navig Mixte
20	Wellcome	BTR

Source: Authors calculations based on *Management Today* data, December 1992.

pursued growth or profits, the outcome would be the same. It is interesting to consider Table 9.4, which shows the leading European companies ranked by profitability and the leading European companies ranked by growth in its assets.

The information comes from data published in *Management Today*, which, in December 1992, provided a list of 'top' 500 European companies. The list was assembled by ranking companies according to a weighted average of performance measures based on profitability, financial solidity and growth. Details of how this was done can be found in the article recommended in the reading at the end of the chapter.

What appears above in Table 9.4 is taken from the top 50 European Companies only. The first column gives the leading 20 of those 50 companies ranked by profitability. The profitability measure is the return on equity before tax in the previous five years. The second column takes the top 20 of those same 50 companies, this time based on growth. The growth measure is the annual growth of total assets by the company concerned, again over the previous five years.

Only four of the companies appear in both lists. Of the top nine by growth only one appears in the top 20 by profitability. So there does seem to be a case for saying that there is not a high correlation between growth and profitability.

e Surveys of British attitudes

Another possible source for discovering the attitudes of senior management to profit maximisation is surveys. Several surveys have been conducted in which management has been asked to fill in questionnaires concerning their attitudes. One such survey was published in 1993, under the title 'How ethical is business?' (see under Further Reading). Three of the many questions asked are given in Table 9.5 below. Of those sent the questionnaire about 16 per cent responded, representing 645 replies. Table 9.5 refers to the 480 replies which came from senior managers and professionals. It records the responses to only three of many statements. What do these responses suggest about attitudes to profit maximisation?

The results are mixed. The first statement shows that few wanted to place environmental friendliness so high that profits were sacrificed. This is consistent with an attitude which is that it is profits which must be maximised. On the other hand, considering the second statement, only 11 per cent of senior managers and professionals were prepared to agree with the view that the only rule for business is to make as much money as possible, that is maximise profits.

One must recognise that there are drawbacks to a questionnaire approach to attitudes. One difficulty is that people may be reluctant to be honest. Some may be

Table 9.5 Percentage of senior managers' and professionals' responses to statements on business attitudes

1	Environmentally procedures should always be followed, even if profits are reduced.			
1	2	3	4	5
1	14	20	53	12
2	There is only one rule for business behaviour – make as much money as you can.			
1	2	3	4	5
37	40	11	9	2
3	Products which use scarce resources should be banned.			
1	2	3	4	5
7	31	30	23	9

Notes: 1 = strongly disagree; 2 = disagree; 3 = neutral 4 = agree; 5 = strongly agree
Source: T. Burke, S.Maddock and A.Rose (1993) 'How Ethical is Business?', University Westminster, Research Working Paper, Series 2, No.1.

unwilling to be seen as 'hard-nosed', although often such surveys' responses can be anonymous. A further major drawback is that attitudes may not be consistent. Look at the third statement. All resources are scarce. If such products were banned, there would be no output and these managers would not have a job at all. Yet only 7 per cent of the respondents strongly disagreed! Surveys may be useful, then, but must be interpreted with care.

9 Conclusion

By no means all economists are convinced that management, in whatever market structure it operates, aims to maximise the welfare of its shareholders. Some economists believe that only the divorce of ownership and control makes such an argument a possibility. They feel that one gains much greater insight into the working of large companies if one focuses on other goals. They do not all agree, however, on what those other goals are. Some economists are still convinced that the profit maximisation models are the most useful. Some argue that even if they are less descriptive, profit maximisation models are still valuable because they yield predictions about firm behaviour.

One way in which you might help your own thinking about these issues would be to think through again what we learned in Chapter 8. Would the models we have examined in this chapter be able to cast more light on firms behaviour in the European airline industry? But be in no doubt if you take the question seriously you will find it very hard work!

See pp 153–7

10 Questions for discussion

1 What factors would you expect to determine the size of the mark-up in the full cost pricing model of business behaviour?
2 Check back to Chapter 8. Now explain the criticism of the Baumol model that says it does not matter whether firms maximise profit or sales revenue, their price/output decision is the same.
3 In the sales revenue maximisation model we saw that firms make a higher output at a lower price than if management were seeking to maximise profits. Since the socially optimal price/output decision is a greater output at a lower price does it follow that sales revenue maximisers come nearer to social optimum pricing than profit maximisers?
4 Not all studies have found that the companies who get taken over are those with a low valuation ratio. Why do you think this might be?
5 How can Galbraith sustain the view that people do not really want the things they buy? If there is a demand, must this not be because people gain utility from the goods they purchase?

See pp 153–6

6 If one is interested in the motives of firm's managers, what are the problems associated with asking them what their goals are?

7 How easily can firms in oligopolistic markets increase demand for their products?

11 Further reading

This is not a topic extensively dealt with in introductory economics despite its great importance and interest. As a result there is a limited reference to other books given below. However, given the closeness of the reasoning in this chapter you may well have found that it took you rather longer than some others.

Sales revenue maximisation
Sloman, pp. 276–7

Growth maximisation
Sloman, pp. 277–9

Managerial utility
Sloman, p. 272

Are profits everything?
T. Burke, S. Maddock and A. Rose (1993), 'How ethical is British business?', University of Westminster, Research Working Paper, Series 2, No. 1
'Europe's top 500', *Management Today*, December 1992, pp 38–52

CHAPTER 10

Government spending:
do we get value for money?

[WITH DAVID BIBBY]

The government takes away much of our income in taxes, which it spends on roads, health, education, defence, and so on. Does it spend wisely? Or is much of it wasted? When we spend our own income on things we wish to buy we try to get value for money. How can we be sure that we are getting value for money from our government's spending?

In this chapter we review
- Isoquants and isocosts
- Monopoly

We introduce
- Efficiency
- Public goods

1 Introduction

Some of what most consumers earn they spend on themselves, or their families. A significant proportion of their earnings, however, is taken in taxation and spent by governments. As Figure 10.1 below shows, some of what is taken in tax is redistributed to the poor and the unemployed in social security benefits. Large sums are spent on goods and services which are provided on a non-market basis. Is it well spent? Or is much of it wasted? Is there any way of testing for the efficiency of government spending? These are the questions which we shall address in this chapter.

We can say immediately that there is a body whose task is to raise and answer such questions. It is known as the National Audit Office (NAO). This office describes its role as 'to provide information and advice to parliament on the way government departments and many other public bodies account for and use the taxpayers' money' (NAO Annual Report, 1991, p. 4). The NAO, headed by the Comptroller and Auditor General, is completely independent from Government and the Executive and works closely with the Public Accounts Committee.

There are two facets to the NAO's work: financial audit and value for money audit. Financial audit is the process of checking our accounts for national receipts

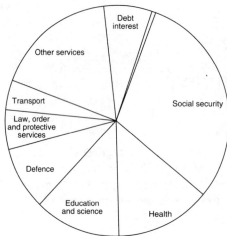

Pence in every £1	
Social security	30½
Health	13½
Education and science	12½
Defence	9
Law, order and protective services	5½
Transport	4
Other services	17½
Debt interest	7
Other	½

Figure 10.1 Government expenditure, 1992–3

and payments. Although this is a very important task we are more interested here in value for money audit.

Our approach to understanding how the NAO operates is this. We shall see how efficiency might be achieved in the private sector. In doing this we shall review some of the concepts raised in earlier chapters. We shall then see how the NAO attempts to see that these aspects of efficiency are achieved for the taxpayer in the state sector.

2 Understanding efficiency

We have already defined economics as the study of how scarce resources are allocated between competing ends. An economy is endowed with a certain amount of resources which can be transformed into a certain quantity of goods and services. How do we know that we have produced as much as we possibly can? Even if we are satisfied that we have maximised production quantities how do we know that we have produced all the different goods and services in amounts that are appropriate for the consumers?

There are, in fact, three separable elements to the efficiency question here. We may refer to them as technical efficiency, cost efficiency and allocative efficiency. Let us examine each of these in turn, asking whether such efficiency will be obtained in the *private* sector. Later, we shall use those concepts to examine the work of the NAO, in its attempts to check for efficiency in the government sector.

a Technical efficiency

Technical efficiency means producing a particular quantity of output using as few inputs as possible, or what amounts to the same thing, to produce the maximum output from a particular quantity of inputs. In plain language waste is being minimised. Garments are made with the minimum amount of fabric on the cutting-room floor, furniture is manufactured with as little sawdust and wood shavings as possible. The labour force should not be making unnecessary journeys and stocks of raw material and finished goods must not be gathering dust in warehouses.

These are just a few of the things that affect the technical efficiency of a firm's operations, but there is also a large number of other factors that have already been taken into account before operations begin from the design of the buildings to the type of machinery used and so on.

Its not easy to be technically efficient and the ability to keep such matters under continual review and recommend improvements is an important part of what managers are paid for!

Let us see how technical efficiency fits in with what you have already learned about production and cost. How do firms make long-run decisions about the right combination of capital and labour needed for producing output? You will remember that we introduced this question in Chapter 5. Let us remind ourselves of what we saw there and then develop the ideas somewhat.

See pp 99–103

Table 10.1 below shows the maximum output of some good that we assume can be produced when a certain quantity of labour and capital is used. In other words, it is a list of technically efficient outcomes.

If we focus on 26 units of output we can see that there is a number of different input combinations that can be used to produce this output. Figure 10.2 shows that it can be done with, for example, 8K + 4L, 4K + 6L or 2K +10L.

Figure 10.2 has been drawn with the assumption that inputs can be divided up into small amounts so that the curve linking all the points representing 26 units is a smooth one. The curve shown is what we referred to in Chapter 5 as an isoquant, a line or contour of constant output. We could have selected any output

See p 99

Table 10.1 Maximum possible output with combination of inputs

Units of capital	Units of labour				
	2	4	6	8	10
10	19	29	37	44	50
8	17	26	34	40	46
6	16	24	30	36	41
4	13	20	26	30	34
2	10	15	19	23	26

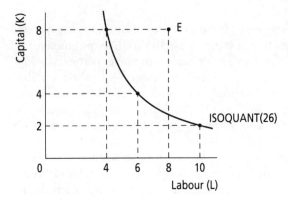

Figure 10.2 Maximum possible output with combinations of inputs

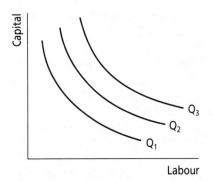

Figure 10.3 Isoquants for successive levels of output

we wished; in each case we would have obtained an isoquant that had a similar shape but was located closer to, or further away from, the origin depending on whether the selected output was higher or lower than 26 units, as Figure 10.3 shows.

If we take point E in Figure 10.2 which represents input quantities of eight units of both labour and capital we would expect to be able to produce 40 units of output as shown in Figure 10.2. However, this is only true if the firm is technically efficient; if it is not, it is quite possible to observe eights units of capital and labour together producing less than 40 units of output.

So to be technically efficient means to avoid waste. It means that for any given usage of one factor we are not using more of another factor if we could use less of it to produce the same output. Figure 10.3 shows a series of isoquants. Each one represents the technically efficient combinations of capital and labour for a given level of output. Notice that technical efficiency says nothing about the prices which must be paid for those factors.

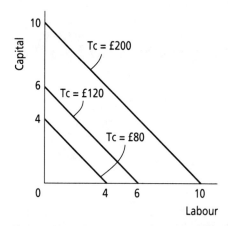

Figure 10.4 Isocost curves: the relative price of inputs

b Cost efficiency

We have shown that any output level can be produced in a technically efficient way if the point is 'on' the relevant isoquant. The isoquant in Figure 10.2 gives us a very large number of possible combinations of capital and labour which can be used to produce our 26 units of output. Which particular input combination should be used? To decide this we need information on the money available to buy inputs and the prices of those inputs. Figure 10.4 illustrates three isocost lines. As their name implies they are simply lines of constant cost; their slope is determined by the relative price of capital and labour. If you have forgotten how we constructed an isocost curve you can refer back to Chapter 5.

See pp 100–1

The next task is to put the information in Figures 10.3 and 10.4 together. This gives us Figure 10.5 which shows the maximum output that can be produced for a given cost outlay at points A, B and C respectively. Looked at the other way around these points also show the minimum cost of producing a given level of output.

Although we consider the nature of isoquants and isocosts in Chapter 5 and the nature of long-run costs in Chapter 6, we did not examine the link between these two concepts. It would be useful for us to do that now.

See pp 99–101, 116–20

The line that links points A, B and C together in Figure 10.5(a) is called an expansion path. When we move from input space Figure 10.5(a) to cost space in 10.5(b) it can be seen that this same line becomes a long-run total cost curve.

Long-run total cost curves do not have to be this particular shape; we have chosen this one for illustrative purposes. Figure 10.5 exhibits constant returns to scale. Doubling inputs doubles output. Then total costs increase at a particular rate. If returns to scale are not constant other shapes for the long-run total cost curve are possible.

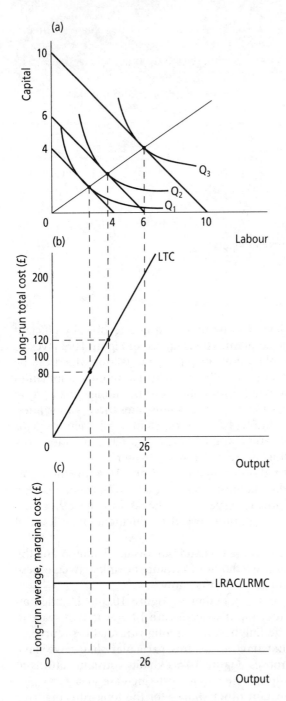

Figure 10.5 Developing the cost curves

Given the total cost curve of Figure 10.5(b), what would this suggest for the firm's average and marginal cost curve? If total costs increase at a constant rate, average costs, costs per unit of output, must be constant. What of marginal costs? Remember, marginal costs are those which tell us the speed at which the total costs are changing. It is clear that total costs are increasing at a constant rate; in other words, marginal cost is constant. What may not be so obvious is that average costs and marginal costs will be the same at all levels of output, as one can see in Figure 10.5(c).

Perhaps the best way of seeing why this must be the case is to remember what we learned in Chapter 5 about graphical techniques for deriving the average cost and the marginal cost from the total. Recall that the slope of the ray from the origin to any point on the total curve gives the average. Average cost, as we have seen, is constant at all levels of output. Remember that the slope of the total curve at any point gives the marginal. Marginal cost is not only constant, but at any point on the total cost curve the ray from the origin has the same slope as the slope of the total cost curve. This is what is plotted in Figure 10.5(c).

See pp 95–6

We could think though, for example, what set of isoquants could produce the shapes of long-run average cost curves given in Chapter 6. In particular, what isoquants give rise to the U-shaped long-run average cost curve? We explained the shape of this curve in terms of economies and diseconomies of scale. We can express the same thing in terms of isoquants. If doubling inputs causes output to increase by more than double, average total costs must fall. If doubling inputs causes output to increase by less than double, average costs must rise. Hence the isoquants will come closer together as output increases for low levels. At higher levels of output the isoquants will become progressively further apart.

Now let us return to our efficiency considerations.

Points A, B and C are 'least cost' points. In terms of our theme of efficiency they can be defined as cost efficient. Technical efficiency means minimising waste and cost efficiency means minimising money cost. Note that in Figure 10.5(a) all points on a given isoquant are technically efficient but only one point is also cost efficient. Thus technical efficiency is a necessary but not a sufficient condition for cost efficiency.

We have seen the least cost points form a long-run total cost curve so it should now be clear that such cost curves presuppose the existence of both technical and cost efficiency. What you should also remember is that this applies not only to the long-run total cost curve but to all the cost curves that you encounter.

All cost curves are in fact boundaries between cost levels that are attainable and those that are not. When looked at in this way we see that it is quite possible for firms to be cost inefficient, that is, operate above their cost curve. Relatively little attention is paid to such behaviour because economists often assume that where output is produced in a market, firms will wish to maximise their total profits and cost minimisation is an important pre-condition for this. You will, of course, remember that we questioned the validity of this assumption in Chapter 9.

See pp 169–87

3 Allocative efficiency

The two dimensions of economic efficiency that have been examined so far relate to how goods are produced or, as businesspeople sometimes say, 'doing things right'. Our third and final dimension is rather different. It refers to what goods are produced and in what relative quantities, that is, 'doing the right things'. The crucial thing to remember is that there is little point in producing goods in a technically and cost efficient way if nobody wants the goods in question. Even if consumers do want some of the goods we must produce them in the right quantities otherwise we will not be making the very best use of our scarce inputs. This last dimension is called allocative efficiency.

The 'right' quantities are those that exactly match the tastes of consumers. But when does such an exact match occur? Consumers' tastes and preferences lie behind the derivation of individual and market demand curves for commodities. Allocative efficiency will therefore have to involve bringing together cost and demand considerations. Although it was not described at the time in efficiency terms, the equality between demand and supply curves in earlier chapters did exactly this!

The equality between demand and supply will only occur in competitive markets and so it follows that only competitive markets can achieve allocative efficiency. To see how this is accomplished consider Figure 10.6 above. The market demand curve DD summarises the maximum prices that consumers are prepared to pay for the different quantities produced. The supply curve SS summarises the minimum prices that producers are prepared to accept for the same quantities. The equilibrium price P* clears the market and satisfies the wishes of both consumers and producers.

See pp 131–2

What has the equilibrium price P* to do with efficiency? You may recall from Chapter 7 that the supply curve is simply all of the marginal cost curves of the firms added together. Remember, too, that these marginal costs are the same thing as opportunity cost. We also know from this chapter that these costs are the lowest

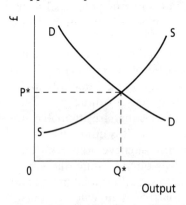

Figure 10.6 An allocatively efficient price and quantity

possible because of the existence of technical and cost efficiency. Thus the market clearing price has ensured that the value of the good to consumers is exactly equal to the minimum opportunity cost of producing that particular output. If less were produced then there would be allocative inefficiency because consumers would value additional units of the good above the cost to society of producing the extra units; if there were more being produced the cost to society would exceed society's value of the extra output and once again, we would have allocative inefficiency. The argument we have developed makes assumptions which may not be realistic. In section 4 we shall consider some of these.

4 Market imperfections

Markets, however, do not always ensure efficiency. We shall consider three possible circumstances where such efficiency is not likely to be achieved.

a Producing too little: monopoly power

If an individual firm faces a downward sloping demand curve for its product then it has a degree of monopoly power. Unlike the competitive firm it will not lose all its sales if it raises its price, and so it is a price maker rather than a price taker. As we saw in Chapter 7, the downward sloping demand curve means that marginal revenue is less than average revenue for any given output, and since all profit maximising firms will wish to equate marginal revenue with marginal cost it follows that marginal cost will be below price at the optimum point. This situation is shown in Figure 10.7.

See pp 143–5

The monopolist's profit maximising price and output (P_m and Q_m) are different from the competitive market's price and output (P_c and Q_c). For reasons we gave in Chapter 7, the value of the underproduction is represented by the shaded area in Figure 10.7, which is often used in economic analysis as a measure of welfare loss. Since the argument which underlies this point is so important for an understanding of efficiency, let us remind ourselves why this is so. The marginal

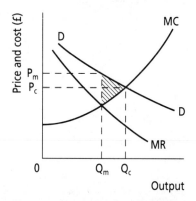

Figure 10.7 Allocative inefficiency and monopoly power

cost curve represents the cost to the firm of producing an extra unit of output. But since it is using up scarce resources, and those resources have an opportunity cost, the marginal cost curve also shown is the value of the output which we could have if those resources were used elsewhere. The demand curve, you will recall, tells us the value we place on the output. Then those units between Q_m and Q_c, which the monopolist will not produce, are valued by society at more than its opportunity cost. The value in excess of opportunity cost on this output, a value which society will not be able to enjoy, is given by the shaded area.

The allocative inefficiency has occurred because the price of the good is not the same as the marginal cost or opportunity cost of producing the last unit.

b Producing too much: external costs of production

Our second case of market failure and allocative inefficiency has the opposite effect to monopoly power and results in over-production. Figure 10.8 illustrates the case of a competitive market which generates equilibrium at price P and output Q. However, unlike the situation in Figure 10.7 this does not result in an allocatively efficient outcome because there are external costs of production.

External costs are costs that are external to the firms but internal to society as exemplified by such things as pollution or congestion.

If external costs are a consequence of production they pose a problem precisely because the relevant firms do not consider them when they decide how much to produce. The firms will only calculate their private marginal costs and will ignore the additional external cost.

If the external cost were added to the private marginal cost we would get what is called the social marginal cost of production, the true full cost to society. In Figure 10.8 this true cost to society is given by MSC, the sum of the social marginal cost curves of all firms in the industry. The cost of the over-production is given by the shaded area in Figure 10.8. Once again we can see that the allocative inefficiency follows directly from the fact that price and marginal social cost are not the same.

See pp 132–4

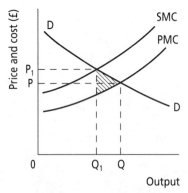

Figure 10.8 Allocative inefficiency and externalities

c No production at all: public goods

Our final case of allocative inefficiency is provided by what we call public goods. Pure public goods have two very interesting characteristics; they are not depleted by additional users (non-depletion) and second it is not possible to exclude anyone from their consumption (non-excludability).

Consider first the characteristic of non-depletion. If *you* use some street lighting, you do not use it up such that *I* cannot consume it. This contrasts with, say, an apple. If *I* eat it then *you* can not. The apple is a private good, street lighting has this characteristic of public goodness which we call non-depletion. Your use of street light does not deplete the amount available for the rest of society.

But, consider also the characteristic of non-excludability. Most goods are excludable. This enables me to say that I will not allow you to consume the apple, unless you pay me. I can exclude you from its consumption. On the other hand, street lighting is non-excludable. It is wholly impracticable to exclude from its consumption those unwilling to pay for its usage.

Not all goods and services fall neatly into the category of public or private. For example, an uncrowded swimming pool has the characteristic of non-depletion. It is, however, clearly excludable. Such goods and services are called impure public goods.

Pure public goods are rare and the 'deterrence' effect of defence expenditure is one of the few examples of a pure public good. However, there is a very extensive list of goods which have significant public goods characteristics such as flood control schemes, police and health services, street lighting and investment in basic research.

The central question that now has to be addressed is, what is the most efficient level of output of the public goods? If we were considering a private good produced under competitive conditions then the benefits would be measured by adding up all the amounts that consumers are prepared to demand at different prices. Similarly, the amounts producers are prepared to supply would be added up and the point where the market demand and supply curves coincide gives us our answer.

In the case of a public good we are again involved with balancing the benefits and costs but the procedure is different in some important respects.

Figure 10.8 represents the benefits and cost of providing a public good. The MV curves are the marginal valuation of the good for three consumers a, b and c. The MV curves are not quite the same as demand curves. They do represent the value that consumers place on different quantities of the public good but this valuation is not measured by the price that they are prepared to pay. Since nobody can be excluded from enjoying the benefits of the good it follows that they do not and can not pay a price at 'the point of delivery'.

Obviously, there is no market for the public good and for this reason it is difficult to measure the benefits even though they exist! There is an additional reason why benefits are difficult to measure; even if all consumers were asked, they would have an interest in understating their true desire for the public good. This understatement is called the free-rider problem. Free-riders exist because of non-excludability, that is, if everyone can enjoy the good regardless of whether they pay for it there is a strong incentive either to avoid paying altogether, or to understate the true amount that you are prepared to pay.

Let us assume that the public good in Figure 10.9 is called protection against flooding. Our three consumers live in a low-lying area in East Anglia that is prone to flooding by the sea. We assume that the MV curves represent their true valuation of protection from this possible event, and the MC curve represents the cost of erecting the sea wall that would ensure this protection; for simplicity the marginal cost of building it is assumed to be constant.

We are now in a position to define the efficient level of provision of flood control. In Figure 10.9, we sum each consumer's valuation *vertically* to get the curve labelled SMV which stands for the social marginal valuation. Allocative efficiency occurs at the optimal point E and quantity Q* where social marginal benefits equate with marginal cost of provision. You may be puzzled by the fact that the SMV curve was obtained by vertical rather than horizontal summation. We sum vertically because the consumers are not getting different units of the public good at a given value (horizontal summation), but have simultaneously a collective value for the same non-rival public good (vertical summation).

Additional consumers could enjoy the flood control service at no extra cost. In other words the marginal or opportunity cost of supplying such additional users is zero, and since we know that for any good allocative efficiency is maximised when price is equated with opportunity cost, it follows that price should be zero!

The above analysis has shown us that we can define allocative efficiency for public goods but it does not explain whether or how they will be produced. Figure 10.9 shows the valuation curves for each consumer well below the cost that would be incurred if the sea wall were actually constructed. This means that the

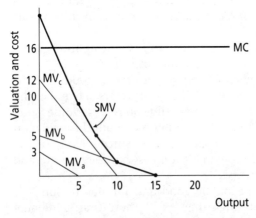

Figure 10.9 An allocatively efficient level of flood control provision

wall may not be constructed even though the social marginal valuation indicates that it would be allocatively efficient to do so.

The production of public goods depends, not surprisingly, upon consumers acting collectively. Getting people together and obtaining sound agreements on these matters is both costly and time consuming. Although it may not always be necessary for provision to be undertaken by local or national governments it is easy to see why it usually is done in this way.

5 Government policy on efficiency

We have seen that under perfect competition both cost and allocative efficiency are realised. Moreover, even under monopoly the drive to maximise total profits was assumed to promote cost efficiency. This represents the intellectual basis for those governments that advocate the market mechanism as an integral part of what is known as industrial policy.

Since 1979 successive Conservative Governments in the United Kingdom have had a fairly consistent approach to the promotion of efficiency in our production of goods and services. The main focus of attention has been on the market mechanism. Privatisation and deregulation have simply transferred publically owned resources to the private sector, while initiatives such as hospital trusts and locally managed schools are created in the belief that economic efficiency is enhanced if decision takers have the discretion to manage funds themselves.

Our analysis of the causes of allocative inefficiency focused on those areas characterised by market failure. It is reasonable to expect that such areas will be of interest to governments, especially Conservative governments that have the market mechanism as the centrepiece of their industrial policy.

Market failure because of monopoly power has traditionally been dealt with by competition policy which covers restrictive trade practices, dominant firm monopolies and mergers that might result in a dominant firm monopoly. Such policy is administered by the Office of Fair Trading whose Director General has the power independent of government to examine restrictive practices and dominant firm monopolies. Mergers are the exceptions to this procedure and have to be referred to the Office of Fair Trading by the Secretary for Trade and Industry.

Like monopolies, mergers and restrictive practices, our second and third categories of market failure, externalities and public goods will also be the focus of government policy and ultimately of government expenditure. How is economic efficiency assessed and promoted in these areas? Central to this question is the work of the National Audit Office (NAO).

6 The National Audit Office: getting value for money

As we said earlier, there are two facets to the NAO's work; financial audit and value for money audit. It is value for money audit that concerns us here.

Table 10.2 Value for money of a hospital building programme

Economy	the tendering, contract and project control procedures to establish how far the hospital and associated facilities had been built to specification, on time and at lowest achievable cost or within approved cost limits
Efficiency	utilisation of wards, beds, theatres and equipment; medical and administrative staff allocations and mix; integration of services; maintenance; management and resource allocation systems; etc.
Effectiveness	results in terms of, for example, reductions in patient waiting lists, increases in operations performed, improved diagnostic and treatment rates and (ultimately) improvements in health and quality of life, reduced mortality rates, etc.

Source: NAO.

Value for money (VFM) has three elements; economy, effectiveness and efficiency. Each of these elements is defined by the NAO in the following way:[1]

- Economy is concerned with minimising the cost of resources acquired or used, having regard to appropriate quality.
- Efficiency is concerned with the relationship between the output of goods and the resources used to produce them. How far is maximum output achieved for a given input, or minimum input used for a given output?
- Effectiveness is concerned with the relationship between the intended results and the actual results of projects. How successfully do outputs of goods and services or other results achieve policy objectives?

Although the NAO only uses the word efficiency once it should be clear from the detailed definitions that the '3Es' are nothing other than cost efficiency (economy), technical efficiency (efficiency) and allocative efficiency (effectiveness).

In other words, the NAO is attempting to achieve for the public sector's spending what markets are supposed to achieve for the private sector.

Table 10.2 summarises the NAO's own explanation of how these concepts might relate to a particular project. Notice again how these areas are ones in which, if a market were operative, the market itself might be able to achieve these goals.

In order to have a better understanding of how the NAO operates we will now select two case studies and see how their assessment work is done.

7 Purchasing defence equipment

The Report of The Ministry Initiatives in Defence Procurement examines the procedures for procuring equipment stores and services for the armed forces. In the five years prior to this Report over £40 billion had been spent on defence equipment and the NAO was evaluating the more commercial approach that has been adopted between the Ministry and the private firms that supply the equipment.

Figure 10.10 below defines the four ways of placing a contract. The essence of the commercial approach is the introduction of an element of competition as a mechanism for ensuring cost efficiency. This is in marked contrast to the cost-plus percentage system which had inadequate incentives for cost minimisation and led to some waste of taxpayers' money.

The NAO assessed how far the commercial system had been introduced, what cost savings had been made, and what might be done in the future.

Figure 10.10 shows the rising trend of contracts led competitively, a rise from 36 per cent in 1882–3 to 67 per cent by value in 1989–90. In the same period cost-plus contracts had fallen from 16 per cent to 4 per cent by value.

The evaluation of cost savings was made by examining the figures from the Government's Statement of the Defence Estimates, 1988. Six projects valued at £2000 million yielded savings of £250 million when put to competition. Net savings of £350 million were made from post-tender negotiation and net savings of £250 million were estimated over the following 20 years through improved reliability and maintainability.

An interesting by-product of the commercial approach was said to be the sharpening of the competitive edge of the UK defence industry which had improved its position in the world league of defence equipment manufacturers.

The Report concluded that for the future, an efficiency enhancing development was the extension of competitive principles into non-competitive tendering. What this means is that as far as is practicable, procurement arrangements for non-competitive contracts should determine the price before the contract is placed. Rather surprisingly this was often not the case for existing contracts and in 10 per cent of cases contracts were still unpriced when all work had been completed!

Calculating an appropriate price is often rather difficult because of the very nature of the non-competitive environment. The NAO stressed the importance of obtaining 'external yardsticks of cost' wherever possible.

The relevance of this Report for our discussion of efficiency is that although government expenditure relates to goods which are not produced by private firms competing with one another, arrangements can be found to mimic the efficiency enhancing effect of the market by a partial introduction of market forces.

8 Coastal defences in England

The 1992 NAO Report on Coastal Defences in England covered both of the categories of work to protect the English coastline namely:

1 Sea defences (including tidal defences) to protect against the flooding of low lying areas. These are usually built by the nine English regional offices of the National Rivers Authority.
2 Coast protection works to prevent the erosion of land and encroachment by the sea. These are usually carried out by 89 maritime district councils.

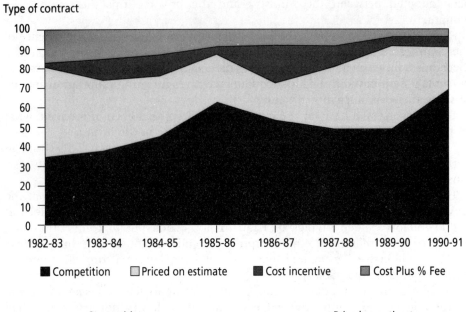

Contracts placed: analysis by type of contract

Type of contract

■ Competition □ Priced on estimate ■ Cost incentive ■ Cost Plus % Fee

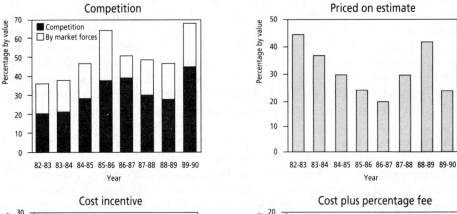

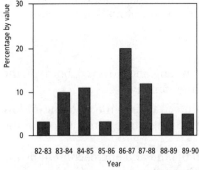

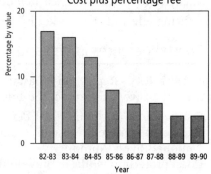

Figure 10.10 Competition statistics, 1982–83 to 1989–90

The Report relates directly to our earlier analysis of flood control as a public good. You may remember that the principles underlying the optimum provision of flood control were straightforward, namely to equate social marginal valuation with the marginal cost of providing the good. This case study is an excellent illustration of the practical problems of applying the theory to the real world.

The NAO employed a team of economists and engineering and environmental consultants to assist them in examining three dimensions of the good:

1 *The Performance of coastal defences and the storm tide warning service.* There is a need to gather and update information on the adequacy and performance of coastal defences. Put a different way, how well do the defences do what they are supposed to do? The NAO found that at the three Authority regions they visited there were no systems of post-project appraisal to assess the performance of schemes against intended standards of protection and the severity of events experienced.

   In addition to physical defences against the sea, coastal defence also involves national and local flood warnings so that suitable precautions are taken to minimise damage. Co-ordinating the various agencies responsible poses operational problems and there was scope for improvements via the introduction of performance indicators.

2 *Planning co-ordination and financing of coastal defences.* Coastal defence relies on sound planning to ensure that the more urgent works have priority and that the funds are available to carry the work out.

   Economic theory does not spend much time on these matters which are usually studied in such disciplines as social and public administration. Real world problems often involve a number of disciplines which is why teams of experts are frequently assembled to deal with them.

   We have seen that coastal defences are administered by a rather large number of agencies. The coordination of these agencies gives rise to what economists call transactions costs. Transactions costs are often reduced if the transactions in question occur within rather than between agencies. Not surprisingly therefore, the NAO recommended a reduction in the number of agencies involved with sea defences. It also advocated reducing transactions costs by more effective transmission of information about financial arrangements.

3 *Engineering, economic and environmental appraisal of coastal defence schemes.* Of the three dimensions considered in this Report this is without doubt the one that is of most interest and relevance to the economist. Coastal Defence is a public good that obviously involves questions of technical efficiency which is why engineers need to advise on such important matters as water levels, erosion damage and project control. The reader may remember that the production isoquant in Figure 10.2 was derived on the assumption that we were not wasting scarce resources by combining resources in ways that engineers would not have approved.

After the engineers have considered the practicable options the NAO was concerned that relevant costs and benefits were identified and correctly valued. Our model of optimal public good provision in Figure 10.9 depicted marginal valuation curves for each consumer and the marginal cost curve of providing the good; in reality there are many reasons why the data necessary to measure accurately these benefits and costs is difficult and costly to obtain. Some of the main reasons are:

1   The free-rider problem may result in consumers understating their true willingness to pay for the good.
2   There are physical and logistical difficulties in obtaining direct information on preferences.
3   Many costs and benefits are intangible, for example, environmental or amenity impacts, risk to life, health and social effects of stress resulting from flooding. It is difficult to estimate what people feel those benefits are worth.
4   The calculation of benefits and costs of coastal defence have to take account of the passage of time. The costs occur immediately. The benefits accrue over a period of many years. Estimating benefits accruing many years into the future raises additional difficulties. We examine this problem in Chapter 14.

See pp 276–80

Allowing for the difficulty of measurement, the government requires that schemes demonstrate a predicted benefit-cost ratio of one or greater to qualify for grant aid, in other words expected benefits must exceed the costs. Figure 10.11 provides data on these ratios.

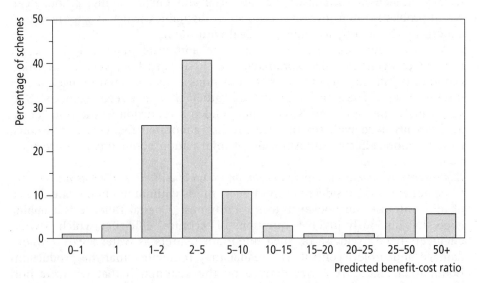

Figure 10.11   Range of predicted benefit–cost ratios for coastal defence schemes, 1986–7 to 1990–91

What does such a benefit-cost ratio imply? To the extent that the number is greater than unity, the benefit to society outweighs its opportunity cost. Almost all schemes, according to NAO were very worthwhile, even though a market would not have provided them.

However, NAO clearly felt that government failure also constitutes a problem. In the eight schemes examined in depth by the NAO consultants their conclusions included the following:

- Maintenance costs were wrongly excluded for three schemes.
- Property damage was generally well addressed but recreational, traffic or services benefits were not adequately assessed in any of the schemes.
- There was confusion over the treatment of benefits to local tourism and caravan sites.
- Significant problems arose with double counting of benefits for one scheme.
- Agricultural benefits featured in three of the schemes but were properly assessed in only one case.

9 Conclusion

This chapter has identified three dimensions that underly the concept of economic efficiency. When firms operate in the private sector the assumption of self-interest in the form of profit maximisation is the mechanism for encouraging efficient operation. We have seen how under certain conditions such efficiency is unlikely to be achieved in the private sector without government intervention.

Since 1979, government policy has attempted to promote efficiency either by privatising previously publicly controlled enterprises. Where this was not feasible, as in the case of defence, there has been a partial introduction of market competition. Some public goods, such as coastal defence, are not even amenable to partial influence of the market and under these circumstances institutional arrangements have to be kept under constant review to ensure value for taxpayer's money. It would appear that the NAO has had some success here. Figure 10.12 shows the increasing amount of savings as a result of the NAO's work. These savings need to be seen against the background of a cost of running

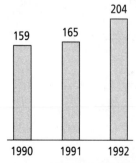

Figure 10.12 NAO value for money savings (£ million)

the office of something less than £40 million. The concept of value for money employed by this increasingly important watchdog, matches those concepts of efficiency which we have developed throughout the book and forms the basis of its attempts to see that we do get good value for government expenditure.

It should now be clear to you that markets are not a guarantee of efficient resource usage and allocation. But neither are governments!

10 Questions for discussion

1 In terms of Figure 10.7, why is the argument about allocative efficiency expressed as an argument about marginal output rather than the degree of abnormal profit?

2 Doesn't the level of profit matter when discussing allocative efficiency?

3 Clearly public goods provide a strong argument for state ownership of assets. Would you categorise the following as public goods?
a Art galleries.
b Police services.
c The weather forecast on TV.

4 What problems will services such as street lighting create for a market system?

5 Can a market system ever produce public goods?

6 Is there any point in analysing whether resources such as flood control have been used efficiently? Should we not be deciding whether to invest in flood control at all? How could we do that?

7 In recent years the government has introduced an 'internal market' in health care. What do you think this means? Are the reforms beneficial?

8 Should a higher or lower proportion of society's output be allocated on a market basis?

11 Further reading

Efficiency
Sloman, pp. 176–85; pp. 399–405; Begg, pp. 256–68; Parkin and King, pp. 288–90

Public goods
Sloman, p. 381; p. 417; Begg, p. 51; pp. 281–4; pp. 284–6; Parkin and King, pp. 458–63

Government spending: value for money
Ministry of Defence Initiatives in Defence Procurement. HMSO, 1991.
Coastal Defences in England. HMSO, 1992.

12 End note

1 A Framework for Value for Money Audits, National Audit Office, 1984, p. 4.

CHAPTER 11

Trade unions:
labour market manipulators?
[WITH ROB THOMAS]

To some people, trade unions are crucial protectors of the weak. To others, they force up wage levels to unrealistic levels and contribute to unemployment. What role do trade unions have in a modern economy? How successful are they in raising the wages of their members? To what extent do they manipulate labour markets?

In this chapter we review
- Indifference curves
- Cartels

We introduce
- The demand for labour
- Wage rate determination

1 Introduction

As we have already seen, market forces play a crucial role in determining the prices of products. Where a large number of suppliers and consumers operate, supply and demand determines an equilibrium price. But we saw in Chapter 7 how suppliers might wish, given certain conditions, to combine to raise price above that equilibrium.

See pp 143–6

In this chapter we consider the determination by market forces of the price of labour services. We also consider the extent to which labour can combine into trade unions to raise wages above the level that would be determined by uncoordinated market forces.

Trade unions are often seen as institutions designed to correct or reverse the unequal relationship between the asset-poor employee and the asset-rich employer. The Conservative governments in the UK since 1979 have viewed unions as a distortion (or friction, as economists often call it) in the working of market forces. These administrations have passed a large amount of legislation to curb the power of unions, directly via their activities in the market-place, and indirectly by changing the democratic processes within unions. It is not the purpose of this chapter to review this legislation and its impact, but you can do so, if you wish, by consulting the additional readings at the end of the chapter.

In this chapter we will investigate the nature and role of unions and then develop an analysis using economic principles in order to assess the impact of these labour market institutions on market pricing, known in this case as pay or wages. These two terms can be used interchangeably to indicate the financial remuneration received by an employee, be this in the form of a wage or salary, with or without fringe benefits such as a company car, company health insurance or employer's pension contributions. The conclusions we reach can help us to understand how wages are determined. It will also help us to consider later some key macro-economic concepts such as unemployment and inflation.

2 Trade unions and industrial relations in the UK

The most widely quoted definition of a trade union is 'a continuous association of wage-earners for the purpose of maintaining or improving the conditions of their working lives'.[1] It is not always a *voluntary* relationship because there are circumstances where there is coercion by fellow workers to join. The term 'wage-earner' in our definition is no longer strictly correct with unions recruiting employers, particularly the self-employed. Nowadays, it can be argued that the aim stated in the definition is too restrictive because unions pursue other causes: full employment (not just of union members) and social issues both domestically and internationally. But as our focus is on unions in labour markets, the definition can be accepted as a first step.

a Types of trade unions

Unions differ in many respects including structure, rules of membership and recruitment policies. This last aspect has been taken as the basis of classifying unions as in Table 11.1. Notice from the table that unions by no means restrict themselves to recruiting manual workers.

Over recent decades, however, due to the changing structure of employment in the UK, fluctuations in union fortunes and shifts in government policy, mergers have reduced the number and, given the decline in union membership indicated

Table 11.1 Classification of types of union

1	craft	recruit only from one, normally skilled, occupation
2	industrial	recruit only from one industry
3	general	recruit from a range of occupations and industries and often concerned with unskilled
4	white-collar	recruit non-manual workers with restrictions on occupation and/or industry in some cases

Table 11.2 Number of trade unions and trade union membership in the UK, 1979–91*

Year	Number of unions at end of year	Total membership at end of year (in thousands)	Percentage change in Union membership since previous year
1979	453	13,289	+1.3
1980	438	12,947	−2.6
1981	414	12,106	−6.5
1982	408	11,593	−4.2
1983	394	11,236	−3.1
1984	375	10,994	−3.2
1985	370	10,821	−1.6
1986	335	10,539	−2.6
1987	330	10,475	−0.6
1988	315	10,376	−0.9
1989	309	10,158	−2.1
1990	287	9,947	−2.1
1991	275	9,585	−3.6

Note: *Figures compiled from returns to the Certification Officer for Trade Unions and Employers' Associations.
Source: Department of Employment, *Employment Gazette*, various editions.

Table 11.3 Relative size of UK trade unions in 1979 and 1991*

Number of members	Percentage of unions		Percentage of membership of all unions 1979	
	1979	1991	1979	1991
Under 1,000	53.7	44.3	0.5	0.4
1,000–9,999	27.6	31.3	3.0	3.1
10,000–49,999	9.5	12.7	8.0	10.1
50,000–99,999	3.3	3.3	6.9	6.2
100,000 and more	5.9	8.4	81.6	80.2

Note: *Figures compiled from returns to the Certification Officer for Trade Unions and Employers' Associations.
Source: Department of Employment, Employment Gazette, various editions.

in Table 11.2, this has enabled the large unions to retain their relative size, as shown in Table 11.3. Union membership 'density', the proportion of the labour force in unions, differs makedly between countries, with the UK now being slightly above the average of OECD countries. In the union merger process, unions have tended to look beyond their traditional craft/industry/white-collar recruitment and the general union, with sections for particular groups of members, has come to dominate.

b Trade union structure

Large unions are often divided into sections or divisions. This structure can be important. First, the sections or divisions are important in large unions because structure helps to retain a sense of loyalty via a unity of purpose within the sub-group. Second, it helps to continue the long-held principle of democracy in unions. This has been an important factor in shaping union structure so that members' views are heard and acted upon. Most unions have some form of local organisation based around the role of the shop steward who represents a group of members working together for the same employer. There is also likely to be a local branch with meetings attended by members from different local employers. In the case of larger firms, the branch may only be for members in that company. From this local level, information and views are passed up and down a regional hierarchy, which stretches to the national executive of the union, its General Secretary and the ultimate rule-making body, the (usually) annual conference. A generalised structure such as this does not apply to all unions but it clearly displays the political nature of unions, a topic to which we will return.

c Structure of collective bargaining

The different levels in the structure of unions tend to be mirrored by the levels at which collective bargaining occurs in the UK. National agreements negotiated between the union leadership and an employers' association representing employers in an industry are largely concerned with setting basic pay rates and standard weekly hours; bargaining at the individual company level will supplement the national agreement or, in the case of large companies which do not belong to an employers' association, will replace national bargaining.

However, agreements at these levels cannot always take into account the particular circumstances of a plant/office or even of a part (known as the 'shop floor') of the local operation. Bargaining at these levels supplement the national agreement by focusing on working practices and incentive payments to meet local needs. Exactly what is negotiated at which level in this decentralised bargaining structure is a matter of historical precedent though surveys carried out during the 1980s indicate a tendency to formalise industrial relations. Written procedures for dealing with grievances have become more prevalent and these have sought to move bargaining away from the shop floor level, thus reversing the post-1945 trend towards decentralised bargaining.

3 Economic analysis of trade unions

a The economic nature of trade unions

Embarking on the economic nature of trade unions immediately brings us to their dual identity. On the one hand, a union operates to supply services which are demanded by members; the services range from bargaining to legal advice and representation, and in recent years have included discount cards and favourable credit terms. Unions compete both with each other to get members to 'buy' via subscription (though this competition is limited among unions that are members of the Trade Union Congress (TUC) by the so-called 'Bridlington Rules') and with other providers of the services in the public and private sectors. In this respect, the union is like a product market firm, except that it would be difficult to justify the assumption that unions seek to maximise profits.

On the other hand, while a union's behaviour in labour markets is often portrayed as being similar to that of a monopoly firm supplying in this case labour, the analogy is difficult to sustain. A union does not supply labour services in the same way as a product market firm; the individual member owns and supplies her/his labour services. Therefore, when combining with others in a union, individuals are doing so in order to exploit their combined market power. This is not so much a monopoly as a cartel.[2]

See pp 156–7

The problem of a cartel, as we saw in Chapter 8, is that while all the participants gain by agreeing to limit supply, it is in the interests of one participant to break the agreement and increase supply, as long as the others continue to abide by the rules. Let us take an example in the context of a union. Suppose an overtime ban to support a pay claim is in force but one union member breaks the ban: she/he would get paid overtime and the rise in pay if the ban produces the pay increase. Of course, the one member working overtime could reduce the effectiveness of the ban, increasing the resolve of the employer. Union rules aim to prevent this 'cheating' though recent changes in the law make it illegal for a union to discipline a member who breaks a strike. However, the individual's fellow workers are likely to have far more effective sanctions (for example, refusing to speak to a strike-breaker).

b Union objectives

To analyse the objectives of a union, we turn to utility analysis which was introduced in Chapter 4, to examine consumer behaviour. A utility function can be specified for each member of the union and these aggregated to give the union's utility function. The aggregation is not straightforward if, as seems reasonable to assume particularly in respect of a general union, the individual member's utility functions differ or even conflict. Consider some possible conflicts. Unskilled members want to narrow the pay differential between themselves and skilled workers while the skilled members oppose such a lowering of their status.

See pp 70–4

Then again, there are the objectives of the union leaders who will be concerned with the survival and growth of the union in financial and membership terms. Despite these problems, economists wish to concentrate on the wage (W) and employment (E) aspects, specifying the union utility function in the following way. Union utility depends in some systematic way upon wage rates and upon the level of employment of members. You may sometimes see the idea of a systemmatic relationship of this kind expressed as:

$$U = f(W, E, ...)$$

where U is union utility;

$f()$ indicates that the variables in the brackets influence union utility though the exact relationship is not being specified;

..... indicates that there are other unspecified influences on union utility such as health and safety, membership growth and the union's public image.

The analysis requires a further assumption, namely that all the unspecified influences can be held constant during the period of study. Some dispute this assumption arguing that a union is a political organisation with the leadership reconciling the various internal pressure groups by continually changing the emphasis given to the objectives.

Holding the assumption allows a union's indifference curve map between wages and employment to be derived as shown in Figure 11.1(a) and (b).

Each indifference curve is drawn to show how different combinations of wages and employment give rise to the same level of union utility; different curves represent different levels of utility with higher utility shown by curves lying further to the right. The view taken in Figure 11.1(a) is that a union will experience the same level of utility if a fall in wages is compensated by an increase in employment and vice versa. The map in Figure 11.1(a) reflects the usual assumptions about indifference curves and indicates a smooth trade-off between wages and employment. Not so in Figure 11.1(b) where the indifference curve

See pp 71–4

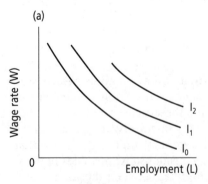

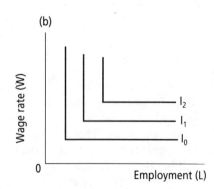

Figure 11.1 Indifference curves showing preferences between wages and employment

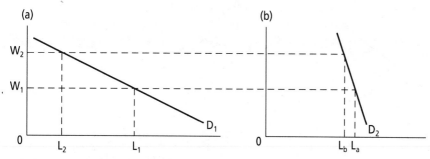

Figure 11.2 Possible labour demand curves

map depicts the limiting case where no increase in the wage rate can compensate for a fall in emloyment levels and vice versa.

c The demand for union labour

Orthodox economic theory does not see the union as being able to move to higher and higher indifference curves and thereby greater and greater levels of utility. There is a constraint on its actions in the form of the demand curve for labour, the derivation of which is explained in Appendix 4. What is important to note at this stage is that the labour demand curve shows the employer's profit maximising employment level for each wage rate: the lower the wage, the more labour will the firm find worthwhile employing. The position and slope of the demand curve is dependent on conditions in the firm's product market and its methods of production. Changes in the degree of competition in the product market or in consumer tastes for the product will alter the position and/or slope; as will alterations in the method of production whereby it becomes more or less labour intensive.

Figure 11.2(a) and (b) illustrate two possible labour demand curves. If a union manages to increase the wage from W_1 to W_2, the union will prefer to face the relatively inelastic[3] (more steeply sloped) labour demand curve shown in Figure 11.2(b) because the consequent reduction in employment (OL_a to OL_b) is much less than when the curve is relatively elastic as in Figure 11.2(a) and the employment decrease is OL_1 to OL_2.

d Pay determination in unionised labour markets

We can now bring the various threads of analysis together and begin considering the impact of a union on pay.

Figure 11.3(a) illustrates both the orthodox economic theory of market forces and the way in which a union is perceived to intrude and alter the outcome. The labour demand (D) and supply (S) curves intersect at A to give the market equilibrium wage (OW_e) and employment (OL_e); without the presence of a union, the market would be expected to settle at A. If a union is then formed it

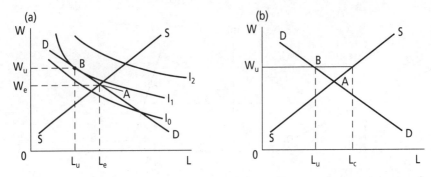

Figure 11.3 Union preferences and the market for labour

will use its cartel power to maximise its utility subject to the labour demand curve constraint; it will force the market to point B, where the highest indifference curve that can be attained just touches (is tangential to) the demand curve, resulting in a higher wage (OW_u) but lower employment (OL_u). Point B is assumed to lie above A on the labour demand curve because it is believed that the union will wish to obtain a higher wage than is set by market forces in order to encourage workers to remain in/join the union. Figure 11.3(b) gives an alternative picture of the situation with the union controlling the going wage (OW_u) so that the supply curve is horizontal at this wage until it intersects with the original supply curve when it takes on its usual positive (bottom left to top right) slope. What Figure 11.3(b) illustrates is how the union's action is believed to increase unemployment so that L_uL_c amount of labour is willing to work at wage OW_u but cannot get a job.

Point B arguably lies above A on the labour demand curve, but how far above? What determines exactly where the union aims to be on the demand curve? And, can it attain its goal? A significant part of the answer is to be found in the constraints upon union activity.

4 The constraints on union action in labour markets

To examine the constraints upon union action we must delve a little further into both the demand and supply sides of unionised labour markets. The aim is to take the analysis beyond the simple, somewhat mechanical application of market forces. We need to understand the institutional structure of the wage bargaining process in order to understand how the two sides of the market interact to produce an outcome.

a The demand for union labour

As already noted, the most obvious constraint on a union's ability to use its cartel potential is the demand curve for labour. It summarises the profit maximising

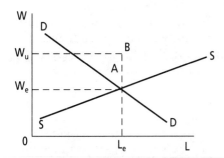

Figure 11.4 Wage rates in the absence of perfect competition in the product market

employer's position and implies that the employer will not be shifted off the demand curve. The reason for this is that with perfect competition in the product market, the employer will earn less than maximum profit and as maximum profit equals normal profit, the firm will go out of business if it earns less profit. However, this is not the end of the analysis.

First, union action can theoretically at least, alter the labour demand relationship. Figures 11.2(a) and (b) show that the union will prefer to face an inelastic demand curve and it can increase the degree of inelasticity by bargaining over manning levels. If unions can obtain agreements or legislation which stipulates minimum crew numbers then this will reduce the ability of employers to decrease employment when the wage increases. Also, if the union can organise the whole of the industry then all the employers will incur the same union-induced wage cost increase and so no single firm need suffer a fall in product demand relative to other firms.

Second, if there is not perfect competition in the product market, the firm may be able to continue trading even if it earns less than maximum profit. An employer could then pay a wage above the perfectly competitive wage and maintain the level of employment, such as at point B in Figure 11.4. Obviously there is a limit to this in that eventually the firm's costs of production would cause the product price to rise to an uncompetitive level; but the limit could lie well to the right of the labour demand curve.

Third, the firm may have labour market power itself. Economists refer to such power as monopsony power. Thus a firm which has product market power or is the major employer in a particular locality can use its position to exert influence in its labour market(s); employers can also group together for bargaining purposes, forming an employers' association. Whichever, firms in such a position will be able to increase profits by paying a wage below the competitive wage and employing less labour. In these circumstances, the monopoly union comes up against the monopsonist employer and the outcome of this 'bilateral monopoly' in terms of supply and demand is indeterminate. Rather the wage (and employment) will be the result of the relative bargaining power of the two sides, a topic to which we will return.

What we can conclude at the moment is that the employer need not just passively accept the union's cartel influence over the wage and then adjust the level of employment. There are circumstances in which the employer or employers' association has the power to resist the union's pay demand.

b Unions and labour supply

Turning to the supply side of labour markets we return to the line of thought that sees unions acting like product market monopolists having complete control of the supply of a product. A union as a cartel, however, only possesses this power if all the members of the labour force are members of the union and they abide by the cartel's decision to alter the labour supply. Difficulties arise for the union in its attempt to achieve this 100 per cent control because of the multi-dimensional nature of labour supply, which comprises:

a the person
b the number of hours supplied
c the amount of effort supplied
d the amount of skill supplied
e the amount of ability supplied

where the distinction between skill and ability is that skill is expertise obtained from some form of training while ability is expertise that is inherent in the individual.

As already noted, individual members of the union do not necessarily hand over control of their labour supply to the union executive. At best, the member agrees to abide by the decisions of the majority following a vote on a particular issue. Even then, the individual member can increase her/his labour supply by accepting the decision of the majority over one dimension (say, number of hours supplied) but altering the supply of another dimension (say, amount of effort supplied). In fact, unions normally do not seek to control all the dimensions of labour supply and much depends on the type of union and the work context of the rank and file members. A craft union will seek to control the number of workers with the appropriate skill via control over an apprenticeship scheme whereby only by successfully completing a minimum number of years of training can an individual obtain work as a 'skilled operative'. Alternatively, the union negotiates the number of hours that comprise the standard working week but leaves it to the employer and employee to agree on the number of overtime hours. Rarely do unions formally attempt to control the amount of effort supplied, although there have been instances where groups of members have taken it upon themselves to limit informally the pace of work.

What the union wishes to achieve can be interpreted as a shift of the labour supply curve to the left, thus raising the wage set in the labour market, though it is at the expense of employment below the competitive level. In doing so the most obvious target for the union is to organise all the workforce via a 'closed shop' agreement. Under this, the firm agrees either to recruit only union members (a pre-entry closed shop) or to make it a condition of employment that the new recruit becomes a union member (a post-entry closed shop). Unions argue that closed shops are justified because they overcome the 'free-rider' problem, that is, non-union workers who benefit from union-obtained improvements in pay and working conditions but do not pay subscriptions nor take part in industrial action. Conservative governments since 1979, however, have legislated to remove closed shops on the grounds that they are the basis of a major form of labour market monopoly.

c Industrial action

So far we have seen that unions have the potential to exercise monopoly-like power in labour markets because they act as a cartel. This enables them to raise wage rates above the competitive equilibrium level. But by how much? In other words, we are concerned with the circumstances under which unions can realise some or all of their cartel potential in raising wages above the level that would be set by the unimpeded forces of demand and supply.

Power lies at the heart of the issue in that power is the ability to do something. In this case we are considering the ability of the union to obtain agreement to its demands. Union power mainly comes from the degree of control it can exercise over labour supply, aspects of which have already been discussed. Now we focus on the power that comes from 'taking industrial action'. This can involve the union members in a 'go-slow', 'work to rule', or withdrawal of cooperation, all aimed at reducing the pace of work and volume of output. Alternatively, it can take more 'headline' forms of industrial action such as an overtime ban or a strike. Notice that all these actions are temporary; rarely will union members withdraw their labour on a permanent basis because it would mean losing the jobs which are their only source of income. Industrial action seeks to impose costs on the firm in order to obtain a satisfactory (from the union point of view) agreement, but the outcome is determined by a wide range of factors that make up the circumstances of the bargaining.

The threat of industrial action hangs over each negotiation between union representatives and those of the firm, even when the negotiations are informal. How potent a threat it is depends first on the proportion of the labour force which is unionised or, if the proportion is low, whether the union members have a crucial position in the production process. These form the basis of the threat but even if a large proportion of the workforce is in the union, it is the individual union members who must be willing to take action. They must therefore believe in the importance of the issue and must agree on the action to be taken; in other words, there needs to be cohesion and unity, a coming together of the individual members. Cohesion, some may use the term militancy, is again a matter of degree which can be related back to the economic concept of the cartel and the ability of the cartel to use its potential power.

Table 11.4 Estimates of the percentage overall union pay gap in Britain 1970–87

Year	% Union pay gap	Year	% Union pay gap	Year	% Union pay gap
1970	26	1976	29	1982	34
1971	28	1977	26	1983	31
1972	31	1978	28	1984	32
1973	30	1979	19	1985	24
1974	22	1980	28	1986	19
1975	33	1981	34	1987	22

Source: R. F. Elliott (1991) *Labor Economics: A Comparative Text*, McGraw-Hill, Maidenhead, England, p. 437.

The final part in the jigsaw of factors determining the potency of the threat of industrial action are the costs incurred by both sides. As Table 11.4 shows, the level of strike activity can be substantial, although it has been rather less so in recent years. A strike is the most obvious form of industrial action in which the rank and file lose pay but the other forms of industrial action listed above can also involve a reduction in earnings (they are sometimes called 'cut-price' actions because the costs to union members are likely to be less). The potency of the threat will depend on the willingness of the members to put up with the hardship of having no/lower income for the duration of the dispute. On the other hand, the employer will also be suffering lost output which will lead to lost profit, though the precise size of the costs to the firm will be lower if it has a stockpile of the product and can continue trading by selling from stock or if the product market is depressed so that the firm would not have sold much anyway. Furthermore, the costs to both sides are reduced if the output can be made up by extra overtime working after the dispute is resolved: the union members receive extra pay to compensate for that lost during the dispute and the firm can sell the extra output (profits may not be fully restored in that the extra overtime would usually be paid for at a premium wage rate above the standard rate).

During the negotiations, the representatives of the union and of the employer will attempt to gauge the potency of the threat. As both sides will incur costs if industrial action takes place, the negotiations can be portrayed as attempting to avoid an industrial dispute with the relatively weaker side giving ground to the other until a settlement is reached. However, should either side fail to recognise their true relative power position, then the threat of industrial action will be tested and its potency measured by how long the action lasts and the extent to which the resulting settlement reflects the final positions of the sides before the action occurred.

d Some tentative conclusions

What is obvious from this discussion is that the ability of the union to capitalise on its potential cartel power and force the employer to pay above the free market wage is circumvented by factors ranging from the cohesion of the union to the general economic climate. The number of 'ifs' and 'buts' make it difficult to apply economic theory but some generalised conclusions can be drawn about the impact of the union on pay.

1 Unions can have different objectives and thereby while some may seek high pay increases others may be more concerned with employment prospects for members. There may be other objectives that the union wishes to pursue (status of the union and its leaders, survival of the union) which also mean the union does not just focus on pay.
2 The cohesion or unity of the members will be important in determining whether the union can achieve its objective(s). No satisfactory measures of this factor exist and so it is not incorporated in empirical studies.
3 The degree of unionisation will be a factor in determining the unions ability to achieve its goal(s). If the union can recruit the whole workforce in an industry then it will be easier for it to push for higher pay as all the firms in the industry will be affected and their relative competitiveness in the product market will remain unaltered by the pay rise.
4 Large firms with product market power offer unions the double prospect of being able to organise employees in the industry at lower cost (not so many employers with which to negotiate bargaining rights) and the firms have the ability to pass on pay increases in the form of price increases so making them less resistant to union demands. This will not be the case, however, if there is product market competition from abroad.
5 Economic conditions can influence the ability of unions to obtain pay increases in several ways. In times of economic prosperity, strikes will be more costly for firms in terms of lost business while it will be easier for the strikers to find part-time work to offset the lost pay. If there is inflation, the firm may be able to pass on the pay rise in higher prices.

5 The empirical evidence

a The sources of data

At first glance there seems to be plenty of data available on which to judge the impact of unions on pay in the UK. The Department of Employment publishes monthly figures for earnings, employment and stoppages of work due to industrial disputes; there are two main sources of statistics on union membership (the TUC and the Certification Officer for Trade Unions and Employers' Associations); and the Labour Force Survey provides annual, and more recently quarterly, survey data.

In the main, these are accepted as accurate measures though there are some problems associated with their use. 'Stoppages of work due to industrial disputes' does not include non-strike actions and in fact does not include all strikes, deliberately omitting small stoppages (where less than 100 working days are lost). The TUC union membership figures only relate to those unions which are affiliated to the TUC while the Certification Officer includes as trade unions some organisations which are not unions in the strict sense of being independent of the employer(s). Therefore, the statistics that relate to the basis of union power need to be interpreted carefully.

b Interpreting the data

It seems such a simple task to complete. We obtain the data on the pay of union members and then compare it with the pay of non-union members; assume non-union pay is equal to the wage that would be set if the forces of demand and supply operate freely; then the difference in pay is the measure of the impact of the union on pay. But things are not so straightforward.

First, there are various reasons, other than the influence of unions, why pay will differ between two people (for example, between males and females, between skilled and unskilled, between different industries and between different geographical areas). The influence of these other causes of pay differentials must be removed so that the data compares like with like.

Second, in the UK, many collective agreements on pay are applied to union and non-union members alike. So, for the purposes of empirical work, do we include those non-union members who are covered by the collective agreement as being union members even though they are not? Or, do we place them in the non-union category when they are paid the union pay rate?

Third, as is obvious from the previous point, non-union pay need not be equal to the competitive market wage. Figure 11.5(a) and (b) illustrate how the emergence of a union in a labour market affects non-union wages.

Omitting the supply curves in order to make the diagrams clearer, Figure 11.5(a) represents the unionised part of the market and Figure 11.5(b) the non-unionised part. Initially, there is no union and the competitive wage is set at 0We in both sectors and resulting employment of $0L_a$ and $0L_b$ respectively. Then the union is formed in sector (a) and it uses its cartel power to raise the wage to 0Wu

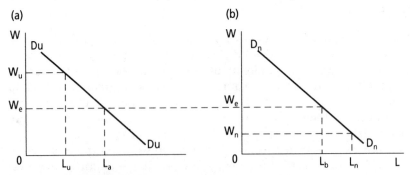

Figure 11.5 Unionised and non-unionised labour markets

and employment in the sector decreases by L_aL_u. This unemployed labour seeks work in the non-unionised sector, bidding down the wage to $0W_n$ (note that all the unemployed labour seeks work in the non-unionised sector so that L_aL_u equals L_bL_n). Obviously in these circumstances the non-union wage does not equal the competitive wage.

That, however, need not be the end of the story. Non-union employers may wish to ensure that their workforces do not become unionised. Therefore, they may be willing to 'buy-off' their workforces by paying a wage just about equal to the union wage (maybe even higher than the union wage) in order to persuade their employees that a union is not necessary.

These so-called 'spill-over' effects muddy the empirical waters but certainly it is not possible to hold that the non-union wage is the wage that would prevail if unions did not exist. The union pay gap is thus to be interpreted as a measure of how much union members gain in pay over non-union workers.

c Assessing the data

A large number of studies have been carried out to discover whether, and by how much, union pay differs from that of non-union employees in the UK. The results are much in line with our previous analysis; that is, the differential varies! However, certain patterns emerge.

First, it is by no means always the case that union pay exceeds non-union pay when comparing similar types of labour in the same broad industry. However, the majority of the evidence points to a positive wage gap in favour of the unions.

Second, the union/non-union pay differential tends to be larger when union pay has been at least partially determined by bargaining at the company, plant or shop floor level. Conversely, where the union pay is set by national bargaining, the pay gap tends to be smaller.

Third, skill level, company size and establishment size appear to influence the size of the pay differential, with unions able to gain greater advantage for the semi-skilled than for the skilled and for those members who work in large companies, especially if those companies have a significant degree of product market power.

Fourth, the size of the overall union wage gap varies over time and the variation seems to be related to the business cycle. This can be seen from the data in Table 11.4 where the estimates for Britain measure the gap as fluctuating between 17 and 34 per cent over the period 1967 to 1987. The percentage gap tends to get smaller during times of economic prosperity but becomes larger during downturns in economic activity.

In general these findings are in line with our theoretical expectations; the exception might seem to be the last one about the influence of economic conditions. The explanation normally given is that the union gap widens in the downturn of the business cycle because while pay falls in the non-union sector, unions will have some success in resisting such pressure, preventing wages from falling.

6 Conclusions

Our analysis and consideration of the empirical results have given few definitive answers to the questions of how and to what extent unions affect relative pay. However, we have built a framework for understanding the role of unions; a framework which seeks to combine the economic analysis with the political nature of unions in order to analyse union behaviour. It is not a rigorous, technical analysis because unions are not susceptible to such an approach. There are too many ifs and buts!

In respect of the impact of unions on relative pay, the theoretical analysis and the empirical evidence lead to the conclusion that overall unions push up wages above the non-union level of pay. 'Overall' should not be taken to mean in every situation because both theoretically and empirically this is not the case.

7 Questions for discussion

1 How do you think unions will react to a leftward shift of the demand curve for its labour? (due, for example, to a fall in demand in the product market). (HINT: What is happening to the union in terms of Figure 11.1?)
2 Why do employees decide to join trades unions? Why do others decide not to do so?
3 Recent legislation in the UK has made it possible for an employer to be taken to court if an applicant is rejected for a job because she/he will not join a trade union. In this way the government is seeking to remove closed shop agreements. But is a closed shop necessarily a bad thing?
4 Under what circumstances can a strike be said to be successful or unsuccessful?
5 What can be concluded about the determination of pay in the absence of unions (either in non-unionised labour markets or where the union is not recognised for bargaining purposes)?

8 Further reading

The demand for labour
Sloman, pp. 306–12; Begg, pp.173–82; Parkin and King, pp. 350–61

Wage rate determination
Sloman, pp. 312–34; Begg, pp. 187–92; Parkin and King, pp. 376–94

Trades unions: labour market manipulators?
W. Brown and S. Wadahani (1990) 'The economic effects of industrial relations legislation since 1979', *National Institute Economic Review*, February.
P. Foley (1993) 'Pay versus jobs in the 1990s', *Lloyd's Bank Economic Bulletin*, July.

9 End notes

1 S. and B. Webb (1965) *The History of Trade Unionism*, reprinted by Augustus Kelly, New York, p. 1.
2 You will recall that we discussed cartels in the product market in the context of airline prices in Chapter 8.
3 Both of the demand curves in Figure 11.2 have an elasticity ranging in value from infinity to zero. However, one can say that at any given wage rate, the value of elasticity for the steeper curve is less elastic at that point. In that sense (a) is relatively elastic compared with (b).

CHAPTER 12

Damaging the earth:
how much does it really matter?

Pollution and the depletion of the earth's resources affect us all. But how serious is the problem? To what extent do such activities reduce our well-being? How much does it really matter?

As we analyse these questions we review
- External costs

We introduce
- The circular flow of income
- National income accounts

1 Introduction

Most people know, at least in general terms, what constitutes pollution and it would be reasonable to suppose that most people do not like it and would prefer less to be produced. Yet people, industry, and governments all over the world have witnessed significant pollution levels emerge, and have tolerated them over a substantial period. The quality of the physical environment is reduced over time by increasing levels of pollution, and this is now increasingly recognised. Since people have votes in many societies, governments view such pollution as a matter of concern. More effective and wide-ranging action to combat increasing pollution levels is possible, and is being actively considered or implemented. But are pollution and the quality of the physical environment genuinely related to the functioning of national economies? As we aim to show in this chapter, the answer is yes. The pollution problem is one of genuine concern to economists and economists are actively involved in examining this whole issue.

Pollution is generated as a result of both household and industry activity in fuel combustion and as by-products of manufacturing processes. There are many different types of pollutants which exist in air, water, land, or in some combination of these environmental media. It is also the case that different pollutants have damaging impacts which are more geographically diffuse than others, and damaging impacts which are discernible over very different periods. The timing of the damage ranges from the almost instantaneous (for some highly toxic dangerous pollutants), to decades and centuries (for example, the anticipated damages via climate changes caused by global warming gases).

Damage to the physical environment caused by pollution has real effects that can reduce household welfare and may directly or indirectly increase production costs to industry. For example, river pollution caused by one factory's discharges may necessitate the installation of special water purification devices for a water using factory further downstream. Alternatively, it may lead to increased water purification charges for all water consumers.

Since these damages generate real costs why do most emitters of pollution not take adequate account of these costs when they are engaged in the production activities that generate the pollution? The key reason relates to the nature of the pollution damage costs. We have already seen that such costs are known in economic terms as external costs or negative externalities. They can be said to exist when an economic activity by one party causes a loss to another group. When an externality is present, the loss of welfare for one party is not compensated in any way. This describes the nature of most polluting activity. The right to pollute the environment is still typically not traded in a market. This is sometimes said to be the problem of missing markets. If there are no established market rights to pollute the environment then pollution emitters perceive that the effective 'market price' is zero. We saw from our understanding of demand curves that if the price of some good or service is free, then usually more of it will be wanted than if its price is higher. So a perceived zero price encourages over-consumption of the services of the physical environment.

See pp 132–4

In this chapter we shall focus on the extent of welfare loss implied in such over-consumption. But we shall not be concentrating on individual markets. Our attention will be at the macro-economic level. We shall examine the problem by considering the extent to which we overstate our level of welfare as a society when we ignore the effects of polluting activity.

But we shall also consider the effects on our welfare of running down the stock of the world's resources, through the consumption of oil, minerals, and so on. This is a separate problem but it is still a concern to environmentalists in that it can be argued to be damaging the earth on which human life ultimately depends.

As we consider these matters we shall begin by seeing how economists usually measure the extent of the welfare that we enjoy from the output produced. We shall see that this form of measurement ignores the problems of pollution. Subsequently, we shall consider how we might modify the traditional measures to take account of environmental concerns.

2 The circular flow of incomes

a The independence of firms and households

The link between welfare and production of goods and services can best be seen in the context of what economists call the circular flow of income. We shall explain this in terms of Figure 12.1. The diagram shows pictorially a simplified economy in

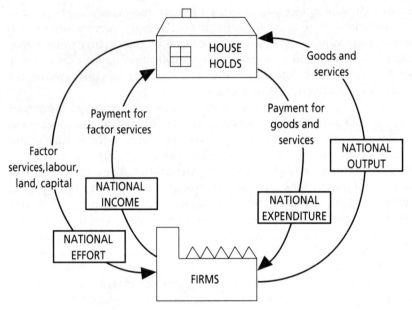

Figure 12.1 The circular flow of income

which is depicted the relationship between household (consumers) and firms. It is in fact a double relationship.

The first relationship is depicted on the right-hand side of the figure. It shows that households purchase a flow of goods and services from firms. Firms provide the products in return for a flow of payments from households.

But how are firms able to produce the output? The left-hand side of the figure gives us the answer. The second relationship is that households provide firms with factor services. For most households this will mean that people will be supplying labour – working for those firms. For others it means supplying capital, through, for example, the purchase of shares. For others it means supplying land. For still other households it may mean the provision of a combination of different factors. In return for the provision of these services firms provide payment as wages and salaries, dividends and rent. These payments provide the income which enables households to purchase goods and services. The relationship is a circular one.[1]

b Measuring the circular flow of income

These exchange relationships are made easier to organise because of money. Money functions as a medium of exchange. Why are you willing to accept money for work done for a firm? The money has no intrinsic value at all! You cannot eat it, travel on it, wear it or live in it. Its value is that it represents a claim on output. It can be used to purchase goods and services which you *do* require. It is the existence of these money flows which have enabled economists to measure the value of goods and services produced and, more controversially, to make a link between such output and consumers' welfare. Let us concentrate first on the measurement of the output. The circular flow of income diagram of Figure 12.1 enables us to see that there are three points at which we can measure this flow of output. First we can measure in money terms the flow of goods and services to households during the year. We refer to this flow of goods as *'national product'*. Second, we can value that flow by considering expenditure upon that year's flow of output. This is called *national expenditure*. Third, we can measure the income earned in producing this flow of output. This is what we call *national income*.

c The place of the environment in the circular flow

We shall need to examine the measurement of national product, income and expenditure and we shall do so shortly. However, first we need to notice that

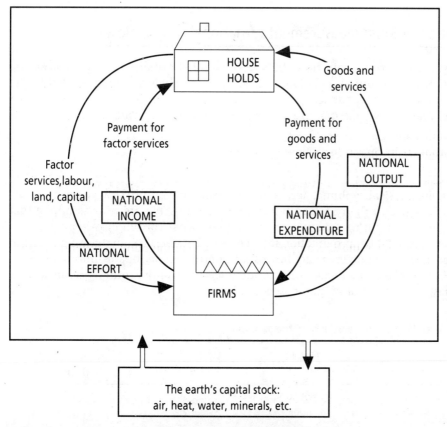

Figure 12.2 The environment and the circular flow of income

what is usually missed from the circular flow of income diagram is any mention of the position of the natural environment.

There is a problem with the circular flow diagram of Figure 12.1. There is an implication that all national output is produced by firms, and that all costs of producing it are met by those firms. In fact this is untrue. Figure 12.2 redraws the circular flow diagram adding in the position of the natural environment. It shows that firms draw upon a 'capital stock' represented by the earth and its resources. Some 'output' is really the selling of that capital stock rather than something which firms have produced themselves. It also shows that some costs of producing output are not met by firms but 'dumped' into the earth's capital stock in the form of pollution of the air and sea and so on.

We turn, in the next section, to how the national output income and expenditure accounts are measured. Having done that we shall be in a position to see how such a procedure might be modified. The purpose of the modification will be to capture the damage done to the environment during the production and consumption of output.

3 The traditional measurement of national output flows

In this section we explain how the size of national product is measured, paying attention to its claim as a measure of welfare. We shall not be interested in the problems of detail that arises in compiling these accounts, but we will concentrate on the major problems that are at issue in producing this data.

a Measuring the flow of output

The basic method of establishing an economy's output is to take each kind of output in physical, volume, terms and to multiply the physical quantity by its price. This gives a figure for output in money terms. We are thus assuming that the value of output to society is represented by what consumers are prepared to pay for it. As a first approximation this seems reasonable. To purchase a good from limited income involves a sacrifice of an alternative, its opportunity cost. So a member of society *must* value the output at least at its price, otherwise the output in question would not be purchased at all.[2]

Table 12.1 Illustrative measure of national output

Industry	Output	Value of output (£ millions)	Value added (£ millions)
Farming	Wheat	10	10
Milling	Flour	25	15
Baking	Bread	55	30

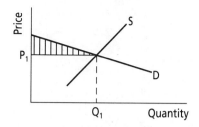

Figure 12.3 Valuing output by price

There is one immediate problem with this assumption. In terms of Figure 12.3, we value each industry's output at P_1Q_1. In fact, as you will recall from Chapter 3, all except the marginal consumer value the output more than that price. This additional value we called *consumer surplus*, shown as the shaded area. The value of the consumer surplus is ignored for the purpose of national income measurement. To that extent the level of national output understates its value to society in terms of its power to satisfy wants.

One way of measuring the value of national output is to consider only output sold to households. Such output is called final output. However, if we listed all final output, we could not observe contributions made by 'intermediate' industries, that is, output sold not to households but to other firms. For example, virtually no steel is bought by households. Most is sold to industries such as the car industry, which in turn sells much to households. So measuring all final output and ignoring intermediate output would imply that the steel industry produces almost nothing whereas the car industry's output is substantial! Both industries contribute to consumer want satisfaction, although the steel industry does it indirectly. So it might be good to present a measure of national output in a way which made clear that this is the case.

An alternative, equivalent, approach to measuring national output, is to list the 'value added' of each industry and this, as the following simple example shows, will give the same value for national output as measuring all final output.

In our example in Table 12.1, farmer Copas grows wheat which sells to millers for £10 million. Miller MacMillan turns the £10 million of wheat into £25 million worth of flour, thus adding £15 million of value. This £25 million of flour is then sold to baker Clarke, who adds £30 million in value and sells it as £55 million of bread. If this were the economy's only output and Copas, MacMillan and Clarke, the only producers, then the national product table would show this national output as in Table 12.2.

This, of course would give the same value of national output as listing only Clarke's bread sales to consumers as £55 million. However, in this form the information we have is much greater.

This 'value added' approach is the one adopted in the official statistics. The values added of all the different industries are given in Table 12.3. The total of all

Table 12.2 Illustrative national product table

	£ millions
Farming	10
Milling	15
Baking	30
National product	55

Table 12.3 National accounts: output measure[1]

	Weight per thousand	1982	1985	1988	1990	1991	1992
Agriculture, hunting, forestry and fishing	19	88.0	95.3	92.1	100.0	103.9	106.0
Production							
Mining and quarrying (inc. oil and gas extraction)	22	124.0	129.4	123.4	100.0	101.0	104.2
Manufacturing (revised definition)	237	77.6	84.5	95.9	100.0	94.7	93.9
Electricity, and gas and water supply	22	81.3	86.5	97.7	100.0	105.9	105.4
Total production	281	80.4	88.0	98.2	100.0	96.0	95.6
Construction	72	65.3	73.0	92.3	100.0	92.1	87.1
Service Industries:							
Distribution, hotels and catering; repairs	142	71.2	81.3	96.9	100.0	95.3	93.9
Transport, storage and communication	84	71.5	80.3	94.2	100.0	97.3	98.6
Other	403	80.5	87.7	98.0	100.0	100.3	100.5
Total services	629	77.1	85.2	97.2	100.0	98.8	98.7
Gross domestic product	1,000	77.4	85.2	97.3	100.0	97.7	97.2

Notes: 1 1990 = 100
Source: CSO, 'Blue Book', 1993.

this output is gross domestic product (GDP). The data is presented not in value terms here (we shall do this when we look at the income and the expenditure method) but in index number form. The years show what has been happening to output in 'real' terms over a period of years. From what we have said so far you will appreciate that over time the value of output can change for two reasons. It can change because the quantity of outputs has changed or because the general level of prices of the outputs has altered. Table 12.3 has removed the effect of inflation and shows changes only if they are the result of changes in the actual level of output. This we call real output. We say that we are measuring the output at constant prices. The value of the output in 1990 for each industry was given the number 100. What has happened over time to real output changes can then be easily established. Take, the first item for example, agriculture, hunting forestry and fishing. In 1990 the index number was 100. By 1992 it was 106. So output in that industry, value added in real terms, rose by 6 per cent over the course of those two years.

Notice that real output does not always increase. For construction, for example the index number for the early 1990s has been less than 100. Real output from that sector rose through the 1980s only to decline in the recession of the early 1990s.

Another thing to note from Table 12.3 concerns a problem of using market prices to establish values for output. Not all products and services are sold through a market. For example one of the item included in services is 'Public Administration, and national defence. However, we cannot measure these items at market prices, since they are not distributed on such a basis. How, then, can we place a value on this output? In the accounts they are valued at the cost of their provision. If a soldier is paid £20,000 per annum as a wage, the assumption is made that he provides £20,000 worth of national security for society during that year. You can decide for yourself how realistic this assumption is. If you think it is unrealistic, you will not find it easy to think of a better alternative!

Gross domestic product represents the value of the output produced within the borders of the UK during a given year. However, some output produced by British resources is produced overseas. Some oil extraction, for example, takes place in other countries with British capital, such as British owned oil rigs. As a result there is an inflow into this country of profit dividends and interest which represents the volume of 'our' output produced outside our borders.

Similarly, some output produced in Britain is produced with foreign owned resources. For example, Japanese car companies produce cars in Britain. Part of this output is British. After all, many British workers contributed to its production. Part of the value of this car output is really Japanese. This part is represented by the flow of profit, dividends and interest *out* of Britain to Japan. So for Britain, as for other countries, there is an inflow of profits, dividends and interest and an outflow. The net flow we call net property income from abroad (NPIA).

Gross domestic product plus NPIA is called gross *national* product (GNP). This figure is not shown in Table 12.3 but *is* shown in the expenditure methods of calculation which we shall consider shortly.

We need to consider one other item in this measure of output, which will form a particularly important part of our thoughts about the damage to the environment shortly. It is this. The measure of the output we have considered takes no account of the wear and tear of machinery in producing output. This is the meaning of the term 'gross'. It means that before allowing for such capital consumption, an estimate is made of the extent to which the value of capital has been reduced in all industries during the year. This can then be subtracted from the gross figure to get net domestic product. Again, this is not shown in Table 12.3, but we will give a value for it when considering the expenditure approach to measuring output. However we shall find that this capital consumption value ignores all the costs of damage to the earth that we mentioned earlier. We shall return to this matter shortly.

b Measuring the flow of income

An alternative way of valuing output is to value the income derived in producing it. Since we are measuring the same flow at a different point on the circular flow diagram of Figure 12.1, we may expect to arrive at the same total value. Income is income earned in producing output.

Let us illustrate, with a particular example, why this must be so. Consider again Miller MacMillan who, as you will remember from Table 12.2, produced flour as her contribution to national output. She received £25 million for the sale of the flour and spent £10 million of it buying wheat from farmer Copas. We recorded her national output contributions as a value added of £15 million. What did she do with this £15 million? She will have spent some of it on the wages of those she employed. Some will have paid for the rent of the land. Some will be left over for profit to distribute to shareholders. In other words, all of the £15 million must be an income to some factor of production involved in the production of the output. Therefore national output will equal national income. There is one important proviso. When calculating national income we must be sure only to count income earned in producing the national product. Incomes to groups such as pensioners and students will *not* be counted because it is not a factor income. It has been transferred from other factors of production whose income has been taxed. Such 'transfer incomes' are excluded from the accounts.

Table 12.4 lists the incomes earned in producing the output. The statistical discrepancy apart, the sum of all these factor incomes, gross domestic income must be the same as gross domestic product. Notice that the data given here is in current prices. No attempt has been made to take out the effects of inflation on the data. So incomes seem to have risen rapidly during the last 10 years or so. However, this is money income. Real incomes, incomes after allowing for the effect of inflation, have risen much more slowly.

Table 12.4 National accounts: income measure at current prices (£m)

	1982	1985	1988	1990	1991	1992
Income from employment	158,838	196,858	255,634	312,358	328,257	341,009
Income from self-employment	21,778	29,929	46,362	60,443	58,139	57,980
Gross trading profits of companies	27,665	48,991	58,631	59,432	59,311	62,469
Gross trading surplus of public corporations	9,099	7,154	7,295	3,681	1,779	1,782
Gross trading surplus of general government enterprises	216	265	−32	12	−36	89
Rent	17,700	21,875	29,904	38,569	43,021	46,846
Imputed charge for consumption of non-trading capital	2,426	2,830	3,634	4,391	4,363	4,207
Statistical discrepancy (income adjustment)	663	—	—	—	−10	212
Gross domestic product at factor cost	238,385	307,902	401,428	478,886	494,824	514,594

Source: CSO, 'Blue Book', 1993.

You may well feel that you are not interested only in the size of the income but in its distribution. Have all gained equally from rising incomes? The tables do not help with such a question but it is an important one which we shall consider further in Chapter 16.

See pp 310–29

Gross *national* income can be found by adding the net property income from abroad. Net national income can then be found by subtracting capital consumption. The value of these items we shall discover when we consider our third and last measure of national output, the expenditure method.

c Measuring the flow of expenditure

The final method of calculating the value of output produced is to examine *expenditure* on that output. Since all output is purchased by some person or agent the value of national output will be equal to the value of national expenditure.

We can see the items of national expenditure with reference to Table 12.5.

Who purchases the output which Britain produces? Most of it is purchased by households, listed in the table as consumers' expenditure. This item covers a vast array of expenditures on food, clothing, travel, entertainment, and so on.

Some output is purchased by government, some of it by central government, the rest by local authorities. Some is purchased by firms as capital equipment – buildings, machinery, and so on. This is called gross domestic fixed capital formation. It is 'gross' in that it makes no distinction between the replacement of

Table 12.5 National accounts: Expenditure measure

	1982	1985	1988	1990	1991	1992
AT 1990 MARKET PRICES						
Consumers' expenditure	249,852	276,742	334,591	347,527	339,993	339,941
General government final consumption	102,146	105,097	108,612	112,934	115,797	116,002
of which: Central Government	64,260	66,241	67,588	70,108	71,950	72,189
Local authorities	37,886	38,856	41,024	42,826	43,847	43,813
Gross domestic fixed capital formation	68,404	81,575	104,726	106,776	96,265	95,241
Value of physical increase in stocks and work in progress	-2,084	1,336	5,532	-1,118	-4,722	-1,773
Total domestic expenditure	417,916	464,316	553,461	566,119	547,333	549,411
Exports of goods and services	94,996	109,163	121,197	133,284	132,114	135,547
of which: Goods	68,724	80,250	90,508	101,718	102,898	105,165
Services	26,441	28,883	30,689	31,566	29,216	30,382
Total final expenditure	512,372	573,567	674,658	699,403	679,447	684,958
less Imports of goods and services	-88,146	-105,957	-137,443	-148,285	-140,248	-148,271
of which: Goods	-67,771	-84,825	-111,360	-120,527	-114,101	-121,611
Services	-20,849	-21,189	-26,083	-27,758	-26,147	-26,660
Statistical discrepancy (expenditure adjustment)	-840	–	–	–	-430	-427
Gross domestic product	425,252	468,071	537,215	551,118	538,769	536,260
Net property income from abroad	1,899	2,458	4,872	1,630	319	5,742
Gross national product	426,585	469,976	542,087	552,748	539,088	542,002
AT 1990 FACTOR COST						
Gross domestic product at market prices	425,252	468,071	537,215	551,118	538,769	536,260
less Factor cost adjustment	-54,846	-60,310	-71,469	-72,232	-71,049	-70,614
Gross domestic product at factor cost	370,493	407,844	465,746	478,886	467,720	465,646
Net proprty income from abroad	1,899	2,458	4,872	1,630	319	5,742
Gross national product at factor cost	371,804	409,714	470,618	480,516	468,039	471,388
less Capital consumption	-52,001	-56,214	-59,780	-61,200	-62,642	-63,489
Net national product at factor cost (national income)	319,803	353,531	410,838	419,316	405,397	407,899

Source: CSO Blue Book, 1993.

Note: Amounts are in £million at 1990 prices.

worn out capital stock and new additions to capital – both are included. It is 'domestic' in that it is for firms in this country. It is 'fixed' in that it is the purchase of plant and machinery as distinct from investing in stocks of finished goods.

All these items taken together consumption, government expenditure and investment, represent *domestic* expenditure. However, some of our output is purchased by foreigners. So foreign demand exports are also included as national expenditure. The sum of all these items gives total 'final' expenditure. It is expenditure on final output. It does *not* include expenditure by firms on the purchase of 'intermediate' goods, or goods bought by one firm from another.[3]

Some consumers' expenditure, government expenditure and investment expenditure has been made on foreign goods and services. These are *not* items of expenditure on British output. To the extent that we import we have overstated the amount of such expenditures on British firms' output. Hence the table shows a subtraction of import expenditure. If this seems odd at first, remember that we are not measuring expenditure by British citizens but expenditure on British output.

So the sum of expenditure by consumers investment government and exports minus import expenditure gives us gross domestic expenditure. Subtracting NPIA as before gives gross national expenditure, where all these expenditures are at the appropriate market prices, the prices actually paid by those who purchase.

However we still have to consider the meaning of the heading 'Factor Cost Adjustment'. We have argued in earlier chapters that the logic of a market system is that prices should reflect opportunity cost. We have shown that opportunity cost will be the opportunity cost of the factor incomes used in producing output. But governments distort that relationship when taxing certain goods and subsidising others.

For national income accounting purposes we wish to value expenditure as the expenditure at the factor cost of producing, say, a packet of cigarettes. This might be about 80p for a packet of 20, but the tax means that the market price is £2.20. The expenditure items in the accounts have so far been valued at market prices, which includes the tax. The factor cost adjustment therefore removes these indirect taxes, valuing the output at the resource cost.

The mirror image of this problem is government subsidies. The effect of such subsidies is to reduce prices below factor cost. Since expenditure items have been at the 'distorted' price, we have to add subsidies to produce expenditure at factor cost. The adjustment of subtracting indirect taxes and adding subsidies gives us gross domestic expenditure which will be identically equal to gross domestic income and product.

Table 12.5 also shows an estimate for capital consumption. By subtracting this item we get *net* national product, income and expenditure.

d Using national output estimates as a guide to welfare

We have now seen how economists attempt to measure the size of national output. Many economists believe that this measure is the best guide we have on which to base estimates of welfare. Since prices reflect people's willingness to pay, we can value the output produced. All other things being equal, the more output we produce the more welfare society has.

Of course, the usefulness of this measure is limited. We need to know what size of population this output supports. In other words, we need to look at income *per head*. Nevertheless, that figure would still not tell us how income is distributed. Furthermore, it is a measure which ignores other non-monetary sources of welfare. There is no perfect correlation between income and contentment. Nevertheless it is this measure which is widely used as a link to welfare. Thus if we could improve it in some way, it would be most helpful. It is to that which we now turn.

4 Environmental pollution and the national income accounts

One seemingly obvious way of improving the measuring of welfare is to take into account the depletion of the earth's resources and the degradation of the environment which economic activity causes. Much thought has been given, in recent years, to doing just that. As yet there is little to show for the effort. It is a procedure fraught with difficulty. Yet in principle the procedure would appear to be very simple. We already measure 'capital consumption'. To the extent that resources have to be committed to the replacement of worn out capital stock, economic welfare is reduced. Why do we not simply extend this analysis? We could count environmental degradation as a depletion of society's capital stock and show net national product as net of such degradation.

In fact there are substantial problems associated with this seemingly simple idea. We shall consider the main ones. In this section we shall deal with the problems of building estimates of pollution damage into the accounts. Later we shall briefly consider the problems associated with the depletion of mineral deposits, and so on. First, then, let us look at problems associated with measuring the reduction in welfare caused by pollution activities.

a The non-linearity of pollution damage

Machines wear out. When more output is produced from them, the value of that capital stock declines proportionately. Much environmental pollution damage is unlike that. In terms of Figure 12.2 the earth's capital stock can absorb some output waste at minimal cost. But beyond a critical point serious depletion sets in. Two examples will illustrate the point.

Environmental pollution has reduced the thickness of the eggshells of birds of prey. Figure 12.4 shows, in particular, the postwar effects of the pesticide DDT usage on the shell thickness for one bird, the merlin. The effect of the DDT was to reduce thickness by around 15 per cent. Merlins, however, continued to breed, so

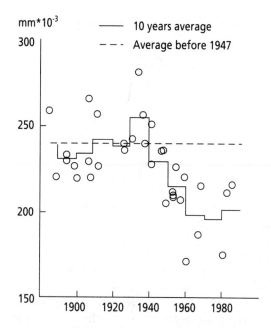

mm*10⁻³ cannot...

Source: OECD, *Economic Survey* of Europe, 1993.

Figure 12.4 Eggshell thickness of the Merlin, 1885–1993.

there appears to be no problem. In fact there is a real difficulty. Such a reduction has brought the shell's thickness close to the point where further deterioration will cause the shell to break when the parents sit on the egg during incubation. Should this happen the chicks will not hatch and the merlin population would be decimated. If the pollution problem were to become a little worse, we could move from apparently minimal effects to catastrophic effects in this instance.

A second, though controversial, example may prove to be global warming. A rise in the ocean's temperature of a part of one degree may be apparently irrelevant. Just a small increase in warming might, at some critical point, cause a rise in the sea level sufficient to engulf a whole island. Again the damage to the environment is non-linear.

Here is our first problem of measuring environmental damage. It is not a linear function of output. So placing a value on the reduction of the earth's capital stock is extremely difficult.

b Avoiding a mess or clearing it up?

There is a second problem in measuring environmental pollution damage. It involves one aspect of the problem of *damage valuation*. The statistical office of the

United Nations has suggested a measure of welfare called 'green domestic product'. This is arrived at in the following way.

GDP – capital consumption (conventionally valued) = NDP.

NDP – natural capital depreciation = green domestic product.

The United Nations Statistical Office (UNSO) then goes on to suggest a method of calculating natural capital depreciation, based upon the cost of avoiding a reduction in the earth's capital stock. At first this seems unambiguous. That is far from the case. Suppose an industry discharges a poisonous chemical into the river, causing damage to fish and making the water unsuitable for alternative uses such as drinking. The United Nations Statistical Office suggestion is effectively that we reduce the value of the natural capital stock by the cost involved in not incurring the pollution. In other words the degradation of the capital stock equals the loss of the output from the resources needed in using a more expensive, less environmentally destructive way of producing the output.

It is possible that the cost of avoiding the pollution would have been quite small. It might have involved rendering the poison harmless by adding some additional chemical. Measured in this way the amount of capital depreciation is small. However, since the firm did not have to incur the clean-up costs – the cost was an external cost – it chose not to be environmentally friendly. The cost of cleaning up the mess once caused was far higher than the cost of prevention.

An alternative approach, then, to the measurement of environmental damage, would be to reduce the green capital stock by an amount equal to the cost of clearing up the mess. This could be argued to be a more realistic alternative if the damage has already been done. This gives a much higher figure than UNSO's.

c International pollution

When governments consider the level of welfare enjoyed by their citizens, they may well want to know how much that welfare is reduced by the capital stock depletion costs we have been considering. Knowing what these costs are enables appropriate action to deal with the problems. Sometimes, however, governments are virtually powerless to do anything about it. This is because the pollution is created by output generating activities in other countries! One severe case of such a problem is that of Scandinavia.

Consider Tables 12.6 and 12.7. They give estimates of the production of some key pollutants, oxides of sulphur, SO_x and oxidants of nitrogen, NO_x which react with water to create acid rain. These acids are responsible, among other things, for damage to forests, a matter of particular concern to Scandinavian countries. Notice that the countries who do the emitting are not always those doing the receiving! Norway emitted, in 1990, 21,000 tons of SO_x and received 159,000 tons mostly borne from Europe on the prevailing winds. The EC was a net 'exporter' of such pollutants, emitting 6,316,000 tons of SO_x and 2443 tons of NO_x in 1990. It received less at 3,799,000 tons of SO_x and 1134 tons of NO^x.

Receivers	Norway	Other Nordic	EC United Kingdom	West Germany	East Germany	Other EC	USSR	Eastern Europe	Poland	CSFR	Other Eastern	Others	Total
							Emitters						
Norway	8	4	70 36	14	4	15	11	12	7	4	2	54	159
Other Nordic[2]	3	76	120 36	45	11	29	66	53	35	13	5	104	422
EEC	0	2	3,092 653	856	244	1,339	15	294	80	126	88	396	3,799
United Kingdom	0	0	508 478	7	3	20	1	3	2	2	0	37	548
West Germany	0	0	710 16	643	28	23	2	73	19	52	2	19	804
East Germany	0	0	436 49	120	161	105	3	62	23	35	4	40	551
Others	0	1	1,438 111	86	52	1,190	9	156	37	37	82	291	1,895
USSR	1	32	375 52	228	32	63	1,924	727	404	128	196	557	3,617
Eastern Europe	0	3	777 42	537	55	144	68	2,628	895	580	1,153	223	3,700
Poland	0	2	4126 26	328	28	34	20	910	741	130	40	60	1,409
Czech and Slovak Federal Republic	0	0	171 8	130	15	19	3	474	68	357	50	26	675
Others[3]	0	1	190 8	80	12	90	44	1,244	87	93	1,064	137	1,616
Others	8	45	1,882 619	266	82	917	241	560	183	120	258	1,560	4,295
Total	21	162	6,316 1,438	1,945	428	2,506	2,325	4,274	1,603	970	1,701	2,893	15,992

Notes: [1] Amounts are in 1,000 tons, 1990. [2] Finland, Iceland, Sweden. [3] Bulgaria, Hungary, Rumania, Yugoslavia.
Source: The Norwegian Meteorological Institute.

Table 12.7 Sources of emissions and deposits of NO$_x$ in Europe[1] (1,000 tons, 1990)

Receivers	Norway	Other Nordic	EC	United Kingdom	West Germany	East Germany	Other EC	USSR	Eastern Europe	Poland	CSFR	Other Eastern	Others	Total
Norway	6	5	60	26	3	12	18	2	5	3	2	1	21	98
Other Nordic[2]	7	38	95	28	11	27	29	17	18	12	5	1	39	213
EEC	2	3	897	155	47	229	466	5	64	21	28	15	163	1,134
United Kingdom	0	0	78	56	2	6	14	0	1	1	1	0	14	94
West Germany	0	1	91	10	17	42	22	1	11	4	7	0	9	113
East Germany	1	1	225	30	14	103	78	1	15	6	9	1	25	267
Others	1	1	503	60	14	78	352	3	35	10	11	14	116	660
USSR	4	38	241	37	46	86	72	332	185	112	40	33	168	968
Eastern Europe	1	6	344	29	67	124	123	19	267	99	73	95	85	722
Poland	1	4	156	18	40	62	37	6	95	61	27	7	26	287
Czech and Slovak Federal Republic	0	1	71	5	14	33	19	1	42	13	22	7	12	128
Others[3]	0	1	117	6	14	30	68	12	130	25	25	81	47	307
Others	13	30	807	236	40	150	380	49	102	39	30	33	413	1,414
Total	33	119	2,443	512	214	629	1,088	425	640	286	177	178	890	4,550

Notes: [1] Amounts are in 1,000 tons, 1990. [2] Finland, Iceland, Sweden. [3] Bulgaria, Hungary, Rumania, Yugoslavia Institute.
Source: The Norwegian Meteorological Institute.

In one sense it does not matter much where such pollution was created. Its presence in Norway still reduces the country's net welfare. In another sense it matters a great deal. If the purpose of constructing green accounts is a first step towards a national decision-making process of *doing* something about the problem, it matters greatly if governments are unwilling importers of other people's pollution.

It seems then that pollution damage can have serious effects on welfare. Clearly, some acknowledgement of those effects in estimates of national output would be of benefit to policy makers. Alas the problems of incorporating such estimates into the tables are formidable.

5 Resource depletion and the national income accounts

A related but separate problem is that raised by our extraction and use of the earth's stock of oil and mineral deposits. Are we not depleting the earth's capital stock while pretending that we are not doing so, if our national income accounts make no mention of such activities? It is this issue that we now examine.

a The case for doing nothing

The argument for taking a relaxed view of the decline in natural resource stocks is based on a confidence in the market system to deal with scarcity. Suppose oil stocks are run down rapidly. The reduction in the available supply will drive up the relative price of the product. A higher relative price will draw forth alternative sources of energy not previously profitable at the lower price. For example, the USA has vast resources of shale oil, which is not at present worth exploiting because the costs are too great relative to the price. But if oil prices rise sufficiently, the output from such sources will become profitable.

One could widen the argument to include other sources of energy. Wind power, wave power and solar power are all sources of energy that could be used. At present they are used very little, since energy prices are lower than the opportunity costs of the resources involved in enhancing such power. If other, cheaper, energy sources are nearing exhaustion, relative price changes will bring forth these alternative supplies.

Pessimists have for years concerned themselves over a future 'energy gap'. This concern is based on estimates that the demands for energy will grow faster than its supply. Some might argue that this will only happen if relative prices do not alter. However, such an energy gap will alter energy prices sufficiently to eliminate the gap. Shortages are simply a reflection of disequilibrium relative prices. On this view, the problem of resource depletion can be ignored.

Others remain unconvinced. Sir John Hicks argued that income should be considered as whatever one can consume while remaining as well off at the end of the period as at the beginning. In other words, capital depletion does matter to society. The problem is that even for those who *do* believe that resource depletion is a serious problem, there is little consensus about how to measure it, as we shall now see.

b Measuring changes in the natural capital stock

If we are going to count resource depletion as part of capital depreciation to help produce a 'green GDP', how we are going to value the decline in such stocks? There are many possibilities but there are three main options which we can illustrate from Figure 12.5 with respect to UK oil and gas reserves.

Option one is to assume that the nation's capital stock has been reduced by whatever is the value of the output oil and gas. This suggests that capital depletion with respect to oil and gas was around £20 million per year in 1985.

Option two shows a lower figure for national capital depreciation. Not all the value of the output is national capital. Part of the value is man-made. It came from the use of man-made oil rigs and oil pipelines. People were involved in taking the naturally occurring oil and 'adding value' to it. On this view, only the value of the oil and gas should be included in the depreciation estimates. The 'value added' by the industry is *not* part of such natural capital consumption. Two different methods of calculation are given for this option, shown in Figure 12.5 as 'depreciation' and 'excess profit'.

A third and final option remains to be considered. This is the 'user cost' option, which as you can see from Figure 12.5, gives the lowest value to the extent of

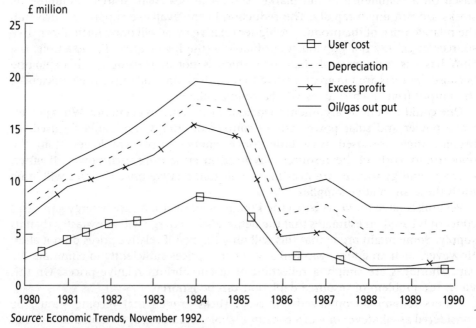

Source: Economic Trends, November 1992.

Figure 12.5 Evaluating oil and gas reserve depletion

resource depletion. Not all of the used natural capital stock is 'wasted'. Some income can be reinvested in other forms of capital equipment. This will produce a flow of income for society. Hence part of the resource depletion is not depletion at all. It is changing one form of capital into another. If this argument is accepted, the extent of measured capital depreciation will be smaller.

You can see, then, that the degree of concern about the effect of production and consumption on the environment varies between economists. But even within the increasingly large group expressing concern about these effects, there is no unanimity about how all this should be represented in the national accounts. The differences of outlook produce very different estimates. For example, between 1977 and 1990 welfare measured by GNP per head rose by about 30 per cent in the UK. The New Economics Foundation, a green economics think-tank, measures welfare by its 'Index of Social Welfare'. This is an index based on a variety of measures of welfare, including environmental degradation, noise, pollution levels and the cost of commuting. This index, which was broadly in line with the more conventional measure for the previous 27 years, suggested a fall in welfare of 4 per cent between 1977 and 1990.

6 Conclusion

We have seen that economists do have a measure of welfare of a country's citizens. It is based upon valuing the flow of output that is produced. That flow can be measured at any of three points in the circular flow of income. This gives us national product, national income and national expenditure, which will all be identically equal.

The best measure of welfare is national output per head of population. That output should be after allowance has been made for capital depreciation. In recent years attention has been given to attempts to incorporate environmental degradation in the estimates of capital depreciation, but this is fraught with difficulties. As yet there is no agreement about how this should be done. Since governments are always interested in making comparisons of their own country's economic performance with other countries, we are unlikely to have in the near future published environmental accounts that are taken seriously. This will require international agreements about how to incorporate such information into the data. Meanwhile, we must make do with an imperfect measure of welfare based on traditional national income accounting.

7 Questions for discussion

1 The ignoring of consumer surplus in the calculation of national output is an example of how the figures *understate* the level of a country's welfare. Ignoring the damage to the earth *overstates* it. What other factors make the use of national output a poor judge of welfare?

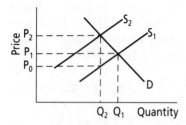

Figure 12.6 Taxing a pollution creating firm

2 A government imposes a tax on a competitive industry on which is polluting the environment. This changes its price output decision as shown in Figure 12.6. According to the national *expenditure* tables what is the value of the output (a) before the tax (b) after the tax?

3 One way for government to tackle the problem of ecological damage is to make society aware that it is in its own interest to behave responsibly towards the environment. Why are most economists sceptical about this particular kind of appeal to self-interest to reduce such damage?

4 Why do economists sometimes refer to pollution as an 'untraded' interdependency. (HINT: When firms trade between themselves in the production of intermediate goods, this is a traded interdependency.) What light does this shed on methods of dealing with polluting activities of firms?

5 Re-read section 4(b). Suppose environmental tax was placed on the river polluter. Which measure of valuation of green capital stock depletion would be greater?

6 Is a zero level of pollution a desirable goal?

8 Further reading

The circular flow of income
Sloman, pp. 14–15; 295–6; 529–33; Begg. pp. 343–5; Parkin and King, pp. 560–6

National income accounts
Sloman, pp. 579–95; Begg. pp. 345–58; Parkin and King, pp. 566–77

Damaging the Earth: How much does it really matter?
E. Lutz and M. Munasinghe (1991) 'Accounting for the environment', *Finance and Development*, March.
C. Bryant and P. Cook (1992) 'Environment issues and the national accounts', *Economic Trends*, November.

9 End notes

1 We said that Figure 12.1 represents a simplified economy. The main simplifications are (a) individual households spend all income received, making no provision for saving, (b) all income is actually received. In reality some is taken by government in taxation, (c) there is no international trade. Income is spent on domestic production and domestic firms receive no orders from overseas. All these simplifications will be removed in a later chapter.

2 We have assumed here an optimal distribution of income. Recall from earlier chapters, particularly Chapter 4, that the demand curve reflects not only willingness to pay, but also ability to pay.

3 The existence of international trade will, as we have already said, mean that the circular flow diagram needs to be a little more complex. We shall make Figure 12.1 more realistic in the next chapter.

CHAPTER 13

Unemployment:
what can the government do?

Millions of people in Britain and throughout Europe have no job. Many want one but they feel that there is little prospect of finding one. Unemployment is not simply a waste of resources but a human problem of considerable proportions. What can the government do? Is there no way in which government policy could improve the situation?

In this chapter we review
- National income accounts
- The circular flow of income

We introduce
- Keynesian unemployment equilibrium
- Injections and withdrawals
- The multiplier
- The paradox of thrift

1 Introduction

a The scale of the problem

Unemployment is a serious social problem. It has a dramatic effect upon the living standards of the people and their families involved. It can also have the debilitating effects of making people feel worthless and inadequate. On a national scale it is a waste of resources. The opportunity cost of increased output is zero. This, of course, is true of any resource, including unemployed land or capital but at least a machine has no feelings of despair about the future.

Some ideas of the scale of the problem of unemployed labour can be seen from Figure 13.1 where some important aspects of the problem are illustrated. Consider the position in the UK. First, unemployment can be very high. For substantial periods over the last 10 years it has been over three million, or over 10 per cent of the workforce. Second, the level of employment can vary greatly over time; at least for some parts of the world. In the UK, it was only around half a million in 1973. Third, the position can change very quickly, for example, in the third quarter of 1992, 382,000 jobs were lost, representing a 1.75 per cent decline in

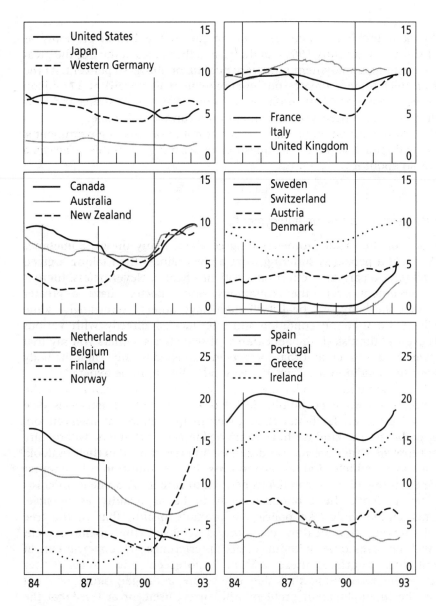

Source: BIS Annual Report, 1993.

Figure 13.1 The unemployment picture (percentages)

three months. Finally, the problem appears to be worsening over time. Even during a boom in the late 1980s in Britain unemployment remained at over 1.5 million, three times its 1973 level. In the European boom of the late 1970s, EC unemployment was 5.4 per cent. At the subsequent 1990 peak it was 8.3 per cent.

Unemployment problems, then, are not unique to the British economy as Figure 13.1 shows. In the early 1990s, of the 12 member states of the EU, the great majority have had unemployment rates very near to, or above 10 per cent. At the beginning of 1994 some estimates put unemployment in the EU at 17 million people. It is not even a problem confined to Europe. Canada, Australia and New Zealand all have experienced unemployment on a considerable scale.

To say that there is a real problem, however, is not to say that a government is in a position to do much about it. The question we wish to raise is this: *what* can a government do about it?

b Economists' perspectives on unemployment

Most members of the medical profession agree about many things. Sometimes they agree that if a person is suffering from a given illness then taking a given medicine will have a particular effect on a patient's health. Nevertheless, there is much less agreement over other conditions. Some doctors have a greater confidence that the body will heal itself than have others. Accordingly, some doctors will advise that the condition must be tackled directly with various treatments even at the risk of the appearance of side effects. Others will say that the important thing is to see to it that the person is in good health. Then the body can deal with the condition itself. In that way side effects can be avoided.

One could say something similar about the problems being diagnosed by the economics profession. Some economists feel that markets, left to themselves, deal with almost all problems far better than government attempts at intervention. Only a few problems, the kind we have examined in earlier chapters, will require government control. Other economists are more 'interventionist' in their outlook.

Now one issue which divides economists is the question of whether unemployment is one of those conditions best left to cure itself. Some economists feel that the 'patient', the economy, needs to be as healthy as possible. Governments should undertake policies to promote health, that is, the free working of markets. If a healthy economy is achieved, the unemployment problem will be overcome without direct interference by government. If government does interfere, there will be unforeseen side effects. Other economists, while recognising that side effects are a danger, simply do not believe that the unemployment problem will correct itself, or at least that the correction process is far too slow.

There is a view, then, that markets can do many things but that they cannot be relied upon to bring about full employment at a reasonable speed. Government involvement is required. This is a view that was expressed most forcefully by John Maynard Keynes. Those who share this basic outlook, while not in agreement about everything, are known as Keynesians. In this chapter we shall examine the Keynesian view. We shall see how it can be argued that a market system can give rise to lasting unemployment, and that governments can intervene, helping to eliminate it. An alternative view, critical of the Keynesian position will be considered in a later chapter.

See pp 302–6

c Major reasons for unemployment

In Britain the amount of unemployment in the economy is measured by the Department of Employment. The figures quoted by this department are adults who are not employed and who are claiming unemployment benefit. Why do millions of people find themselves in this position? Several reasons can be found.

First, there is *frictional* unemployment. Markets do not work instantaneously. Some people may leave one job and not take up another for a period of weeks. Meanwhile they claim benefits as unemployed people.

Second, there is *seasonal* unemployment. Many find work in the summer in tourist areas but are unemployed in the winter months. A proportion of those employed in the construction industry are out of a job if the weather is severe in the winter.

A third category is *structural* unemployment. If demand for the output of an industry falls rapidly, labour inputs are no longer required. A fall in product demand causes unemployment in that industry. The decline in the demand for coal causing a large amount of unemployed miners is a problem we have already considered in Chapter 7. Some of the problems of regional unemployment which we examined in Chapter 5 are structural in origin.

See pp 128–48

See pp 88–108

Fourth there is *voluntary* unemployment. Some are unemployed because they do not wish to work at the wage rate being offered to them but would prefer to do nothing and live on state benefits. Much controversy surrounds the question of the extent of this kind of unemployment. It is an issue to which we shall return in Chapter 16.

See pp 317–23

There is another, fifth, kind of unemployment upon which we shall focus in this chapter, namely *demand-deficient* unemployment. By this we mean that people can be unemployed because the volume of demand for goods and services in the whole economy, what we refer to as 'aggregate' demand is simply not high enough for all those seeking a job to be able to find one. It is important to understand that it is not the lack of demand in one particular area of economic activity that is the problem, but the lack of demand in the economy as a whole. If the demand for output is, in some sense, too low, the demand for labour, which is a demand derived from the demand for output, will also be low. Under these circumstances this unemployment will need government policies to change that demand for output. That is the concept that forms the heart of this chapter. It is a controversial concept. Some economists, those whose views are especially Keynesian, accept the proposition that governments must manipulate the volume of demand for aggregate output. Others, whom we might call *classical economists*, believe that government attempts to deal with the problem of such unemployment through 'demand management' are worse than useless. It is to give a patient a medicine with unpleasant side effects when he would recover naturally and unaided. Much of this chapter follows the logic of the Keynesian argument and explains how demand might be manipulated, although we will indicate why the classical economists dissent from these views. In later chapters we shall develop the neoclassical view more fully.

2 Equilibrium output in Keynesian thinking

a Planned and actual demand

See pp 230–37

If you think back to Chapter 12 you will recall that we saw that national expenditure is always of the same value as national output. Whatever is produced there is an expenditure on it by someone or some organisation. However, not all that expenditure is necessarily intended. If a car manufacturer produces a car, it is included in the national output table. Suppose nobody wanted to buy it and the car remained unsold? In the national expenditure account the car appears as a stock item. Essentially, then, it is regarded as an item that the firm itself has purchased as part of its stocks for selling later. The firm may not have *intended* to 'purchase' the car for holding as stocks; it may have wanted to sell it. Actual output was not equal to *planned* expenditure. However, actual output was equal to actual expenditure. Now what is true of the company's car production can be true of an economy's output. The national income accounts will always show that actual national output equals actual national expenditure. But what happens in an economy if *plans* to purchase output, *planned* expenditure, is not equal to the actual output produced?

We can examine this question by referring to Figure 13.2. Consider first the curve labelled 'planned aggregate expenditure'. Plans to purchase output come from consumers, firms (as demand for investment goods), governments, and foreigners who wish to buy British goods (export demand). To the extent that part of the demand for output is met by import demand, planned expenditure on British goods and services is reduced by the amount of planned import demand. Now, the higher national income is, the higher will be plans to purchase output. This is shown in Figure 13.2. The figure illustrates the aggregate of planned expenditure at all possible levels of national income.

Notice that this relationship is shown such that even at a low income there is some expenditure. Some forms of government spending take place whatever the level of income even if it means borrowing. Similarly individuals must spend on basic needs whatever their income, either by borrowing or 'dissaving', that is running down assets that they previously acquired. Such planned spending which is independent of the level of income we call 'autonomous expenditure'. The expenditure which economic agents are induced to make as income rises we refer to as 'induced' expenditure.

Now consider the line in Figure 13.2 drawn at 45°. It will have the same value on the horizontal axis as on the vertical axis. In other words, it shows the actual

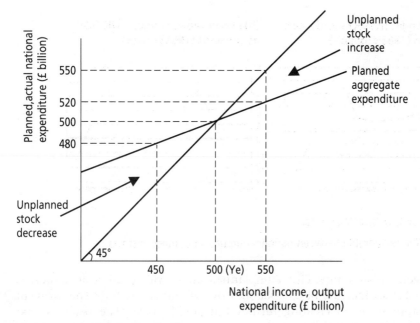

Figure 13.2 Equilibrium national output

output must equal actual expenditure. So, for example at a national income of £550 billion *actual* national expenditure must also be £550 billion. But we have seen that for an economy to be in equilibrium planned expenditure must equal actual output. Is there any value of national output at which plans to spend will be the same as real output? You can see from the diagram that there is only one such level, and that is £500 billion. At this level of output plans to purchase are equal to the amount of output being produced. This is the equilibrium level of output, Ye. The economy is in equilibrium because the amount people wish to purchase equals the amount firms wish to produce.

b Stable equilibrium

Before we see the significance of this for unemployment there is one other point we must note because it is of great importance. Ye is not only an equilibrium level of output, it is also a stable equilibrium. In Chapter 2 we defined equilibrium as a state of rest and stability as a condition such that movements away from equilibrium were self-correcting. We can see the same principle at work here in a different context. Suppose national output were to rise from £500 billion to £550 billion. Planned expenditure is now £520 billion (see Figure 13.2 again) and actual expenditure is £550 billion. So £30 billion more output is being produced than

See p 36

(a) UK Changes in stocks and work in progress (1985 £ billion)

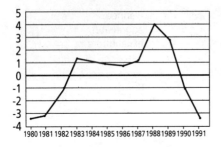

(b) Percentage change in UK GDP at constant (1985) prices

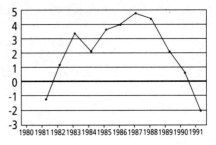

Source: Based on CSO 'Blue Book' data.

Figure 13.3 The relationship between national output and changes in stocks

economic agents wish to buy. Firms' unplanned stocks will be rising since there is an unplanned stock increase of £30 billion. How will firms respond? They will cut back on output to avoid creating further unwanted stocks. The result is that national output will fall. Only at a national output of £500 billion will this problem disappear.

What if national output were to be only £450 billion? You should be able to see how equilibrium is restored. We shall not stop to deal with this question now, since you are asked to work it out for yourself in the questions for discussion at the end of this chapter.

Some idea of the relationship between national output and changes in stocks can be seen in Figure 13.3. Notice how the recession in the British economy of the late 1980s and into the 1990s is clearly visible. Stock levels were building to a peak in 1988. By 1990 stock changes were negative, that is stock levels were falling. National income fell back sharply as firms cut back on stocks and reduced output.

c Equilibrium and unemployment

We have now established that given the relationship between income and expenditure, there is a unique level of equilibrium national output to which the economy will tend. The Keynesian argument is that the equilibrium level of national income is by no means certain to be a level at which there is full employment of labour. In terms of the opportunity cost curve we studied in Chapter 1 the economy could be at equilibrium inside the curve! There is nothing in the nature of the market system which will see to it that the economy tends quickly towards a full employment level of output. It could be stuck at Ye (the equilibrium level of national income) for a substantial period. We considered this possibility in Chapter 7 in the context of the coal industry.

See pp 6-7

See pp 138–40

High unemployment can be seen as an excess supply of labour. But if there is an excess labour supply, one might expect the price of labour services, that is wage rates, to fall. This labour market adjustment might continue until all who want a job have one as discussed in Chapter 5. But Keynesian economists believe that labour markets do not quickly respond in this way. This leads them to the conclusion that the economy can suffer from demand deficient unemployment which requires government intervention. The form that intervention might take is something we shall consider shortly. Before that, however, we can use and extend the above analysis to see why changes in people's attitudes to savings and consumption expenditure can create difficulties for employment prospects.

See pp 90–4

3 The paradox of thrift

a Injections and withdrawals

A country with a high level of savings is one with some real advantages. As we saw in Chapter 1, if a country refrains from consumption (saves) it can invest, raising consumption in future years. So a high savings ratio, that is a high proportion of a country's income which is saved, makes funds available to firms for investment purposes. This increases national income in future years. However, in the Keynesian view, a high level of savings can, given certain conditions, damage a country's economic well-being and worsen a country's unemployment problem. Let us develop our analysis of the economy. We shall then be in a position to see why increased 'thrift' by society, or increased willingness to save, may create a problem for unemployment. We shall also see in what sense it represents an apparent contradiction, or paradox.

See pp 9–10

In Figure 13.4 we return to the circular flow of income diagram from Chapter 12. We said there that firms will need to produce sufficient output to meet the flow of consumers' expenditure. In fact firms must produce more than sufficient to satisfy consumption demand. There are other demands made upon their output, as we saw in Chapter 12 when examining the national income accounts. There are demands upon firms from government, government expenditure (G), from firms wanting to purchase investment goods (I), and from foreigners in the form of export demand (X). These expenditures are in addition to those of households. They are shown in Figure 13.4 as 'injections' into the circular flow of income. Output must be sufficient to meet all these demands.

See pp 227-30

On the other hand, not all the income households receive from firms is spent on demands from firms for their output. Some of that income leaks out of the circular flow. What income do households receive which is not spent on current output from firms? What part of their income is withdrawn from the circular flow? One such leakage is savings (S). People choose not to spend all their income. But that is not the only withdrawal. Another is taxation (T). Not all the income households receive is available for consumption since government demands part of it as taxes.

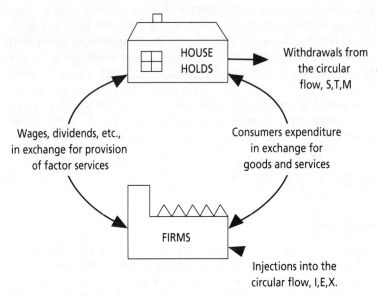

Figure 13.4 *Injections and withdrawals into the circular flow of income*

A further leakage is import demand (M). To the extent that people use their income to buy imports, they are purchasing goods and services, but it is not domestically produced output. Savings, taxes and imports, then, constitute the leakages, or withdrawals from the circular flow of income. To the extent that households do not use their income for consumption purposes, it reduces the amount of output which firms must produce if aggregate demand is to be satisfied.

Now these injections into and withdrawals from the circular flow of income are represented in Figure 13.5. Look first at withdrawals from the circular flow. As national income increases, people save more, pay more taxes and buy more imports. This gives the positively sloped relationship S + T + M. What about injections? For simplicity we will assume that injections into the circular flow of income are autonomous. In other words, whatever the level of national income, government expenditure, G, investment expenditure I and export expenditure, X, are assumed to remain the same. This is shown in Figure 13.5 as I + G + X.

What we can now see is that equilibrium income for the economy is that level of national income at which injections into the circular flow (I + G + X) are equal to withdrawals from it (S + T + M). This is shown in Figure 13.5.

If output is to be enough for the demands made upon it, it must be sufficient to satisfy consumption demand plus the injections, less the withdrawals. This is £500 billion for the economy of Figure 13.5. We can see in the following way why this must be the case. Suppose this were not so. Let us imagine that national income were, say £550 billion. Since planned leakages are greater than planned

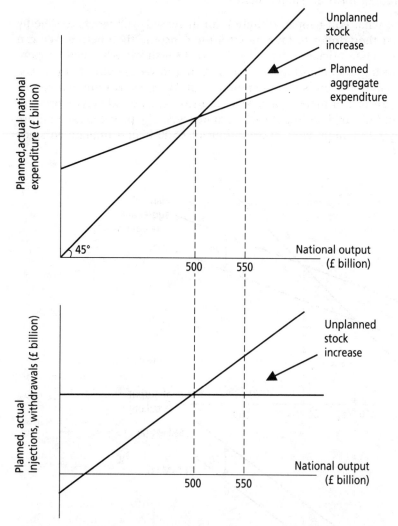

Figure 13.5 Injections and withdrawals: Equilibrium national income

injections, the amount of demand for output is less than the output being produced. Hence there is an unplanned stock increase shown in both parts of Figure 13.5.

We have already seen from the top part of the diagram what happens when unplanned stocks increase. Firms will reduce output. Equilibrium is restored where planned aggregate expenditure equals national output. Expressing the same idea in a different way, equilibrium is at the level of output at which injections into the circular flow of income equal withdrawals from it.

b Effects of increased thrift on employment

Now we can ask what will happen if there is an increased willingness to save by society, such that they prefer to save more of their income then before. We can trace through the effects diagrammatically. Figure 13.6 shows what will happen. We start with an initial equilibrium of £500 billion and we assume that this is a level of output where there is some unemployment. We now assume that people decide to save £20 billion more at any level of income. Alternatively expressed, they plan to spend £20 billions less at each income level. The planned expenditure function falls by £20 billion. Now at an output of £500 billion unplanned stock

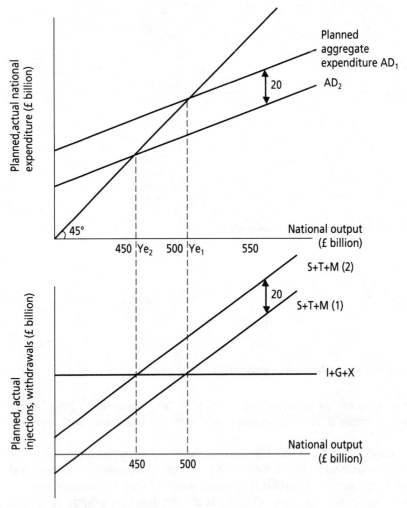

Figure 13.6 Effects of an increase in thrift by society

levels rise. Firms respond by reducing output causing workers to be unemployed. Only when output has fallen to £450 billion is equilibrium restored.

The same effects can be seen on the lower part of the diagram. Since the lower part shows leakages including savings, increased thrift is shown as an upward shift in the withdrawals function. Again, one can see the resulting unplanned stock increase, and the fall in national income to its new lower equilibrium of £450 billion.

Under these circumstances increased thrift has reduced aggregate demand, lowered equilibrium output and increased unemployment. One thinks of saving as a good thing to do, and for the individual who does, so it is. He may want a pension or some insurance against losing his job. It can also have advantages for society at large as we have already seen. However, under certain circumstances, its effects on society can be harmful. Output falls, unemployment rises.

It can be argued that there is a tendency for increased thrift to appear at exactly the wrong time for an economy. If an economy is at full employment higher aggregate demand can create inflation, and increased willingness to save can reduce inflationary pressure. But suppose for some reason unemployment is high

Annual average, as a percentage of disposable income

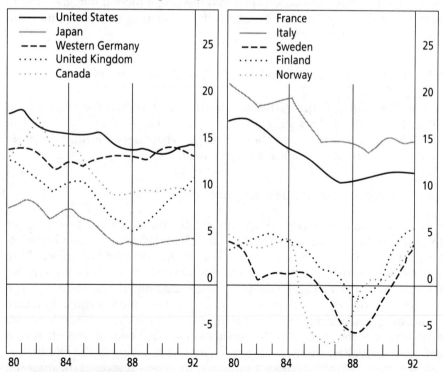

Figure 13.7 Personal savings ratio over time

or rising, the *fear of more unemployment* can cause those who have a job to increase their savings. This will reduce aggregate demand compounding the problem. You have seen something of the unemployment problem of the late 1980s and early 1990s in Figure 13.1. Observe in Figure 13.7 how this was mirrored in the rising savings ratio (and thus falling consumption demand) of the same period. The chart shows personal income net of tax, that is personal disposable income minus consumer spending, measured as a percentage of income. Observe the sharp rise in the savings ratio in the UK during the period in which the economy moved into recession and unemployment was rising. The same trend can be observed in many other countries. It is very evident in the Scandinavian countries, somewhat less marked in some others, such as France and Canada.

c Effects of increased thrift on savings

A particularly surprising result of increased thrift in the circumstances described is its effect on the volume of savings. They may not increase at all. In Figure 13.6 households took a decision to increase savings. But the aggregate effect was to reduce output and therefore income. They may now be saving a higher proportion of their income but they have less income. They may therefore not have increased the *volume* of savings at all. It is this phenomenon that gives rise to the name the 'paradox of thrift'. Intentions by a nation to save more may not result in increased saving at all!

4 Government action on demand-deficient unemployment

British gross domestic product (GDP) has clearly been less than full employment GDP. The Keynesian analysis suggests that some unemployment is a result of demand deficiency. We can now think through what the government can do about it and what its effects on the economy might be.

a Possible remedies for demand-deficiency unemployment

Any measure to stimulate aggregate demand can be considered as a possibility for raising output and therefore reducing demand-deficient unemployment. Referring back to Figure 13.5, anything that shifts the planned expenditure function upwards can be used to achieve the desired effect. We can say this another way. Looking at the lower part of the diagram the government can attempt either to lower the withdrawals function or raise the injections function.

We shall list some possible ways of raising the planned expenditure function. We shall leave to the questions for discussion at the end of the chapter a consideration of whether these measures equate to a lowering of the withdrawal function or a raising of the injections function in the lower section of the diagram. Let us list the main options for raising aggregate demand.

Consumption can be increased. This might be achieved by cuts in taxation. Cuts in tax might be a reduction of direct tax, the tax on people's income. Alternatively, it could be cuts in indirect tax, the tax on items of expenditure. The main form of indirect tax is value added tax (VAT), but there are other indirect taxes such as tax on petrol and cigarettes. Consumption can also be increased by lowering interest rates. Some forms of expenditure are particularly sensitive to such a change. Large items of consumer expenditure, such as cars and household goods are often bought on credit. Lowering interest rates effectively makes such goods cheaper to purchase on credit[1].

Investment can be increased. This can be private or state investment. The government can increase its own spending. Expenditures on hospital buildings, roads, school buildings and police stations are examples of this. Alternatively, it can encourage private sector investment. Lower interest rates will make it cheaper for firms to borrow money for investment. Alternatively, it might offer subsidies for investment, as we saw in Chapter 5. Either way the attempt can be made to boost expenditure via increases in investment.

See pp 98–103

Another approach is to increase government current expenditure. It might, for example, employ more nurses or teachers, although such a policy might prove difficult to reverse if the economy were subsequently to be fully employed. Again the effect is to boost aggregate expenditure.

Britain is an open economy, which is to say it engages in international trade; indeed, it has a very large international sector. We shall spend much of Chapters 19 and 20 examining international trade. Here, however, we note that if governments can boost export demand this will also raise national output. We shall not stop here to consider how that might be done. But notice also that aggregate demand can be increased by *reducing imports*. Since any part of consumers' income spent on the purchase of imports reduces the amount spent on domestically produced goods and services, switching demand away from imports can raise aggregate demand and therefore the level of unemployment.

See pp 370–411

As we shall see in Chapters 19 and 20, there is no way in which this can be done which is not controversial. Here we simply note that it is difficult for one member of the EU to do this. Part of the commitment of each country to the EC is to allow free trade between member countries. Reducing imports by, for example, taxes on imports are therefore politically difficult in the extreme. Even without a political constraint, there will be problems in pursuing such a policy. It is distinctly possible that, say, a UK decision to restrict imports will create retaliation by the government of the country whose export industries are affected by a fall in their export demand. That retaliation will then have its effects on British exports and employment.

b Measuring the size of increase in expenditure: the multiplier

There is a very important consideration for a government wishing to increase aggregate demand for the purpose of reducing employment. That consideration concerns the appropriate *extent* of the demand increase. One reason this is important is that a given boost to demand will increase expenditure by more than the original increase. In other words national output will rise by a multiple of any increase in demand. There is a 'multiplier' effect on output. To understand why this is so we shall examine Figure 13.8 below. This is the circular flow of income diagram which you encountered earlier in the chapter as Figure 13.4.

Let us assume that this economy has an 'unemployment equilibrium'. Planned injections are equal to planned withdrawals. Expressing the same idea differently, planned demand is equal to the available output. However there is a significant level of unemployment which the government wishes to eliminate by increasing aggregate demand. Let us assume that the attempt to do this is through increasing government investment in hospitals, roads, schools to the extent of £20 billion. We must now think through the effects on the economy using Figure 13.8 to do so.

Since an additional £20 billion of output is being demanded by government, construction companies and other firms will increase output by £20 billion. This will raise household incomes by £20 billion, since some people will be employed and receive wages, others who own shares in the companies will receive increased dividends from the profits.

Remember from Chapter 12 again that national output must be identically equal to national income. What will households do with the £20 billion of income

See pp 230–7

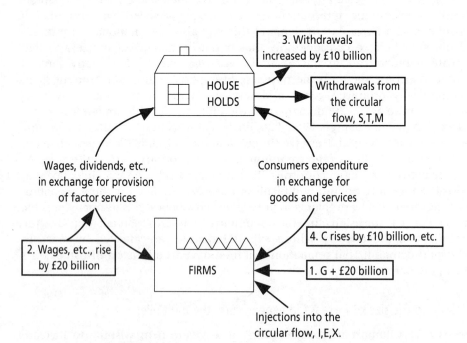

Figure 13.8 Injection of £20 billion into the circular flow of income

Table 13.1 Effects on national output of an increase in government spending of £20 billion

Period	Increase in national output	Increase in planned consumption	Increase in planned withdrawals (S+T+M) (£billions)
1	20	10	10
2	10	5	5
3	5	5	5
4	2.5	2.5	2.5
n	40	20	20

that they receive? Some will be taxed away from them; some they will choose to save; some they will spend on imported goods. Let us suppose that 20 per cent goes in income tax, 20 per cent on imports and 10 per cent on increased saving. The other 50 per cent, or £10 billion will be spent, further increasing the demand for output by firms.

So in the next period firms will increase output by £10 billion to meet this increased demand. That output represents household incomes, half which will be withdrawn from the circular flow as taxes, savings and imports. This leaves £5 billion to be spent – and so on.

What will the end of the process be? Table 13.1 summarises the position. There will eventually be an increase in national output of twice the original increase in government spending. This is because part of the increase in national income is spent on further consumption. What is true of increases in government spending will be true for decreases also. Decreases in government spending will reduce output and therefore incomes causing a multiple reduction in output.

What is the size of this 'multiplier' effect? In the economy illustrated in Table 13.1 the multiplier is 2. A change in government spending led to a change in output of twice that amount. But the multiplier will be different for different economies. Indeed it may be different for the same economy at different times. We can however establish a general principle. The principle is as follows. The multiplier $k = 1/w$ where w is the proportion of any increase in household income not spent but withdrawn from the circular flow. The term w is usually called the 'marginal propensity to withdraw'. In this case since half of any additional income received by households is withdrawn from the circular flow the multiplier, $k = 1/0.5 = 2$. In a different economy where withdrawals from the circular flow are smaller, the multiplier is higher.

Suppose tax is only 10 per cent of income. Suppose, furthermore, that we save only 5 per cent of any additional income we receive and that only 10 per cent of any increase in income is spent on imports. The multiplier would then be as follows:

$$k = \frac{1}{0.1 + 0.05 + 0.1} = \frac{1}{0.25} = 4$$

A formal proof of this general multiplier relationship is given in Appendix 3.

c Using the multiplier for reducing unemployment

In principle, then, unemployment in an economy can be controlled by changes in government expenditure. The government *can* do something by adding to aggregate demand where it is too low. One way in which it can do this is by increasing its expenditure. But it will need to have an idea of the size of the multiplier. It will also need to be aware of the extent to which increases in output leads to an increase in the demand for labour.

See pp 88–108

We can extend our analysis to the problem of regional unemployment that we considered in Chapter 5. If unemployment is high in one part of the country, increased regional expenditure on roads, hospitals, and so on, etc. can raise income in that part of the country through the multiplier. The size of the multiplier will again be determined by w, the propensity to withdraw spending from the circular flow. Again this will be dependent upon the tax rate, willingness to save out of increased income and willingness to 'import' not only from abroad but from other areas of the country too. The extent to which Scottish output will rise, if government increases spending there, is determined partly by whether Scots spend their additional income on Rover cars manufactured in the Midlands!

5 Problems in controlling unemployment

As we shall see in subsequent chapters, some economists do not believe that Keynesian management of aggregate demand is necessary or desirable. Now we consider two great problems for governments who *do* believe that such control is beneficial.

a Time lags

Clearly, if the policy is to be successful it has to be applied at the right time. If the level of economic activity and unemployment is fluctuating, aggregate demand must be increased when activity is low and reined back when it is high.

However, it takes time for the government to be aware of the economic situation. Data is collected and is available weeks or perhaps months after the event. Further time then needs to be given over to analysing the situation and formulating a policy that appears to be appropriate. Time will then pass while policy is being implemented.

The effect of these time lags might be that by the time government has recognised an unemployment problem, analysed it, and released funds to boost demand, a recession may be ending and demand may be rising. Government policy might then prove to be worse than useless.

b Funding the expenditure

Suppose a government decides to stimulate demand by increasing government spending. Unless at the time it takes the decision, it is receiving more in taxes than it is spending, it will have a deficit on its own account that it must fund. It will have to borrow. The extent of this borrowing requirement is called the public sector borrowing requirement, or PSBR. If the government spends more than it receives in taxes, the PSBR is positive. If it spends less than it receives, the PSBR is negative. A negative PSBR is referred to as a PSDR, the public sector debt repayment. The government has accumulated debts in past years. Part of this debt can be repaid if the PSBR in any given year is negative.

Part of the logic of Keynesian demand management policy is that during a recession when unemployment is high there should be a PSBR. On the other hand, when there is a high level of economic activity, there should be no need for a PSBR at all.

During a recession, if government increases its spending, how will it be funded? Some of it will be funded by increased government income raised by the increase in economic activity. Let us illustrate this by reference to Table 13.2. Government spending, G was assumed to increase by £20 billion. Output rose, through the multiplier by £40 billion. But remember that government was assumed to receive taxes of 20 per cent of national income. So 20 per cent of the increased national income or £8 billion is received in extra tax. Thus the increase in G is £20 billion, the increase in T is £8 billion. The PSBR will only rise by £12 billion.

Table 13.2 Effects on the PSBR of an increase in government spending of £20 billion

Initial increase in government spending (£ billions)	Eventual increase in national output (£ billions)	Eventual increase in planned withdrawals (£ billion)	Eventual increase in planned withdrawals (£ billion)	Eventual increase in taxation 20% of increase in national output (£ billion)	Eventual change in PSBR (£ billion)
20	40	20	20	8	12

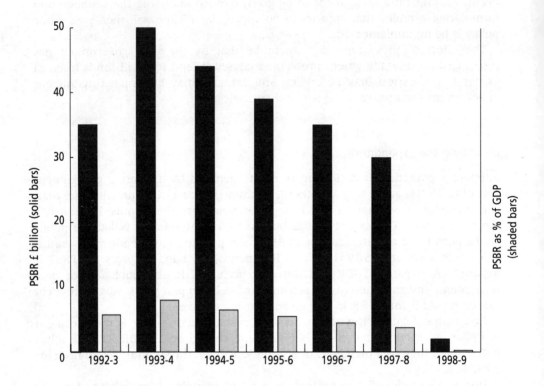

Source: Treasury

Figure 13.9 UK PSBR, actual (1992–3) and forecast

In reality the position for a government will probably be better than this. A significant part of G goes on unemployment benefit. If unemployment is reduced, this aspect of G will also fall.

Nevertheless, a significant rise in the PSBR will be inevitable if government wishes to increase expenditure. Figure 13.9 shows the extent of the PSBR in Britain. Notice how for 1993–4 the government was seeking to finance a borrowing requirement of 8 per cent of GDP, an amount approaching £1 billion per week! If you look back at Figure 10.1 you will see just how expensive this can be. In 1993, it consumed 7p in every £1 of government income to pay interest on this debt – over half of what is spent on health care and over three-quarters of what is spent on national defence.

Persuading people to lend such sums may be very difficult. It also diverts those savings away from other uses. Therefore, firms may find it more difficult and more expensive to borrow money for investment purposes. We shall have cause to return to this point in later chapters.

See p 190

6 Conclusion

If unemployment is high, can the government *do* something about it? Keynesian economists certainly think that, in general, they can. Unemployment can be an indication of a shortage of demand in the economy. The reason for this state of affairs continuing is that markets, especially labour markets, do not adjust quickly. Governments should not therefore wait for markets to clear. They should act. Governments, Keynesians believe, can act to influence aggregate demand and hence unemployment. There are problems and costs involved but, to return to our medical analogy, if the patient is seriously ill, the medicine must be administered and the costs accepted.

In later chapters we shall see why some economists believe an economy with unemployment to be like a person who is sick, for whom the best remedy is not simply to leave him alone to recover but to improve his fitness, so that his resistance to future illness is that much greater.

But let us close this chapter with a word of warning. We have not said all there is to say about unemployment. In particular, we have not yet given much consideration to its relationship with other macro-economic variables, especially inflation and the balance of payments. Neither have we yet explained the objections of some economists to the whole notion of manipulating aggregate demand to affect employment. On the other hand, we have said a good deal. We have seen why some economists do believe that governments have a significant responsibility for short-term demand management for influencing unemployment in the modern economy.

7 Questions for discussion

1 According to Figure 13.1, what is the level of autonomous demand in the economy? What is the level of induced demand if Y is £600 billion? What is the multiplier?
2 Explain how 'equilibrium' is restored to the economy of Figure 13.1 if national output were to fall to £450 billion.
3 Suppose there is substantial unemployment in the economy which government plans to reduce by increasing aggregate demand. What do you believe to be the relative benefits of raising aggregate demand via changes in consumption, investment, government spending, exports and imports?
4 Which of the proposals for increasing aggregate demand mentioned in question 3 raise the injections function? Which lower the withdrawals function?
5 Suppose the government were to redistribute income towards equality raising direct taxes on higher income groups to pay for increased benefits for lower income groups. What is such a policy likely to do to

a the planned expenditure function?

b the level of unemployment?

6 The text suggests that the main determinant of consumption (and saving) is income. But there are other factors influencing the level of domestic consumption. What do you think they are? How significant might they be for the level of employment?

7 How much does it matter if a government has a large PSBR?

8 To what extent is the present British government Keynesian in its attempts to control unemployment?

8 Further reading

Keynesian unemployment equilibrium
Sloman, pp. 530–43; Begg, pp. 360–73; Parkin and King, pp. 620–30; pp. 651–60

The multiplier
Sloman, pp. 651–8; Begg, pp. 369–70; Parkin and King, pp. 661–70

Paradox of thrift
Sloman, pp. 657; Begg, pp. 370–2; Parkin and King, pp. 657–9

Unemployment
J. Philpott (1993) 'Getting back to full employment', *Economics and Business Education*, Autumn.
D. Pierce (1992) 'Unemployment: meaning and measurement', *British Economic Survey*, Autumn.

9 End note

1 Changes in interest rates also affect the distribution of income. One sometimes gets the impression from the press that lowering interest rates improves the welfare of everyone. In fact, one significant part of its effect is to redistribute income between savers and borrowers. Lower interest rates make it cheaper to borrow. But pensioners living on interest from their savings will be worse off, if interest rates fall.

CHAPTER 14

Does Britain invest enough?

By comparison with its European neighbours, Britain is not a rich country. Average income is higher, for example, in France, Germany, Italy and many other countries, whereas in the early postwar years this was not the case. A commonly cited reason for the change is that Britain does not invest enough. Is that true? What ought we to do about it?

In this chapter we review the following concepts
- Opportunity cost
- Keynesian equilibrium

We introduce
- The rate of interest
- Investment analysis
- Human capital

1 Introduction

During our studies of micro-economics we were often concerned with the concept of opportunity cost. Any action undertaken means that the next best alternative is foregone. The opportunity cost of your trip to the bowling alley last night is not only that you cannot spend that money on something else but that perhaps you are late reading this chapter. If firm A produces output it uses land, labour and capital which are then not available for the production of something else. The foregone output is the opportunity cost of firm A's output. For an economy the opportunity cost of investment can be seen as the current consumption foregone. Land labour and capital devoted to buildings and machinery for next year's consumption cannot produce current output, the output of food or haircuts that we could consume now.

In Chapter 1 we introduced these ideas in terms of an opportunity cost curve, or production possibility curve. There it was in the context of an Eastern European economy, but the principles hold for any society. The economy is represented in Figure 14.1 by an opportunity cost curve AB. This society has full employment and is at point P. It is thus enjoying OC_t^* of current output, whereas it could enjoy OA current output. But it is choosing to forego consumption of $A - C_t^*$ in order to invest. This investment will produce consumption in the next period of OC_{t+1}^*. In other words, investment for future consumption involves an opportunity cost in

See pp 6–10

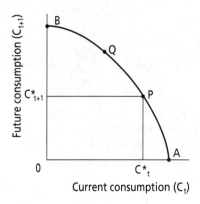

Figure 14.1 Opportunity cost curve: current and future consumption

terms of current consumption. Now many people believe that Britain should be at, say, Q. This will mean foregoing more current consumption, investing more, raising future consumption and thus standards of living. But are they correct, or are these things better left to be decided by market forces?

2 The market for investment goods

See pp 252–5

What determines whether an economy, instead of being at P, is at, say, Q with a greater volume of resources committed to investment? This is a matter of some controversy. As we saw in Chapter 13, Keynesian economists say that there is nothing in the nature of the system even to suggest that an economy will be in equilibrium on the opportunity cost curve. In Keynesian equilibrium, aggregate output (Y) will be sufficient to meet all planned demands upon it. You will recall that these demands are consumption (C), investment (I), government current demand (G) and export demand (X) minus import demand (M). Alternatively, expressed equilibrium output, Ye, is where planned injections into the circular flow (government investment and export demand) are equal to planned withdrawals from the circular flow (savings, taxes and imports). This may not be at full employment output as Figure 14.2 below indicates, since full employment Y may be greater than Ye.

Governments choosing to move the economy towards full employment can in principle do so by raising any item of autonomous demand including investment. This will, through the multiplier, help to decide where on the opportunity cost curve of Figure 14.1 the economy is located. Notice that in this simple Keynesian model investment is autonomous, that is, it is independent of the level of income.

By comparison the classical view is that any unemployment constitutes only a short-term problem and that markets will always tend to push the economy on to the opportunity cost curve frontier where there is full employment. After all,

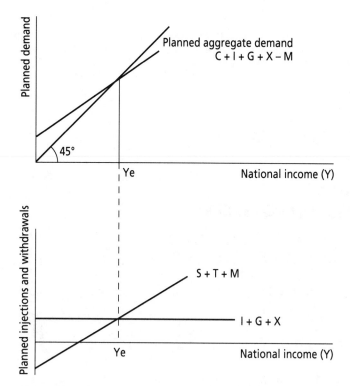

Figure 14.2 Keynesian macro-economic equilibrium

unemployment means an excess supply of labour services. Given a free labour market, as we saw in Chapter 5, the price of labour services, wage rates, will fall and equilibrium, including full employment will be restored. The classical criticism goes further than that. Not only do market forces ensure full employment of labour in the long run but markets also bring about an optimum volume of investment. The volume of investment will be optimally determined without government intervention. The mechanism that ensures that this happens is interest rates. We can use supply and demand analysis to see how it happens. Consider Figure 14.3 below, which can be regarded as a market for investment funds where interest rates are the price of using those funds. The higher the interest rate the more willing people will be to save since consumption has a higher opportunity cost. Hence the upwards sloping savings function (S).

The lower the interest rate the cheaper it is for firms to borrow for investment purposes and so the greater is the quantity of funds demanded. This is shown by the demand curve (D). We shall examine this demand curve in more detail shortly. So if interest rates are allowed to find their own level, they will be established at r^*, a level where the supply and demand for loanable funds are in

See pp 91–3

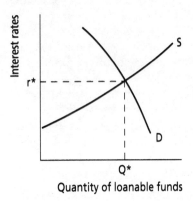

Figure 14.3 Equilibrium in the market for loanable funds

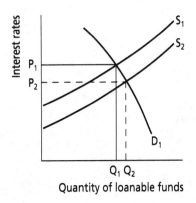

Figure 14.4 Increased willingness to save and its effect on interest rates

equilibrium. The volume of investment will thus be optimal. Society will obtain the best possible level of welfare from its limited resources.

Let us use the diagram of Figure 14.4 and see how markets adjust in classical equilibrium with respect to investment when society's preferences alter. People have preferences between current and future consumption expressed by the supply and demand curves for loanable funds. Suppose society is now inclined to be more thrifty. People wish, on average, to have more future consumption. They are prepared to sacrifice current consumption to make this possible. In terms of Figure 14.4 the supply curve for loanable funds shifts to the right, from S_1 to S_2. People are more willing to save than before at each level of interest rate. Banks have more funds available to lend. However at the present level of interest rate, P_1, there is an excess quantity of these funds supplied. To encourage the use of these funds, the banks will lower the interest rate. The price of these funds now finds an equilibrium at P_2. Firms are encouraged to invest more. The quantity of loanable funds for investment rises from Q_1 to Q_2. Firms use these funds to bid resources away from current consumption. More resources are committed to investment because that is what people want. Again the mechanism is relative prices. This time the key price is the rate of interest.

Since society gets the volume of investment that it wants, Britain cannot be investing too little. It may invest less than other countries but that is because its citizens have a greater preference for current consumption, which it has expressed through markets. Shortly we shall look more closely at why firms invest more when interest rates fall.

Now few economists believe that markets work as perfectly as the above suggests but it provides a framework for analysing problems of alleged investment inadequacies in Britain that we shall look at later. Before we do that, however, we need to develop our understanding of what investment is and what problems are encountered in measuring its extent.

3 The meaning of investment

Investment is often referred to as gross domestic fixed capital formation (GDFCF), an excellent term for picking out its key features.

a *Gross*. During the year some capital is worn out and needs replacing. This is called replacement investment. Some investment is new, in the sense that it increases the size of the nation's capital stock. Gross investment includes both replacement investment and additions to the capital stock. You can gain from Table 14.1 an idea of the extent of Britain's investment. We have chosen one particular year, 1992, from the national income accounts that we met in Chapter 12, Britain's GNP by expenditure. We can see that gross domestic capital formation represented about 20–21 per cent of gross national product (GNP) at that time. How much was that investment simply replacing worn out capital? Capital consumption was recorded as £63,489 million, so net investment was only about 7 per cent of GNP. Of course these percentages will vary somewhat from year to year. You can see how much for yourself by looking up the data in the national income accounts and undertaking similar calculations on other years' figures.

See pp 230–7

b *Domestic*. Some investment by British firms is undertaken in other countries, and some investment in this country is made by foreign firms. For example, Japanese car companies have factories making cars in Britain. The figures above refer to investment in Britain, not investment by British firms.

c *Fixed*. Firms 'invest' in stocks of their own products. Sometimes intentionally to meet unforeseen changes in demand, sometimes unintentionally when demand falls suddenly and they are left with unsold, unplanned stocks. These stock items will not be included in GDFCF since this only includes the purchase of capital items such as machinery and buildings.

Table 14.1 Investment in Britain 1992 (£ million)

	Value (at current prices)	Approximate percentage of national product
Gross domestic fixed capital formation at current factor cost	95,241	20–21
Gross national product at factor cost	471,388	
Less capital consumption	−63,489	13.5
Net national product at factor cost	407,899	
Net domestic capital formation	31,752	6.5–7

d *Capital formation*. It is the formation of capital that investment involves. It is not the stock of capital in an economy, but the flow that changes to that stock represents. Note also that investment is done by firms and governments not by individuals. What is often referred to as financial investment, such as the purchase of shares, is really saving. The only kind of investment that is made by individuals is the purchase of new housing. The purchase of cars or even washing machines could in principle be seen as investment. After all it represents the acquisition of assets that will produce a flow of benefits over several years. However, for statistical purposes these items are regarded as consumer durables, and we assume that the whole value of the product is consumed during one year. One obvious advantage of this unreal assumption is that it avoids the need to work out the extent to which wear and tear on washing machines, and so on, has reduced the value of the nation's capital stock.

One thing in particular should be remembered about the above data. The percentages refer to proportions, not absolute amounts. In absolute terms Britain's investment performance would be worse than another country with the same percentage if the other country had a higher GNP.

4 The extent and direction of UK investment

a The extent of UK investment

The national income table referred to earlier gave us an idea of the extent of investment in the British economy for one year. Let us look at the proportion of

Table 14.2 GDFCF as a proportion of GDP for selected economies

Year (average)	UK	West Germany	Japan	OECD (total)
1960–67	17.7	25.2	31.0	21.0
1968–73	19.1	24.4	34.6	22.3
1974–79	19.3	20.8	31.8	22.3
1980–84	16.3	21.1	29.6	21.0
1985–89	16.3	19.1	30.1	20.5

Source: OECD, *Historical Statistics.*

GDP represented by investment in Britain over a longer period and compare it with other countries. Table 14.2 gives a clear indication of the relatively low volume of investment in Britain compared with some other advanced countries. However, you should bear in mind when you look at the figures that this is not investment volumes, but investment proportions. In absolute terms UK investment performance is worse than it appears in that the UK has a lower level of national income than many other advanced countries. Many commentators feel that Britain should, in terms of Figure 14.1 be at, say, Q rather than at P. Of course, as we have already argued, Britain could be at P because British people have chosen to be current consumption orientated. It could also be that the market mechanism is not working well. This is a point to which we shall return later.

However, studies have shown that there is a far from perfect correlation between the volume of individual and growth in GDP. Since there is nowhere near a perfect correlation between the two it suggests that there are other important factors to consider. The most obvious one is the efficiency with which capital resources are used. The Eastern European economies of the 1980s had, as we saw in Table 1.2, much higher ratios of investment to GDP. Yet they had substantially lower living standards.

See p 5

b The direction of UK investment

There are also some interesting developments over the last 10–15 years with respect to the direction of investment. Table 14.3 enables us to see some of the most important of these. During the 1980s the relative importance of public sector investment fell very significantly. This fall reflected the Conservative government's desire to reduce government spending, and the shifting of assets out of public into private ownership via the privatisation programme. However, during the early 1990s the greater effect of the recession on private sector spending reversed this trend.

Having seen some of the features of British investment, we now consider the factors affecting such investment. Concentrating on private investment we begin

Table 14.3 Gross domestic fixed capital formation at constant (1990) prices

	Total gross domestic fixed capital formation	Private sector	General government	Public corporations
1986	83,685	67,877	9,163	6,645
1987	92,260	78,013	9,027	5,220
1988	104,726	92,043	7,579	5,104
1989	110,503	94,778	10,054	5,671
1990	106,776	89,162	12,659	4,955
1991	96,265	79,697	12,688	3,880
1992	95,241	77,052	13,765	4,424
1993 Q1	24,236	18,704	4,143	1,389
Q2	23,763	18,981	3,765	1,017

Source: Economic Trends, December 1993.

with the relationship between private investment decisions and the rate of interest.

5 Investment decisions and the rate of interest

a Making investment decisions

Suppose that we are a firm trying to decide whether a project is worthwhile as an investment – that is, will it be profitable? Let us see how we might go about making such a decision. There will be an initial capital cost (C) but because of the investment we expect to receive a flow of income from the sale of the product that the investment will produce. This income will arrive over a period of years until the capital is worn out or needs replacing.

There will be much uncertainty about this cash flow. In particular, there is uncertainty about how much output will be bought, what price we can charge for it and about all the other costs such as the wage bill and the tax liability. We must do the best we can, though, and produce our best estimate of this potential income. When we have done it, it might look like this:

Year	0	1	2	3	4
	−31,700	10,000	10,000	10,000	10,000

This shows the initial outlay, C, as a minus, since we shall be paying out to purchase the capital. Then we show the 'cash flow' as positive amounts since this represents the income we expect to receive. The cash flow will represent the income from the sale of the product less costs of labour, materials and so on. The

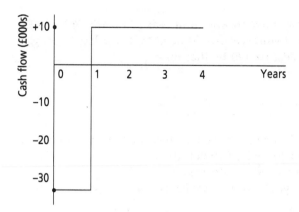

Figure 14.5 Cash flow profile

machinery might be worth something as scrap at the end of its useful life. If so, we would add that to the cash flow in the last year. Here we will assume for simplicity that the scrap value is nil.

You can plot this information on a diagram to give what is referred to as a cash flow profile. We have done this in Figure 14.5.

Let us decide now if the project is worthwhile. To keep things simple, let us assume that we can (a) be quite certain we have got our numbers right (b) there will be no inflation over the period. These are huge assumptions but at least it keeps the size of the problem manageable.

Can we say that it costs £31,700 but will get back more (£40,000) so it must be worth it? No, because money earned in the future is less than it is worth if we had it now. If we had it now, we could put it in a bank and it would earn interest. If we have to wait for a year (or more) to obtain the cash flow, we will lose this interest. So we need some way of adjusting the numbers to allow for that.

The way this is done is to 'discount' the cash flow. For example, take the £10,000 earned in year one. We ask the question: 'What amount of money do I need now to be able to invest it at a given interest rate to turn it into £10,000 in a year's time?' We discount the £10,000 using the formula $A\frac{1}{1+r}$, where A is the cash flow and r is the interest rate per annum.

Suppose r is 10 per cent then in our example we get

$$\pounds 10,000 \times \frac{1}{1+(0.1)} = \frac{10,000}{1.01} = \pounds 9090$$

That is, if we had £9090 now we could put it in a bank at 10 per cent interest and it would be worth £10,000 in a year's time. So the 'present value' of £10,000 in a year's time is, assuming a 10 per cent interest rate, only £9090. To put it another way we would be indifferent between £9090 now and £10,000 in a year's time since the £9090 now is capable of producing £10,000 a year from now.

What of the £10,000 for which we have to wait until year 2? Clearly, it is worth less to us. Its present value is lower since we would need to invest less at 10 per cent for two years to have acquired £10,000 by that time.

The formula would be

$$A_2 \frac{1}{(1+r)} \times \frac{1}{(1+r)} \quad \text{or} \quad A_2 \frac{1}{(1+r)^2}$$

where A_2 = cash flow in year 2. Which gives £8260 since I need £8260 now to invest at 10 per cent for two years to make £10,000 then.

So what is the present value of the whole cash flow?

The formula we use is one that you can now probably guess. It is

$$A_1 \frac{1}{1+r} + A_2 \frac{1}{(1+r)^2} + A_3 \frac{1}{(1+r)^3} + \ldots A_n \frac{1}{(1+r)^t}$$

In our example we have the discounted cash flows as

Year	0	1	2	3	4
	−10,000	9090	8264	7513	6830

What is the present value of all the cash flow? If we add up all the cash flows from year 1 we get the gross present value (GPV) which, with slight rounding, becomes £31,700.

We can now decide if our project is worthwhile. We are going to borrow £31,700 and invest in a project with an expected return of, in present value terms, £31,700. Clearly, it is a very marginal project. If the GPV is greater than C it is worth the investment. If GPV is less than C it is not. The difference between the capital cost and the discounted value of the cash flow is called the net present value (NPV). Hence NPV = GPV − C. If NPV is positive the project is worthwhile. If NPV is negative it is not. This approach to the investment decision is referred to as the NPV method.

However, we could look at our investment problem in a different way. We could ask what is the rate of return implied in our project? It is usually called the internal rate of return (IRR). We could do that by asking: what is the interest rate that would just discount the cash flows back to the size of the initial outlay? Formally:

$$\text{IRR} = \text{the rate}, r, \text{ such that } \sum_{k=1}^{n} A_k \frac{1}{(1+r)^k} - C = 0$$

In our example we know that it is 10 per cent. We could then ask ourselves this question: is it worth investing in a project which gives us a 10 per cent return when it costs us 10 per cent to borrow the funds? Again, this is a marginal project. If the IRR exceeds the cost of borrowing the project is worthwhile, if IRR is less, it is not worth investing in the project. Basically, the IRR and NPV methods are equivalent.

b Investment decisions and interest rates

You should now be able to see when a lower interest rate implies more investment. More projects will become worthwhile. Consider Figure 14.6 below, which shows what is called a marginal efficiency of investment schedule (MEI). In essence it is a demand curve for investment. It shows the relationship between the price of investment (r) and the quantity of investment demanded.

If interest rates are at r_1, all projects are worthwhile down to the marginal one at point A. If interest rates fall to r_2, the project at r_1 is no longer a marginal one and investment expands to I_2 with the marginal project at B. The lower the interest rate the more projects are worthwhile for firms and the higher the volume of investment.

The market mechanism, then, should see to it that we get the right volume of investment. It should also see to it that these investment goods are used efficiently. Assuming that firms wish to maximise profits, they will choose only those projects where consumers value the output highly enough to cover the opportunity costs of the resources used. We shall examine some evidence shortly and see whether this seems to work in practice.

We have not considered all the factors involved in investment decisions. Just like any other demand schedule the 'price' of investment funds is not the only factor affecting demand. We shall consider some other possible factors in section 6 of this chapter.

See pp 283–6

c Real or money rates of interest?

So far we have simply referred to interest rates. However, we need to distinguish between what we call nominal rates of interest and what are called real rates. What is the difference? The nominal rate of interest is the one quoted in the market at any given time. The real interest rate is the nominal rate minus the inflation rate. Let us see why we need to make this distinction. £100 left in a bank

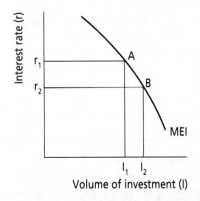

Figure 14.6 Interest rates and the demand for investment

for a year at a nominal interest rate of 10 per cent has become £110. But suppose inflation is at 10 per cent. The real rate is zero in that the £110 now buys only the same amount of output as the £100 would have bought the year before. Saving for future consumption has in this case not increased at all the amount one can consume. When people make savings decisions, they may not be willing to forego current consumption unless it enables greater future consumption. This requires positive real interest rates. In other words, the nominal rate must exceed the rate of inflation. The analysis in this chapter focuses on real interest rates.

d Investment analysis in action: the Channel Tunnel

The private sector sometimes undertakes enormous investment projects and interest rates are a crucial consideration. The biggest private sector investment project in Britain is the Channel Tunnel link between Dover and Calais. It is being run by Eurotunnel. They contracted the building of it to a British and French building consortium of companies known as Transmanche Link. Since the government is not providing any of the funds, Eurotunnel had to raise the large sums to finance it from a large number of banks plus the floating of some shares.

There were arguments for government funds to be put into the project. However, the then Prime Minister, Margaret Thatcher, believed in the power of the market. If the project was worthwhile funds would be made available. Subsequently the present government has been willing to consider investing funds along with the private sector in the rail link between London and Dover.

What did the cash flow profile for the Channel Tunnel project look like in 1987? Eurotunnel estimated the capital costs from the start of building until completion at around £4.7 billion. They estimated that the tunnel would open in the summer of 1993. The cash flows would be determined by many factors. The main ones would be the size of passenger and freight traffic from 1993 onwards, the expected proportion of that traffic that could be won in the face of competition, especially the cross-channel ferries, and the price they could charge. The price also would depend upon competition. Eurotunnel might be able to offer a superior journey, perhaps a faster or more comfortable one, and therefore ask a higher price. Alternatively, if the journey were very similar they could match or undercut the ferries' price, but clearly the severity of the expected competition would be a consideration.

Obviously, there are enormous problems in estimating the return on an investment of this length and size. In Table 14.4 we give some idea of the problems, by looking at what happens if we change some key assumptions. The IRR is the expected rate of return to shareholders investing in the project in the public share offering of 1987 using various assumptions as explained.

What are the assumptions on which the table is based? The Eurotunnel base case is the sort of return projected before construction work began. The other estimates are not Eurotunnel's, but are based on the same kind of model.

Table 14.4 Rates of return to Eurotunnel shareholders under various assumptions

	Approximate IRR %	Year of first dividend
Eurotunnel base case	15	1994
Assumption A	11.9	2003
Assumption B	10.5	2006
Assumption C	9.1	2008

Assumption A is that Eurotunnel faces competition from a rival tunnel from 2022, capital costs have been understated by 12.5 per cent and the tunnel opens one year late, but all other factors are the same as the base case.

Assumption B is that assumption A is correct except that the rate of passenger growth traffic is half that which Eurotunnel originally estimated.

Assumption C is that assumption B is correct except that Eurotunnel only gains half the expected share of the car and coach market it anticipates.

In the event, cost and time overruns occurred and a 12.5 per cent cost overrun was optimistic. Present estimates of the capital cost will be in excess of £10 billion. The tunnel becomes fully operational during 1994. The greatest uncertainty is now the revenue projections. Some regarded Eurotunnel's initial projections as optimistic, but Eurotunnel itself believes that its original figures now look likely to be a significant underestimate and that the revenue projections will cover the significant cost overruns.

Clearly, it requires some years from the tunnel's opening before some reliable forecasts can be made of its likely revenue. Meanwhile one can see just how uncertain the returns are on large investment projects. However, as we have seen, interest rates are crucial to the whole project, and indeed to any investment.

e Empirical evidence

Does empirical evidence support the argument we have been developing concerning the relationship between investment and interest rates? Does a lower interest rate produce more investment? An article by W. W. Easton[1] in the *Bank of England Quarterly Bulletin*, suggests that it does. Table 14.5 shows the Bank of England's estimates of the effects of a 1 per cent rise in interest rates on a number of key variables, including investment. A rise in interest rates produces a fall in the volume of investment. The evidence is, however, that some of the strength of the relationship is between residential investment and interest rates. The evidence is not so strong if one concentrates on private investment *net* of residential investment, as Table 14.5 shows.

Table 14.5 Bank model simulation: all interest rates +1% point (exchange rate fixed) (percentage differences from base, except where stated, after specified)

	1	4	8	12
GDP (output measure)	—	−0.4	−0.7	−0.9
Domestic demand	−0.1	−0.7	−1.1	−1.4
Consumers' expenditure	−0.1	−0.6	−0.9	−1.2
o/w durables	−0.1	−3.5	−4.5	−3.6
Investment	−0.1	−1.3	−2.2	−2.8
o/w private residential	−0.9	−3.2	−3.1	−4.1
GDP deflator	—	−0.1	−0.2	−0.5
Retail price index	0.4	0.3	0.2	—
Average earnings	—	—	−0.1	−0.4
Current account (£bn) [a]	—	0.6	1.5	2.0
Unemployment (000's)	—	12	35	58
Effective exchange rate	—	—	—	—

Note: [a] Quoted effects are over the year to the specified quarter
Source: Bank of England *Quarterly Bulletin*, May 1990.

What is perhaps particularly interesting is that earlier studies did *not* find much support for the relationship between interest rates and investment. Easton argues that this might be explained by the deregulation of financial markets in the later 1980s. The relationship may have looked less real when governments regulated the availability of finance as well as its price. Now there is virtually no attempt to control the availability of finance except through its price, which is to say, interest rates.

The other piece of empirical evidence relates to UK investment performance relative to that of other economies. Table 14.6 makes interesting reading. As a proportion of GDP, UK investment is comparatively low. One can argue that even if this makes for lower levels of output, it reflects UK society's preferences. Look now at the second column. The Conservative administration of the 1980s was keen to allow market forces to operate more widely. These figures suggest that it may have improved the UK's investment level, even though it looks poor against Japan where market forces are given less scope. The most worrying column is the last one. How much extra capital is needed to produce a marginal increase in output? The answer is that it requires far more in the UK than elsewhere. This suggests that, whatever one might say about the volume of UK investment, the efficiency with which it is used leaves much to be desired.

Table 14.6 Investment : Some international comparisons, 1986–91

	Average share of GDFC in GDP	Annual growth in private (non-residential) investment	Incremental capital/output ratio
France	22.2	5.2	1.9
Germany	20.8	7.5	2.3
Japan	26.8	11.3	2.5
UK	17.6	5.9	3.1
USA	14.2	0.6	0.3

Source: OECD and National Accounts.

6 Investment and other factors

We have argued that there is a relationship between investment and interest rates. Why is the evidence that there is not a better fit? The answer is that other things influence the business community also. We shall briefly consider some of them.

a Business expectations

Business confidence about the future will clearly affect the size of the cash flows predicted from an investment project. The higher the level of confidence the further to the right the demand curve for investment, the MEI schedule, will be. Is there any way in which we can measure such a nebulous thing as the level of confidence? One way is to ask businesses about their future investment plans. The Confederation of British Industry (CBI) does this quarterly. The results are published in *Economic Trends*. How good a guide is the survey to actual business investment decisions? *Economic Trends* measures the results of the surveys against the volume of investment in plant and machinery that was actually undertaken a year later. Look there and you will see that it shows a good but far from perfect fit. In other words, it does have some value in predicting what is likely to happen to investment volumes in the near future. There is also similar data for investment in buildings and works.

b Profitability

Profitability may be positively associated with investment either because profits increase business confidence or because companies find that it is cheaper to use past profits for investment purposes than to seek finance elsewhere. So a firm using an IRR calculation to find the value of an investment may use a lower interest rate as its marginal 'cut-off rate' if it has past profits available. It will never

Table 14.7 Rates of return on private business capital in selected OECD countries

	UK	USA	Germany	Japan
1980–87	9.4	14.6	12.4	14.3
1988–91	9.8	16.6	14.2	15.8

Source: OECD, Economic Outlook.

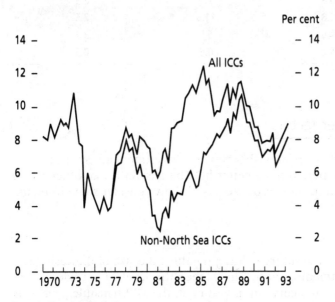

Source: Treasury Bulletin.

Figure 14.7 Profitability of industrial and commercial companies

regard the appropriate cut-off rate as zero. Those funds still have an opportunity cost. Table 14.7 may then reveal a part of the explanation for relatively low investment levels in Britain. British companies, on average, consistently make lower rates of return on their investment than other major countries' private sector. Figure 14.7 shows that the level of profitability can vary considerably over time, the rate of return on capital being very variable. The trend in recent years is upwards. The rate of return in the last recession is little less than in the boom of the late 1970s.

c Changes in national income

Unlike the simple model with which we began investment must depend partly on the level of income. If income is higher, demand will be higher, so a higher volume of capital is required to meet that demand. However, it can be argued that investment is also a function of the rate of change of income. The accelerator principle suggests that firms have a desired stock of capital to meet the volume of demand. Since the value of the capital stock will need to be several times as great as the value of the output produced from it, it follows that small changes in national income can produce relatively large changes in investment. A rise in national income of say £100 may mean the need to increase the capital stock by several hundred pounds worth to meet the additional demand. Certainly, investment is the most unstable component in aggregate demand but attempts to find a close fit between changes in national income and the volume of investment have never been very successful, even if one allows for the inevitable time lags.

d Short-termism

One factor that some commentators believe affects investment in Britain, and a commonly asserted reason investment in Britain is lower than in many other developed economies, is that Britain suffers from 'short-termism'.

Short-termism can take the following form. Companies can be reluctant to engage in investing in projects where the pay-off is some years ahead even if the IRR for the project is high, since the high cost of capital will reduce profits in the short term. They may be reluctant to do this if shareholders, particularly institutional investors, are unwilling to wait and therefore choose to sell the shares of such firms. This will depress the price of those companies' shares and render them liable to takeover. Companies will therefore choose to concentrate on short-term projects. This may have a high cost to the country in that some forms of investment may suffer. One obvious form of investment that would be susceptible is research and development, where the pay-off may be many years ahead. For example, pharmaceutical companies invest millions of pounds. Even if a promising drug is discovered, the period of time before it receives a cash flow from the investment may be 10 to 20 years!

Another form of short-termism may be under-investment in training. Governments may be reluctant to encourage industry to train its workforce if the rewards of such investment are only going to appear many years later, perhaps after the next general election.

It is, however, possible to argue that short-termism exists only because markets operate in the context of imperfect knowledge. Patrick Foley,[2] for example, argues that the problem is really one of inadequate information. Part of his argument goes as follows. Management may not be short-sighted. It may be that they are reluctant to reveal information beyond the minimum required by law lest it give some advantage to a competitor. A side effect of this reluctance is that shareholders are therefore denied information. Given their lack of information they may be induced to sell shares in a company that they would have held on to, had they been aware of all information including its long-term prospects. Hence the difficulty is not that there is a problem of short-termism as such, rather that there is a problem of inadequate information on which investment decisions can be made. Not all economists agree about whether short-termism is a difficulty for the British economy. The difference of viewpoint mainly reflects confidence, or lack of it, in the power of markets to allocate resources effectively.

7 Weaknesses in the market case?

See pp 132–4

There is one other area in which we can make out a strong case for saying that the market will not bring about an optimal volume of private investment and might explain why British investment levels are too low. It is an application of ideas we have met earlier.

We have seen how the presence of externalities creates a problem for a society leaving its pricing decisions to the market. This is true for investment as well as for pricing. We have seen how there may be external benefits in production that markets ignore. One such example might be investment in education and training. Education and training spending can be seen as a kind of investment in 'human capital'. By increasing people's skills and knowledge one commits resources with an opportunity cost in the hope of a return, over a period of years, of an increase in output. When the value of this output is discounted at an appropriate interest rate, it shows the investment to be worthwhile.

Firms may be unwilling to invest adequately in training its workforce since the people it trains may decide to move and be employed elsewhere. Society will gain from the training but the firm itself may not do so. Therefore, left to a market the volume of investment in such human capital may be less than optimal. Britain spends much less on education and training than most other advanced nations.

A paper by Leo Doyle[3] of Kleinwort Benson Securities argues that there is a reasonably close positive relationship between investment in education and training and economic welfare. The more a country spends on education and training, the higher its welfare tends to be. This, of course does not show the direction of causality. Do countries who invest most in education have the highest output? Or is it that countries with the highest GNP can afford large volumes of educational expenditure? Perhaps the most plausible answer is that there is a 'virtuous circle' into which the UK needs to break.

The paper goes on to argue that educational investment should be increased and that if the UK could reach the best attainment level of the OECD, one million people would be removed permanently from the unemployment register. If this were so it would suggest that such an investment would be very worthwhile.

See pp 248–68

The idea of human capital might also lead us to the view that unemployment is an even worse problem than we saw in Chapter 13. If someone is out of work for a long time his or her skills are likely to diminish. The value of the human capital thus declines. Not only does unemployment involve an opportunity cost in terms of lost output while the person is unemployed, it may reduce the output that he or she can produce when finally returning to the labour market.

It is easy to see why a government might suffer from short-termism. If the payback to the investment were to be more than five years away, it might feel unwilling to commit such resources through higher taxation. In terms of our investment calculations the NPV must be much higher because cash flows beyond about five years will be ignored. The government might not win the next election. It can be argued that our election cycle causes governments to be short-termist.

Notice that to the extent that under-investment in education and training is a problem for the British economy it will have an effect on growth and output. It will not show up as a problem in conventional 'investment' statistics such as one given in Table 14.2 since these figures refer only to physical investment.

8 Conclusion

So does Britain invest enough? Given that investment uses resources with an opportunity cost, there is clearly an optimal volume of investment for a country to have. Some of that will inevitably be done by governments since part of that expenditure is in public goods. Whether the volume of private investment can be safely left to the market to decide is a question of some controversy. However, you should now be in a position to think through for yourself the extent to which you consider that market forces can be left to determine the level of private investment in an economy.

You should be able to see that much of the debate at the macro level about the levels of investment in Britain revolves around one's confidence, or lack of it, in the market system that we have been analysing in earlier chapters.

9 Questions for discussion

1 Why is it that only the purchase of a *new* house constitutes investment? After all, even if a house is five years old, it will still produce a flow of benefits over a long period.

2 A company has produced the following cash flows profile of a potential investment project. Using NPV (net present value) and assuming that interest rates are 10 per cent, would you recommend that the company goes ahead with the investment? Would it make any difference if interest rates were 15 per cent?

Year 0	Year 1	Year 2	Year 3
−£20,000	£6000	£12,000	£7000

3 The project given in question 2 has a rather different cash flow profile than the one given in the text. Which do you think would be more typical and why?

4 Since cash flows are only estimates of incomes the firm might receive, how could a firm cope with the problem of uncertainty in measuring the cash flow? Consider a major project such as Eurotunnel's in particular.

5 Is there so much value to an economy if some of its investment is made in another country? If not, should such outward investment be restricted? Should the government encourage inward investment such as the setting up of Japanese car firms in Britain?
6 What do you see as the major advantages of government being actively involved in the investment decisions of private firms?

10 Further reading

Investment analysis
Sloman, pp. 342–5; Begg, pp. 431–4; Parkin and King, pp. 631–40

Human capital
Begg, pp. 198–204; Parkin and King, pp. 377–9

Does Britain invest enough?
W. W. Easton (1990) 'The interest rate transmission mechanism in UK and overseas', *Bank of England Quarterly Bulletin*, 30, 2, May.
P. Foley (1990) 'Short-termism', *Lloyds Bank Economic Bulletin*, September.

11 End notes

1 W. W. Easton (1990) 'The interest rate transmission mechanism in UK and overseas', *Bank of England Quarterly Bulletin*, 30, 2, May. We shall use this model again in Chapter 20 when we are considering aspects of the international economy.
2 P. Foley (1990) 'Short-termism', *Lloyds Bank Economic Bulletin*, September.
3 L. Doyle (1992) *The Economic Cost of Being Bottom of the Class*, Kleinwort Benson Securities.

CHAPTER 15

Beating inflation:
is it really worth it?

Inflation in Britain is endemic. Prices have risen continually – although at different rates – since the Second World War. British inflation in recent years has been very low. In this chapter we ask whether government commitment to its defeat is worth the cost.

In order to do this we review the following concepts:
- **Absolute and relative prices**
- **Investment analysis**

We introduce the following concepts:
- **Aggregate supply and demand**
- **The Phillips Curve**
- **Rational expectations**

1 Introduction

The present government has invested a great deal of its credibility in beating inflation. During the late 1980s the then Chancellor of the Exchequer, Nigel Lawson, said that the government's inflation record was 'the judge and jury of economic policy'. The government of John Major the 1990s had at one time set as its goal a zero inflation rate. Since the government believes that in defeating inflation there are costs to pay – even increased unemployment is, according to another former Chancellor, Norman Lamont 'a price well worth paying' – it seems necessary to ask: what are the benefits that justify bearing such costs? Does inflation really matter? If it does, one thing is clear, the task faced by some governments is much greater than others. Table 15.1 shows that a wide variation in inflation rates exists in the world. Inflation in postwar Britain has never approached the levels of some countries given below, although it has often been high by European standards. During the 1990s British inflation performance has improved substantially. On one measure, inflation in November 1993 reached a low not seen since 1968.

We shall discover that virtually all economists agree that there are benefits in defeating inflation, but there is significant disagreement about the extent of the costs involved in doing so. However, before we consider what the costs and benefits are we must begin by being clear about what inflation is.

Table 15.1 Inflation in selected countries

| Countries | 1982–89 | 1990 | 1991 | 1992 | | | | 1993 |
| | | | | Mar. | Jun. | Sep. | Dec. | Mar. |
	Annual percentage changes, based on end-of-period figures[1]							
USA	3.7	6.1	3.1	3.2	3.1	3.0	2.9	3.1
Japan	1.4	3.8	2.7	2.0	2.3	2.0	1.2	1.2
Germany[2]	1.6	2.8	4.2	4.8	4.3	3.6	3.7	4.2
France	4.6	3.4	3.1	3.2	3.0	2.6	2.0	2.2[3]
Italy	7.3	6.4	6.0	5.4	5.4	5.1	4.6	4.2
UK	5.3	9.3	4.5	4.0	3.9	3.6	2.6	1.9
Canada	4.3	5.0	3.8	1.6	1.1	1.3	2.1	1.9
Australia	7.4	6.9	1.5	1.7	1.2	0.7	0.3	1.2
Austria	2.7	3.5	3.1	4.1	4.0	3.9	4.2	3.9
Belgium	3.4	3.5	2.8	2.7	2.6	2.3	2.4	2.9
Denmark	4.7	1.9	2.3	2.6	2.3	2.0	1.5	1.1
Finland	5.5	4.9	3.9	2.8	2.7	2.6	2.1	2.7[3]
Greece	17.7	22.9	18.0	18.3	15.1	15.3	14.4	16.4
Ireland	5.0	2.7	3.6	3.7	3.6	2.8	2.3	1.9
Israel	89.6	17.6	18.0	17.3	12.2	8.0	9.4	10.8
Netherlands	1.3	2.6	4.9	4.2	4.0	3.4	2.6	2.3
New Zealand	9.6	4.9	1.0	0.8	1.0	1.0	1.3	1.0
Norway	6.4	4.4	2.9	2.5	2.5	2.0	2.2	2.5
Portugal	16.1	13.7	9.2	8.5	9.5	9.1	8.4	7.3
Spain	7.8	6.5	5.5	6.9	6.2	5.8	5.4	4.0
Sweden	6.3	10.9	8.1	2.6	2.1	2.5	1.9	4.9
Switzerland	2.4	5.3	5.2	4.9	4.2	3.5	3.4	3.6
Turkey	50.8	60.4	71.1	78.7	65.8	67.7	66.0	58.0
Average[4]	4.5	5.8	14.1	4.0	3.7	3.5	3.2	3.2

Note: [1]Quarterly figures for Australia, Ireland and New Zealand. [2]Western Germany only. [3]New index. [4]Weighted average, based on 1990 exchange rates and consumption weights.
Source: Bank for International Settlements (BIS), Annual Report, 1993.

2 Inflation: what do we mean?

By inflation, we mean a general and persistent rise in the 'average' level of prices. Prices, on average, continue to rise. To put the same thing in a different way, we could say that the value of money is falling. With inflation, a given amount of money income buys less over time. But we shall need to do better than that. We need to measure more accurately the extent of the change in the price level. We shall show how this is done by way of an example taken from Table 15.2. The process involves the use of index numbers.

Since these are based on the number 100, it makes percentage changes in the price level immediately apparent. The calculation for changes in the price level in Britain uses the price changes of many hundreds of goods and services. The Central Statistical Office (CSO) collects about 130,000 observations on these different commodities from various outlets each month to produce the data, which are then grouped into the main areas of consumer expenditure shown in Table 15.2.

We observe the change in price of each good over whatever period we are interested in. In Britain this is done monthly as well as annually. We illustrate here the change in the UK price level for the 12 months to November 1993. Each price change will not have the same significance to consumers. Price changes of those goods on which consumers spend more are more important so we attached larger 'weights' to these changes reflecting that significance.

Look at the 'weights' column in Table 15.2. It can be interpreted in the following way. For every £1000 of expenditure the average consumer spends £21 on seasonal food or 21 thousandths of his/her income. Hence the weight is 21.

Table 15.2 Constructing the retail price index

Category of expenditure	Weights	Change in price in years to Nov. 93	Change in price X expenditure weights
Seasonal food	21	−0.6	−12.6
Non-Seasonal food	123	+1.9	233.7
Catering	45	+5.0	225.0
Motoring	136	+3.5	476.0
Travel	21	+4.3	90.3
Housing	164	−5.4	−885.6
Household goods	79	+0.9	71.1
Household services	47	+3.5	164.5
Leisure goods	46	+1.2	55.2
Leisure services	62	+4.2	260.4
Fuel and light	46	−1.6	−73.6
Clothing and footwear	58	+1.4	81.2
Personal goods and services	39	+4.1	159.9
Alcoholic drink	78	+3.6	280.8
Tobacco products	35	+8.6	301.0
Total	1000	34.6	1427.3

Source: CSO.

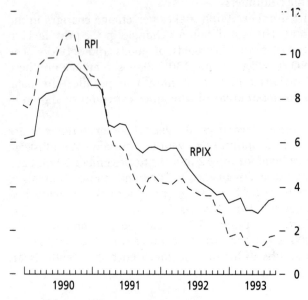

Increase on prices on a year earlier

Figure 15.1 UK inflation in the 1990s

Since rather more, £136 out of every thousand pounds, is consumed by motoring costs, this receives the appropriate higher weighting.

The process used to establish the price index is as follows. Each change in price of a category of goods is multiplied by its weight. For non-seasonal food, prices increased by 1.9 per cent in the year to November 1993. We multiply that change by its weight: $1.9 \times 123 = 233.7$. This is shown in the final column of Table 15.2 where similar calculations have been done on all of the other categories of consumer expenditure. We now add all the figures in that column. This gives 1427.3. We then divide that number by the sum of the weights: $1427.3 \div 1000$ gives 1.4273. Hence prices have risen by 1.4273 per cent in the 12-month period 'on average'. The price index rose by 1.4 per cent, approximately.

Notice what would have happened if we had not weighted the price changes. The unweighted average price change would have been as follows. The sum of the (unweighted) changes was 34.6 per cent. We divide that by the number of categories of consumer expenditure. This gives $34.6 \div 15 = 2.3$ per cent. The reason for this higher inflation figure is that we have failed to attach sufficient importance to the large fall in housing costs which occurred over the period. Such an unweighted measure is so unrealistic that it would not be calculated at all.

Some prices have risen by more than the average and some by less. Relative prices have altered. Seasonal food has fallen absolutely and relatively. But notice that in this period household goods have also fallen relatively because they have risen less than the average price level. If we were looking at household goods and trying to explain the change using micro-economic analysis, we would be seeking to explain why their price was declining, not why they were rising.

The most commonly quoted measure of inflation in Britain is provided by the retail prices index (RPI) produced by the CSO. It is the one we have just calculated. It is frequently called the 'headline rate'. Also published is the figure called the 'underlying rate' referred to in Figure 15.1 as RPIX. What is the difference between the two and which is the better measure? The difference is that the underlying rate excludes an item that is quite volatile, namely mortgage interest payments. This is a large item of expenditure for millions of people buying their own homes but is an item that can vary significantly with changes in interest rates in the economy. So when interest rates are increasing the RPI is rising more quickly than the underlying rate, but falling more quickly when interest rates fall, which is exactly what happened in the year to November 1993. The reduced volatility of the underlying rate can easily be seen in Figure 15.1. It was this rate which reached a 26 year low in November 1993.

There are two main arguments for concentrating on the underlying rate. The first one is that mortgage repayments are not simply a reflection of living costs. People who pay mortgages are acquiring a house which is an asset. It is a form of saving. The second is that most other countries, including Europe produce a price index that excludes mortgage interest payments. Hence comparisons with European countries are more realistic using the underlying rate.

However, it is important to remember that mortgage interest does partly reflect living costs. If one were to produce an RPI from which mortgage repayments are excluded, it would be necessary to put into it some element of housing costs since it is such an important element of a family's expenditure. The government's 'preferred' measure is the underlying rate.

There is one other thing that might well have occurred to you as you studied Table 15.2. The weights are for average expenditure. This means that for some groups neither the RPI nor the underlying rate is very realistic. So, for example, if student representatives wish to make out a case for more generous treatment with grants, they could construct a different index based on average weights for student expenditure. This might well show a different change in the cost of living for students as compared with the average household.

3 The costs of inflation

It is not obvious that inflation is a problem. If money incomes rise as fast as the price level, living standards are not falling. Indeed, if you recall the logic of national income accounts, it should be clear that a price increase for one person is an income increase for someone else. Nevertheless, there are costs to inflation. We shall look briefly at most of them and then concentrate on the most controversial aspect of inflation – its link with unemployment. First, however, we shall consider other costs of inflation.

a The political costs to government

Some have suggested that governments have a vested interest in inflation. The higher prices rise the less is the real value of government debt. However, postwar history in Britain tells a different story. The relationship of movements in the price level to general election results suggests that the electorate judges a government very much on its inflation record. In the last British election in 1992 the Conservative government won an election during a period when growth was negative, unemployment was rising, the balance-of-payments account was in deficit and interest rates were high (though falling). Nevertheless, the rate of inflation, although positive, was falling. This was not an isolated occurrence.

It is likely that over time this aversion of the electorate to inflation will continue. Those on retirement incomes fear that inflation will erode their savings. The proportion of the population that is of retirement age is increasing. It is therefore likely to be politically as well as economically shrewd to place a high priority on the defeat of inflation. There is some economic logic too, as we shall see.

b The waste of scarce resources

There are several different ways in which inflation imposes costs on society, in that resources are used up which could have been put to more valuable ends.

It could be argued, for example, that much of the time spent by management and unions on the bargaining associated with the annual pay round is a function of a positive rate of inflation. Resources are committed simply seeing to it that there is no change in the relative price of labour. The argument needs to be treated with some care. At least part of all this resource usage would be necessary even with zero inflation. The market mechanism still requires some change in relative wage rates over time. It could be argued that some inflation 'oils the wheels' of such changes in that where market forces dictate a lower equilibrium real wage unions may find this more palatable if they receive a smaller 'increase' rather than, as would be the case with zero inflation, a cut in the nominal wage rate.

An alternative possible resource waste could be working days lost through strikes. The higher the inflation rate, the more frequently labour bargains for increases in nominal wage rates. This increases the danger that the outcome of bargaining will be some strike action. Figure 15.2 suggests that there is indeed a positive correlation between inflation rates and working days lost by strikes, at least in advanced industrial economies.

However, a waste of resources through inflation is possible not only in the labour market. Resources are also committed, in a society with a permanent inflation rate, to the production of services whose main function is to protect

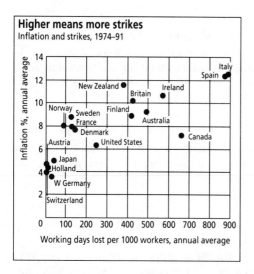

Higher means more strikes
Inflation and strikes, 1974–91

Source: *The Economist*, 7 November 1992.

Figure 15.2 Inflation and strikes

against inflation. For example, speculative purchases of gold are attributable to people's perception that inflation erodes away the real value of savings. Resources are then committed to producing a service that would be irrelevant in a society which did not suffer from inflation. This is not to suggest that gold has no intrinsic value. But many purchases of the commodity are not to enjoy its intrinsic worth, but because of its perceived hedge against inflation.

c 'Menu' costs

During periods of inflation the nominal price of those goods and services whose relative price is not changing still has to be altered. This involves costs. For example, a restaurant owner must go to the expense of altering the prices on the menu. Price lists of many products will need changing. The faster the rate of inflation the worse the problem will be. This problem manifests itself partly through additional resources being committed to the coverage of these 'menu' costs and partly through the reduction in information available. With a stable price level firms are willing to advertise with the price of the product included in the advertisement. During an inflationary period the high menu costs prevent so much information being available.

d 'Shoe leather' costs

There is one other cost of inflation that would be small if inflation rates are of the level of, say, Western Europe. Higher inflation tends to mean higher interest rates.

Since money in circulation gains no interest, the opportunity cost of holding such money increases. This encourages people to hold less cash and make more trips to their bank or building society. Such actions impose costs on the individual directly – they are sometimes called 'shoe leather' costs! – but also indirectly. Banks' and building societies' transactions costs increase if people come often for a little cash rather than fewer times for more.

The above costs are imposed on society during a period of inflation, even if the inflation is correctly anticipated. However, one could argue that economic agents do not correctly anticipate inflation. If this is so, further costs are imposed on society. It is to these that we now turn.

4 Imperfectly anticipated inflation

As we shall see, the costs of imperfectly anticipated inflation are likely to be very much greater than those costs discussed so far. In this section we consider four possible costs of imperfectly anticipated inflation, namely redistributional effects, balance-of-payments problems, increased uncertainty and the problem of hyper-inflation.

a Redistributional effects

See pp 279–80

One problem for an inflationary economy is the capricious way it tends to redistribute income. Recall that in Chapter 14 we made a distinction between nominal and real interest rates. Real interest rates are nominal rates minus the rate of inflation. The main reason for the redistributional effect of inflation is that nominal interest rates rarely respond fully to the effects of rising prices. Although there is generally some upward movement of nominal interest rates during an inflationary period, it is rarely sufficient to see to it that real interest rates are constant. Therefore when an economy suffers from any more than mild inflationary pressures, income is redistributed from creditors, those who are owed money, to debtors, those who have borrowed. Two illustrations of this process will suffice.

Most people who purchase a house borrow the money from a bank or building society. Really, of course, they are borrowing from other people who save with these institutions. The institutions themselves are simply intermediaries who make a profit by reducing the transactions costs involved.

Now if inflation is high and interest rates do not rise fully to reflect it, the real value of the mortgage debt falls. Correspondingly, the real value of the savings of the creditor also falls. Income is therefore redistributed through inflation. Of course, the problem is one of imperfectly anticipated inflation. If the creditor had correctly anticipated future events, he would have found an inflation-proof method of saving. The problem, then, is a combination of inflation plus imperfect knowledge.

A similar process occurs when inflation reduces the value of the government's debt. Since, with rare exceptions, governments spend more in any year than they receive in taxation, and so on there is a public sector borrowing requirement adding to the national debt. Most of that debt is with its own citizens in the form of national savings, bonds and bills. If interest rates are less than inflation and people are willing to buy government debt because of failing to anticipate inflation correctly, income will be distributed away from private citizens, and possibly companies, towards government.

These redistributional effects can have secondary consequences that may be overlooked. As we have already seen on several occasions efficient markets require mobility of labour. Unanticipated inflation can reduce that mobility.

A typical contract for professional labour includes a pension entitlement. The size of the pension depends upon the number of years service with the company and the salary at retirement or at the time the employee leaves the company. Inflation erodes away the real value of the salary earned at the time of leaving. In a strongly inflationary economy a person who leaves a firm at, say, 35 to work for another, may discover that at retirement the real value of the pension from the first firm is virtually worthless. This may act as a strong disincentive to change jobs.

Another way of viewing these redistributional problems is to see it as an illustration of the problem mentioned in Chapter 1. Relative price changes can be confused with absolute price changes during inflation. If this happens it can have consequences for the efficient working of the market system.

See pp 12–15

b Balance-of-payments problems

Frequently the British government has argued that inflation control is crucial to retain balance-of-payments equilibrium. If Britain inflates faster than the rest of the world, import prices become cheaper relative to export prices. Exports fall as foreigners substitute other goods for British ones. Imports rise as domestic consumers switch to cheaper substitute imported goods. The conclusion is that the inflation rate must not be allowed to be greater than that in other countries. This is an argument that many economists would not accept and deserves careful consideration. However, we shall not discuss it further now. It is dealt with in Chapter 20.

See pp 393–4

c Increased uncertainty

Recall what we said in Chapter 14. Investment decisions taken by firms, we said, are made by estimating the initial capital cost and the future revenue stream. Then the revenue stream is discounted at an appropriate interest rate to see if the project is worthwhile. We assumed that there was no inflation in the economy. Now suppose there is inflation but future inflation rates are entirely predictable. Any correctly anticipated inflation can easily be built into the investment

See pp 276–9

equation. Thus, we would have

$$IRR = \text{the rate, } r, \text{ such that } \sum_{k=1}^{n} A_k \frac{(1+s)^k}{(1+r)^k} - C = 0$$

A = cash flows
C = capital cost
r = nominal interest rates
s = anticipated inflation

Note that if the nominal interest rate is the same as the inflation rate, the real rate of interest is zero. Assuming that a rise in the price level is not anticipated, it is then a matter of indifference when the cash flows are earned. There is no opportunity cost involved in waiting for the cash flows.

But unanticipated inflation creates problems. It may reduce the volume of investment because of the increased uncertainty associated with inflation. That is to say, firms are aware that they cannot perfectly anticipate inflation. They may therefore make a greater allowance for risk reducing the chances that the project will be undertaken. Furthermore, the higher the level of inflation, the greater the likely variation in its rate. This again increases uncertainty and may decrease investment.

Is there any evidence to suggest that this is the case? First, there is evidence that a lower rate of inflation means less variability. Figure 15.3 plots the relationship between the rate of inflation and a measure of its variability for advanced industrial countries. There is clearly a strong positive correlation.

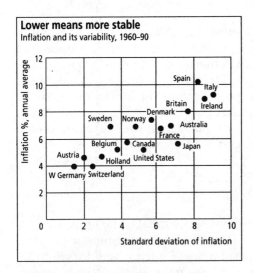

Source: The Economist, 7 November 1992.

Figure 15.3 Inflation and its variability

But does a higher level of inflation lead to less investment? We can measure this correlation indirectly. Since more investment should, *ceteris paribus,* lead to a higher growth rate of gross national product (GNP), we can ask if there is a correlation between inflation and growth.

The evidence here is weak. We can again compare the performances of advanced industrial economies in this respect (see Figures 15.4 and 15.5 below).

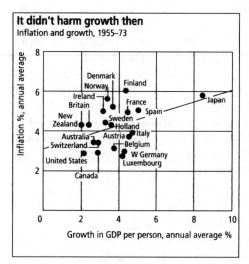

Source: The Economist, 7 November 1992.

Figure 15.4 Inflation and growth, 1955–73

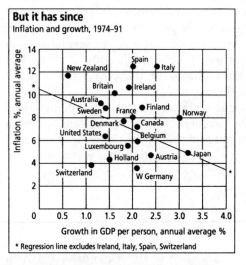

Source: The Economist, 7 November 1992.

Figure 15.5 Inflation and growth, 1973–91

First, consider what happened in the period 1955–73 when inflation was low for most of these countries. If a correlation exists, it is a positive one. That is, higher inflation countries achieved higher rates of growth. However, if one removes Japan from consideration, there appears to be no correlation at all.

What do we find if we examine the relationship between inflation and gross domestic product (GDP) growth in the period 1974–91? *The Economist* claims that it shows inflation harming growth. As you can see from Figure 15.5, the correlation is again poor. However, it is certainly much improved, though hardly compelling, if one ignores Italy, Spain, Ireland and Switzerland. The reason for ignoring these countries is as follows. Italy, Spain and Ireland began the period with relatively low average incomes per head. They had, therefore, more potential for growth than the others and so had a high growth rate despite having relatively high inflation rates. Switzerland, on the other hand, had the highest income per head and thus had less scope for growth. You must decide for yourself whether the argument for ignoring some countries is convincing. Does national income in different countries converge over time? If not, it is difficult to argue that, for example, Switzerland has little scope for growth.

d Hyper-inflation

Some regard any inflation as harmful because it tends to increase. If left unchecked, it produces high rates of inflation known as hyper-inflation. As the saying goes, a little bit of inflation is like a little bit of pregnancy – it is liable to increase. Whether this is true is far from certain. What is certain is that if inflation does lead to hyper-inflation, an economy will experience enormous problems. The costs of hyper-inflation are very high. Perhaps the most valuable function of money is that it acts as a medium of exchange and removes many transaction costs associated with the barter economy. If people lose confidence in money, for example in Germany in the early 1920s when inflation reached several million per cent per week, a market economy cannot function efficiently, if at all. Not even the emerging democracies of Eastern Europe or the economies of Latin America have approached this level of difficulty with inflation.

What we have said so far may cause you to feel that inflation is not painless and that its defeat should be a priority for a government. However, one cannot form a judgement on the matter without examining one more crucial issue. How does inflation affect unemployment? It is to this central question that we now turn.

5 Inflation and unemployment

a Aggregate demand and supply

Demand and supply curves for individual markets show the relationship between the price of a good and the quantity of it demanded and supplied. By now this is familiar to you. Here we will find it useful for understanding the working of the

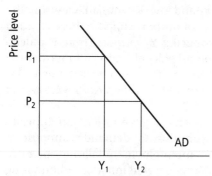

Figure 15.6   The price level and aggregate demand

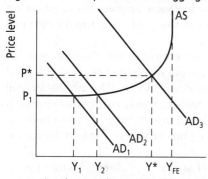

Figure 15.7   Aggregate demand and a Keynesian aggregate supply curve

economy at the macro-level, if we use aggregate demand and supply curves. Essentially this means that we look at the relationship between the price level of all goods and services and the amount of output of all goods and services demanded and supplied. What would these relationships look like? Consider first the aggregate demand curve in Figure 15.6, which shows a greater quantity of goods and services being demanded as the price level falls. Why would this happen?

The answer is that at a lower price level the real value of money will be greater, so people will wish to buy more. Furthermore, it may be that at a lower price level for our goods and services people will switch out of buying imports into buying home produced output. Thus, for a lower price level, say a decline from P_1 to P_2, the quantity of national output demanded increases from Y_1 to Y_2.

The shape of the aggregate supply curve is much more controversial. We shall consider two possible shapes, the first of which is given in Figure 15.7.

Back in Chapter 13 we considered the question of unemployment. We saw the Keynesian view that unemployment can be dealt with via an increase in aggregate demand. We said little about the effect of this increase in demand on the price

See pp 260–4

level. Figure 15.7 will now help us to understand the Keynesian view on the matter. Y_{Fe} represents the full employment level of output. Suppose there is much unemployment, since the economy is only producing Y_1 output. There is a deep recession. Aggregate demand is low, at AD_1 the price level is at P_1. Suppose now aggregate demand is stimulated and that it shifts to AD_2. Output increases to Y_2. Firms increase output to meet the increase in demand. Yet the price level stays at P_1.

But there is still unemployment. What happens if government attempts to remove that unemployment via a further stimulus to demand? Suppose it increases demand to AD_3. Output expands to Y^*, unemployment falls but the price level has increased to P^*. Moving towards Y_{FE} has generated inflation. Eliminating unemployment altogether would only be possible with substantial inflation. In other words, the aggregate supply curve suggests that there exists a trade-off between inflation and unemployment. Why Keynesians believe this to be so we shall consider shortly. Another possible shape of the aggregate supply curve is given below in Figure 15.8.

The vertical aggregate supply curve represents the basis of the classical view.[1] It says that there is a full employment level of output in the economy. That is a level of output where everyone who wishes to work will do so. The economy will always tend towards that position because the market mechanism will see that it does. Suppose there was unemployment. Unemployment must be, by definition, an excess supply of labour. What happens in a market where there is an excess supply? The price will fall. In other words, real wage rates would decline until all those wanting a job have got one. In essence that is what full employment is.

See pp 359–61

If governments control inflation which, as we shall see in Chapter 18, can be done by monetary policy, we can have the benefits of lower inflation at no great cost in terms of unemployment. There may be some temporary unemployment for reasons we shall see shortly, but that will be something that markets can quickly correct. A reduction in aggregate demand from AD_1 to AD_2 will reduce

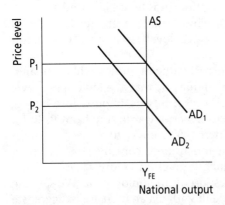

Figure 15.8 Aggregate demand and a vertical aggregate supply curve

inflation, that is reduce the price level, from P_1 to P_2. Unemployment, however, will not result. It is this disagreement over the shape of the aggregate supply curve which we will now consider further.

b Developing the Keynesian perspective: the Phillips Curve

Support for the Keynesian perspective represented by Figure 15.7 came as the result of empirical observations made by A. W. Phillips. He noted that if one plotted over a period the recorded observations of unemployment and the rate of change of money wages for the British economy, one obtained a picture suggesting a relationship as described by Figure 15.9. Note that this is not a theory, it is a recording of observations. He noted that in years when unemployment was high, the rate of change of money wages was relatively low. The speed at which money wages were changing served as a good proxy for inflation. Not all the observations were exactly on the line, but the line represented a good fit.

Now what could give rise to such a relationship? The Phillips argument was as follows. When unemployment is high and there is a pool of labour seeking employment, trade unions power to gain wage increases is low. If the pool of unemployed labour is smaller, and the labour market tighter, trade unions can negotiate larger increases in money wages.

The next step in the argument is simple. Governments have the power to regulate the volume of aggregate demand in the economy. If they believe the costs of inflation to be high, they can prevent that inflation by tightly controlling aggregate demand. The price they must pay is a higher level of unemployment. If the government feels that the costs of inflation for an economy are low, it can gain the advantages of fuller employment via a higher volume of aggregate demand. The government can assess the costs and benefits of inflation control and act accordingly.

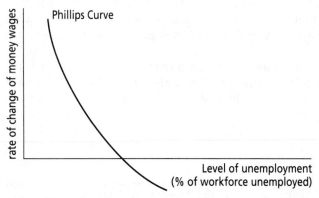

Figure 15.9 The Phillips Curve relationship

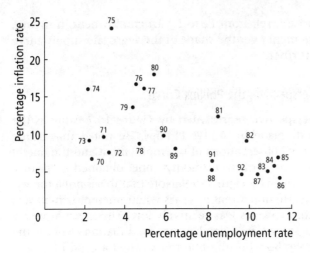

Figure 15.10 Annual observations of unemployment and inflation

c The Phillips Curve: a criticism

The Phillips Curve was based on observations of the British Economy up to 1957. One criticism that can be made of it is that more recent history has shown it to be out of date. Look at Figure 15.10. Observations of recent years are very far to the right of the original curve. The original curve suggested that with an unemployment level of only 5.5 per cent there would be no change at all in the average level of money wages.

The Keynesians have an interesting response to the criticism. It goes like this. The original Phillips Curve was developed during a period of low inflation. Therefore when unions negotiated wage increases, they were using what had been happening to prices in the recent past as a basis for wage claims. Once inflation is clearly higher, unions begin to anticipate what will happen to prices in the coming year, and negotiations proceed on that basis. Higher inflation thus becomes a self-fulfilling prophecy as higher wages chase higher prices in an inflationary spiral. The Phillips Curve still holds but expectations of inflation can push the curve to the right.

Plausible though this is, it still admits of an empirical problem. In the last few years expectations are that price inflation will be only around 2–4 per cent per annum. Even so, the curve does show little sign of shifting back inwards to its original position.

d Two classical perspectives on inflation

Not all Keynesians think exactly the same. There are variations on the Keynesian model, although the Keynesian school of thought can be said to cover those economists whose perspective is that markets do not clear quickly in the way that classical economists believe. Similarly, not all classical thinking is identical, though there is this basic perspective that markets will adjust and do a better job maximising welfare than governments will do by macro-economic intervention. We shall now look at two different views of the relationship between inflation and unemployment, both of which are in the classical mould.

The first school of classical thinking is happy to accept the existence of a Phillips Curve, but not its policy conclusion. The reason for this is based on what has become known as the 'rational expectations' hypothesis. Remember that the classicals believe markets clear quickly. So, as we have seen before, we have a vertical aggregate supply curve. Does this mean zero unemployment? Not quite. There is a natural rate of unemployment, comprising people who choose not to be working at the going level of real wages. It is voluntary unemployment since markets clear. Anyone who wants a job at the going wage rate for their particular skill can find one. In Figure 15.11 we show that natural rate at an assumed 8 per cent. We can have that at any level of inflation. Remember that in classical thinking unemployment cannot be traded against inflation. To have a lower level of unemployment the government must reduce the natural rate of unemployment. This may be possible as we will see in Chapters 16 and 17. How then can the Phillips Curve be accepted? The argument is an interesting one.

See pp 310–47

Suppose the economy is at point A in Figure 15.11. There is zero inflation and a natural rate of 8 per cent unemployment. Suppose then that the government, following a Keynesian model, decides that unemployment is too high. It expands aggregate demand, thinking that the cost of a lower unemployment rate of 6 per cent is worth the 9 per cent inflation it will cause. It therefore shifts the economy to point B on the diagram. The problem, according to this school of thinking is that

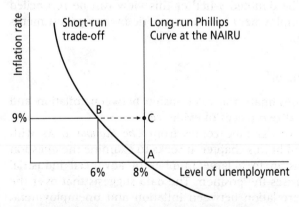

Figure 15.11 Classical view of the Phillips Curve

the economy cannot and will not remain there. What has happened is that some people have been persuaded into employment since they believe that the higher wage rates being paid because of government stimulus to the economy make it worth their while. Soon they will realise that they have been misled. Money wages are higher, real wages are not, since the price level is higher. Once they realise that real wages have not increased they will leave the labour market again and the economy will be at point C. Notice that we now have 9 per cent inflation, with all the costs that imposes on the economy and the same level of unemployment as before – the natural rate.

Now, of course, you cannot fool all the people all the time. The government will not be able to keep stimulating the economy and permanently fooling people into thinking that real wages are increasing. Rational expectations suggests that they will incorporate a 9 per cent inflation rate into their thinking. Next time the government may be able to fool people again, but since people have adjusted to thinking in terms of inflation at an annual rate of 9 per cent, it may take an inflation rate of, say, 12 per cent, to do it. To get unemployment below 6 per cent it will require, not a positive rate of inflation, but an accelerating rate of inflation. That is why the natural rate of unemployment is sometimes called NAIRU – a Non-Accelerating Inflationary Rate of Unemployment. In the long run the benefits of zero inflation are available at zero cost. In the short run there is a trade-off between inflation and unemployment.

A second strand of classical thinking takes a different approach. It takes the view that economic agents do not have to wait until inflation figures are announced. They can anticipate changes in the inflation rate from freely available information on such data as changes in the money supply.[2] On this view any attempt by governments to trade off inflation for unemployment will not work even in the short run. You cannot fool any of the people any of the time. Markets will therefore clear very quickly and there is not even a short run trade-off. The Phillips Curve is of no value at all. Governments should forget about unemployment problems and concentrate economic policy on the elimination of inflation. However, it must be doubted whether this view can be reconciled with the evidence of rising unemployment over a long period when governments attempt to bring inflation down.

e Empirical evidence on the trade-off

Economists have attempted to estimate the relationship between inflation and unemployment. We shall look at two pieces of evidence.

The first piece of evidence we examine comes from *The Economist*. As with previous evidence we considered in this chapter, it seeks to examine the question with reference to the relationship in a large number of advanced industrial countries. Figure 15.12 summarises the position. The data suggests that over the long run there is a positive correlation between inflation and unemployment. Overall, countries with the higher inflation rates tend to have higher

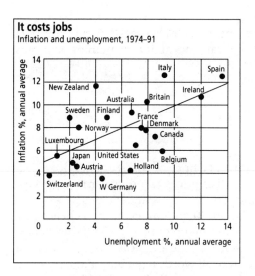

It costs jobs
Inflation and unemployment, 1974–91

Source: *The Economist*, 7 November 1992.

Figure 15.12 Inflation and unemployment

Table 15.3 Estimated natural rate of unemployment in Britain

1956–59	1960–68	1969–73	1974–81	1980–87
2.2	2.5	3.6	7.3	8.7

Source: S. Nickell (1990) 'inflation and the UK labour market' *Oxford Review of Economic Policy*, Vol. 6, No. 4. Reproduced by permission of Oxford University Press.

unemployment levels, although as you can see the relationship is not particularly close.

The Economist therefore argues that it is worth fighting inflation since in the long run it will decrease unemployment and increase national output. The article goes on to argue that if inflation is reduced there will be some short-term increase in unemployment since, as the Keynesians suggest, labour markets do not adjust quickly. Therefore at the same time that the government seeks to reduce inflation, it should try to undertake policies to reduce the short-term costs involved. We shall return to this point in the next chapter.

The other piece of evidence comes from the Oxford economist Stephen Nickell. He argues that there is a natural rate of unemployment for the British economy, but that this rate has been changing. Applying various statistical techniques to data for the British economy, he argues that this natural rate has risen over time as shown in Table 15.3.

This 'natural rate' is the one that he argues to be consistent with a constant rate of inflation and balanced international trade. Reducing the rate of inflation will

See pp 314–17

require a still higher level of unemployment. Nickell also seeks to consider what factors are responsible for this rising natural rate, but that is something that must wait until the next chapter.

6 Conclusion

Inflation is a general rise in the weighted average price of goods and services. Even if the absolute price level does not rise, relative prices can do so. There are costs imposed on a society that suffers inflation. There is considerable debate as to the costs of government policy to control inflation. Keynesian economists believe the costs to be those associated with the increased unemployment, which they believe is the result of markets failing to clear. Some of the classical school of thought believe that the costs of inflation control are well worth paying in that they are of a short-term nature only. Other classical economists believe that there are not even short-term costs to pay in that markets can clear very fast. The severe, and sometimes lasting, nature of recessions makes this last view difficult to believe. As with other questions, your own view of this debate will be largely determined by the extent of your enthusiasm for the market mechanism and its ability to restore equilibrium speedily.

7 Questions for discussion

1 How should an accurate consumer price index reflect a change in government taxation policy which switches from direct to indirect taxes?
2 Why might the way the RPI is calculated overstate price inflation during a period of recession in the economy? (HINT: Compare the CSO selection of goods which forms the price index and the selection of a typical shopper looking for the best value goods.)
3 To what extent is the view of the labour market expressed in the Phillips Curve relationship consistent with the explanations given in Chapter 11 for the decline in trade union membership?
4 What arguments would Keynesian economists give for rejecting the view that labour markets clear quickly? Are these arguments convincing?
5 We saw that Stephen Nickell expresses the natural rate of unemployment as one consistent with a zero change in inflation. Why does he also express it as one consistent with an international trade balance? (HINT: If demand increases does it necessarily lead just to increased prices at home?)
6 How convincing do you find the argument that beating inflation has no cost in terms of increased unemployment?

See pp 210–12

8 Further reading

Aggregate supply and demand
Sloman, pp. 547–54; Begg, pp. 447–67; Parkin and King, pp. 588–612

The Phillips Curve
Sloman, pp. 571–3; Begg, pp. 494–501; Parkin and King, pp. 854–8

Rational expectations
Sloman, pp. 848–64; Begg, pp. 563–570; Parkin and King, pp. 842–51

Beating inflation: is it really worth it?
S. Soteri and P. Westaway (1993) 'Explaining price inflation', *UK National Institute Economic Review*, May.
'How low is low enough?' *Economist*, 07/11/92, pp. 21–4.

9 End notes

1 We have used the word 'classical' to describe economists whose views are that markets do clear reasonably quickly, and that therefore government intervention to manipulate aggregate demand is not necessary. The process by which markets clear, the speed at which it happens, and the extent to which governments should assist markets to work quickly is a matter of some debate among 'classicals'. Hence this term embraces a large group of economists who may differ over many things. But they do agree that markets will adjust with a reasonable speed and in this sense have a view quite distinct from Keynesian economists.

2 The use of the money supply data to predict inflation rates is dealt with in Chapter 18.

CHAPTER 16

The rich get richer and the poor get poorer . . .
the supply-side revolution

In the last 15 years taxes on high income earners have been cut dramatically. Meanwhile, some at the bottom of the income scale are worse off. How can such a policy change be justified? The idea behind this policy change is to improve incentives to work, thus raising output in order to improve living standards for all.

In this chapter we examine this argument, we review the following concepts:
* Indifference theory
* The supply curve of labour
* Aggregate supply and demand

We introduce the following:
* Income and substitution effects
* Average and marginal tax rates

1 Introduction

During the postwar years most Western economies experienced a period of unparalleled prosperity. Sustained growth was accompanied by relatively full employment. This was widely attributed to Keynesian macro-economic policies. As we have seen, these emphasised government responsibility in controlling the volume of aggregate demand with little attention paid to aggregate supply. The aggregate supply curve was taken as given. A key element in the control of demand was taxation. When demand was thought to be too high, threatening inflation, taxation could be increased. Alternatively, it could be lowered if demand was thought to be too low and excessive unemployment was a danger.

During the 1970s such Keynesian policies were increasingly criticised. When the Conservative party returned to power in 1979, it had rejected the Keynesian position. Aggregate demand could look after itself. Markets would see to it that the economy tended towards full employment. The key to successful macro-economic policy was improving aggregate supply. In essence this meant that policy should be aimed at raising output from a given volume of resources. Various measures were introduced because of this belief. They included attempts to increase competition in markets where it was felt to be too limited. This covered, for example, pressures in the Economic Union to liberalise air transport, which we considered in Chapter 8. Another policy measure was to transfer state industries to the private sector. This is the focus of Chapter 17. Confidence in markets also resulted in another very significant policy measure, on which we shall now concentrate. One very important means of stimulating the supply side of the economy was believed to be reducing the burden of direct taxation. Less taxation meant a greater stimulus to work effort. This would raise output and the economy would grow faster.

See pp 149–68

See pp 330–47

In this chapter we examine the rationale for this view. It raises several important issues. How has the tax system altered as a result of this view? What is the macro-economic model of the economy implicit in such policies? Is the view it presents of the labour market correct? Does the evidence suggest that policy has been successful? It is these important questions that we wish to address now.

2 The tax system in Britain

a The nature of the tax system

Our first task is to see what is the burden of taxation that falls on UK citizens who work for their living and how this burden has changed in recent years. Of all taxes paid to the government only part of it is 'direct', that is to say, we pay taxes in part directly to the government out of what is called our factor income. For most people that means tax on income from our labour, a direct tax on wages and salaries. If we own capital, we pay tax on dividends and interest. If we own land, there is a direct tax on the rent received. Similarly, firms pay direct taxes to the government out of the factor income, capital, in the form of profits tax.

However, some part of government revenue is received as an 'indirect' tax. When we purchase many goods, a computer for example, to the price received by the supplier is added $17^1/_2$ per cent value added tax (VAT). The value added tax is indirect in that it does not come directly from our incomes to government. It is only when people spend their incomes that the tax is paid. VAT is the major but not sole form of indirect tax.

Direct tax can be seen from Table 16.1 to be the largest single source of government revenue. Of all direct taxes the two most important ones are those borne by suppliers of labour, income tax and National Insurance contributions. Not all National Insurance contributions are paid by employees. A large part of them is paid by employers.

There are still other forms of revenue received by the government which are listed below. One of these is receipts from privatisation, part of 'other' in Table 16.1 on which we shall have more to say in the next chapter.

Since governments must raise taxes, what is the best way of doing it? One consideration is the cost of administration. Income taxes are cheap to collect in

Table 16.1 Sources of government revenue 1994–5

	£ billion	% of revenue
Income tax	64.4	22.2
National insurance contributions	42.8	14.8
Corporation tax	17.6	6.0
Value added tax	43.1	14.9
Excise duties	27.1	9.3
Other receipts	57.4	19.8
Borrowing	37.9	13.0

Source: Treasury Bulletin.

administrative terms, whereas VAT is expensive. However, there are two other considerations that must weigh heavily when considering how to raise revenue. One is that it should be fair. In deciding upon taxation policy there is an equity consideration. The other is that it should not be such as to discourage people from working, that is, there is an efficiency consideration. The difficulty is that if we believe that taxation policy has considerable efficiency effects, we may be faced with a trade-off between efficiency and equity.

b Progressive and regressive taxes

Before we examine any possible trade-off of this kind we have to understand a distinction to be drawn between regressive, proportional and progressive tax systems. A *progressive* tax is one where as income rises, the proportion of a person's income paid in taxation increases. So higher income earners pay a higher proportion of their income in tax. This is illustrated in Table 16.2, which shows the position of a single man paying tax, ignoring National Insurance contributions, to the government in the last full year of a Labour administration. The average earnings then were around £4280 per annum. A man earning about a quarter of that could earn £985 without paying income tax, but on each additional pound earned he paid 25 per cent. The proportion of his salary taken by the government in income tax was thus 1.3 per cent, but each additional pound earned would be taxed at 25 per cent. As his income rose, the proportion of it going in tax would also rise. The tax rate on the last pound earned we call the marginal rate. A man earning something near to average earnings, say £5000 per annum, could have his first £985 free of tax, the next £750 was taxed at a rate of 25 per cent and the rest at 33 per cent. Therefore, 25.3 per cent of his earnings were taxed away. The very high income earner on £40,000 per annum, that is nearly 10 times average earnings, found the marginal tax rate rising such that the last pounds earned were being taxed at 83 per cent. If he had 'unearned' income that is income from interest, dividends from shares, or rents on property, the marginal rate was 98 per

Table 16.2 Income tax payable by a single person, 1978–9 tax year

Income per Annum	Average tax rate*(%)	Marginal tax rate (%)
1,040	1.3	25
2,080	14.5	33
4,000	23.4	33
5,000	25.3	33
15,000	37.8	65
40,000	63.2	83
100,000	75.1	83

Note: * Excluding National Insurance Contributions.
Source: Budget 'Red Book'.

cent. The steeply rising average tax rate implies a strongly progressive tax, reflecting the view that the rich should bear the heaviest burden.

The incidence of the whole tax system was less progressive than implied in the rate, since part of government revenue is indirect tax. Indirect tax tends, by its very nature, to be less progressive. The rich spend a lower fraction of their income than the poor. A proportional tax is one where as income rises, the amount of tax paid rises but the proportion of one's income going to the tax man stays constant. A regressive system is regarded by most people as very inequitable. It means that as income rises the proportion of an individual's income taken in tax decreases. Notice that the amount paid in taxation may still increase in a regressive system.

Now let us examine the situation after the November 1994 budget and see how things have changed. With inflation average incomes are much higher. Average earnings are around £15000 per annum.

Table 16.3 shows the income tax position for the tax year 1994–5. It indicates that several significant changes have taken place since the end of the 1970s. Although the income tax system is still progressive, its degree of progressiveness is markedly more mild. Those on low incomes pay a slightly lower proportion of income in direct tax than in 1979, those on very high incomes pay a far lower proportion than 15 years previously. The highest marginal tax rate has been cut from 83 per cent to 40 per cent. Two other of the systems features are not obvious from the table. One is that the overall burden of direct tax has fallen less than would be indicated by the tables since National Insurance contributions paid by employees on average earnings have risen from 6.5 per cent to 10 per cent. The combined marginal tax and National Insurance rate for an average earner in 1979 was 39 per cent. It is now 35 per cent. The other is that government revenue relies somewhat less on direct tax than it used to do, and more on indirect tax. For example, in 1979 the standard rate of VAT was 8 per cent. It is now 17.5 per cent. Since indirect tax is less progressive than direct tax the overall incidence of the tax

Table 16.3 Income tax payable by a single person, 1994–5 tax year

Income per Annum	Average tax rate* (%)	Marginal tax rate (%)
3,000	0	0
5,000	6.2	20
7,000	10.6	25
15,000	18.3	25
30,000	23.1	40
50,000	29.8	40
100,000	34.9	40

Note: * Excluding National Insurance Contributions.
Source: Budget 'Red Book'.

system is now even less progressive than in 1979. Direct tax cuts have been concentrated, then, on high income earners.

This significant switch is argued by the government to be necessary to increase incentives to work. Although less equitable, output is stimulated leading to a higher absolute living standard for all than would otherwise be possible. We shall examine this view in section 4. First we consider the assumptions of the underlying macro-economic model on which these tax changes are based.

3 Tax and effects on output

a Tax and aggregate demand

One major reason that 'supply siders' reject the idea of Keynesian equilibrium that we saw in the last chapter is their view of the labour market. In the Keynesian system the economy can be in equilibrium while significant unemployment of resources exists. One criticism of this view is that if unemployment exists, that must mean, by definition, an excess supply of that resource. But if there is an excess supply of, say, labour, the price of labour will fall in the long run to an equilibrium where there is no such excess. In other words, the economy will always adjust towards full employment output.

See pp 300–3

Let us remind ourselves of the argument that we began to consider in Chapter 15. Figure 16.1(a) is a way of representing the simple Keynesian equilibrium which we saw in the last chapter. If the economy is at AD_1, cuts in taxation will shift it to AD_2 and output will rise – but the cost is a higher price level – yet there is still some, though less unemployment. Governments are therefore faced with a trade-off. Reduced unemployment is only possible with a higher price level.

Figure 16.1(b) reminds us of an alternative view. It is labelled in the diagram 'classical' because in essence it represents a market orientated view of the

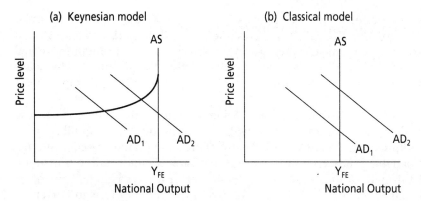

Figure 16.1 Keynesian and classical equilibrium

economy. The classical model argues as follows. Left to themselves, all markets clear and an equilibrium is always found. This, as we saw above, includes labour markets. Thus all resources including labour, will be productive, given time for the market to adjust. What of the present level of unemployment of labour? Some simply choose not to work. For others who do wish to, the problem is only a short-term one. Wage rates are too high for equilibrium in some markets, and given time the market will take care of the problem. Even then there will always be some friction in the system, which will mean that at any given moment some are out of a job. This is the 'natural rate of unemployment' which we met in Chapter 15. In Figure 16.1 it is represented as Y_{FE}. Essentially this means that there are always impediments to freely adjusting markets such as minimum wage legislation, trade union activity, and social security payments. In the classical view it is part of the government's task to reduce the effect of such impediments so that markets can reach equilibrium quickly and easily.

See pp 304–6

Markets then will tend to adjust to the full employment level of output whatever the price level. Stimulating the economy by lowering taxation must have only one long-run effect. It will raise the price level without changing real output. If the government stimulates aggregate demand as in Figure 16.1(b), money wages will rise. Some people who do not wish to work at the present wage level will think that *real* wages have risen. They will enter the labour market. In time they will discover that given the higher price level, real wages have not changed. They will leave the labour market. Y_{FE} is unchanged in the long run. 'Over-full employment' in the short term has been bought at the expense of higher prices. This is the view which we examined in the last chapter. Here the important point to grasp is this. In classical thinking changes in taxation to stimulate aggregate demand cannot work to increase output and decrease unemployment. Stimulating demand will only serve to stir up inflationary pressure.

Now, as we have already seen, equilibrium for an economy must be where planned injections into the circular flow of income, government expenditure (G),

See pp 252–7

See pp 270–3

investment expenditure (I), and export expenditure (X) are equal to planned withdrawals from the circular flow represented by savings (S), taxes (T) and imports (M). We saw in Chapter 13 how injections are brought to equal withdrawals, in the Keynesian view, by changes in national output. This leads Keynesians to say that equilibrium output is not necessarily full employment output.

We saw in Chapter 14 that classical economists reject this argument because they believe that injections and withdrawals are not brought into equilibrium by changes in output at all. Savings and investment are brought into equilibrium in a market for loanable funds via changes in interest rates. Exports and imports tend to equalise through various ways to be looked at in a later chapter, but often through foreign exchange markets via changes in the value of foreign currency.

b Tax and aggregate supply

All this leads to some important conclusions. If markets see to it that S = I and that X = M, it is the government's responsibility to see to it that government expenditure, G, equals government income, T. If the government fails to do this and allows G to be greater than T, aggregate demand will rise. Since the aggregate supply curve is vertical the effect will not be to raise the equilibrium level of output, but to cause inflation. The government then must balance the budget.

However, this simply argues that the government's account should not be in deficit. It does not tell us, by itself, how any deficit should be corrected. So, if at present the government is spending more than it is receiving in taxes, a correction can be made, either by increasing T or reducing G. Which of these is better? In classical thinking, cuts in government expenditure are very much to be preferred to increases in taxation as a way of reducing any public sector borrowing requirement (PSBR).

Why is this? Keynesian thinking is that taxation can be used for manipulating aggregate demand. But, at least in older Keynesian models, the aggregate supply curve is unaffected by tax changes. The classical view is that by reducing taxes people will be willing to work harder, since they have more incentive if they can keep more of their earnings. This raises potential output in the economy. In other words, income tax cuts will cause the aggregate supply curve to shift to the right. This means that there is value in improving the supply side of the economy rather than simply taking it as given. So starting from a position of deficit in the PSBR, the preferred classical remedy is to cut G at least until the budget is balanced. Better still would be larger cuts in G. Taxes could then be lowered without creating a deficit in the public finances. Lower income taxes are not the only means of improving the supply side but they are an important means, so a policy of steadily reducing the tax burden over time has become a cherished aim of UK government policy.

If T is to fall over a long period to stimulate aggregate supply, and the budget has to be balanced, G must fall too, either in absolute terms or at least as a proportion

Table 16.4 Top rates of taxes for selected countries, 1986–93 (%)

	1986	1993
Japan	70	50
France	65	57
Italy	62	51
UK	60	40
Australia	57	47
Germany	56	53
USA	50	31

of gross domestic product (GDP). This will probably mean, among other things, that in the short term we shall have poorer school buildings, reduced funding for hospitals and unrepaired roads, although to some extent one can compensate for less direct tax by increases in indirect tax and more private expenditure on these things. The cuts in G may not have to be as severe as one might at first think. If a cut in T raises national output, tax revenue will rise also.

Such a policy will also mean making the distribution of income more uneven. We saw in Chapter 4 how that income is now less evenly distributed than 10–15 years ago. The motivation behind this policy change should now be clear. It is all part of the 'supply side' revolution.

See pp 77–9

c Supply side tax reforms in other countries

Is the policy of reducing direct taxes, especially on higher income groups a peculiarly British phenomenon? The evidence suggests that it is not. Table 16.4 shows a consistent picture of Western governments reducing top rates of tax though some by more significant amounts than others.

We want to be very sure, then, that reducing the tax burden does produce incentives to increase output so that the aggregate supply curve really does shift. Then out of that increased national income hospitals, schools, roads, and so on, can be improved. Whether tax cuts are likely to achieve this is something we now examine.

4 The supply of labour: willingness to work

Let us use our indifference curve analysis, which we introduced in Chapter 4, to build up a picture of how people behave with respect to their willingness to work. Work will result in income being earned, albeit at an opportunity cost, that is leisure must be foregone. You once watched the TV programme *Eastenders* in the happy thought that it was virtually costless to you. Now as an economist, you

See pp 70–4

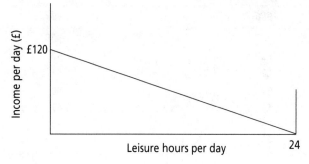

Figure 16.2 Relative price of leisure and income

have come to realise that although no money changes hands, it can be expensive to watch TV. It may be that you could have worked and earned an income during that time.

How much does an hour's leisure cost? Clearly it depends upon the rate per hour that could be earned. All options open to a supplier of labour are described in Figure 16.2 by the budget line. Assuming a wage rate of £5 per hour, the possibilities open to him are 24 hours per day leisure and no income, £120 per day (24 × £5) and no leisure, or some combination of leisure and income described by the budget line. A higher wage rate would imply a steeper budget line with its horizontal intercept still at 24 hours. Which combination will he choose? That will depend upon the budget line and upon his preferences.

Now, different people will have different preferences but it seems reasonable to suggest that for the vast majority there is a diminishing marginal rate of substitution of leisure for income as there is between goods. Therefore we have the familiar shape of the indifference curves in Figure 16.3. This figure also shows the budget line from Figure 16.2 and a labour supplier's preferred combination of income and leisure. He can just reach IC_2 by choosing 16 hours leisure per day and thus eight hours work per day. This gives him £40 per day income.

So if the wage rate is £5 per hour he supplies eight hours of labour per day to the market. How much would he supply at other wage rates? We can see this quite easily by changing the budget line from $Y_1 24$ to $Y_2 24$. Obviously a steeper budget line implies a higher wage rate. Given the nature of his preferences something interesting happens. If wage rates are raised from a low level, leisure becomes relatively more expensive. The opportunity cost of watching *Eastenders* rises. Thus he substitutes out of some leisure, since it is now relatively expensive, into more income. All this can be seen from Figure 16.4. When the wage rate changes, as shown in the move from budget line $Y_1 24$ to $Y_2 24$, leisure is reduced from L_1 to L_2 and thus work supplied increases for 24 minus L_1 to 24 minus L_2. Of course the higher wage rate increases his utility – he is on a higher indifference curve.

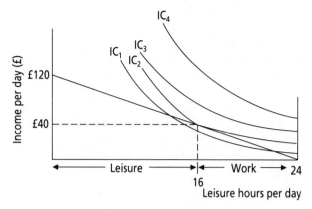

Figure 16.3 Optimising leisure and income

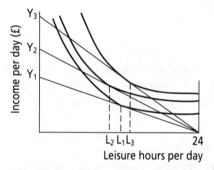

Figure 16.4 Effects of increased wage rates on willingness to work

Suppose now that wage rates are raised even higher, shown by the move from budget line $Y_2 24$ to $Y_3 24$. Again the increase in the wage rate increases his utility. He is on a higher indifference curve than before. Now his best amount of leisure is L_3 where he takes more leisure, offering fewer hours to the labour market. So when the wage rate rose from a very low level, he took more income and more work, and therefore less leisure. However, when the wage rate rose from a higher level to an even higher one, he took more income but less work and more leisure. These effects are shown in Figure 16.5 where we represent his supply curve for labour.

Why does he behave in this way? The answer is that when the wage rate rises there are two effects on his behaviour. The first effect is a 'substitution effect'. Consumers will always substitute out of relatively dear goods into relatively cheap ones when relative prices alter. In this case, leisure has become relatively expensive because of the increase in the wage rate. He will thus tend to reduce his leisure consumption and shift into income as the wage rate increases.

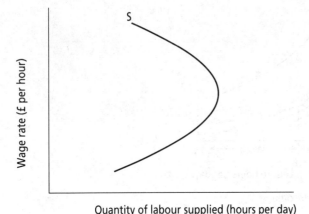

Figure 16.5   A backward-bending supply curve for labour

There is also an 'income effect'. The rise in the wage rate makes him better off. It causes his real income to rise. When his income is rising he can buy more other goods and take more leisure also. So these two effects work in opposite directions. When wage rates rise, the substitution effect is encouraging him to work more, the income effect causes him to work less. These two effects are always present when wage rates rise, but the nature of the diminishing marginal rate of substitution of leisure for income suggests that at lower wage rates the substitution effect will outweigh the income effect. At higher wage rates, however, the income effect will be increasingly likely to be stronger than the substitution effect. This gives us the backwards sloping nature of the supply curve. This theory of labour supply has important implications for policy on direct taxation.

5 Direct taxation and its effects on incentives

We want now to incorporate government direct tax policy into this model of labour supply. The analysis of section 4 made a quite unreal assumption which you may have noticed. The earner of income paid no tax on his earnings! So how do we modify the analysis in the light of taxation policy? Direct taxation will have no effect on the indifference curves – they simply represent preferences as between income and leisure. It does affect the budget line by altering what is possible. The present tax system in Britain moves the budget line for a supplier of labour as shown in Figure 16.6. For simplicity we ignore National Insurance contributions.

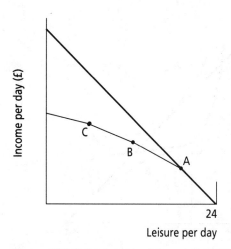

Figure 16.6 Income tax and the relative price of leisure and income

We begin with the familiar straight line budget line that assumes no direct tax. How will the introduction of income tax change it? All labour suppliers can earn several thousand pounds per year and pay no tax, so the lowest part of the line remains the same. As income rises above that level, 20 pence in the pound is payable in tax, so possible income is less than it would have been from point A.

Now the higher the income the bigger the gap between what one can earn and what one *could* have earned, since tax is paid on every marginal pound earned. The marginal tax rate is higher at some level of income. At point B the slope of the post-tax budget line changes since marginal tax rates are increased to 25 pence in the pound. Finally, at well above average incomes, point C in Figure 16.6, the top rate of tax (40 pence in the £) applies and the actual budget line becomes still flatter. Government policy has been aimed at pushing the lower budget line up towards the higher one, especially closing the gap at the left-hand end. Remember, the marginal tax rate in 1979 was 83 pence on earned income. Will the policy increase the supply of labour and thus increase national output and income?

There are two things to say by way of answer to that question. The first, as we show in Figures 16.7(a) and (b) is that it may or it may not, depending upon the nature of labour supplier's leisure preferences. In each of the two diagrams in Figure 16.7 a cut in marginal income tax rates is shown moving the budget line upwards. We choose an extreme example – direct tax is abolished altogether. In each case the cut in tax enables the supplier of labour to reach a higher indifference curve. In each case he has a higher level of income.

However, note that in case (a) the effect is to cause him to take less leisure, L_1–L_2, and therefore work harder just as government policy intended that he should. On the other hand, in (b) his response is to take more leisure, moving from L_1 to L_2!

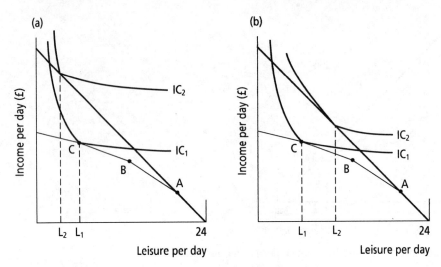

Figure 16.7 Possible effects of income tax on attitudes to work

Why do we get the difference in reaction? It is simply that the income effect for labour supplier (b) is greater than his substitution effect, whereas for labour supplier (a) it is smaller.

We are therefore driven to the conclusion that government policy towards reducing direct taxation is far from certain to succeed. However, there is a second thing that we can say. While cuts in direct tax are not certain to increase output, *the higher the income level the less likely it is to succeed*. We have already shown how indifference analysis has led us to the backwards sloping supply curve for labour, redrawn in Figure 16.8.

Cuts in tax rates are effectively increasing the wage rate of the labour supplier. If the wage rate is increased by a tax cut from W_1 to W_2 more labour is supplied. The increase is from Q_1 to Q_2. If the tax cut applies at higher wage rates, a backwards bending supply curve is more likely. A raise from W_2 to W_3 decreases labour supply from Q_2 to Q_3.

The conclusion, of course, is that concentrating tax cuts at the top end of the income scale may succeed in increasing the labour supply of high earners – but it is less likely. We cannot say, simply from drawing diagrams, at what point the supply curve will bend backwards. That is an empirical matter, and very hard to test. So while theory can tell us that eventually the income effect will outweigh the substitution effect as wage rates rise, it cannot tell us at what wage rate that will occur for most people. Nevertheless, we can say that the higher the income group whose marginal tax rate is being cut, the less likely is the policy to succeed in increasing hours worked.

All this argument assumes that, meanwhile, other things remain equal. They may not do so. The Conservative government of the 1980s and early 1990s felt

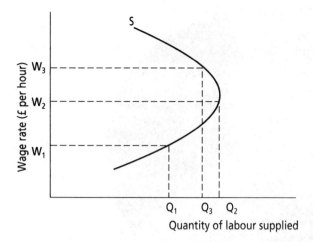

Figure 16.8 Tax rate changes and willingness to work

that there were other reasons for thinking that cuts in top marginal tax rates may increase labour supply. One consideration is that labour can migrate. High marginal tax rates may encourage high income earners to leave the country and seek employment abroad. Another possibility is that capital might migrate. High marginal tax rates encourage wealth owners to seek offshore tax havens where tax is not payable to the British government at all. Lower marginal rates of tax may increase government revenue by dissuading people to seek these tax havens.

6 Income support and its effects on incentives

We have concentrated efforts to increase labour supply by changes to taxation policy. We now turn to attempts to increase the supply of labour with changes in income support. Implicit in government policy is the view that some people choose not to work because they would rather be idle and live on state handouts. Of all government expenditure, around one-third goes on social security. Figure 16.9 indicates the major kinds of state benefits available. Pensions and disability benefits would be the only major categories of social security spending unrelated to unemployment.

The argument can easily be seen from Figure 16.10. Given that it is possible to get income support the original budget line does not represent the choice of a labour supplier. The bottom part is done away with. However little he chooses to work he can get something from the state, shown as Y_0 in Figure 16.10.

Given his preferences as between income and leisure this man's reaction to income support is to choose 24 hours per day leisure and Y_0 income from the state. Had this not been available he would have chosen Y_1 income and $24 - L_1$

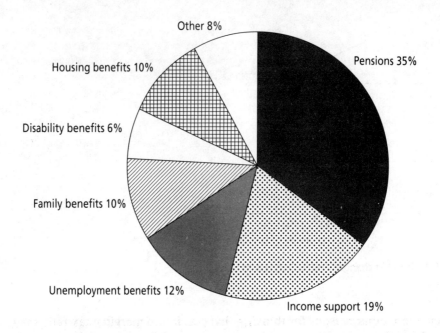

Source: *Treasury Bulletin*

Figure 16.9 Categories of social security expenditure

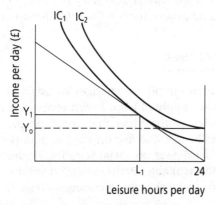

Figure 16.10 Income support and willingness to work

labour. The conclusion, of course, is that one can reduce the volume of unemployment, by getting the idle poor to work. It simply requires a reduction in income support. Politically, the government has not found it possible to reduce many forms of support in money terms. However, the same thing can be achieved by raising benefits annually by less than the rate of inflation.

One other thing may create severe disincentive effects. It is the poverty trap. This occurs when an increase in earned income reduces actual income. The person is trapped in poverty. Suppose a previously unemployed person takes a job and earns some income. He may find that he has lost entitlement to rent rebates, free school meals for his children and other state handouts only available to very low income groups. He may then find that his actual income is lower for having taken the job. The poverty trap means that it is not simply a question of the additional income from a job not being worth the loss of leisure time. Work actually reduces his income. Changes in the operation of the social security system in recent years have reduced this problem, but many disincentives to work remain for the lower income groups.

Can it be justified to reduce benefits to such lower income groups to stimulate willingness to work? As so often, the answer is that much depends upon one's macro-economic view of the economy. Remember that from a classical perspective any unemployment is voluntary since markets, including labour markets, always clear quite quickly. A Keynesian perspective gives a different answer. First, it is possible to be unemployed because there is no job available. There is unemployment equilibrium. Second, cuts in income support will *reduce aggregate demand*. Low income groups spend all their additional income. They have a marginal propensity to consume of one. If the government revenue saved is then given in tax cuts, the recipients of that income will save part of it. They have a lower marginal propensity to consume. Thus aggregate demand will fall, which may exacerbate the unemployment problem.

7 Strands of evidence

a Tax rates and the PSBR

Is there any evidence that reductions in the marginal rate of tax on higher income groups has produced any improvement in economic welfare? As in so many areas a difficulty arises in isolating the effect of a particular policy change from all other factors that have an influence. Bearing this in mind one can proceed cautiously in saying that its effects on the PSBR are not encouraging. A commonly expressed opinion of 'supply-siders' is the view that income tax cuts have such an effect on incentives that output rises significantly. If output and therefore incomes rise significantly, government may increase its income. This is because although it takes a smaller share of national income, it is a smaller slice of a larger pie.

This can be expressed more formally in terms of what is known as the 'Laffer Curve' of Figure 16.11, which shows the claimed effect of government revenue changes in income tax. If income tax rates rise from low levels, 'tax take' increases. Government revenue rises. However, it rises at a slower rate as the disincentive of taxation begins to take effect. The disincentive effect is so high at very high marginal rates of tax that government revenue declines. At a 100 per

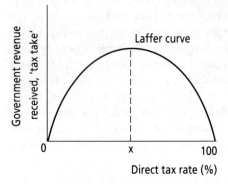

Figure 16.11   The Laffer Curve

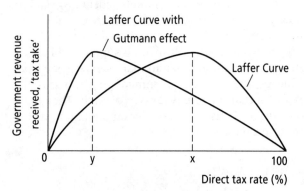

Figure 16.12   The Laffer Curve and the Gutmann effect

cent income tax rate no one would do anything and government tax revenue would thus be zero! So in principle tax cuts can increase revenue. All other things being equal this will reduce the PSBR. This assumes, of course, that the present tax rate is higher than x in Figure 16.11, x being the optimal tax rate for the purpose of raising revenue.

If the curve accurately reflects reality, it will still not follow that the curve is symmetric. One of several possible reasons for asymmetry is the reason behind the skewed Laffer Curve of Figure 16.12, which describes the Gutmann effect. The reasoning behind the skew is as follows. As marginal tax rates are lowered there is another group from whom income tax revenues will be received. These are the people who have been working in the 'black economy'. The black economy refers to those activities earning income which are not declared for income tax purposes. Failure to declare such income is illegal. Those caught risk jail sentences. Many take the risk when the amount they must pay in taxes is high. If marginal tax rates are lowered, some will feel the risk to be no longer worth taking. Some will declare their income and pay the tax. Thus, as the Laffer Curve of Figure 16.12

shows, governments may be able to cut marginal taxes down to quite low levels and still increase their tax take as more are drawn into paying income tax. The optimal tax rate for raising revenue is thus y, where y is significantly lower than x.

We can say that both the British and American governments have begun to be sceptical about the Laffer Curve argument. Marginal tax rates have been substantially reduced, but the PSBR is enormous in each country. The President of the USA and the Chancellor of the Exchequer in the British government have both used tax increases as well as cuts in government expenditure as part of a strategy to hold down the PSBR.

b Tax, benefits and the 'natural rate'

A second strand of evidence comes from the article by Stephen Nickell on the natural rate of unemployment, which we considered in Chapter 15. You will recall his argument that the natural rate had risen during recent years. We now look a little more closely at his evidence. He also sought to produce some estimates of the contribution of different factors to this unemployment rate. If we look at the period from 1980–7 we can see in Table 16.5 what his estimates were. Since these are difficult to determine, they are estimates that he regards as 'very rough and ready'.

See pp 304–8

See pp 380–1, 383–5

North Sea oil and terms of trade effects we shall consider in a later chapter, but the other four measured factors referred to in the table are of interest now. Mismatch refers essentially to frictional employment referred to in Chapter 13. In particular, it suggests that it is skilled labour that is scarce relative to unskilled labour. 'Unions' refers to the effects of unions in trying to raise wage rates above market wage rates.

See p 251

Table 16.5 The contribution of various factors to equilibrium unemployment in Britain, 1980–87

Natural rate	8.7
North Sea oil	−2.86
Terms of trade effects	2.26
Mismatch	2.53
Benefit system	1.12
Unions	1.50
Taxation	−0.20
Unmeasured	1.95

Source: S. Nickell (0000) 'Inflation and the UK labour market', Oxford Review of Economic Policy, 6, 4. Reproduced by permission of Oxford University Press.

Notice in particular the other two factors. The fall in direct tax rates during the 1980s has improved the labour market and reduced the natural rate. The sign is negative, but it is a very small number. If these 'rough and ready' estimates are somewhere near correct its value is nowhere near as large as the cost of the benefit system in discouraging work effort. Again, though, it has to be stressed that even if reducing benefits were to improve the working of the labour market, the government might still legitimately choose not to act in this area. It could take the view that the effect on low income groups would be too serious to justify the cuts in benefits.

8 Conclusion

It is never easy for governments to cut taxes. There are always enormous demands made upon the Treasury for state spending. The Conservative administration since 1979 has managed some cuts in income tax to encourage the growth of output. The most dramatic cuts in marginal tax rates have been at the top end of the income scale making the distribution of income more uneven. Micro-economic theory does not give great support to this view suggesting that cuts in tax rates further down the scale are more likely to succeed.

Certainly there is no evidence yet that in the end lower income groups also benefit from these cuts through increased national output. Some of those on lower incomes are relatively *and* absolutely worse off than they were 15 years ago. There is some evidence that the Conservative government of the 1990s has begun to accept this. In recent years there have been no further cuts in top rates of tax and most tax cuts have been concentrated at the lower end of the income scale.

A choice that any government has to face is this. A strongly progressive tax system will tend to give relatively lower average income tax rates but relatively higher marginal ones. This may create disincentives to work but produce a more even distribution of income. On the other hand, a less progressive tax system will give higher average tax rates but lower marginal ones. This may have good incentive effects and therefore helps to raise national output. But it does mean that we shall have a more uneven distribution of income, which depending upon one's perspective, might be regarded as less just.

As far as income support rates are concerned, economic theory would suggest that a cost of establishing an income support scheme is that some will choose to be idle. How serious this problem is cannot be easily ascertained.

9 Questions for discussion

1 Suppose you were offered an increase in your grant of 10 per cent and all other students on the course also received 10 per cent. As an alternative you were offered a 15 per cent increase but all your colleagues received a 100

per cent increase. Which of these options would you prefer? Why? What does this have to do with the issues discussed in the chapter? (HINT: Look at the definition of Pareto optimality given in Chapter 5, and the distribution of income implicit in direct taxation policy as shown in this chapter.)

2 The Conservative administration of the 1980s believed that governments should in all circumstances balance the budget. So in the early 1980s with high unemployment the government chose not to stimulate aggregate demand by tax cuts, but to reduce its deficit by raising taxes. The Conservative administration of the 1990s says it believes in a balanced budget in the medium term. What changes in policy does this imply? What do you think might have altered its position?

See pp 79–80

3 Refer back to Table 16.5. Stephen Nickell sees frictional unemployment as a significant difficulty. Would further reductions in marginal tax rates help? Remember that the main mismatch problem is skilled labour shortages. What other policies would help to deal with the problem?

4 In Chapter 1, Table 1.4, we saw that there was no close correlation between the volume of taxation received by a government and growth of GDP. In the light of what you have read in this chapter, do you find this surprising?

See pp 16–17

5 'It is a curious policy which encourages the rich to work harder by giving them more – and the poor to work harder by giving them less.' How fair is this as an assessment of government taxation policy?

10 Further reading

Income and substitution effects
Sloman, pp. 152–7; Begg, pp. 83–9; Parkin and King, pp. 172–5

Income and substitution effects with respect to labour supply
Sloman, pp. 392–3; Begg, pp. 182–4; Parkin and King, pp. 817–8

Average and marginal tax rates
Sloman, pp. 373–4

'The rich get richer . . .
G. Kopits (1993) 'Reforming social security systems', *Finance and Development*, June.

CHAPTER 17

Privatisation:
a supply side improvement?

Fifteen years ago many of the basic goods and services we purchased were provided by the state, including gas, electricity, water, telephone services. The assets which produce this output are now in the private sector where they are being used for private profit.

Has the public gained or lost from this change?

In this chapter we review.
- Efficiency
- The public sector borrowing requirement (PSBR)

We introduce
- Efficiency with declining long-run average cost (LRAC)
- Privatisation policy

1 Introduction

For over 30 years after the Second World War British economic policy concentrated primarily upon controlling the overall level of economic activity by attempts to manipulate the volume of aggregate demand. This involved increasing government spending and cutting taxes during a downturn in the trade cycle and reversing the policy in the upturn. The 'supply side' was left, to some extent, to look after itself. In other words' macro-economic policy was essentially Keynesian in orientation.

See pp 310–29

The Conservative government from 1979 onwards shifted its emphasis away from the management of aggregate demand towards improving the supply side of the economy. One aspect of this policy we considered in Chapter 16. One other aspect of this procedure that we consider now is the programme of privatisation. It was believed that assets in private hands would in some sense be more productive than in state hands. More output would come from a given volume of resources. Furthermore, areas of economic activity would be opened to market forces. Remember that the supply side view is that macro-economic policy is primarily concerned with seeing to it that markets work properly. In the last chapter we focused on a resource market, labour. In this chapter we concentrate on markets for goods and services. You should not be surprised if much of this chapter focuses

Table 17.1 Major privatisations since 1979

Year	Company	Revenue (£ million)
1979	BP (part)	276
1981	BP (part)	200
1981	Cable and Wireless (part)	182
1882	Britoil (part)	627
1983	BP (part)	543
1983	Cable and Wireless (part)	263
1984	BT (part)	3,916
1984	Jaguar	297
1985	Britoil (part)	449
1985	Cable and Wireless (part)	900
1986	British gas	5.600
1987	British Airways	900
1987	Rolls Royce	1,100
1987	BAA	600
1987	BP (part)	7,200
1988	British Steel	2,400
1989	Water Companies	5,240
1990	Electricity Distribution Companies	5,200
1991	Electricity Generators (part)	3,200
1991	BT (Part)	2,900
1993	BT (Part)	5,000

Source: Financial press, Financial Statistics.

on micro-economic issues. Supply side policies are about returning to confidence in markets, rather than upon macro-economic demand management.

What are the arguments for privatisation? What has happened? What has been the result? These are the issues we are about to examine. The size of the privatisation programme has been remarkable. Table 17.1 gives an indication of the extent of the process with a selection of some of the largest sales.

Although the idea of shifting resources out of the state sector is not new, the scale of the procedure in the UK has revolutionised the thinking of many concerning what can be produced within the private sector.

For example, it would surely have been inconceivable during the 1970s for serious debates to take place in which health and education were seen as possible candidates for privatisation. Although the present conservative administration has backed away from full scale privatising in these areas, the political atmosphere has altered so much that the privatisation of BR, coal, London Underground, the prison service and even the fire and ambulance services are regarded as real possibilities. However, to say that more privatisations are feasible is not to say that they are desirable. It is to the likely major effects of the policy generally rather than the effects upon any one industry in particular that we now turn.

What exactly is privatisation? It is a wide-ranging term. Howard Vane[1] suggests that it covers three areas (a) denationalisation, selling publicly owned assets to the private sector; (b) contracting-out, franchising to private contractors the production of (state financed) goods and services previously produced in the public sector; and (c) deregulation, removing various restrictions on competition previously given to statutory monopolies. Clearly all three aspects are important, but it is the first of these three areas that is the main subject of our attention.

Even within this area, namely the sale of publicly owned assets to the private sector, the means of achieving it have varied. So, for example, many industries, such as water and steel, have been sold to members of the public in the form of a public share subscription. Others have taken a different form. For example, the Rover car group was sold to British Aerospace with no opportunity for the public to purchase the assets directly.

The first questions we must ask are these. Does it matter who owns the assets from which output is produced? If so, why?

2 Public ownership of assets: the arguments in favour

Those who see advantages of keeping assets within public ownership will usually express the argument in one or more of the five following ways.

a Efficiency

The industries involved are all those where firms have some degree of monopoly power. That power varies between industries. In no case is it absolute. Electricity competes with gas. Water has few substitutes, but even here power is not absolute. Where water meters are introduced, quantity demanded falls. Some industries are natural monopolies. That is to say, as output increases in the long run, unit costs of production fall. This means two things. One is that the high level of financing of capital projects may be difficult for private firms. It will require public sector financing to see that adequate investment takes place in such industries. Obvious examples of such industries would include electricity with huge investment in the national grid system, and the water industry.

The other thing that follows from a declining long-run average cost is that consumers will be exploited. Given the cost structure described above, the formation of a monopoly is almost inevitable. Consider Figure 17.1. Since the long-run average cost curve (LRAC) falls we can never expect competition to take place. If there were to be more than one firm it would pay these firms to merge, increasing output and lowering unit costs.[2]

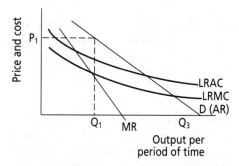

Figure 17.1 Monopoly power and a declining LRAC curve

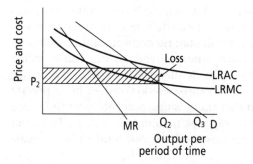

Figure 17.2 Socially optimal price output decisions with declining LRAC

See pp 143–5

What price would the monopolist charge? Profit is maximised at Q_1P_1 such that all output is made where addition to cost (LRMC) is less than addition to revenue (MR). The appropriate profit maximising price is clearly the maximum one that consumers are prepared to pay for that output. Now let us ask what would be the output and price that would maximise consumer welfare. Clearly, it would not be Q_3 output and a zero price, even though that would give the greatest output at the lowest price. The reason for rejecting Q_3 output is that the production of output uses resources which have an opportunity cost. The marginal opportunity cost is found in the marginal cost curve. Therefore the socially optimum volume of output is at Q_2 in Figure 17.2 where the additional value to society of the last unit produced is equal to the marginal opportunity cost of the resources used in producing it.

Notice that if Figure 17.2 accurately represents the cost and revenue conditions faced by an industry, the decision to set a socially optimal price will inevitably result in a loss (shown by the shaded area). This must be the case. A falling LRAC implies LRMC below LRAC. Hence LRMC = D, where LRAC is higher than D. Thus total revenue, output x average revenue must be less than total cost, output x average cost. Since no private firm will be willing to operate in a way which means it cannot make a normal profit, state ownership is required if resources are to be allocated optimally. The loss can then be funded out of general taxation.

Even if LRMC does not fall continuously, but rises at some level of output, the argument still holds if D intersects LRMC on the downwards sloping section of LRMC.

b Externalities

To show that MC = D is a socially optimal price/output decision it is necessary to show that long-run marginal private cost (LRMC) is equal to long-run marginal social cost (LMSC). This condition does not always hold. In such circumstances resources would be better owned by the state sector, which will allow for the external effect that produces this divergence.

See pp 132–4

See pp 138–40

Let us illustrate with an example. British Steel closed the Ravenscraig steel plant in Scotland because it adjudged that revenues from the sale of its steel were less than the incremental costs of production. It will take no account of the additional unemployment benefit payable to those unemployed or to those made unemployed through the multiplier effects in Scotland. There is a divergence between social and private cost that a state enterprise could consider but a private producer will not. We have already seen that there is much debate over the speed of resource adjustment that takes place in response to demand changes. However quick it is, there will be some adjustment costs, which will tend to fall at least partly on the state.

c The distribution of income

State produced services such as education and health can be seen as part of the 'social wage'. Higher income groups contribute more taxation through a progressive tax system, so lower income groups consume more than they pay for. This redistributes income towards equality.

There is no economic distinction between nationalised industries and departments of state in this respect. Therefore, one way of benefitting lower income groups is to produce electricity, gas, water and other basic commodities in the public sector at subsidised prices. State owned assets can therefore be a means of distributional change. One should bear in mind, however, that subsidies can, in some cases, be largely of benefit to the middle classes. Telephones might be one example of this kind.

d Macro-economic control

See pp 260–62

Governments have a responsibility for macro-economic stability. Suppose that aggregate demand is too high, generating inflationary pressures in the economy. We have seen that one approach to the problem is to reduce such demand by, for example, taxation policy to control consumption demand or interest rate policy to affect consumption and investment. A more direct method would be to reduce government expenditure. A large state sector makes it possible to engage in such a policy by ordering investment expenditure in state industries to be reduced or postponed. The policy could be reversed if aggregate demand were to be too low, and was threatening to cause an unacceptable volume of unemployment.

Clearly the larger the state sector the more potential there is for direct control of the volume of investment and the volume of aggregate demand. Notice that this is a Keynesian view of macro-economic policy, a point to which we shall return later in the chapter.

e The provision of public goods

See pp 199–201

A market system cannot provide an optimal volume of public goods. Let us remind ourselves of the meaning of public goods in order to see why.

As we saw in Chapter 10, public goods have several characteristics. One important feature will illustrate the argument that says that the provision of such goods cannot be left to market forces. A public good is one which is consumed equally by all of a country's citizens, or by a group of them. One example we considered was street lighting. If it is provided the output is not divided between those who wish to consume it. All the citizens consume all of it. Consider the diagram, Figure 17.3. For a private good the market demand curve is the horizontal summation of all individual demand curves. The social optimum output (in the absence of market power or externalities) is Q_0. But if the good is a public good the analysis is meaningless. Q_0 output is not divided between the citizens according to individual demand. *All* consume Q_0 street lighting.

To be sure, it will be difficult for a government to decide the optimal provision of a public good, but if it is left to the private owners of resources, as we have seen already, the best level of output for society is most unlikely to be provided. Government ownership of assets is therefore more likely to maximise economic welfare in this area than is the private ownership of resources.

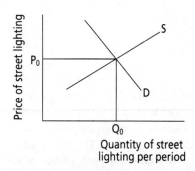

Figure 17.3 The problem of pricing a public good

3 Private ownership of assets: counter arguments

Since the late 1970s the Conservative government has, as we have seen, continued to shift resources into the private sector. In the light of what we have said above, on what grounds has it been done? The arguments given above have been almost completely rejected. The exception is the public goods case. There appears to be no enthusiasm for privatising national defence or street lighting, for example. The other four grounds we examined are regarded as unacceptable arguments. We shall consider the efficiency arguments in more detail in the next section. Let us first see why the other three arguments have been rejected.

a Externalities

Externalities are regarded as irrelevant from the standpoint of resource ownership and the privatisation debate since it is possible to 'internalise' externalities even if resources are in the private sector. Consider the case in Figure 17.4 below. Assume that industry is tipping effluent into streams and imposing costs on society that it is not bearing itself. The externality has caused a breakdown in the identity between private and social costs. The identity can be restored by imposing a tax on the firm, shifting up the MPC to coincide with the MSC. It does *not* require that the firm's assets be in the public sector. If the external effect were to be an external benefit an appropriate subsidy can be found, shifting MPC down to coincide with MSC.

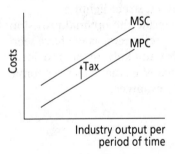

Figure 17.4 Externalities private and social cost

b The distribution of income

There are various ways in which income can be redistributed, the most obvious example being a progressive tax system. This is supplemented in Britain by social security payments of various kinds. If income is not thought to be sufficiently evenly distributed, it would be better to increase benefits and make the tax system more progressive. This is because a combination of artificially low prices plus subsidies distorts relative prices and misallocates investment.

The argument, then, is not that income redistribution should not be undertaken. It is that keeping assets in the public sector to keep prices down artificially is an inefficient means of achieving such a redistribution. Nevertheless, as we saw in Chapter 16, supply side economists worry about any policies to redistribute income because of its effects on incentives.

See pp 310–29

c Macro-Economic Control

If macro-economic control of the economy is thought to be appropriate, it can be argued that interfering with individual industries is an unfortunate way of achieving it, for it inevitably misallocates resources. Let us illustrate. One particularly ineffective attempt to use state assets for macro-economic control was the effort to control inflation during the Conservative administration of Edward Heath in the early 1970s. Nationalised industry prices were artificially restrained during a period of inflationary pressure in an attempt to break an inflationary spiral. Subsidies to those industries had therefore to be increased. The provision of those subsidies imposed pressures on the PSBR which proved to be inflationary! The link between the PSBR and inflation is something we shall explore in Chapter 18. Not only was it therefore self-defeating but it also misallocated resources by providing inappropriate relative price signals.

See pp 359–64

4 The claimed benefits of privatisation

So far we have seen why nationalised industries might not be seen as a superior alternative to privatisation, although we have not dealt with the key question of efficiency in the use of resources. We turn now to examine the three areas in which the privatisation programme has a claim to being a means of bringing positive benefits to the economy. In doing so we shall deal with the argument yet to be examined, which concerns efficiency.

The three claims for privatisation of assets are first, it is a *more* efficient use of resources if assets are owned privately. Second, the sale of state assets provides an income to the government that can be used for increasing welfare. Third, privatisation can widen the ownership of wealth with positive benefits to society at large.

As we look at each of these three arguments in turn, we shall discover that to some extent each of them is dubious and confidence in the correctness of these arguments must to some extent be a matter of faith. The first issue we consider is the claim that privatisation, far from reducing efficiency, actually increases it.

a Benefit one: efficiency

The efficiency argument for privatisation is based partly on cost efficiency and partly on allocative efficiency. Let us remind ourselves of the distinction. When we talk about cost efficiency, we mean that the firm will produce any given level of output at the lowest possible long-run average cost *for that level of output*. In other words, the firm will be on its cost curve and not above it. Allocative efficiency means producing output in the quantity that reflects society's preferences. It means to produce output where (in the absence of externalities) MC = D.

Privatisation is often argued to improve cost efficiency. Nationalised industries suffer from low morale, so output is lower than it need be. Management has no incentive to reduce waste and improve cost efficiency since it will not be rewarded with increased profits. Only the incentive of improved rewards will lower costs. Privatisation makes that possible.

All this is arguable. Does the evidence support it? Are private firms more cost efficient than state firms? We have to say that there is no convincing way of demonstrating the matter one way or the other. Whatever attempt we make to examine the evidence is likely to prove futile. For example, one way we might try is to compare the pre-privatisation and post-privatisation performance of an industry, say British Steel. Remembering that British Steel was privatised in 1988, consider Table 17.2 below. What does it tell us about the effects of privatisation? The question is not as easy to answer as we might think.

The productivity figures are impressive. On the other hand, we do not know what would have happened in the absence of privatisation. Perhaps some or even all this improvement would have taken place because of increased competition from abroad and the introduction of better technology. We need to assume that all other factors affecting productivity were held constant.

The profit figures are also impressive at first sight. After all, one can hardly claim that the improvement is due to more consumer exploitation as privatisation approached – that prices were being increased to 'fatten up' the industry prior to the public share offering. Steel is very competitive within Europe. Such a point would have more force, of course, in an industry such as water where there are few substitutes and monopoly power is considerable.

Table 17.2 Record of British Steel Corporation - Selected years

	1980–81	1983–84	1986–87	1989–90	1991–92
Turnover (£ millions)	2,954	3,358	3,461	5,113	4,303
Net profit (loss) (£m) before tax	(1,020)	(256)	178	733	(149)
Productivity (man hours per tonne)	14.5	7.1	6.2	4.8	4.2

Source: British Steel Corporation, Reports and Accounts, various years.

Nevertheless, the profitability figures still represent difficulties in interpretation. The change in profit levels in recent years certainly reflects the effects of recession as well as the effects of privatisation.

To summarise, then, cost efficiency *may* improve with privatisation. There is no certain way of demonstrating it. However, the figures above make a strong prima facie case for saying that privatisation can improve cost efficiency.

We turn now to the important matter of allocative efficiency. Why do some think that this is better achieved if resources are in private hands?

One aspect of this question is access to capital markets. A nationalised concern has to go to government to ask for funds for investment. Whether they will be granted will depend not only on the merits of the case itself but other wider considerations of the Treasury – the size of the PSBR, for example. In the private sector, industries such as water and electricity will compete for funds on an equal footing. If consumer demand is strong enough to justify investment, it will be forthcoming. The industry no longer has to concern itself with the political problems inherent in state intervention.

An equally important aspect of allocative efficiency is the question of pricing. Advocates of privatisation argue that there is no reason one cannot achieve pricing efficiency in the private sector. Let us examine the argument with reference to Figure 17.5.

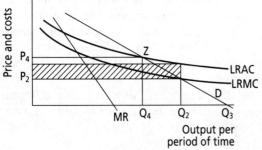

Figure 17.5 Socially efficient prices and the private sector

There are two points to consider. First, if as is usual the LRAC slopes downwards, one can argue that MC = D is not allocatively efficient. The logic of allocative efficiency is that it is the point at which all mutually beneficial trades have taken place. In other words, the assumption is the usual Pareto-optimal idea that all exchanges have taken place where someone's welfare is improved without making anyone else worse off. However, MC = D implies a loss represented by the shaded area, as we have already seen.

Since with MC = D losses are made and there is a consequent redistribution of income, it cannot be Pareto optimal. If, for example, this situation were to describe BR, then setting a price where MC = D and subsidising BR means redistributing income from the general taxpayer to railway users. It would be difficult to see how this could be regarded as Pareto-efficient. The best we can do, therefore, is to see that the price/output decision is Q_4, the nearest we can get to MC = D while avoiding losses and a consequent income redistribution.

That leads us to the second point. A price/output of $Q_4 P_4$ is achievable in the private sector with a suitable price control at P_4. A profit maximising monopolist operating under a price ceiling of P_4 would choose just that price/output level. This explains why the government has privatised some industries that face little effective competition but has imposed a price control.[3] Let us take two such examples. First consider BT. The company was privatised but had to work under a pricing formula as follows. Each year BT could raise its charges by the retail price index less 3 per cent (RPI − 3 per cent). The view was that technological progress would, over time, move the LRAC downwards so that BT could breakeven, even with a falling price level. Subsequently, the formula was tightened to RPI − 4 per cent, then to RPI − 6.25 per cent, then in June 1992 to RPI − 7.5 per cent.

Second, look at the example of the water industry. This industry was given a price ceiling of RPI *plus*, the size of the plus varied from one water company to another. The idea of allowing these companies to increase water charges in real terms was to enable them to be sufficiently profitable, that it could attract large sums from capital markets. These sums would be needed to engage in large programmes of repairing crumbling water pipes, and so on.

Notice the difficulty involved in deciding whether the policy is successful. Many would argue that water and electricity companies, among others, have done far better than break even. Now recall that 'break even' means covering all costs including normal profit. That is, they must make a rate of return on capital comparable to other similar risk industries. Whether their profits are equal to, or greater than that is a matter for debate, but it is clearly difficult to obtain an agreed figure as to what contributes a normal profit.

See pp 190–6

You will recall from Chapter 10 the distinctions we drew between different kinds of efficiency. It would appear that privatisation may lead to an improvement in the efficiency of those industries involved. That said, it would be extremely difficult to demonstrate the fact in any convincing way.

There are other claimed benefits of the privatisation programme to which we now turn.

b Benefit two: increased government revenue

One apparent advantage of the privatisation programme is the revenue that it generates. Table 17.1 gives an indication of the revenue received from the largest asset sales and Table 17.4 gives the total amounts received from all privatisations. The increase in revenue is more apparent than real. There are three reasons why this is so.

The first reason can be understood if we ask ourselves why anyone is willing to buy these assets from the government. The answer is, of course, because of the expected stream of revenue that will be produced in the form of profits or

Table 17.3 First day price premiums on selected privatised companies

Company	Date	Part paid offer price (p)	First day price (p)	Gross profit (%)
BT	Dec. 1984	50	91	80
British Gas	Dec. 1986	50	68	34
BAA	July 1987	100	146	45
Servern Trent Water	Dec. 1989	100	131	30
Northumbrian Water	Dec. 1989	100	157	56
London Electricity	Dec. 1990	100	142	41
Manweb	Dec. 1990	100	166	65
National Power	Mar. 1991	100	137	36
Powergen	Mar. 1991	100	137	36

Source: P. Curwen and D. Holmes (1992) Returns the small shareholders from privatisation, National *Westminster Bank Quarterly Review,* February.

Table 17.4 Privatisation receipts (£ billion)

Year	Proceeds	Year	Proceeds
1979–80	0.4	1986–87	4.5
1980–81	0.2	1987–88	5.1
1981–82	0.5	1988–89	7.1
1982–83	0.5	1989–90	4.2
1983–84	1.1	1990–91	5.3
1984–85	2.1	1991–92	7.9
1985–86	2.7	1992–93	8.0*

Note: *Estimate.
Source: Treasury statistics.

dividends. As we saw in Chapter 14, the value of the capital will be the discounted value of the expected income stream. Then the government is simply replacing a stream of earnings in the future with a one-off receipt of revenue now. It is not increasing its revenue, merely altering the timing of its receipts.

See pp 276–9

Of course the government may feel that the income generated will enable it to make a better investment. It could use the sales to build more schools or hospitals, for example. Critics have argued that it has in fact been used for tax cuts. This may not necessarily be a valid criticism. The tax cuts may improve the supply side of the economy by increasing output sufficiently fully to justify the decision to privatise the assets. Whether tax cuts do stimulate the output of the economy in this way is a matter we examined in Chapter 16.

See pp 310–29

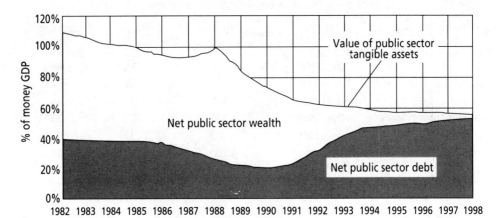

Source: Lloyds Bank *Economic Bulletin*, October 1993.

Figure 17.6 Projections of public sector net wealth

One thing we can say, however, is that since 1979 the public sector's balance sheet has changed significantly. Figure 17.6 records the position. You can see there how the value of the public sector's assets as a proportion of GDP has fallen sharply through the 1980s. This reflects partly the sale of assets to the private sector. It also reflects government policy to reduce state capital spending. It is easier to cut capital expenditure – road building, school buildings, prisons, etc., than to cut current spending – pensions, unemployment benefit, and so on. It is these two factors, reduced capital spending and the privatisation programme, which account for the decline in public asset values. Public sector debt fell too but by much less, so the difference between the two, net public sector wealth, was substantially reduced. Even in 1988 the net assets of the public sector were about 60 per cent of GDP. By 1993 it was 20 per cent. The Lloyds Bank forecast shows it to be approaching zero by 1988. However, this calculation, made in the Autumn of 1993, assumes that the government is willing to allow the PSBR to stay high for much of the 1990s thus increasing public sector debt. Present government policy is, as we have already seen in Chapter 13 that the PSBR will fall rapidly during the 1990s so that the public sector debt will not rise so rapidly.

See p 266

The second reason the increased revenue is more apparent than real is this. There is a strong case for saying that the assets have been underpriced. Table 17.3 gives an idea of this criticism. The government fixed the price of the shares of each of these companies and offered them to the public and to the institutions. In most cases there was excess demand for the shares and applications were scaled down. Excess demand, of course, suggests too low a price. What was the equilibrium price? One idea would be to look at the price at which the shares changed hands on the stock market at the end of the first day of trading. As you can see, there was often a substantial premium to be earned.

The above criticism has been made of other forms of privatisation also. For example, the Rover group was sold to British Aerospace at an agreed price, but the government did not accept bids from other interested parties. It is quite conceivable that had it held an auction, the price obtained would have been substantially higher. British Aerospace sold Rover to BMW for a large profit in 1994.

The third reason for thinking that the state's assets could have been sold for more is that there is a basic inconsistency between two of the government's stated aims of the sales. One aim is to get efficiency in the use of resources. Part of this aim means allocative efficiency which, in turn, it can be argued, means that price controls are necessary for reasons given earlier. But the way to have maximised revenue was to have had no price controls! The huge monopoly profits then available to some of these industries would have enabled the government to get a much higher price for the sale.

Selling the assets and stipulating no price ceiling for the industry's output is something that should be seriously considered. Remember that monopoly power is a cost when resources are transferred. The new owners would have been prepared to pay a much higher price for industries such as gas and water because they would have been willing to buy the right to the monopoly profits. By preventing the appearance of such profits, revenue from the asset sales could not be maximised.

One other issue about revenue might be considered here. The logic of maximising revenue for the sale of assets is that they should be sold to the highest bidder. In Germany the government has tended not to do this, but to sell shares to those who are employed in the industry.[4] This clearly has a claim to be better from an equity point of view but, by severely restricting the market for the shares it would increase the problem of not getting the best price for the assets.

c Benefit three: wider share ownership

The last claimed benefit of the privatisation programme is the wider spread of wealth ownership that has taken place.

This is arguably the government's most important aim in its privatisation programme in that it has the long-term objective of changing attitudes to wealth creation through greater individual ownership of capital. As we have seen, one of the great criticisms that has been levelled at the government over its policy of privatisations has been that it has consistently under-priced the assets involved. It is one thing to sell the family silver. It is another thing to fail to get the best price for it. But it is certainly possible for the government to argue that the under-pricing of assets to members of the public has been worthwhile. The consequent loss of Exchequer revenue is a small price to pay when set against the benefits obtained by spreading share ownership more than was previously thought possible.

The government is proud of its record at this point, since by the middle of 1991 it was able to say that one-quarter of the adult population owns shares. This means that the proportion of the population of which this is true has increased over 350 per cent since 1979, whereas it has gone up by only 50 per cent over the same period in the USA. In France, where privatisation is only in its infancy, the percentage of adults owning shares is thought to have increased from 5 per cent only to something over 10 per cent over the same period. There can surely be no doubt that the predominant explanation for this phenomenal and unique rise is government policy towards asset sales. This can be seen from the fact that six million people hold shares in at least one privatised company.

Is this leading to a situation in which people are now buying and selling non-privatised shares, as the government clearly hoped? The evidence suggests that they are not. It is true that in 1987 around 8 per cent of adults in Britain owned shares in at least four companies, whereas in 1991 the figure was 14 per cent. However, this largely reflects an increase in the number of privatised shares that there now are.

See p 182

There has also been no discernible effect in slowing the trend towards an increasing proportion of shares being in the hands of the institutions (as we saw in Table 9.2). This steady upward trend over the last 10 years has been entirely unaffected by privatisation. That said, some individuals who have been encouraged through state asset sales to invest in shares, have taken their share ownership through the unit trusts, and so on, rather than involve themselves directly in the purchase of shares. It is, of course, possible, that the effect of the privatisation policy is cumulative and that it is too early for such effects to take place. The dramatic increase in the individual ownership of shares appears only to have begun in 1984–5. However, it does seem as though the process has a long way to go before it slows the movement of shares towards the institutions. It looks as if it will take more than further privatisations to affect the trend. A significant change of attitude towards risk bearing is also required, and it is just such a shift in attitude that the government seeks.

5 Deregulation

We saw earlier in the chapter a key criticism of the privatisation process. Monopolies, with their power to misallocate resources, are transferred from the public to the private sector. We saw also that those privatised companies where substantially monopoly power exists have that power curtailed by a price control. A further technique for controlling monopoly power is that of deregulation. Most of the natural monopolies within the public sector have been protected from competition to ensure the benefits of economies of scale. This is still true for some industries. For example, the Post Office, still publicly owned, has a legally determined monopoly power over the delivery of letters (although competition is allowed in parcel deliveries). When an industry is privatised it can be deregulated. One illustration of deregulation is the allowing of such companies as Mercury access to BT's cable network so that BT has now some competition. Another is

Table 17.5 Welfare effects of deregulation (1990, $US billions), a range of estimates is denoted as (A, B). Positive indicates a welfare gain

Industry	Consumers	Producers	Total	Additional benefits if deregulation achieves optimality[1]
Airlines	(8.8, 14.8)	4.9	(13.7, 19.7)	4.9
Railroads	(7.2, 9.7)	3.2	(10.4, 12.9)	0.45
Trucking	15.4	−4.8	10.6	0.0
Telecommunications	(0.73, 1.6)	—	(0.73, 1.6)	11.8
Cable television	(0.37, 1.3)	—	(0.37, 1.3)	(0.4, 0.8)
Brokerage	0.14	−0.14	0.0	0.0
Natural Gas	—	—	—	4.1
Total	(32.6, 43.0)	3.2	(35.8, 46.2)	(21.65, 22.05)

Notes: [1] The additional welfare gains are based on assuming regulatory reform actually generates optimal pricing and, where appropriate, optimal service.
Source: C. Winston. 'Economic Deregulation: Days of Reckoning for Microeconomists'. *Journal of Economic Literature*, Sep 1993.

allowing regional electricity distribution to buy power from any source they choose.

Deregulation and privatisation are separate issues, but they are closely related. Deregulation is a way of controlling monopoly power in the private sector and encouraging competition to move price/output decisions in industry closer to the social optimum. Is it effective? The most comprehensive attempt to answer this question is provided by Clifford Winston from his collection of researches into the effects of deregulation on American industry.

The results for those who believe in the power of deregulation are encouraging. They suggest that substantial welfare gains can be achieved as Table 17.5 shows. Consumers gain from lower prices and better services. Notice that this effect is not simply a transfer of welfare from producers to consumers. There are overall gains. Competition improves efficiency. Notice also that in some cases, consumers and producers both gain. Cost efficiency is improved by competition. Prices fall but by not as much as costs. Producers increase profits, consumers get lower prices.

The last column in Table 17.5 indicates that, while the process has improved things for society in the United States, prices in those industries do not reflect a welfare optimum. There is given there an idea of the further benefits available if it were possible to get price and output to reflect that optimum.

The results of the study, then, suggest that deregulation is a powerful way to improve welfare. It is a particularly important means of controlling the monopoly power of privatised industries.

6 The future

Clearly, the claimed benefits of privatisation is a matter of great debate, but the Conservative party's victory at the April 1992 election suggests that the process is set to continue in Britain for some years to come. Its ramifications go far beyond Britain. Britain was not the first to shift assets out of the state sector, but the scale of the process in Britain has captured the imagination of many other governments. It is to privatise or not to privatise a debate that will not go away. Nevertheless, we can say two things with a reasonably high degree of confidence.

First, while the concepts around which the arguments revolve are clear, the empirical evidence does not enable us to resolve the privatisation arguments convincingly. It does suggest that for monopolies which are transferred to the private sector deregulation of the industries involved will be of great benefit to society. Second, the driving force behind the privatisation process was the supply side belief that macro-economic problems are best dealt with by micro-economic policies designed to make markets work effectively. Your view of macro-economic policy cannot be divorced from your view of the key micro-economic issue: how effective are markets at allocating resources efficiently?

7 Questions for discussion

1 If a public sector monopoly faces a downwards sloping demand curve but an upwards sloping LRAC, and sets a socially optimal price/output, will it make losses, break even or make a profit?

2 Refer back to Figure 17.5. Suppose a privatised firm has to operate under a price ceiling of P_4. How much output would it make and what price would it charge?

3 Can you think of ways of testing for the effects of privatisation on an industry's efficiency? What problems do you see with these ideas?

4 Until 1994 value added tax (VAT) on domestic fuel was zero. By 1995 it will be at 17.5 per cent. What will happen to domestic fuel prices? Was the decision to impose VAT on domestic fuel the right one?

5 How might the government defend itself against the charge that the state's assets were underpriced?

6 Do you consider the benefits of the privatisation programme to have outweighed the costs?

8 Further reading

Efficiency with declining LRAC
Sloman, p. 503; Parkin and King, pp. 508–12

Privatisation policy
Sloman, pp. 486–512; Begg, pp. 313–25

Privatisation: a supply side improvement
S. Ison (1992) 'British rail privatization', *British Economic Survey*, section 11, pp. 40–3, Spring 1992.
R. Frydman and A. Rapaczynski (1993) 'Privatization in Eastern Europe: is the state withering away?', *Finance and Development*, June.

9 End notes

1 Howard Vane (1992) 'The Thatcher years: macroeconomic policy and Performance of the UK economy, 1979–1988', *National Westminster Bank Quarterly Review*, May, p. 34.
2 Of course, if there were to be several private firms in the market who were prevented from merging to preserve competition, it could be argued that resources would be wasted. The situation would not allow the exploitation of scale economies.
3 There is a frequently unrecognised problem here. If a company such as BT knows that a decrease in costs and an increase in profits will lead to a tightening of its price ceiling, it may come to the conclusion that efforts to reduce costs are rather pointless. Then the policy will no longer be achieving cost efficiency.
4 See Richard Hawkins (1991), 'Privatization in Western Germany, 1957–1990', *National Westminster Bank Quarterly Review*, November, pp. 14–22.

CHAPTER 18

Does the UK want an independent central bank?

In recent years a feeling has grown in Britain that running the economy is too important to be left in the hands of the politicians. Could an independent central bank do for Britain what it appears to have done for Germany, provide economic stability?

In this chapter we review:
- **Keynesian equilibrium**
- **Fiscal policy**

We introduce:
- **Money market equilibrium**
- **Monetarism**

1 Introduction

See pp 289–93

As we saw in Chapter 15, Britain's inflation record in postwar years has not been good. By comparison with Germany, widely regarded as the strongest economy in Europe, it has been particularly poor. Table 18.1 illustrates the extent of the problem. Between 1985 and 1992 the UK price level rose by 41.1 per cent, Germany's 9.9 per cent and the Economic Union (EU) as a whole 28.4 per cent German inflation rates have been substantially better than Britain's over almost the whole period, the fall in the external value of the pound against many of these currencies being an inevitable consequence. The British inflation record in the context of the whole of the EU is clearly not good. According to Eurostat estimates, only Portugal, Greece and Spain have faired worse in recent years. That said, as we saw in Chapter 15, the recent past has been much better in this respect. Figure 18.1 clearly displays the extent of that relative improvement.

Whereas the UK inflation rate has tended to be relatively high, it has fallen below the community average only in the recent past. It is unclear whether this relative improvement will be sustained. It has been suggested that one reason for Britain's poor inflation record over a long period is to be found in the nature of its central bank. In Britain, the central bank, the Bank of England, is an arm of the government policy. The government decides upon its policy and can then instruct the Bank of England to carry it out. In Germany the equivalent organisation, the Bundesbank, has a large measure of independence. It is charged with the task of

Table 18.1 EU consumer price index 1992 (1985 = 100)

EU	128.4	Ireland	120.6
Belgium	113.8	Italy	139.3
Denmark	124.1	Luxembourg	111.7
Germany	109.9	Netherlands	107.4
Greece	259.3	Portugal	189.5
Spain	143.2	UK	141.1
France	119.4		

Source: OECD.

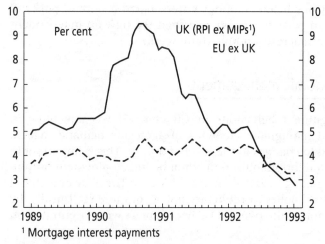

¹ Mortgage interest payments

Figure 18.1 UK inflation relative to European Union

achieving price stability and has to undertake the appropriate policies to achieve it. The state then has to conduct its policy against that background.

Now the suspicion is that the British system has a problem in that governments sometimes have a vested interest in inflation. In the short term it might find that stimulating the economy before an election can induce temporary growth of output. Falls in unemployment, with the associated inflation, will only become apparent after polling day. In the longer term a further advantage of inflation for government is that the real value of government debt can be reduced over time. This assumes that the inflation rate is greater than interest rates, which has often been the case. In the British system governments can oblige the central bank to undertake policies to achieve these advantages. With the German system this is impossible. But what is it that central banks do? How do their policies affect inflation? We shall discover that the answer is tied up with money and monetary policy.

In this chapter, therefore, we shall be extending our analysis of government macro-economic policy to include policy on money. We shall discover that most Keynesian and classical economists are divided upon this subject as on others we have already examined. Enthusiasm for central bank autonomy depends largely upon the perspective on the monetary issues of macro policy we shall consider.

There are two aspects to the question of central bank independence. One is whether the Bank of England should be independent. The other aspect is the question of independence of a European central bank if there is to be a common currency for at least part of Europe. We shall leave this second aspect until Chapter 20 and restrict our discussion in this chapter mainly to issues raised in a closed economy, that is, one that does not engage in international trade.

See pp 390–412

First, let us examine how one believes money enters macro-economic policy, if one has a broadly Keynesian perspective. We can then see how an independent central bank fits into such a macro-economic framework.

2 Keynesian macro-economic management

See pp 260–4

When we examined investment behaviour in Chapter 13, we saw how, in principle, governments can manipulate elements of aggregate demand, which, through the multiplier, lead to changes in the level of output. This is important in Keynesian thinking since equilibrium output may not be full employment output.

How is that manipulation of aggregate demand achieved? The answer is that it can be done primarily by fiscal policy or monetary policy, or more realistically, by some appropriate combination of the two. (In earlier chapters we concentrated on fiscal policy.)

a Fiscal Policy

Essentially fiscal policy is the use of taxation and/or government expenditure. Such a policy has a number of aims. Clearly one of them is to affect the overall level of economic activity. For example, if an increase in output is required, cuts in taxes on consumers can be used to attempt to raise consumption. Alternatively, as we saw in Chapter 13, increased government expenditure can achieve much the same thing. The government sector is sufficiently large to make substantial changes in economic activity through a multiplier effect. In principle, the reverse is also possible. If inflation is a problem, increased taxes and/or decreased government expenditure can reduce aggregate demand. In practice this is more problematic, since to reduce expenditure or to increase taxes is politically difficult.

See pp 260–4

Increasing expenditure or decreasing taxes may seem easy politically but this also has problems. It may well lead to a deficit in the government's budgetary position. A deficit, a situation in which government spends more than it receives in taxation, and so on, means that government will be obliged to borrow. We called that borrowing requirement the public sector borrowing requirement or

PSBR. How it will be financed is an issue to which we return later in the chapter. We shall come back to the matter of fiscal policy again shortly then, but we want to focus now on monetary policy. To do that we need to know what is meant by the term 'money'.

b What is money?

The most important feature of money is that it represents a claim on output. You work to provide for yourself or your family, goods and services. Now bartering, offering to work for a basket of clothes, books and food is highly inefficient. Money represents a claim on output which you can hold until you are ready to exchange it for goods and services. It thus functions as a medium of exchange. In modern society the main form of money is not notes and coins but bank and building society deposits against which you can write cheques. Accordingly, there are two ways of defining money given in Table 18.2. These are perhaps the most important but there are other definitions also. Wealth can be stored in other ways. For example we can have a deposit account at a bank against which we cannot write cheques, although it is easy to change it into a 'liquid' form for purchasing items. We can also change shares into liquid form but not so easily and not with such a certain value. Thus there are many definitions of money according to how liquid the asset is which we treat as money.

As you can see from Table 18.2, control of the money supply will need to focus on the ability of the banking system to lend. It is that credit creation that is such a significant factor in determining the amount of money in circulation.

Notice that in the wider definition of the money supply banks create money. Bankers sometimes say that they do not create money, simply make loans. In reality they are the same thing. Suppose Alex has saved £1000 from the part-time job at McDonald's, and has deposited it with the bank. The £1000 is still available to Alex for spending, and is therefore money.

Table 18.2 Main definitions of the money supply

Measure	Includes
Narrow definition: M_0	Notes and coins in circulation and operational deposits of commercial banks with the Bank of England
Broad definition: M_4	Notes and coins with the general public and UK private sectors; sterling sight deposits with UK banks; sterling time deposits of the UK private sector with UK banks and building society holdings of private sector *less* building society holdings of deposits with UK banks

Suppose the bank now feels able to make a loan of £800 to Fennella to change her car. You may feel that the bank has simply lent Fennella some of the money that belongs to Alex. Certainly the bank is performing a function in acting as a middleman. It is bringing together one who wishes to lend and one who wishes to borrow. The exchange is improving the welfare of both or they would not be willing participants in the exchange. But in creating the loan it has created money. Fennella has £800 to spend but Alex still has available to her the money she deposited. The bank, in making the loan has created money.

c The supply of money

Most Keynesian models assume that the supply of money can be determined by the government. We have drawn a supply curve for money in Figure 18.2. If it wishes to move the supply curve, a government can do so through the Bank of England by affecting the banks' ability to land. Suppose it wished to reduce the supply from S_1 to S_2, in Figure 18.2, it could do it in a number of ways. We shall mention briefly three of these ways. First, the central bank can demand that the banks have a higher liquidity ratio. That is to say, commercial banks must keep more of their assets in a form easily turned into liquid assets. The extent to which banks can lend will depend upon the volume of their liquid assets. They must retain sufficient liquid assets to meet demands for cash from their customers. The less liquid assets they have, the less they will feel able to lend. Clearly if the banks can now lend less, the supply of money is reduced. This is not a method that has been used in recent years. Second, the government can sell securities, for example long-term debt such as bonds. When people buy the bonds, they pay for them with cheques drawn on their banks, thus reducing bank liquidity and hence the money supply. Third, the central bank can insist on special deposits from the commercial banks. The banks are obliged to deposit some of their funds with the Bank of England. Again the effect is to reduce bank liquidity leading to a reduction in the money supply.

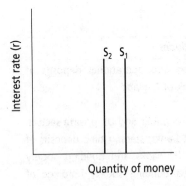

Figure 18.2 Reducing the supply of money

So in principle the supply of money can be determined by government, working through the Bank of England, the Bank being an instrument of government policy.

d Demand for money in Keynesian thinking

What determines the demand for money? To put the question another way, why would people wish to hold their wealth in liquid form rather than in an illiquid form such as shares or government debt such as bonds? There are said to be three motives. First, there is a 'transactions' motive. People wish to hold money so that they can purchase goods and services. Holding all one's wealth as a Goya painting makes buying sausages at the grocers a difficult business. It can be argued that such a motive is unlikely to be affected by interest rates. If that is so the transactions demand for money (D_t) will be as in Figure 18.3. Alternatively, one could take the view that as interest rates rise, the opportunity cost of holding one's wealth in the form of money increases, in that a greater amount of interest is foregone. It will certainly be the case that Dt would shift to the right with a rise in income. More money is needed for steak than is needed for sausages.

But there is a second motive for holding money, the 'precautionary' demand (D_p). People demand money to be ready to meet unforseen expenditure, such as an unexpected bill to repair a car such as a mini. This is probably not interest rate sensitive either, so we show it on Figure 18.3 as interest inelastic just as we did for the transactions demand. Again, however, this would shift right as incomes rise. An unforeseen repair bill for the Mercedes Benz will require more money than one for the mini.

The third and final motive for holding money, according to Keynesian theory is the 'speculative' motive. Holding wealth in illiquid form such as shares, antiques or bonds has an advantage in that capital gains can be made if their value appreciates. Wealth in the liquid form of £10 notes under the bed has no such

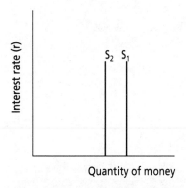

Figure 18.3 The transactions and precautionary demand for money

advantage. On the other hand, such illiquid assets have a disadvantage – their value may fall and one may sustain a capital loss. In Keynesian theory people take this into account when deciding how liquid their assets should be, and that decision is affected by interest rates. Let us see why.

We chose one illiquid asset, the '2.5 per cent consol', and establish the principle, though what we say about this asset is, in essence, true of all assets. This 2.5 per cent consol is government debt. The holder of this bond is paid £2.50 per annum, representing 2.5 per cent of its face value of £100. The bond is irredeemable, that is the government is never going to pay back the original £100. If one wants to sell it, one has to find someone else willing to buy it. What will the market price be for such a bond? The answer is that it depends upon interest rates. Suppose the present rate of interest is 10 per cent, what is the bond worth? The answer must be about £25. If one paid £25 for the bond and received £2.50 per annum interest, that represents a 10 per cent return on the investment. Since 10 per cent is available at the bank, no one is likely to pay more than £25 for the bond. Suppose interest rates were to be 20 per cent. Clearly no one would pay more than £12.50 for the bond, since that lower bond price would be needed in order that the buyer received a return equal to available returns elsewhere. In general, then a rise in interest rates will cause a fall in bond prices and vice versa.

Now consider Figure 18.4. Suppose interest rates are high, at r_1, in the diagram. Most people will anticipate that the next move in interest rates will be downwards. They, therefore, expect bond prices to rise in the future. If bond prices are going to rise they will wish to hold their wealth in the form of bonds in order to make a capital gain – so the speculative demand for money (labelled 'D_{spec}' in the figure) will be low. Conversely, at low interest rates, since most people will anticipate an upward move in r and therefore a fall in bond prices, it makes sense to hold wealth in liquid form. Therefore, the speculative demand for money is high when interest rates are low, for example at r_2 when the interest rate is at Q_2.

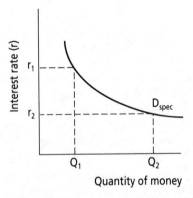

Figure 18.4 The speculative demand for money

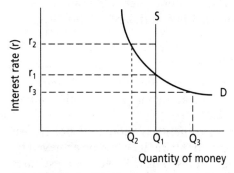

Figure 18.5 Equilibrium in the money market

e Keynesian money market equilibrium

We are now in a position to see how money market equilibrium is found and how the government can affect that equilibrium through the actions of the central bank.

Money market equilibrium can be seen in Figure 18.5. The supply of money, as we have seen, can be controlled by the central bank. The demand curve, D, is simply the horizontal summation of D_t, D_p and D_{spec} to give the total demand for money, sometimes known as the liquidity preference schedule. Market forces will ensure an equilibrium rate of interest at r_1. If interest rates are at r_2 there is an excess supply of money $Q_1 - Q$, that is to say an excess demand for bonds. Hence, bond prices rise and interest rates fall. At r_3 the excess demand for money, $Q_3 - Q_1$, that is the excess supply of bonds, depresses bond prices and raises interest rates.

We now know, how, in Keynesian thinking, money market equilibrium is reached. We can easily see how government can manipulate conditions in the money market. It has two options. It can influence the money supply and hence influence interest rates. For example, if it wishes to see lower interest rates, the Bank of England can increase the money supply in ways we have seen, shifting the supply curve of money to the right. Lower interest rates will follow. Unfortunately, this has a problem. One needs to know exactly where the liquidity preference schedule is, to move the money supply the correct distance rightwards.

As a result, in recent years the alternative option has been favoured. The Bank of England can set the chosen level of interest rates and then supply whatever money is necessary to bring money markets into equilibrium at that rate. As a result of this change in policy, announcements of the money supply figures, once seen as measuring the success of government policy in controlling monetary conditions, are now more often seen as indicating the demand for credit from the general public and hence a measure of economic activity.

Now we shall turn to see how the monetary sector, and government control over it, has influences on the real sector. Having done that, we shall see how Keynesian economists would view an independent central bank.

f Interrelationships between the real and money sectors

We saw earlier how governments could manipulate the volume of aggregate demand via fiscal policy changes. We can now make two important points about aggregate demand control.

See pp 276–80

The first is that an alternative to fiscal instruments is monetary policy. An upward shift in the aggregate demand function, for example, could be achieved by relaxing monetary conditions and lowering interest rates. Lower interest rates may stimulate investment demand as we considered in Chapter 14. Alternatively, it may raise consumption demand, since lower interest rates reduce the cost of purchasing many consumer durable items such as cars and furniture that are frequently bought on credit. Most Keynesian economists would argue, however, that the extent to which demand is stimulated by lower interest rates is difficult to predict and that fiscal policy is therefore of more value in controlling aggregate demand.

The second point is that the effects of fiscal control cannot be isolated from the monetary sector. There are important interrelationships between the two sectors. We shall illustrate this by looking at what happens if governments choose to stimulate economic activity by fiscal means. Figure 18.6 shows an economy with equilibrium in both the real and monetary sectors. Let us assume that the equilibrium in the real sector is with substantial unemployment. Government thus gives a fiscal stimulus to the economy in an attempt to raise output to full employment output, assumed to be at Y_2. Provided that it knows the value of the multiplier, it can calculate the correct increase in, say, government expenditure that is required and raise aggregate demand from AD_1 to AD_2, thus moving the economy to a full employment output.

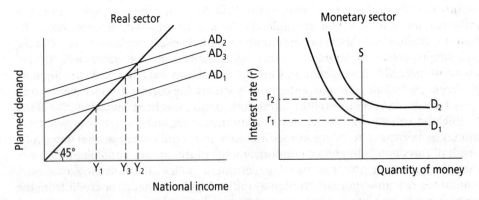

Figure 18.6 Money and its effect on the real sector

Notice, however, what happens in the monetary sector. As output, and hence income, begins to rise through the multiplier the transactions and precautionary demand for money increases, shifting money demand from D_1 to D_2. Assuming the Bank of England does not alter its monetary stance by changing the money supply, interest rates rise. Rising interest rates will choke off some of the expected aggregate demand increase in the real sector. Therefore AD_1 shifts, not to AD_2 as intended, but only to AD_3, leaving the economy with some unemployment at Y_3.

The government will, as a result, be faced with a choice. It can give a larger fiscal stimulus to the economy and accept higher interest rates, or it can operate an accommodating monetary policy. That is, it can get the central bank to allow the money supply to increase sufficiently so as not to increase interest rates.

See p 300

In all this one must remember what we said in Chapter 15 concerning inflation. The government cannot in reality find a level of Y corresponding to full employment without inflationary pressures in the system. It must choose some optimal mix of inflation and employment.

3 Central bank independence in Keynesian economics

We have covered much ground since we first questioned whether the Bank of England should be free from political control of the government. But the ground we covered was necessary. We are now in a position to see why many Keynesian economists would be reluctant to allow central bank independence. Many would accept that central bank independence would overcome the problems mentioned at the beginning of the chapter, namely the manipulation of the economy for electoral advantage and government tendency to use inflation to erode the real value of its debt. However, there are five significant potential disadvantages for macro-economic policy in an independent central bank.

a Non-optimal policy goal

See pp 300-3

We saw in Chapter 15 the Keynesian conviction that there exists a trade-off between unemployment and inflation. The government may come to the conclusion that a higher level of employment is justifiable even at the cost of some increase in inflation. The rationale of an independent central bank is that it should be charged with creating stable monetary conditions and a stable price level as a backdrop against which the economy functions. A stable price level may entail a higher level of unemployment than government thinks is optimal. Yet the government may find itself unable to do anything about it because it has had removed from it the freedom to 'buy' higher employment with increased inflation.

b Non-optimal macro policy mix

The government needs both fiscal and monetary policy for macro-economic control. It has some freedom with respect to the mixture of those policies. For example, as we have just seen, it can stimulate an economy with monetary means, with fiscal means plus an accommodating monetary policy, or with a fiscal policy accepting that monetary conditions will tighten as it does so. At different times it may feel that a different mix is appropriate. An independent central bank reduces government options. A monetary stance is decided by the central bank and thus has to be taken as given. The government will have no power to order the central bank to alter monetary conditions. Government has only fiscal policy as a weapon and may find itself in a position of being unable to operate what it feels is the best mix of fiscal and monetary policy for the economy.

c Constrained fiscal policy

So far one might feel that although an independent central bank will mean that government has no power over monetary policy it will at least retain complete freedom over fiscal policy. This is not so. An independent monetary authority will severely curtail fiscal policy also.

Suppose a government, faced with an independent central bank operating a tight monetary stance, decides to give the economy a fiscal stimulus. Unless it is at present running a surplus on its own expenditure it will need to fund that extra debt that will be incurred. If it borrows more, it must borrow from somewhere. In other words, it will increase its public sector borrowing requirement (PSBR). If it approaches the central bank and asks the bank to fund the debt, it may well be refused. The central bank may well feel that this will increase the money supply and thus be inflationary. If the government borrows extra funds from the private sector it will compete with other institutions for loanable funds and, therefore, raise interest rates, mitigating the effects of the fiscal stimulus.

A government cannot even operate an unconstrained fiscal policy, then, if it has to deal with an independent central bank.

d Waste of resources

Since government macro-economic policy is so severely restrained, it must spend time attempting to guess how the central bank will react to changes in economic policy. Even if it can guess what policy will be adopted, it will be difficult to predict the timing of changes, so that more economic forecasting will be needed. Producing economic forecasts uses scarce resources.

e An undemocratic structure

Some regard central bank independence as essentially undemocratic. Such a bank cannot be independent if it is run by executives who are government elected. If they are not elected by government, citizens unhappy with their performance have no opportunity to do anything about it. At least one can vote for a change of government every five years. Obviously it would be possible to make the central bank accountable in some way but the more accountable it is, the less its independence is guaranteed.

4 An alternative perspective: monetarism

We have already seen that classical economic thinking departs from Keynesian orthodoxy in several respects. We have seen that it rejects the Keynesian view that there is such a thing as an unemployment equilibrium. In the classical view, markets will always adjust, given time, to full employment output. We have seen, furthermore, that there is no trade-off between unemployment and inflation. The choice for government is between high and perhaps accelerating inflation or zero inflation. The zero inflation option does not involve a cost in terms of increased unemployment, except perhaps temporarily. On the other hand, government is responsible for inflation, which as we shall see is in the classical view, essentially monetary. This school of thought is often called monetarism. Some but not all the monetarists are of the classical school. We shall assume, for simplicity, that the classical view is identical with monetarism. We have already seen some of the ways in which classical thinking can differ over some issues.

See pp 305–6

We can briefly and easily explain the idea behind monetarism and then proceed to show what a difference such a perspective gives to the question of central bank autonomy.

a The equation of exchange: a tautology

The monetarist perspective begins with an uncontroversial statement from which it develops an argument that is very controversial. Let us first examine the statement which we shall derive from a simple example.

Four people are on a desert island. They each produce three units of a commodity per year, each unit being worth £1, not for consumption but for exchanging with others. So there is a total of £12 of output or gross domestic product (GDP) in this economy. We found the total by multiplying the number of transactions, T, in the economy by the average price of the goods entering into exchange. In this case, 12 units of output were produced and each one was worth, on average, £1. So GDP equals PT. $12 \times £1 = £12$.

On this island money is used to make the exchanges possible, but there are only six £1 coins. Will those be enough to enable all the trade to take place? The answer of course is yes, provided that each coin is used more than once during the course of the year. In fact, of course, each coin will have, on average, to be used twice, since 12 exchanges will take place. In other words, the money stock, M, multiplied by the average velocity of its circulation, V, gives us six £1 coins x 2.

MV equals £12, which must by definition equal the value of the output. Hence MV equals PT.

In general this must hold for any economy. Its money stock multiplied by the average velocity of circulation must be equal to the value of national output. This is one form of what is known as the equation of exchange.

b The monetarist argument

Since the above is true by definition we can build an argument from it with respect to monetary control. Consider first the size of GDP. In the long run the level of output is going to grow in real terms as improved technology, and so on makes greater output possible. In Britain, for example, GDP growth has averaged around 2.5 - 2.75 per cent per annum over a long period. Now, assuming that real output, T, grows at that rate and we want the price level, P, to be stable, PT will grow by 2.5 per cent or so per year. In the long run the velocity of circulation, V, will, in the monetarist view, be fairly constant, so provided that M is allowed to increase by around 2.5 per cent per annum, it follows that the price level will stay constant.

See pp 302–3

All that is required is for government to restrict monetary growth in this way and that will ensure a stable price level. When monetary conditions are tightened, temporary periods of unemployment may develop. After all, if banks can lend less and people borrow less, aggregate demand will fall. Nevertheless, for reasons we explained in Chapter 15, any increase in unemployment will soon disappear. In the end, then, inflation reflects government failure, since it is in the hands of government to eliminate inflation through monetary control.

The Conservative government followed the policy implied in the above argument for much of the 1980s. Their policy was embodied in the medium term financial strategy (MTFS) where the intention was that over time monetary targets of a tighter and tighter nature were set to squeeze inflation. Controversy has always raged over the extent of the policy's success.

See p 306

Does the monetarist believe that there will be no unemployment at all if government behaves in this way – that stable prices can be achieved with no unemployment at all? The answer is no, for as you will recall from Chapter 15 the argument is usually expressed in terms of there being a 'natural rate of unemployment' – one in which some do not have a job because of friction in the system, but one in which there is no *demand-deficient* unemployment.

c Monetarism and the aggregate demand curve

See pp 304–6

We can now look back at the classical view of inflation as explained in Chapter 15. We saw there that if aggregate demand rises, it leads to inflation. The effects on output were effectively zero, except possibly in the short run. We can now see what might cause AD to shift. The answer, in the classical view, is that it is always a monetary phenomenon.

Let us suppose that government attempts to shift AD outwards via an increase in government spending without accompanying increases in taxation. In other words, the government increases the PSBR. What happens? There are two main possibilities. One is that it will borrow. Since it has to compete for loanable funds, this will tend to push up interest rates. The result will be reduced investment spending as we saw in Chapter 14. The effect of the PSBR has been to raise interest rates, choke off private sector spending and so leave the volume of aggregate demand unaffected. The AD curve has not shifted.

See pp 276–80

However, there is a second possibility. In order not to raise interest rates the government can borrow from the central bank and use this credit to increase its spending. In other words, it increases the money supply. Then AD does shift. The shift is a monetary phenomenon.

There is, however, little evidence that an increased PSBR does increase interest rates if the money supply is not expanded. The probable explanation is that governments can borrow not only from their own citizens, but from abroad. An increased PSBR in, say, Britain would make little impact in a world market for loanable funds that is very large indeed.

d The velocity of circulation: is it really stable?

As we have seen the view is an argument developed from a tautology. $MV = PT$ is a definition. But the argument developed from it makes some crucial assumptions. That PT is an assumption we have already considered. Another assumption is that increases in M will affect P because V is constant. Is this correct? Is there any evidence to suggest that it is so? Perhaps the most impressive empirical support comes from the German economy where central bank autonomy is regarded as crucial for effective control of the economy.

Figure 18.7 is taken from an unpublished working paper written by Dr Joachim Scheide for the Institut fur Weltwirtschaft in Kiel, Germany. It shows the relationship between German GNP/M3 a measure of the money supply since $MV = PT$, and since $GNP = PT$, then $GNP/M3 = V$ the velocity of circulation.

Notice several points. First, the chosen money supply measure is M_3. In our definitions of the British money supply figures earlier we concentrated on M_0 and M_4. So why is the German data for M_3? And what is the difference between M_3 and M_4? Britain used to have a definition of the money supply called M_3. This represented the same measure as the present M_4 with one exception. M_4 includes building society current account deposits which function in the same way as the bank's current account deposits. Since Germany has no such financial bodies, German M_3 is the equivalent of the British M_4 measure.

Next, observe that the trend shows a good fit supporting the monetarist argument, at least for the German economy. For any given period of time the 'fit'

German velocity of circulation (GNP/M3) 1972–92 (in logs)

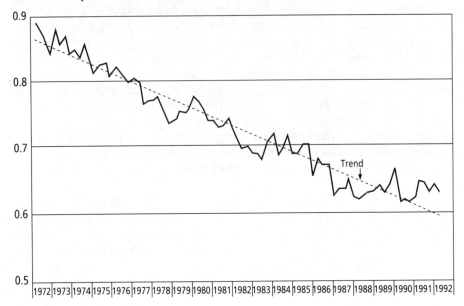

Source: J.Scheide. Unpublished working paper

Figure 18.7 German velocity of circulation

may not be very good. For example, there does not appear to be a good fit in the period 1987–92. However, the argument is not that V is stable but that V is stable in the long run. Short-run deviations from the trend are of no consequence.

Note, too, that V is not constant. It declines at a rate of about 1 per cent per annum. Does this constitute a problem? The answer is no if it is predictable. The German central bank can control monetary conditions because it can predict reasonably accurately the *trend* in the value of V. You might care to plot the same kind of information for the British economy. Sources such as *Economic Trends* will give you velocity of circulation of both M_0 and M_4 over any time period you choose. If you do this you will see that the relationships appear less stable than for the German economy.

One further problem for monetary control occurs when the size of changes in the money supply varies according to which definition one is using. Consider Figure 18.8, which shows the way in which M_0 and M_4 were changing over a period of one year in the British economy. According to the wider definition, M_4, the money supply was declining in late 1992 and early in 1993. On the other hand, M_0 was increasing. One possible explanation for this can be found in the falling interest rates of that period. Lower interest rates lower the opportunity cost of holding money in savings accounts, increasing narrow money in circulation.

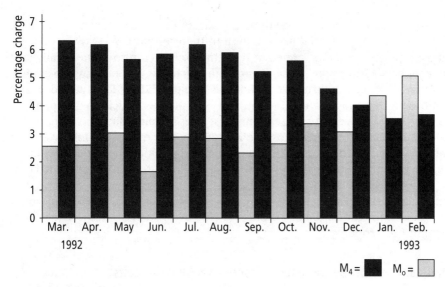

Source: Economic Trends

Figure 18.8 Monthly changes in the money supply

5 Monetarists and central bank interdependence

It should now be clear that monetarists tend, on the whole, to have more enthusiasm for an independent central bank, and that many of the Keynesian arguments we examined in section 3 would be regarded by monetarists as unimpressive. We can express the benefits of a Bank of England free from government interference in three propositions.

a Governments do not need discretionary monetary policy

Monetary policy is not a discretionary weapon for ironing out fluctuations in the real sector. Any such fluctuations can be best left to the market mechanism. Monetary policy is to be aimed at providing sound money by monetary control. An independent central bank is unlikely to be tempted to manipulate monetary conditions for short-term advantage and can be given unambiguous terms of reference: keep tight control of the money supply and hence inflation.

b Fiscal restraint on governments is wholly beneficial

We have seen the Keynesian fears that central bank independence also restricts the degree of fiscal discretion open to governments. To a monetarist such restrictions are wholly beneficial. Recall what we saw in Chapter 15. In the longer

See p 358

term there can be no unemployment as a result of demand deficiency. There is, therefore, no need for artificial fiscal stimuli to the economy. We saw in Chapter 15 that fiscal policy should be aimed at reducing taxes to improve the supply side of the economy. To make this possible there needs to be cuts in public expenditure. The only alternative would be a high PSBR. This would either increase the money supply and be inflationary – a process which an independent central bank could prevent, or increase interest rates by increasing the demand for loanable funds. This would be a possible route for a government to follow even if it were operating in the context of central bank autonomy. But it would be undesirable in that it would take resources from the private sector and 'crowd out' private sector investment.

From a monetarist perspective, then, reduced room for fiscal discretion would indeed follow from central bank autonomy. However, such an occurrence could only benefit the economy.

c Central bank independence reduces economic adjustment costs

See p 306

Suppose an economy is suffering from inflation and government wishes to reduce it. Monetarists, of course, believe that the appropriate way to do so is by reducing the money supply. Given what we saw in Chapter 15 about expectations on the part of economic agents, there may well be some short-term costs in increased unemployment. This will only be temporary. When economic agents, firms, trade unions, and so on, realise that the price level is coming down they will adjust their actions accordingly.

Crucial to this procedure is the belief by such agents that if unemployment develops, the government will not lose its nerve and relax monetary policy. It is essential that there is a conviction that this will not happen if the transition costs of increased unemployment are to be temporary.

This is where central bank independence can be so valuable. Economic agents may find it difficult to believe in the determination of governments, particularly near to a general election. They are far more likely to believe in the policy of an independent central bank that does not have the political pressures to bear.

Economic adjustment to lower inflation will thus be faster and less painful especially in terms of unemployment and lost output.

6 How independent is independent?

So far we have assumed that a central bank is either entirely under the government's control or entirely independent. Clearly this is not so. There are degrees of independence. So how independent is independent? One attempt to quantify it is that by Alesina and Grilli (1991, see Table 18.3). They suggest that there are degrees of economic independence in areas such as the determination of interest rates and control over the banking system, and political independence in

Table 18.3(a) Measures of political independence

Central Bank	1	2	3	4	5	6	7	8	9
European Central Bank		*		*	*	*	*	*	6
Germany		*		*	*	*	*	*	6
Netherlands		*		*	*	*	*	*	6
Italy	*	*	*		*				4
Denmark		*					*	*	3
Ireland		*				*		*	3
France		*		*					2
Greece			*					*	2
Spain				*	*				2
Belgium				*					1
Portugal					*				1
UK					*				1

Note: 1 Governor not appointed by government; 2 Governor appointed for 5+ years; 3 Executive not appointed by government; 4 Executive appointed for 5+ years; 5 No mandatory government representative on executive; 6 No government approval of policy decision required; 7 Statutory requirement for central bank to pursue price stability; 8 Explicit conflicts between central bank and government possible; 9 Index of political independence (sum of asterisks in each row).

Table 18.3(b) Measures of economic independence

Central Bank	1	2	3	4	5	6	7	8	9
European Central Bank	*	*	*	*	*	*	*	*	8
Germany	*	*	*	*	*	*	*	*	8
Belgium		*	*	*	*	*		*	6
UK	*	*	*	*		*	*		6
Denmark		*			*	*	*		4
France				*	*	*	*		4
Ireland		*	*	*		*			4
Netherlands				*	*	*	*		4
Spain				*	*			*	3
Greece				*		*			2
Portugal				*		*			2
Italy				*					1

Note: 1 Government credit from central bank not automatic; 2 Government credit from central bank at market interest rate; 3 Government credit from central bank for temporary period only; 4 Government credit from central bank limited in amount; 5 Central bank does not take up unsold government bond issues; 6 Discount rate set by central bank; 7 No government qualitative controls on commercial bank lending since 1980; 8 No government quantitative controls on bank lending since 1980; 9 Index of economic independence (sum of asterisks in each row).
Source: A. Alesina and V.U. Grilli (1991) 'The European central bank: reshaping monetary politics in Europe', *Discussion Paper Series*, No. 563 Centre for Economic Policy Research.

areas, for example, such as the appointment of governors. Tables 18.3(a) and (b) give their attempts to measure the different degrees of indepenence enjoyed by different European central banks.

Of course, one should be aware that no attempt can be perfect and there are criticisms that can be made of their classification. Two are perhaps most obvious. One is that one has to assume that each of the chosen measures is equally important in arriving at a summary measure – in practice this may not be so. The other is that there may be informal links and pressures which formal measures fail to pick up. For example, the German Bundesbank is clearly regarded generally, and in terms of Tables 18.3(a) and (b), as essentially independent. Indeed, Article 3 of the Bundesbankgesetz, or bank statutes, says that the bank is, in the execution of its tasks, independent of orders from the central government. Yet the statutes also say that the Bundesbank must support the general economic policy of the federal government. So when East Germany was incorporated into West Germany the Bonn government allowed an exchange rate of one Ostmark for one Deutschmark for formerly East German citizens. The Bundesbank certainly had no enthusiasm for such a move but was obliged to accept it despite the fact that there were clear monetary implications that it did not like.

Despite the weaknesses of such a system of measurement, the classification in Tables 18.3(a) and (b) does enable us to test whether central bank independence is likely to help macro-economic policy in the realm of inflation, unemployment and growth. It is to that question that we now turn.

7 Central bank independence, prices and growth: some evidence

Using the ideas of independence measurement above Alesina and Grilli sought to see whether such independence was successful in producing price stability and growth in the major industrialised countries. Figure 18.9 summarises their findings. There is clear evidence of a correlation between central bank autonomy and inflation.

Furthermore, since it is sometimes said that business prefers a stable environment in which to operate it could be argued that low variability in inflation rates is desirable. Central bank autonomy would appear to give that also. Monetarists would obviously find such evidence encouraging.

What the evidence also shows equally clearly is that it has not led to a high growth rate of output. There appears to be no relationship between central bank independence and high growth rates. This evidence, then, gives no support to the monetarist argument that low inflation can be achieved at no long-run cost in terms of output or unemployment.

The Keynesians might argue that even the evidence regarding price stability does not undermine their position. One might argue that there is a trade-off between inflation and unemployment. Some societies, however, value price stability very highly. One might think of Germany, many of whose senior figures

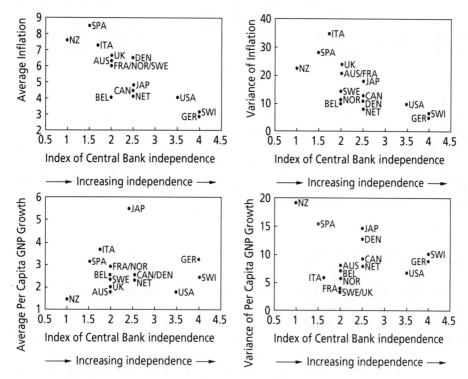

Source: A. Alesina and L. H. Summers, (1993) 'Central Bank Independence
and Macroeconomic Performance: some comparative evidence',
Journal of Money, Credit and Banking, 25,2 (May).

Figure 18.9 Central bank independence, inflation and growth

still remember the appalling hyper-inflation of the interwar years. Such societies
are willing to see central bank autonomy to produce price stability, even at some
cost in terms of growth or unemployment. Other societies, such as Britain, are
more tolerant of inflation. To impose central bank autonomy and low inflation on
such a society at the cost of higher unemployment would be quite unacceptable.
Alas, then, the empirical evidence continues to be inconclusive.

8 Conclusion

We began by arguing that views of central bank independence cannot be detached
from views about other economic issues. In particular they will be influenced by
attitudes towards the suitability of government macro-economic intervention in
the economy and about the trade-off between inflation and unemployment. If
one sees macro-economic intervention as justified and a long-run unemployment

inflation trade-off existing, then central bank independence reduces the scope of government macro-economic room for manoeuvre and harms economic welfare.

On the other hand, some take the view that macro-economic intervention, except for control of the money supply, is unnecessary. Markets will bring full employment in the long run. Macro-economic policy should be aimed at price stability. From that perspective there is much to commend central bank autonomy.

There is one thing, however, that we have not seen. We have concentrated our discussion on issues assuming a closed economy, that is, that there are no significant factors to take into account with respect to the international economy, especially the external value of the currency. Therefore we shall return to the subject of central bank autonomy in Chapter 20 when we have examined the monetary implications of international trade.

See pp 390–412

9 Questions for discussion

1 If the Bank of England reduces the money supply through selling government debt, does it matter:
   a Who purchases the debt?
   b What kind of debt is sells?
   c What it does with income received from its sale?

See pp 276–80

2 Given what we saw in Chapter 14 with respect to the influence of interest rates on investment, how much reliance would you place on monetary conditions for influencing the volume of investment?
3 Attempts have been made to resolve empirically the argument that controlling the money supply leads to a stable price level. These have not always been conclusive. Why do you think that is so?
4 How convincing do you find the attempts to measure the extent of independence central banks have from governments?
5 Do you think that an independent central bank for Britain would be beneficial for the British economy?

10 Further reading

Money
Sloman, pp. 696–703; Begg, pp. 391–404; Parkin and King, pp. 680–705

Money market equilibrium
Sloman, pp. 736–49; Begg, pp. 411–23; Parkin and King, pp. 737–41

Monetarism
Sloman, pp. 600–11, 722–36; Begg, pp. 453–55, 503; Parkin and King, pp. 705–10

Does the UK want an independent central bank?
M. Castello-Branco and M. Swinburne (1992) 'Central bank independence', *Finance and Development*, March.
P. Howells (1993) 'Institutional changes and the money supply aggregates', *British Economy Survey*, Spring.

CHAPTER 19

Manufacturing trade:
not made in Britain
(WITH DR MICHAEL ASTERIS)

British homes tend to be full of foreign produced goods – Japanese television sets, German toasters, Italian washing machines. Many politicians and industrialists believe that Britain's manufacturing sector is in decline and that the country's balance-of-payments difficulties are a reflection of government failure to deal with this problem. The link between manufacturing and the balance of payments is the issue we now consider.

In this chapter we review:
- Opportunity cost
- Efficiency

We introduce:
- The balance of payments
- The law of comparative advantage

1 Introduction

Once Britain was known as the 'workshop of the world' because it dominated world trade in industrial goods. However, its share of world manufactuing trade has declined markedly during the past 40 years, while imported manufactured goods have claimed a growing share of the home market. Indeed, since 1983 Britain has been importing annually more manufactured goods than it has been exporting. This imbalance has fuelled fears of British 'de-industrialisation' – the sharp decline in the significance of manufacturing in total production.

In this chapter we examine the reasons for the deterioration in the UK's manufacturing trade balance and consider its importance. In order to place the issue in context, we will begin by looking at the structure of the balance of payments. This will be followed by a review of trends in the manufacturing trade balance and an examination of the law of comparative advantage which determines the quantity of goods exported from and imported into the UK. Thereafter, the focus will be on the extent to which the deterioration in manufacturing trade is a cause for alarm. We will see that much depends on how trends in the balance of payments over the longer term are interpreted and, as with other questions we have examined, how much confidence there is in the power of markets to allocate scarce resources optimally.

2 The balance of payments

a Basic concepts

The object of the balance-of-payments accounts is to provide a systematic record, during a specific period of time, of all transactions between residents of the recording country and residents of other nations.

The accounts are analogous to a double-entry book-keeping system in that every balance-of-payments transaction involves equal credit and debit items. However, instead of arranging in credit and debit columns which add to the same total, balance-of-payments entries are listed in the same column but given different signs so that the accounts sum to zero. Hence, in a book-keeping sense the balance of payments must always balance. In an economic sense, however, balance-of-payments problems do arise. As we shall see, the degree to which *individual components* of the accounts are in surplus or deficit can give cause for concern.

b The structure of the UK accounts

Now that we have established the general nature of the balance of payments, let us look specifically at the UK accounts. Table 19.1 presents a summary of the UK balance of payments for the period 1983 to 1992. It consists of two main sections: the current account and the capital account.

The current account (the upper part of the table) records all transactions of current goods and services. It, in turn, is subdivided into the balance of visible trade and the balance of invisible trade.

Exporting goods results in receipts of money from abroad. They are thus regarded as *credit* items and are recorded with a plus sign. Imports, on the other hand, cause outflows of money when the goods or services are paid for. They are therefore viewed as *debit* items and are given a minus sign.

The visible trade balance measures the difference between those *goods* which are exported and those which are imported. Foodstuffs, raw materials and manufactured goods are included under this heading. It is clear from Table 19.1 that the visible trade balance which was in surplus in the early 1980s was in deficit in each of the years 1983–91. Of itself, this run of deficits is of limited significance because since the early nineteenth century the UK has rarely recorded a visible account surplus. What matters is the *size* of the deficits.

The invisible balance records the trade balance in services, interest profit and dividends and transfers. The services heading includes transactions relating to shipping, civil aviation, insurance and banking. The heading 'interest profit and

Table 19.1 UK Balance-of-payments account (£ million)

	1983	1986	1989	1991	1992
Current account					
Visible balance	−1,537	−9,559	−24,683	−10,284	−13,406
Invisibles					
Services balance	3,829	6,223	3,361	3,657	4,069
Interest, profits and dividends balance	2,830	4,622	3,388	320	5,777
Transfers balance	−1,593	−2,157	−4,578	−1,345	−5,060
Invisibles balance	5,066	8,688	2,171	2,632	4,786
Current balance	3,529	-871	−22,512	−7,652	−8,620
Capital transfer	—	—	—	—	—
Transactions in UK assets and liabilities					
UK external assets	−30,378	−92,489	−90,089	−18,925	−84,976
UK external liabilities	25,818	89,316	109,503	25,652	93,295
Net transactions	−4,562	-3,173	19,415	6,728	8,319
Exchange equalisation account loss on forward commitments	—	—	—	—	—
Allocation of special drawing rights	—	—	—	—	—
Gold subscription to IMF	—	—	—	—	—
Balancing item	1,033	4,044	3,097	924	301

Source: CSO, United Kingdom, Balance of Payments 'Pink Book', 1993.

dividends' embraces earnings from overseas branches of domestic companies and income paid to foreign investors in the UK. 'Transfers' covers a range of currency flows across the exchanges including government aid and contributions to the European Union.

In contrast to visible trade, the invisible account has been in substantial surplus for most of the period since the end of the Napoleonic wars. Hence, the size of the current account surplus or deficit (visible plus invisible balance) is decided by the extent to which the invisible surplus exceeds or is exceeded by the deficit on visible trade.

Turning to the other major section of the balance of payments, the capital account, this records transactions in UK assets and liabilities. Included under this heading are overseas transactions by banks in the UK and changes in Britain's official reserves.

It also includes the purchase and sale of assets in other countries. It may be direct, such as if BP builds an oil rig in Alaska or a Japanese car company like Toyota builds a car plant in Derbyshire. Alternatively, it might be indirect, for example the purchase by a UK resident of shares in a German engineering company.

In theory the overall balance of payments – the combined current and capital account – should sum to zero. In fact, since the methods of estimating transactions are neither complete nor precisely accurate, there is a need to include a balancing item to reflect the sum of all errors and omissions and thus bring the total of all entries to zero.

Combining the current and capital accounts serves to emphasise that, for a while at least, a country need not worry too much if it has a current account deficit provided that it is able to finance the shortfall by means of capital inflows. A simple analogy may help to explain. Suppose you are a student with a current account at the bank. The bank manager is concerned that you are overdrawn in that your expenditure during the term has been greater than the amount of money in your account makes possible. Although you have spent more than was available in the account in the last term, you might reasonably respond that it should be of little concern to him. After all, (a) he is being paid interest on the overdrawn account and (b) you have a large savings account which can easily fund the deficit on the current account.

The bank manager may accept your explanation, but he is less likely to be so content if he can see that the rate at which you are spending in excess of your income is unsustainable given the limited size of your capital account.

It can be argued that the same is true of a country. The current account deficit is a potential problem if it is large in proportion to overseas assets or if the long-term trend is one which is unsustainable.

c Trends in the visible trade balance

Following our examination of the UK's overall balance-of-payments structure let us now take a closer look at the visible account items with specific reference to trends in the manufacturing trade balance.

Table 19.2, which provides a commodity analysis of UK visible trade for the years 1983–92, gives us the details behind the first row of figures in Table 19.1. The constant deficits for food, beverages and tobacco and basic materials should not occasion any surprise, Britain has long had deficits in these items. In contrast, the credit entry for oil is a relatively recent development. Until North Sea oil came on stream in substantial quantities during the late 1970s, Britain was a major net importer of the fuel. In the space of a few years, however, Britain emerged as a

Table 19.2 Trade on a balance of payments basis: commodity analysis (£ million)

	1983	1986	1989	1991	1992
Exports					
Food,beverages and tobacco	4,230	5,450	6,455	7,654	8,673
Basic materials	1,653	2,112	2,343	2,008	1,946
Oil	12,486	8,189	5,873	6,757	6,566
Other mineral fuels and lubricants	602	464	256	353	304
Semi-manufactured goods	15,864	20,818	26,689	29,195	30,354
Finished manufactured goods	24,284	33,618	48,241	55,604	57,144
Commodities and transactions no classified according to kind	1,581	1,976	2,297	1,842	2,060
Total	60,700	72,627	92,154	103,413	107,047
Imports					
Food,beverages and tobacco	7,259	9,436	10,765	11,604	12,609
Basic materials	4,251	4,636	5,934	4,588	4,613
Oil	5,541	4,119	4,616	5,549	5,079
Other mineral fuels and lubricants	1,274	1,877	1,482	1,613	1,555
Semi-manufactured goods	16,003	21,761	31,036	30,391	31,157
Finished manufactured goods	26,878	38,825	61,159	58,035	63,691
Commodities and transactions no classified according to kind	1,058	1,532	1,845	1,917	1,749
Total	62,237	82,186	116,837	113,697	120,453
Visible balance					
Food,beverages and tobacco	−3,029	−3,986	−4,310	−3,950	−3,936
Basic materials	−2,598	−2,524	−3,591	−2,580	−2,667
Oil	6,972	4,070	1,257	1,208	1,487
Other mineral fuels and lubricants	−672	−1,413	−1,226	−1,260	−1,251
Semi-manufactured goods	−139	−943	−4,347	−1,196	−803
Finished manufactured goods	−2,594	−5,207	−12,918	−2,431	−6,547
Commodities and transactions no classified according to kind	523	444	452	−75	311
Total	−1,537	−9,559	−24,683	−10,284	−13,406

Source: CSO, United Kingdom, Balance of Payments 'Pink Book', 1993.

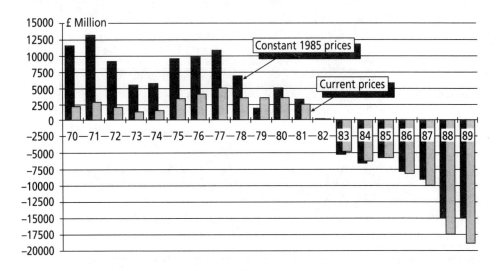

Source: CSO, United Kingdom : Balance of Payments 'Pink Book'.

Figure 19.1 UK balance of trade in manufactured goods, 1970–89

major oil producer. Imports of oil declined and the UK became one of the world's largest exporters of high quality light crude. In 1976 there was a £4.3 billion trade deficit in oil. By 1980 the deficit had been eliminated and in 1985 the UK enjoyed an oil surplus of more than £8 billion.

Figure 19.1 concentrates on these two critical decades, since it was during this time that Britain moved from being a substantial net exporter to a position of being a substantial net importer of manufactured goods. Notice that the balance-of-payments data of Tables 19.1 and 19.2 are at current prices, Figure 19.1 shows the effects of netting out inflation. The picture which then emerges is of an even more dramatic reversal in the fortunes of the manufacturing sector. It is this change from surplus to deficit in the trade balance of both semi-manufactures (such as chemicals and textiles) and finished manufactures detailed in Table 19.2 which is, arguably, the most dramatic transformation in the external accounts. The stark nature of the change is highlighted in Figure 19.1, which shows the UK balance of trade in manufactured goods for the period 1970 to 1989 at constant (1985) prices and current prices. In 1970 the surplus on this trade constituted 30 per cent of the average value of exports and imports; as recently as 1980 the proportion was 12 per cent. In 1983, however, the UK had a peace-time deficit in manufactures for the first time since the Industrial Revolution and the shortfall has persisted to varying degrees ever since.

d Trends in manufacturing output

To a considerable extent the balance-of-payments statistics we have examined reflect what has been happening to the performance of the British manufacturing

Source: Lloyds Bank *Economic Bulletin*, July 1993

Figure 19.2 UK productivity in manufacturing

sector. So we now consider the main trends in manufacturing industry with particular reference to the period since 1979.

First manufacturing output at constant prices was very little different from what it had been in 1979. The recession of the early 1980s caused output to drop substantially. Although it rose during much of the 1980s, the recession of the early 1990s left real output little higher than in 1979. Furthermore, as a proportion of GDP manufacturing output has declined sharply since the tertiary, or services, sector of the economy has grown quite rapidly.

The above should not, however, lead you to imagine that manufacturing output *per worker* has followed a similar pattern. What has in fact happened is that labour productivity, output per person employed, has increased. Hence manufacturing output is now being produced with considerably fewer people. Over 7 million people worked in the manufacturing sector at the beginning of 1979. By 1992 the number had fallen to well under four million.

Even so, since we are interested in examining British international trade performance the above data needs to be set in context by asking how the UK's experience compares with that of other countries. The decline in the proportion of output taken by manufacturing is common to most advanced economies, although the extent of the decline is greater in Britain. Productivity has increased in all countries. As can be seen from Table 19.3 Britain's performance was relatively poor in the 1960s and 1970s but improved significantly in the 1980s. The reverse was true of Germany.

Figure 19.2 shows that Britain has improved its performance substantially in recent years. As you can see, manufacturing productivity has been higher in the 1980s and 1990s than in previous decades and better than other sectors of the economy. Nevertheless, according to the Institute of Economic Affairs,[1]

Table 19.3 Average annual percentage change in manufacturing value added per person

	1960–68	*1968–73*	*1973–79*	*1979–90*
Belgium	4.9	8.2	5.0	4.7
Japan	9.0	10.4	5.0	4.6
Britain	3.4	3.9	0.6	4.1*
United States	3.2	3.5	0.9	3.3*
France	6.8	5.8	3.9	2.4
Italy	7.2	5.6	2.9	1.6
Western Germany	4.7	4.5	3.1	1.1

Note: * 1979–86
Source: OECD, *Economic Outlook.*

manufacturing output per person is still a little less than in Germany or France, and much lower than in the United States.[2]

3 The basis of international trade

In examining whether the British deficit in manufacturing trade is of great consequence, it is helpful to understand why countries engage in trade at all. As we shall see later in the chapter, our judgement about the seriousness of the position will depend much upon our confidence in the market mechanism. Hence we need to see how the principles of trade within a country can be extended to trade between countries. The heart of the answer as to why countries trade is to be found in the 'Law of Comparative Advantage'.

a Understanding comparative advantage

The essence of the Law of Comparative Advantage can be understood if we construct a simple model of international trade. Our model will contain some unrealistic assumptions! Nevertheless, it will be sufficient for us to understand the great attractions of engaging in trade with other countries.

In our model we shall assume just two countries, Britain and Germany. Furthermore, we shall assume that each country's citizens are interested in the consumption of only two kinds of output, which we shall call manufactures (M) and services (S). There are no government restrictions such as tariff barriers on trade between these countries. We shall also assume that the markets are competitive in each country. Now let us make some assumptions about the relative abilities of these countries to produce these goods. In Table 19.4 below the output of each of these goods in each country requires only labour inputs. Each country has only 40 units of labour.

Table 19.4 Assumed relative abilities of England and Germany

	Britain		Germany	
	Manufactures (M)	Services (S)	Manufactures (M)	Services (S)
Labour input required per unit of output	4	2	2	2
Possible production level with no international trade	5	10	10	10
Possible total output and consumption without international trade	15	20	—	—

These units have an opportunity cost. If individuals spend all their time producing services, they cannot produce manufactures. The table shows the assumed amount of labour inputs needed to produce a unit of a given output for each country. In our example Britain can produce a unit of services for the same labour input as Germany but needs twice the labour input to produce a unit of manufactures.

Now what quantity of manufactures and services can each community enjoy, assuming no international trade? The answer, of course, is that there is a whole series of possibilities, depending upon the proportions of labour devoted to different kinds of production. Table 19.4 shows one possibility among many. It shows the output produced in each country if half of the labour resources are devoted to manufactures and half to services.

World output is then 15M + 20S. But since there is no international trade, Britain enjoys the consumption of 5M + 10S and Germany citizens 10M + 10S.

At first thought it might be supposed that Germany has nothing to gain from trade with Britain. After all, it is just as effective at producing service output and far better at producing manufactures. However, this supposition would be incorrect. Germany would be willing to trade because the two countries' relative abilities are different. Britain is relatively good at producing services; Germany is relatively good at manufacturing. To produce a unit of service output in Britain requires the sacrifice of half a unit of manufactures. In contrast, for Germany to produce a unit of services requires the sacrifice of a whole unit of manufactures. It would be better then for each country to concentrate on producing the good in which it has the comparative advantage, and then to exchange those goods internationally. Let us see how this works out in terms of our example. Look at Table 19.5.

Britain is now producing less manufactures but more services, since it is the latter in which Britain has the comparative advantage. With Germany concentrating on the area in which it has the comparative advantage, total

Table 19.5 Production and consumption with international trade

	Britain		Germany	
	Manufactures	Services	Manufactures	Services
Labour input required per	(M)	(S)	(M)	(S)
unit of output	4	2	2	2
Possible production level				
following an agreement	0	20	20	0
to trade				
Possible total output and				
consumption with	20	20	—	—
international trade				

Table 19.6 Production and consumption without complete specialisation

	England		Germany	
	Manufactures	Services	Manufactures	Services
Labour input required per	(M)	(S)	(M)	(S)
unit of output	4	2	2	2
Alternative possible production				
level following an agreement	0	20	18	2
to trade				
Alternative possible total				
output and consumption with	18	22	—	—
international trade				

output from the two countries can be greater than would be possible without trade. In the case of Table 19.5 we have more manufactures available for consumption but the same volume of services. With different allocations of resources it would be possible for aggregate output to be at a level where services and manufactures are higher than would be possible without trade.

Table 19.6 shows just such a possibility. With Germany slightly less specialised, total output with trade is 18M + 22S. This compares with a no trade output of 15M + 20S.

Hence international trade can allow consumption patterns which reflect higher living standards than would be possible without such specialisation.

Whether the increased output is in the form of services or manufactures, or both, will be determined by consumer preference expressing itself through markets.

b Increasing opportunity cost

Although manufacturing output is smaller in Britain than it used to be, it still exists and will continue to do so. Why, given what we have seen above, do we produce any manufactured items at all? Why do we not produce services and import all manufactures? One of the most important reasons is the principle of increasing opportunity cost.

We assumed in our model of Table 19.4 that whatever the level of output, the opportunity cost of producing an M in Britain was 2S. But as we saw in Chapter 1, this is not likely to be the case. The more output of a good that is being produced the higher its opportunity cost. Suppose Britain is producing mainly services and decides to produce even more of them. Marginal resources will have to shift from manufacturing, where they are relatively suited, into services where they are relatively unsuited. The complete specialisation referred to earlier is thus unlikely. But partial specialisation following international trade is inevitable.

See pp 6–9

c The terms of trade

Whatever the increased output made possible by such specialisation the question now remains as to which country will enjoy the benefits of that output. We are assuming that labour is not required to transport this output between countries. If the transport costs involved in trade were to be more than the potential increase in output, the benefits of international trade might be entirely undone! Let us assume this is not the case.

The terms on which the countries trade will have to be such as to give both countries some share of the output gain, otherwise they will not be willing to trade at all. How these terms are established we shall consider further in Chapter 20 but for now the principle can be made clear.

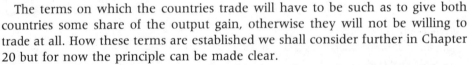

See pp 391–4

As we have already seen in earlier chapters, the market mechanism brings about an identity between the price of a good and its opportunity cost. Hence in Britain before trade the price of manufactures would have been IM : 2S. The price of a manufactured good would have been twice the price of a service item. In Germany manufactures would have been relatively cheap, IM : IS reflecting the lower opportunity cost of manufacturing output.

What happens to price if countries engage in trade? Since manufactures are relatively cheap in Germany the British will buy German manufactures. This will mean that German manufactured prices will increase. This increase in price will encourage some German resource owners to switch production from services to manufactures.

In the meantime, the opposite will happen in Britain. Germans will wish to buy relatively cheap British services. Service output will rise in response to this demand increase. British resource owners will respond by producing more services and less manufactures.

Notice that the relative prices in Britain and Germany were different. But trade has moved them towards each other.

d Some results of comparative advantage

Two conclusions follow from the Law of Comparative Advantage. The first is that a declining manufacturing sector is not in and of itself a problem. If it reflects increasing specialisation in the production of goods and services in which we have a comparative advantage, the change can be beneficial. The problem occurs when, instead of service output increasing to pay for rising manufactured imports, markets fail to adjust. Instead of increased service output there is unemployment and a balance-of-payments problem.

The second point which emerges is that inefficiency in production is not a barrier to international trade. If we produce less output from a given volume of inputs than is possible, we shall have lower living standards. However, other countries will still wish to trade with us. We do not require an absolute advantage in the production of any commodities. We need a comparative advantage.

e The benefits of free trade

Governments are not always willing to allow the law of comparative advantage to operate. The European Union (EU) operates a policy of free trade between its members but there are substantial restrictions imposed upon trade between the EU and the rest of the world. Such restrictions reduce welfare. We illustrate the point first with reference to trade between the EU and Eastern Europe.

As we saw in Chapter 1, Eastern Europe is still a very inefficient producer. But as we have seen in this chapter free trade will still allow mutually beneficial trade to take place based upon comparative advantage. The EU fears that some of its producers will suffer if competition with Eastern Europe is allowed. These fears are very well founded.

See pp 17–19

Eastern Europe has very restricted access to EU markets. If the restrictions were to be removed, many EU producers may suffer, at least in the short run, if their protection from competition is removed. EU consumers will switch to relatively cheap imported substitutes. They will gain from the lower prices available on Eastern European goods.

The gains to consumers, however, are far greater than the loss to producers. Even if imports from Eastern Europe were to increase massively, the loss to producers is far smaller than the gain to consumers.

We have considered only a tiny part of world trade. The data in Figure 19.3 refer not only to the benefits to the EU and the substantial benefits to Eastern Europe of free trade. It refers to the benefits of substantial reductions in international trade restrictions in GATT – the General Agreement on Tariffs and

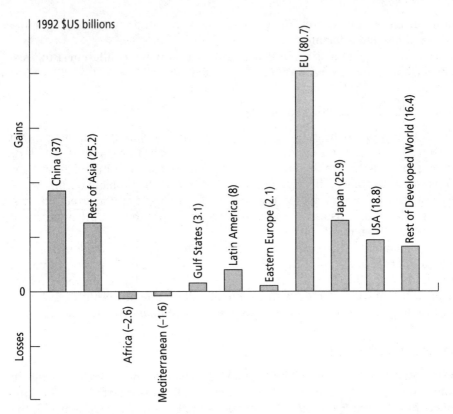

Source : OECD/World Bank

Figure 19.3 Estimated annual gains by 2002 from liberalising world trade (in 1992 $US billion)

Trade. In previous decades it has encouraged world trade liberalisation. In December 1993, most world governments agreed further mutual reductions in trade barriers. The values given in Figure 19.3 are OECD/World Bank estimates of the increases in output that will obtain in 10 year's time as a result of such an agreement. This shows that there will be 213 billion dollars' worth of extra real output then as a result of the agreement. This is, in all probability, a considerable understatement of the benefits flowing from a further liberalisation of trade. The study calculates only the effects on manufactures, but the GATT round for the first time draws other spheres of activity, notably services, into the arrangement. The Law of Comparative Advantage suggests possible improvements in the world output from specialisation in any area of economic activity, not just manufacturing goods. Another study suggests that the benefits from the liberalisation of service trade will be as large as that for manufactures. Note that almost every part of the world would gain. Any losers could easily be compensated by the gainers. It is sad that although there are ways in which economies can be helped which would bring net benefits to the world as a whole, political considerations mean that there is a great reluctance to allow the Law of Comparative Advantage to operate.

Armed with an understanding of the benefits of international trade we can now turn to analyse further the problems of British manufacturing trade.

4 How significant is the deficit in manufacturing trade?

That there has been a marked deterioration in Britain's trade balance in manufactures in recent decades is clear. That said, to what extent is this deterioration a cause for concern? Broadly, it is possible to discern two contrasting schools of thought on this question. These can be termed the 'market approach', which is favoured by the present Conservative administration which stresses the self-correcting nature of market forces, and the 'interventionist approach' adopted by many government critics. The interventionist approach argues that urgent action on the part of government and other bodies is required since the market will not restore equilibrium at all, or at best do it too slowly. Let us look at each of these views in turn.

a The market approach

We have seen that the Law of Comparative Advantage will enable countries to benefit from engaging in international trade. These advantages are, however, fully realised only under quite restrictive assumptions. In essence they are the conditions required for optimal resource allocation within a country plus the absence of barriers between countries, such as import restrictions of various kinds.

The market view is that markets can correct for any misallocation of resources given time. Economies are not always in equilibrium, but they will move towards it if conditions are right.

In the context of the British balance-of-payments problem with respect to manufacturing trade, industry was once far too protected from international competition. Since the supply side improvements initiated in the early 1980s markets have become more open and productivity has increased faster than that of most of our competitors. The requirement during the 1990s is to continue with these reforms, seeing to it that the EU does not impose high tariff barriers against the rest of the world. In short, prices must reflect opportunity costs of production.

Overall, in the government's judgement markets are already operating increasingly effectively. Let us consider two illustrations of this view, beginning with the effects of North Sea oil.

The long-term decline both in manufacturing as a share of GDP and in the balance of trade in manufactures can be seen, in part at least, as a response to the advent of North Sea oil. The alternative to taking the benefits of oil as an increase in net manufacturing imports would have been either to accumulate huge

Table 19.7 Estimated UK North Sea oil reserves

	Proved reserves at end of (thousands million tonnes)	Reserves/production ratio
1985	1.7	13.6
1986	0.7	5.5
1987	0.7	5.5
1988	0.6	5.2
1989	0.5	5.5
1990	0.5	5.6
1991	0.5	5.8

Source: *BP Statistical Review of World Energy,* various issues.

surpluses on current account, and/or to have accepted an even bigger rise in the sterling exchange rate than actually occurred.

In the event, manufactures rather than, for example, services took much of the strain of adjusting to a massive change in the balance of trade in oil because the UK's comparative advantage was weakest in this sector and market forces were permitted to take their course.

Table 19.7 shows the decline in the stocks of North Sea oil over recent years as extraction has been at a level higher than the discovery of new fields. Proved reserves of oil are those quantities which geological and engineering information indicate with reasonable certainty can be recovered in the future from known reservoirs, using existing economic and operating conditions.

The reserves/production ratio can be explained as follows. If reserves remaining at the end of a year are divided by that year's production, the result is the length of time that those remaining resources would last, if production were to continue at the then current level. So in 1991, at the then level of extraction, the UK had less than six years' supply. In reality, the likely discovery of new fields and improved extraction technology will mean that oil from the UK sector of the North Sea will be available until well into the next century. However, it will almost certainly be extracted in reduced quantities.

One estimate of UK oil production into the next century is given in Figure 19.4. Oil output is expected to continue at around its present level until the late 1990s. After that, however, the decline in production levels seems likely to fall sharply.

See pp 390–412 The decline in North Sea oil output will, according to the market view, automatically be compensated for by an improvement in the non-fuel trade balance, including that for services and manufactures, via a fall in the exchange rate. However, as we shall see in Chapter 20, government policy towards the exchange rate has not always been entirely clear.

A second area in which the government sees the market mechanism bringing automatic corrective forces into play is the area of direct inward investment. The

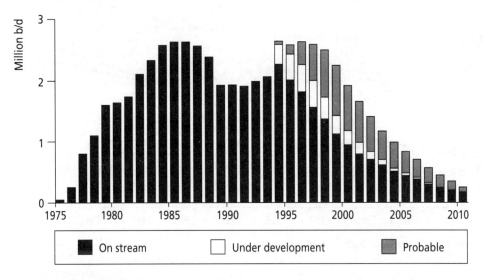

Source: Wood McKenzie

Figure 19.4 North Sea oil output, actual and potential

role of foreign investment, particularly Japanese, in rejuvenating British manufacturing is seen by government as vindicating its relatively relaxed non-interventionist approach towards the manufacturing trade balance.

The UK is a comparatively open economy. This openness enabled imports of, for example, cars and televisions to replace UK products. However, supply–side reforms in the period since 1979 combined with membership of the EU have made the UK an attractive location for multinational firms, especially those from Japan. Consequently, the UK is home to more than 40 per cent of Japan's EU investment. This investment has been instrumental in improving the performance of UK manufacturing because Japanese practices have been disseminated throughout industry in general. In the government's view, the car industry provides an excellent example of how the presence of new Japanese production plants will help to close the gap in Britain's manufacturing trade. Motor vehicles, which were the most important contributor to the growing manufacturing trade deficit of the 1980s, are likely to show a trade surplus by the middle of this decade, as can be seen from Figure 19.5.

The gap between the value of car exports and car imports was closing in the late 1980s and exports will probably exceed imports by value in the mid-1990s. Much of this change is the result of Japanese inward investment. Many of the cars manufactured in Britain by Japanese producers will be exported to the rest of the EC.

b The interventionist approach

We have considered the view that markets provide the best way of dealing with the problems of British manufacturing. However, we must now consider the

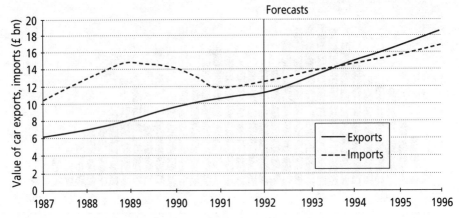

Figure 19.5 Balance of trade in motor vehicles

alternative view. The interventionist approach is inherently pessimistic. It is epitomised by the House of Lords Select Committee on Overseas Trade which in November 1985 published a report on 'the causes and implications of the deficit in the UK's balance of trade in manufactures'. The committee took the view that the decline in manufacturing and in the trade balance in manufactures 'constitute a grave threat to the standard of living and to the political stability of the nation'.

The Committee's report argued that there are two reasons why urgent action is required to revive manufacturing and encourage trade in manufactures. First, because there will not necessarily be a resurgence of manufacturing as North Sea oil diminishes. Second, service industries cannot substitute for manufacturing because many of them are dependent on manufacturing and only 20 per cent of services are tradeable overseas.

The Committee contended that unless the manufacturing base is enlarged, import penetration combatted and manufactured exports encouraged, the country will face adverse effects which will worsen with time. These effects will include:

1 A contraction of the manufacturing sector to the point where the successful continuance of it is put at risk.
2 An adverse balance of payments of such magnitude as to require severe deflation of the economy.
3 A stagnant economy and rising inflation driven by a falling exchange rate.

In the light of their dire predictions, their Lordships made a number of suggestions as to how the government could improve matters. The proposed measures encompassed the promotion of investment, exports, education, training, and research and development expenditure.

We have already examined the logic of the interventionist case in earlier chapters. Here we comment on the predictions made by the committee.

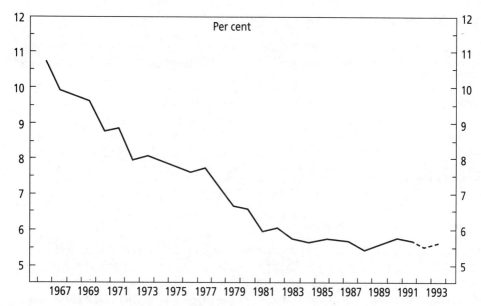

Figure 19.6 Share of British trade in manufactures of volume

Clearly, there has been a long-term contraction of manufacturing in Britain, as we have seen. However, in defence of the official market approach two points can be made. First, UK productivity has risen faster than that of its competitors in the years following the Committee's report. Second, the proportion of world trade in manufacturing taken by Britain has remained steady during recent years as can be seen from Figure 19.6.

In other words, it can be argued that it is government supply side reforms which is turning the situation around without the need for resource misallocation through subsidies.

5 Conclusion

Which of the two views we have been examining is correct? It is difficult to say with any degree of certainty which represents the more realistic interpretation of future trends in Britain's manufacturing trade balance, but a verdict will inevitably be coloured by the degree of enthusiasm for the market mechanism.

In support of the interventionist view, it can be pointed out that manufacturing earns almost two-thirds of all our foreign currency. Arguably, therefore, the decline in the manufacturing trade balance which, as we noted earlier, has been a remorseless feature of the past four decades is a cause for concern. Simple extrapolation of some historical trends would indicate that the future will be

Table 19.8 Changes in international labour costs, 1980–92

% increase	GDP per person	Average earnings	Consumer prices	Real earnings	Unit labour costs	Real unit labour costs
USA	10	80	70	5	63	−4
Japan*	36	69	29	32	25	−3
Germany	17	55	40	11	33	−5
France	27	130	92	19	81	−6
UK	26	167	108	28	111	1

Note: *1992, third quarter.
Source: Lloyds Bank calculations, *Lloyds Bank Economic Bulletin*, July 1993.

much like the past. The UK will encounter a rapidly deteriorating trade balance in manufactures once it attempts to expand the economy at anything more than a snail's pace. In short, this will mean an all too familiar replay of the dismal 'stop-go cycle' which has afflicted the British economy since the Second World War.

The case for pessimism is reinforced by the fact that whereas during the cyclical trough of the early 1980s Britain had a current account surplus of 2.5 per cent of GDP, during the trough of the early 1990s there was a deficit of 2 per cent of GDP.

One interesting possibility is that the British problem lies largely with its labour markets. Table 19.8 refers not to manufacturing specifically, but to the whole economy of each country. Productivity in Britain has improved in recent years. This should, *ceteris paribus*, make Britain more competitive internationally. GDP per person has grown faster in Britain than in the USA or Germany and about the same as that of France. But the real earnings column shows that wage rates net of inflation have tended to rise faster. Hence real unit labour costs have actually risen in Britain while falling in the other countries mentioned in the table. This makes Britain less competitive than previously, despite its productivity record. The evidence could suggest, then, that it is not so much a British manufacturing problem as a British labour market problem.

There are, however, some encouraging signs that the future may not simply be more of the past: the deterioration in the manufacturing trade balance may be halted or even reversed during the second half of the 1990s. The UK is a powerful magnet for inward manufacturing investment – around two-fifths of total US and Japanese corporate investment in the European Community is located here. Much of the output generated by this investment is destined for export. Moreover, British manufacturing as a whole is better managed than in the past, and as we have seen since 1979 there has been a dramatic improvement in value added per employee as a result of reduced labour inputs. But if government had taken a more pro-active view of industrial intervention in the past 15 years, would things have been better?

6 Questions for discussion

1 'Imports from Eastern Europe should be restricted. Their much lower wages means that the competition is unfair.' Assess this view.
2 What are the effects of large-scale Japanese investment in Britain on (a) manufacturing industry and (b) the balance-of-payments account? Should such inward investment be encouraged?
3 Why do you think British manufacturing productivity bears better comparison with that of other European countries than with the USA?
4 Does the poor productivity of British manufacturing relative to that of, say, the USA make trade between the two nations more difficult?
5 If one were to take an interventionist approach, in what ways might government best help manufacturing industry?
6 To what extent is it a good idea to subsidise manufacturing industry?

7 Further reading

Law of Comparative Advantage
Sloman, pp. 916–50; Begg. pp. 577–82; Parkin and King, pp. 940–62

Balance of payments
Sloman, pp. 555–60; Begg, pp. 513–9; Parkin and King, pp. 963–74

Manufacturing trade: not made in Britain
Tony Thirlwall (1992) 'The balance of payments and economic performance', *National Westminster Bank Quarterly Review*, May.
W. Eltis (1993) 'How macroeconomic policy can best assist UK industry', *Economics and Business Education*, Vol. 1, Pt. 1, No. 2.

8 End notes

1 Institute of Economic Affairs. Can deindustrialisation seriously damage your wealth?
2 Remember that productivity refers to the amount of output from a given volume of inputs. So a rise in productivity allows the possibility of increased output. However, it may simply lead to more unemployment, in that the same output can be produced from fewer inputs.

CHAPTER 20

Giving up sterling:
too high a price to pay?

Many European countries tie the value of their currencies to others. Is this sensible? Several are considering the abandonment of their own individual currencies for a European one. What are the costs and benefits of such a move? Does it make sense for Britain to give up the pound sterling and join such a currency union?

In this chapter we review
- Supply and demand
- Speculation
- The balance of payments

We introduce
- Exchange rate determination
- European exchange rate mechanism
- European monetary union

1 Introduction

The postwar economic history of Europe has seen increasing cooperation between many of its member countries. The European Union (EU) began with agreements on coal and steel in the early 1950s. Later it moved towards the establishment of a community between which there were no tariff barriers, and in which there was cooperation on matters of trade, agriculture and regional matters. Subsequently political institutions of a pan-European nature have been established by the EU, and the number of its members enlarged.

There is one important agreement not common to all trading blocs. This is the agreement by most governments concerned to fix against one another the relative values of their currencies. This process began in 1979 with the establishment of the exchange rate mechanism (ERM). The intention has been that by the end of the century this process would have evolved such that some countries will have given up their individual currencies to be replaced by a common currency. In this chapter we will examine the main economic implications of such a monetary union. We shall do so in three stages. We shall begin by asking what determines the relative values of individual national currencies, with particular emphasis on the balance-of-payments account. Next, we shall consider the advantages and problems associated with the kind of fixed exchange rate system exemplified by the ERM. Finally, we shall consider the additional issues raised by moving from a fixed exchange system to a single currency for a group of countries. It is at this point that we shall reconsider the question of an independent central bank, first raised in Chapter 18 in the context of a closed economy.

See pp 348–69

2 Exchange rates and the balance of payments

a The supply and demand for foreign currency

Let us begin our examination of these issues by considering how the value of a currency such as sterling is decided if governments make no efforts to influence its rate against other currencies. In other words, how is the price of currency determined in a free market? Such a currency is often called a 'floating' currency.

When we wish to import goods or services into Britain, the importer must buy the currency of the country from which these items come. If goods are being imported from Germany, the German firm that is selling them wishes to have German marks not pounds. The British importer must acquire the appropriate number of marks from the foreign exchange market. He sells pounds and buys marks. This market consists of a large number of traders willing to swap marks for pounds (or vice versa if Germans are buying goods from Britain). At what rate will the foreign exchange market set the price of the two currencies to be exchanged? In other words, what is the rate of exchange between the two countries and how is it decided? In essence we have a competitive market with large numbers of buyers and sellers. So we can use supply and demand analysis to determine how this value is established.

Consider Figure 20.1 below. It shows the market for sterling at a given time. Look first at the supply curve. Why does it slope upwards? The higher the price of sterling in terms of marks the more marks are available for a pound. The more marks to the pound, the cheaper it is to buy German goods. Suppose, for example,

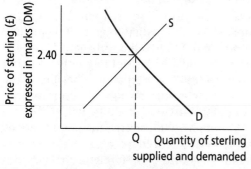

Figure 20.1 The market for sterling

the exchange rate is £1 = 2DM (Deutschmarks). To buy a German car costing 40,000 DM will cost a Briton £20,000. If the exchange rate is £1 = 4DM, the same car would cost the Briton only £10,000. The cheaper are German goods the more we shall wish to import. The extent of that willingness will be determined by the price elasticity of demand for German imports. The more German goods we wish to import the greater the quantity of sterling will be offered in the foreign exchange market in return for marks.

Now examine the demand curve for sterling. The lower the price of sterling the greater the quantity demanded. This is because at a lower price of sterling, Germans find English goods cheaper. At a rate of £1 = 2DM a German must spend 2DM to acquire a £1 bar of British chocolate. At a rate of £1 = 4DM the same chocolate bar will cost the German consumer only 50 pence. The lower price of sterling will, all other things being equal, encourage Germans to purchase more sterling. This is just what the demand curve in Figure 20.1 shows. The extent of the increase in the quantity demanded will depend upon the German price elasticity of demand for British goods.

We have considered this principle in terms of the demand for goods and services. It will apply also to the purchase of capital goods, of shares, or any transaction of an international nature.

b Finding an equilibrium value

Just as for any commodity, the equilibrium price of a currency will be the one at which the price of the currency equates quantity demanded with quantity supplied. If a disequilibrium price were to form temporarily, the excess supply or demand would encourage foreign exchange dealers to adjust price back towards equilibrium, assumed in Figure 20.1 to be at 2.40DM.

In reality the price that is established will be a mid-price between a 'buy' and 'sell' rate. Currency dealers have to cover costs of engaging in the transactions. Therefore the prices at which they will buy currency will differ from the rate at which they will sell it.

Table 20.1 gives some idea of the size of these variations. It shows the rate at which an English individual can expect to pay to buy or sell currency for the purpose of taking a foreign holiday. Suppose Louise wished to go to Italy in June 1993. She changed £1000 into lira and received 221,000 lira, calculated from the 'bank sells' rate. When she changed her mind and decided not to go, she took her lira back to the bank. She was able to buy £928.57 by exchanging her lira at the 'bank sells' rate. As you can appreciate, the decision to change her mind was an expensive one! The rate we use to show equilibrium in Figure 20.1 will be the rate midway between the buy and sell rate. Although we illustrated the point there by using marks, the same principle will apply to any currency.

Large companies purchasing considerable volumes of foreign currency can negotiate better deals than those indicated in Table 20.1, since large foreign

Table 20.1 Selected main currency rates, 17 May 1993

Country	Currency	Bank sells	Bank buys
France	Franc	8.06	8.76
Germany	Mark	2.41	2.62
Italy	Lira	2210.00	2380.00
Japan	Yen	170.50	189.00
Spain	Peseta	181.50	195.00
USA	Dollar	1.50	1.63

Source: High street banks.

currency deals involve lower transaction costs. For such companies the spread between the buy and sell rate will be smaller.

You will probably be aware that these equilibrium values can change quickly. The banks change their tourist rates daily. Sometimes changes can be dramatic enough to make headline news. The reasons for such sudden changes will be considered shortly.

c Equilibrium exchange rates and the balance of payments

There is something that may not be obvious to you from Figure 20.1. One can argue that the equilibrium value we found there is one that will tend to bring an equilibrium to the balance of payments on current account. In other words, it is the one that sees to it that the value of exports is equal to the value of imports. Let us try to see why this should be so. It is usually expressed in terms of what is known as the purchasing power parity (PPP) theory.

In essence the theory says that the purchasing power of, say, a pound sterling, that is, what that pound will buy, should be the same as the amount bought by the exchange rate equivalent of its marks in Germany. Suppose the only good bought and sold in Britain and Germany were to be a McDonald's Big Mac. The fact that the Big Mac is identical wherever it is sold, and is available in most countries of the world, makes it a useful commodity for illustrative purposes. Table 20.2 shows that in Britain in April 1993 the Big Mac cost £1.79 and in Germany 4.60DM. Then the exchange rate at that time should have been 4.60/1.79 = 2.56. In other words, £1 should have exchanged for 2.56DM. This would be the PPP exchange rate. Since the actual exchange rate was around 2.47DM the pound was a little undervalued against the mark, according to the Big Mac index.

The argument now goes like this. If a country's exchange rate is significantly different from its purchasing power parity, economic forces will push exchange rates back towards the equilibrium rate. If a country's exchange rate is undervalued, its producers have a competitive edge in foreign markets. They will export more. The result is a current account balance-of-payments surplus for

Table 20.2 The Economist's Big Mac index: the hamburger standard

	Big Mac prices		Actual	Implied PPP†	Local currency
	Prices in local currency*	Prices in dollars	exchange rate 13/4/93	of the dollar	under (-)/ over (+) valuation **,%
UNITED STATES‡	$2.28	2.28	—	—	—
Argentina	Peso3.60	3.60	1.00	1.58	+58
Australia	A$2.45	1.76	1.39	1.07	−23
Belgium	BFr109	3.36	32.45	47.81	+47
Brazil	Cr77,000	2.80	27,521	33,772	+23
Britain	£1.79	2.79	1.56‡‡	1.27‡‡	+23
Canada	C$2.76	2.19	1.26	1.21	−4
China	Yuan8.50	1.50	5.68	3.73	34
Denmark	DKr25.75	4.25	6.06	11.29	+86
France	FFr18.50	3.46	5.34	8.11	+52
Germany	DM4.60	2.91	1.58	2.02	+28
Holland	F15.45	3.07	1.77	2.39	+35
Hong Kong	HK$9.00	1.16	7.73	3.95	−49
Hungry	Forint157	1.78	88.18	68.86	−22
Ireland	I£1.48	2.29	1.54‡‡	1.54‡‡	0
Italy	Lire4,500	2.95	1,523	1,974	+30
Japan	¥391	3.45	113	171	+51
Malaysia	Ringgit3.35	1.30	2.58	1.47	−43
Mexico	Peso7.09	2.56	3.10	3.11	+11
Russia	Rouble780	1.14	686§	342	−50
S.Korea	Won2,300	2.89	796	1,009	+27
Spain	Ptas325	2.85	114	143	+25
Sweden	SKr25.50	3.43	7.43	11.18	+50
Switzerland	SwFr5.70	3.94	1.45	2.50	+72
Thailand	Baht48	1.91	25.16	21.05	−16

Source: The Economist, 17 April 1993 and correction 15 May 1993.
Original source: McDonald's. *Prices may vary locally. †Purchasing-power parity; local price divided by price in United States. **Against dollar. ‡Average of New York, Chicago, San Francisco and Atlanta. ‡‡Dollars per pound. §Market rate.

that country. Conversely, an overvalued currency leads to a deficit on the current account. Such a situation cannot continue indefinitely. A surplus or deficit implies an excess supply or demand for the country's currency on the foreign exchange market. The market will then adjust the price back to the PPP equilibrium.

Before we leave this aspect of our argument we need to establish that there is a real problem about using the Big Mac index. The PPP argument is based on the relationship between exchange rates and the (weighted) average of all prices in the relevant countries. The Big Mac index is only a guide insofar as the price of the Big Mac is representative of the price level in an economy. Nevertheless, it is an interesting idea that makes exchange rate theory more digestible (*The Economist's* pun, not mine!).

d Exchange rates and the capital account

The PPP theory is a long-run concept. A country's balance of payments on current account can be in deficit for some years, as we saw in Chapter 19 with reference to Britain. How is this possible? You will recall that a balance-of-payments deficit is analogous to an individual's running down a savings account. If the account is healthy enough, the individual can 'overspend' for some time by using his/her capital account. In the long run, however, one must live within one's means. Take the illustration further. Overspending can occur by running down assets or by borrowing, or by some combination of the two. So a fall into deficit on the current account will not create a serious problem for a country in the short run, if it has sufficient overseas assets or if foreigners are willing to lend. As we shall see shortly, governments may be able to persuade foreigners to lend by raising interest rates. However, PPP theory suggests that this can only be a short-term possibility.

See pp 371–5

Nevertheless, PPP theory suggests something very important. To the extent that it represents a valid description of reality, governments need not concern themselves with the balance-of-payments account. The market will adjust the account in the long run towards equilibrium via changes in the exchange rate. In the short run, current account disequilibrium will be dealt with via changes in the capital account.

3 The European exchange rate mechanism

Despite the apparent advantages of a 'floating' exchange rate, most governments indulge in attempts to manipulate the external value of its currency in various ways. Such a policy can take several forms. It may be that a government makes an independent decision to target a value for its exchange rate but is willing to see it deviate from the target, if sticking too rigidly to a particular value prevents the realisation of other policy goals. Alternatively, it may take the form of entering into formal agreements with other governments to fix the exchange rate in some way. An example of this latter type of arrangement is the exchange rate mechanism (ERM) of the European monetary system.

We shall examine the key features of this mechanism and in so doing see why governments often reject the floating system considered above. We shall also see how governments may attempt to fix a rate when market pressures are pushing for a different equilibrium value. So what advantage accrues from a fixed exchange rate?

a The desire to reduce uncertainty

See pp 377–83

The first explanation of government attempts to fix an exchange rate is its desire to reduce uncertainty. We have already seen in Chapter 19 how engaging in international trade can bring benefits in terms of increased consumption of goods and services. For firms engaging in such trade, floating exchange rates can provide considerable uncertainty. Imagine a German firm agreeing to sell a machine to an English company, when the exchange rate was £1 = 3DM. The English company agrees to pay £1000 (or 3000DM) when the machine is made and ready for export from Germany in a year's time. One year later the exchange rate is £1 = 2DM. If the contract has specified the payment of 3000DM, the price of the machine to the English company has risen to £1500. Alternatively, if the contract specified a price of £1000, the German company which thought it would receive 3000DM for its machine, will receive only 2000DM when it exchanges the sterling payment in the currency market.

A potential movement in the exchange rate, then, could, if it is large, mean the difference between profit and loss for firms engaging in international trade. One argument behind a fixed exchange system is that more trade will take place than under a floating system because the uncertainty of exchange rate movements is eliminated.

If countries engage in large amounts of trade with one another, the attractions of such a fixed exchange rate mechanism are considerable. The members of the EU do trade largely with one another, as Table 20.3 so clearly shows, and share of trade between members is taking an increasing proportion of its total trade. The exchange rate mechanism attempts to fix exchange rates of its participating members against one another but not against other countries. Such a scheme, though it may be desirable, is not essential. Some other trading groups do not fix their exchange rates.

There are, however, objections to governments' intervening in exchange rate determination for this purpose. Two principal objections are that the costs of intervention are too high, and that the goal of reduced uncertainty is not achieved anyhow. Let us examine these two in turn.

The first objection to a fixed exchange system such as the ERM is that it may only be possible to hold an exchange rate at a given level at a very high cost to the economy concerned. An illustration of the argument can be seen with reference to the British experience of ERM. Britain entered the system in 1990 at a rate of £1 = 2.95DM. It had a balance-of-payments deficit and there were fears that the rate would need to be lower to restore external balance. However, joining ERM involves a commitment to attempt to fix this rate, at least in the short term. So

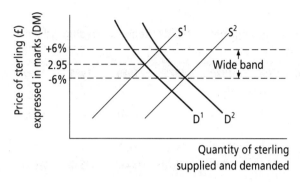

Figure 20.2 Foreign exchange markets and interest rates

how can a government respond when the market wishes to push the value of sterling down? One key weapon is interest rates.

By raising interest rates sharply, there is an effect on the foreign exchange market described in Figure 20.2. $S_1 D_1$ shows the equilibrium price of sterling at entry. The wide band shows the range within which the government agreed to fix the sterling exchange rates. Strictly speaking, this means a band of not more than 6% higher than the next strongest currency, nor 6% less than the next weakest currency. There is also a 'narrow band' of +/− 2.25% that most countries in the system operated until August 1993, but the government felt that, at least initially, it would need the greater flexibility given by the wider 6% band. Fairly soon after entry, however, a worsening balance-of-payments position led to sales of sterling. This position is depicted by a movement of the supply curve from S_1 to S_2. The equilibrium value of sterling would then have been below the permitted range. The government's response was to keep interest rates higher than it wanted. Why did that help to keep the value of sterling up?

Imagine that you wish to save some of your funds and you wish to get the best return on those funds. You will look around for some opportunity of a high interest rate. Suppose further that you are a German saver. You might consider putting your savings into a British bank or another British institution if the interest rate offered were to be attractive enough. You must weigh up the costs of such a decision, especially the costs we considered in Table 20.1 and the potential problem that if exchange rates do alter, your original capital might fall in value. However, you will, all things being equal, be more tempted to put your savings in Britain if the British interest rate differential is increased. Now what happened to British interest rates during its membership of ERM? During the early days of its membership they fell. Indeed, many commentators believed that they needed to fall faster and lower, but that the need to keep the demand for sterling high prevented this from happening. This is illustrated in Figure 20.2. Interest rates were higher than would otherwise have been necessary to shift demand from D_1 to D_2. Interest rates, therefore, protected the value of the pound.

Table 20.3 How have regional trade arrangements fared? Regional trading schemes: intraregional exports and world exports

	Founded	1960	1970	1975	1980	1985	1990
ANZCERTA	1983	5.7[1]	6.1	6.2	6.4	7.0	7.6
		(2.4)[2]	(2.1)	(1.7)	(1.4)	(1.6)	(1.5)
EC	1957	34.5	51.0	50.0	54.0	54.5	60.4
		(24.9)	(39.0)	(35.9)	(34.9)	(35.6)	(41.4)
EFTA	1960	21.1	28.0	35.2	32.6	31.2	28.2
		(14.9)	(14.9)	(6.3)	(6.1)	(6.3)	(6.8)
Canada-US-FTA	1989	26.5	32.8	30.6	26.5	38.0	34.0
		(21.9)	(20.5)	(16.8)	(15.1)	(16.7)	(15.8)
ASEAN[3]	1967	4.4	20.7	15.9	16.9	18.4	18.6
		(2.6)	(2.1)	(2.6)	(3.7)	(3.9)	(4.3)
ANDEAN PACT	1969	0.7	2.0	3.7	3.8	2.4	4.6
		(2.9)	(1.6)	(1.6)	(1.6)	(1.2)	(0.9)
CACM	1961	7.0	25.7	23.3	24.1	14.7	14.8
		(0.4)	(0.4)	(0.3)	(0.2)	(0.2)	(0.1)
LAFTA/LAI A[4]	1960/80	7.9	9.9	13.6	13.7	8.3	10.6
		(6.0)	(4.4)	(3.5)	(4.2)	(4.7)	(3.4)
ECOWAS	1975	—	3.0	4.2	3.5	5.3	6.0
		—	(1.0)	(1.4)	(1.7)	(1.1)	(0.6)
PTA	1987	—	8.4	9.4	8.9	7.0	8.5
		—	(1.1)	(0.5)	(0.4)	(0.3)	(0.2)

Notes: Definitions of regional integration schemes are : ANZCERTA—Australia-New Zealand Closer Economic Relations Trade Agreement; EC—European Community; EFTA—European Free Trade Area; ASEAN—Association of South East Asian Nations; CACM—Central American Common Market; LAFTA/LAIA—Latin America Free Trade area/Latin American Integration Association; ECOWAS—Economics Community of West African States; PTA—Preferential Trade Area for Eastern and Southern Africa. [1]Integrational trade measured by share of intraregional exports in total exports. [2]Share of regional integration scheme in total world exports. [3]It is more a cultural and less an economic association; preferential trading among countries is minimal. [4]LAFTA was founded in 1960, but renewed as LAIA in 1980.
Source: Finance and Development, December 1992.

Table 20.4(a) Total gross reported foreign exchange turnover involving selected currencies on one side of transactions: daily averages

Currency	April 1989		April 1992			Change in share of gross turnover[1,2] 1989–92 percentage points
	Daily turnover in $US billion	Percentage share	Daily turnover in $US billion	Percentage share	Percentage share on a comparable basis[1,2]	
US dollar	838	90	1,114	82	83	−7
Deutschmark	247[2]	27[2]	544	40	38	11
Yen	253	27	313	23	24	−3
Pound sterling	138	15	185	14	14	−1
Swiss franc	n/a	n/a	116	9	9	n/a
French franc	n/a	n/a	51	4	4	n/a
Canadian dollar	n/a	n/a	44	3	3	n/a
ECU	8	1	40	3	3	2
Australian dollar	n/a	n/a	32	2	2	n/a
All other[3]	380	40	269	20	19	n/a
All currencies[4]	1,864	200	2,707	200	200	n/a

Notes: [1]Relates only to the 21 countries reporting data in both 1989 and 1992. [2]Excluding domestic trading involving the Deutschmark in Germany. [3] Identified and non-identified currencies. [4] Because two currencies are involved in each transaction, the sum of transactions in individual currencies comes to twice total reported turnover.

The cost of such protection can be high. Britain had a very high level of unemployment at the time. Raising interest rates reduced aggregate demand and compounded the problem. In other words, defending an exchange rate can involve a level of interest rates inappropriate for a country's internal balance, imposing significant costs upon the economy.

The second objection to a fixed exchange system such as ERM is this. It can be argued that such a system does not reduce uncertainty very much at all. Sometimes currencies are clearly at a disequilibrium rate. Governments formally agree to alter the level at which the currency is fixed. This can be upwards – a revaluation, or downwards – a devaluation. In practice the ERM has almost always involved the governments of weaker currencies devaluing, rather than those with strong currencies revaluing. Furthermore, to the extent that exchange rates are fixed, interest rates will need to vary. This means that in large part the uncertainty is simply transferred from exchange rate variations to interest rate changes.

Table 20.4 (b) Reported foreign exchange market turnover in selected countries: daily averages

| Country | April 1992 | | | | Change in share 1989 - 92: percentage points[4] | |
	Gross turnover[1] ($US billion)	Percentage share[3]	Net-gross turnover[2] ($US billion)	Percentage share[3]	Gross[1]	Net[2]
United Kingdom	369	27 (29)	300	27 (29)	3	3
United States	241	18 (19)	192	17 (18)	-	1
Japan	157	12 (12)	126	11 (12)	−3	−3
Singapore	87	6 (7)	76	7 (7)	-	-
Switzerland	79	6 (6)	68	6 (6)	−1	−1
Hong Kong	73	5 (6)	61	5 (6)	−1	−1
Germany	63	5 (n/a)	57	5 (n/a)	n/a	n/a
France	41	3 (3)	36	3 (3)	-	-
Australia	35	3 (3)	30	3 (3)	−1	−1
All others	208	15 (14)	185	16 (15)	2	2

Notes: [1]Gross of both local and cross-border double-counting. [2]Net of local double-counting; no adjustment for cross-border double-counting. [3] Figures in Brackets show the share of the country's turnover in the total for the 21 countries reporting in both 1989 and 1992. [4]Computed using total turnover in the 21 countries reporting turnover in both 1989 and 1992.
Percentages may not sum to 100 because of rounding.
Source: BIS *Annual Report* 1993.

Even without the increase in the number of interest rate changes, it could be argued that the possibility of larger infrequent exchange rate adjustments involve no less uncertainty. They cause as much uncertainty as smaller more frequent adjustments where markets are free to alter exchange rates without government intervention. If this is the case, a fixed exchange system can impose more costs on an economy than benefits.

b The desire to reduce speculation

See pp 35–6

A further motive for fixing an exchange rate is the desire to reduce speculation. Recall that when in Chapter 2 we considered supply and demand curves in relation to the stock market, we saw that speculation in shares could cause changes in prices. We saw too that such speculative forces could either stabilise or

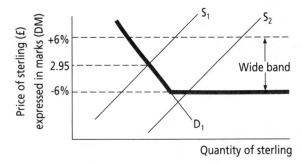

Figure 20.3 Using reserves as an anti-speculative device

destabilise a share price. The same argument can be applied to currency dealings. A currency can change in value not because of its underlying balance-of-payments position but because of speculative pressures.

Some idea of the possible size of such pressures can be gauged from Table 20.4. All transactions in currency markets are speculative to some extent. A trader may buy raw materials from abroad and stockpile it because he thinks this country's currency will fall. He is speculating even though he is engaging in trade. However, the volume of transactions in the foreign exchange markets is hugely greater than that required for the payment of goods and services.

Notice the particularly large turnover in Table 20.4(a) in sterling. The high turnover of currencies in the UK shown in Table 20.4(b) is a huge revenue earner for Britain. However, the high turnover of sterling makes the British economy particularly susceptible to speculative pressures.

The Bank for International Settlements believes that increases in turnover of currencies in recent years are much greater than the increase in trade. In other words, there is a growing proportion of currency transactions which are essentially speculative.

When governments agree to fix exchange rates between themselves, they commit themselves not only to use interest rate policy to defend these values but to use their reserves of currency to fight speculative pressures. Figure 20.3 depicts what this involves. We can use the diagram to see how speculation forced Britain to leave the ERM. In 1992 it was widely believed that sterling was overvalued. Speculators believed it would have to be devalued. If they were correct, profits could be made by selling sterling when its value was high and buying it back after devaluation had made it cheaper. Speculation moved the supply curve from S_1 to S_2. Since the government was committed to a minimum rate of around 2.78DM to the pound sterling, it was forced to act. We have seen that interest rates are a possible weapon. Government dealings in the foreign exchange market are another. The government used its reserves of foreign currency plus borrowings of foreign currency from overseas central banks, notably Germany. It used these

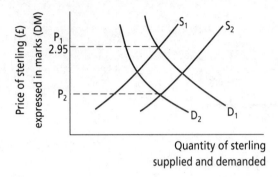

Figure 20.4 The balance of payments and a floating currency

reserves to prevent a fall in the sterling exchange rate below its 'floor'. In Britain's case, the floor was 6 per cent below its central rate.

Effectively it changed the demand curve for sterling to that depicted by the thick line in Figure 20.3. If sterling reached its floor of 2.78DM it had to demand whatever sterling was necessary to stabilise the rate at that level. At that exchange rate the demand for sterling must be infinitely elastic.

The reason for government failure and departure from ERM is plain. It did not have sufficiently large reserves of currency on which to call. Speculative pressures were too great. This was not an isolated event. During the summer of 1993 speculative pressures on several ERM currencies, notably the French franc, forced a major rethink on its members. Bands for most currencies in the system were widened to +/− 15%, effectively devaluing some currencies. Unfortunately, to the extent that bands are widened, the advantages of a fixed system are lost.

It is not always the case that speculative pressure will be irresistible, particularly in the short run. Speculative pressure on the franc was successfully resisted for much of 1993. Nevertheless, not everyone is convinced that it makes sense to fix exchange rates in order to avoid speculative pressures on currencies.

c The desire to defeat inflation

See pp 290–309

Sometimes governments believe that fixed exchange rates are an anti-inflationary weapon. In Chapter 15 we considered the extent to which inflation constitutes a problem, concentrating primarily upon the question of the economy's internal balance, especially the relationship of inflation to unemployment. Now we can extend our thinking to the international economy. In particular we shall consider three possible opinions of a link between a fixed exchange rate system, such as the ERM, and the level of inflation.

The first opinion takes a relaxed view of inflation. This says that there is an adequate mechanism for seeing to it that a faster inflation rate in, say, Britain, does not lead to a long-run balance-of-payments problem. That mechanism is the exchange rate. Figure 20.4 shows the process in operation. We begin with the

Table 20.5 Average money market interest rates, Germany and the UK, 1982–92.

Year	Germany	UK	Implied interest rate 'risk premium'
1982	8.8	12.3	3.5
1983	5.8	10.1	4.3
1984	6.0	10.0	4.0
1985	5.4	12.2	6.8
1986	4.6	10.9	6.3
1987	4.0	9.7	5.7
1988	4.3	10.3	6.0
1989	7.0	13.9	6.9
1990	8.4	14.7	6.3
1991	9.1	11.5	2.4
1992	8.6	9.6	1.0

Source: Calculated from data in International Financial Statistics.

market for sterling showing an exchange rate of £1 = 2.95DM (P_1). If the British inflation rate is faster than in Germany, then over time British people will increase their demand for foreign currency to purchase the now relatively cheaper German imports. To purchase this foreign exchange the supply of sterling increases S_1 shifts to S_2. Since Germans are switching out of relatively expensive British goods they supply the foreign exchange market with fewer Deutschmarks, reducing demand for sterling. The effect is to make the Deutschmark more expensive, and sterling cheaper, with a new equilibrium at P_2. The result is to make British exports competitive again, thus stimulating British exports and choking off the demand for imports. On this view the British balance-of-payments problem of the late 1980s and 1990s is attributable to an overvalued currency. This is either because of a *formal* fixed exchange rate preventing the mechanism operating, or an *informal* one where for some time the government informally fixed the pound at an overvalued rate with excessively high interest rates.[1]

However, there is an objection to this view, held by some, including members of the British government, at the time of ERM entry. It says that the above reasoning is specious. Solving a balance-of-payments problem via a depreciating exchange rate will not work because the process is self-defeating. Higher import prices feed through into a higher retail price index (RPI). This causes increased wage demands leading to an inflationary spiral and further downward pressure on the exchange rate. It will also not work because of expectations. Once an economy has a reputation for solving its inflation problem by allowing the depreciation of its

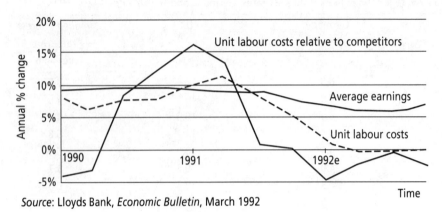

Source: Lloyds Bank, *Economic Bulletin*, March 1992

Figure 20.5 British competitiveness during ERM membership

currency, foreigners will be unwilling to hold it. This creates a further downward pressure on the currency. As a result a fixed exchange rate is preferable.

An alternative way to express the argument is to say that currencies susceptible to periodic depreciation will require higher interest rates to compensate for the added risk of holding them. Such risk premia will impose costs on the domestic economy, notably in discouraging investment.

Table 20.5 indicates that the UK has had consistently to hold its interest rate levels above Germany's in order to give its currency holders a risk premium. Yet these figures understate the problem. The risk premium has not been large enough to prevent a substantial depreciation of sterling against the Deutschmark over this period. To have maintained the value of sterling against the mark would have required an even larger risk premium.

Let us now examine a second view about the relationship between inflation and fixed exchange rates. It says that an exchange rate mechanism such as the ERM can help defeat inflation by tying a country's inflation rate to the lowest inflation rate of the ERM's members. This has tended, in postwar European history, to be Germany.

The argument is as follows. If a country, say Britain, inflates faster than Germany while in the ERM, the temporary effect is, as described in the diagram above, a downward pressure on the exchange rate. Since the ERM commits us to a fixed sterling exchange rate, policy measures will be forced on the government to prevent that inflation continuing. These measures can include a number of possibilities discussed in earlier chapters. Now, when trade unions ask for wage increases, and exchange rates are flexible, employers are inclined to give in to such wage demands. Although it adds to wage costs, employers believe it will not price them out of export markets, since higher prices simply result in a fall in the exchange rate.

A fixed exchange system, however, is an announcement to firms by government that inflationary wage increases will not be validated by a fall in the exchange rate. In this way an ERM-type system can 'stiffen the sinews' of employers to resist inflationary wage demands.

During the period of nearly two years in which Britain was a member of ERM, there was indeed a substantial effect on the wage bargaining process. Britain's membership lasted from October 1990 to September 1992. During that period output per worker rose faster than wage rates. Figure 20.5 shows average earnings increasing at between 5 and 10 per cent per year. However, unit labour costs improved substantially, because output per worker was rising even faster. Figure 20.5 also shows that unit labour costs in Britain improved relative to its competitors during the period of ERM membership. Recall, however, from Chapter 19 that over the period of the 1980s and early 1990s as a whole unit labour costs worsened by comparison with some major competitors.

See p 387

What is open to debate is whether the ERM was responsible for this or whether it was the effect of rising unemployment – a situation that could have been created outside the ERM.

There is a third view about the relationship between inflation and exchange rates. It is a view held by some monetarists. It suggests that if governments fix the money supply and we have a fixed exchange rate, balance-of-payments equilibrium will result in the long run. Let us see how the argument goes.

Assume a fixed money supply and a balance-of-payments deficit. A deficit implies that there is a reduction in the money supply circulating in the domestic economy as some part of that money supply leaves the country for the foreign exchange market. Recall from Chapter 18 that given monetarist assumptions a decline in the money supply (M) will cause a fall in the price level (P). As the price level falls, imports become dearer, exports become cheaper. As a result balance-of-payments equilibrium is restored. Fixing the money supply, then, not only achieves long-run internal balance in the monetarist view, but it achieves external balance also.[2]

See pp 359–61

In the late 1980s an important part of British economic policy was to make sterling shadow the value of the Deutschmark, even though sterling was not then a member of the ERM. The motive was essentially monetarist. Control of the domestic money supply was proving difficult. Control of the external value of sterling was not simple either. It implied high interest rates at times, since it was interest rates that were used to maintain sterling's parity. On the other hand, one could readily see whether the aim was being achieved. In essence, then, targeting the exchange rate was an indirect way of controlling the money supply.

Whatever the desirability or otherwise of the ERM it seems here to stay in some form, although its membership may change and the precise way in which it operates may continue to alter. What is still possible is that the ERM may yet evolve into a fully fledged monetary union between some of its members. It is to the costs and benefits of such monetary union that we now turn.

4 European monetary union

Some members of the EU are actively pursuing a goal of monetary union. The timetable is unclear but the turn of the century is a date to which some aspire. Others, including many in Britain, are sceptical. This is the matter we shall now examine, identifying three areas of potential economic benefit and two areas of potential economic cost.

a Potential benefit one: eliminating transaction costs

The most obvious benefit of monetary union is the elimination of costs involved in transacting business with different currencies. We saw in Table 20.1 that there are substantial costs for tourists changing currency areas. There are considerable costs for businesses also, which could be eliminated. An alternative way of making the same point would be to say that it would free up considerable resources currently engaged in exchanging currencies, enabling them to produce output that would have a greater value to society.

b Potential benefit two: increased economic efficiency

See pp 377–83

When in Chapter 19 we examined the basis for international trade we saw the Law of Comparative Advantage operate under restrictive conditions. The presence, for example, of import taxes, or any indirect taxes, distorts the relationship between price and opportunity cost. Thus the logic of Europe's 'Single Market' is that trade barriers by way of import taxes should be removed. This has been a feature of EU intra-trade for some years. Indirect tax rates are, however, still not harmonised.

A further step to removing distortions in trade is the adoption of a single currency. The absence of monetary union creates distortion by discouraging producers from engaging in international trade. As we have seen this can be because of the uncertainty inherent in free exchange rates. Even fixed exchange rates cannot eliminate this fear since the fixing is not irrevocable. The pound sterling, the peseta and the lira, among others, have all been devalued while in the system. Discouragement to trade can also happen because of the transactions costs to which we referred above.

It can be argued, therefore, that at present, resources move too much towards sectors isolated from international competition and away from goods such as manufactures that are relatively easily traded. One possible indicator of this can be found in Table 20.6.

Since inflation rates are higher in the non-traded sector for all countries, it would suggest that there is less pressure to use resources optimally here. It is easier simply to increase prices. Eliminating exchange rates would not make it possible for all goods and services to enter into international trade. Not many people will fly from Paris to Milan for a haircut! However, the removal of separate currencies should increase the ease of trading in some products.

Table 20.6 Difference in inflation trends in the non-trading and traded goods sectors (a)

Country	1990	1991	1992 (b)	Percentage points Average 1982–86	Average 1987–91	Memorandum items: per cent Inflation in the non-traded goods sector 1992(b)	Inflation in the traded goods sector 1992(b)
Belgium	0.6	1.4	1.8	-0.7	0.1	4.2	2.4
Denmark	-0.1	1.4	3.3	0.9	1.3	3.5	0.2
West Germany	0.7	0.6	2.8	1.6	1.2	5.5	2.7
Greece	3.6	5.0	4.5	0.3	5.5	19.2	14.7
Spain	6.8	7.5	4.3	0.3	5.3	8.8	4.5
France	3.4	1.9	2.9	1.0	3.3	4.5	1.6
Ireland	2.0	1.5	1.4	2.8	1.5	3.9	2.5
Italy	5.4	4.9	4.7	4.5	4.2	7.5	2.8
Netherlands	1.5	2.6	1.5	1.4	1.5	4.1	2.6
Portugal	10.1	7.1	3.8	1.1	3.3	11.2	7.4
United Kingdom	1.6	3.4	3.5	1.4	2.0	7.3	3.8
EEC Average	3.1	3.2	3.4	1.8	2.8	6.6	3.2
EEC Dispersion (c)	2.3	2.1	0.9	1.4	1.5	2.4	1.9

Notes: (a) National proxies supplied by central banks. As proxies differ, cross-country comparisons and the aggregate estimate for the Community should be interpreted cautiously. For Luxembourg, no data are available. (b) Partly estimated. (c) Weighted standard deviation.
Source: BIS, Annual Report, 1993.

c Potential benefit three: the removal of a balance-of-payments constraint

We have already seen what a concern to an economy the balance-of-payments account can be. An economy can have an unemployment problem that suggests an expansionist macro-economic policy, but a balance-of-payments deficit that makes governments fear to stimulate demand for fear of worsening the deficit. Some portion of rising demand will leak into imports, while a reduction in demand will be reflected in a reduced quantity of imports.

Figure 20.6 illustrates an import schedule. It shows imports as a function of national income. The ratio of imports to income is called the average propensity to import. On the other hand, the change in imports associated with a change in income is called the marginal propensity to import. It shows the extent to which increased prosperity is reflected in increased imports.

This relationship is not necessarily proportional because during boom periods, short-term domestic supply constraints may cause a particularly sharp increase in

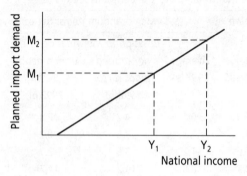

Figure 20.6 Imports as a function of income

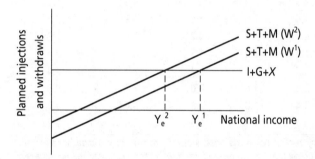

Figure 20.7 Effects of an increase in autonomous import demand

imports. Yet even during a period of high unemployment national income may grow, causing import demand to rise.

The UK has an exceptionally high tendency to devote rises in national income to imports, especially to manufactured imports. When national income moves from Y_1 to Y_2, the increase in imports from M_1 to M_2 is considerable. In other words, the British income elasticity of demand for imports is higher than that of many other countries. This problem is made worse if exchange rates are liable to be adjusted downwards to stimulate export demand.

Now monetary union appears to eliminate this problem entirely! There would be no balance-of-payments accounts for countries with a common currency. Talk of balance-of-payments deficit with, say Germany, would be as meaningless as talk of a deficit between Hampshire and Surrey. A great constraint upon government policy would be removed through entry into monetary union.

While there is some truth in this assertion, things are not quite so straightforward as we can see from Figure 20.7. You will recall from Chapter 13 that in equilibrium injections into the circular flow of income will be equal to

See pp 255–60

withdrawals from it. $S + T + M = I + G + X$. This is plotted in Figure 20.7. Suppose now a country's citizens show an increased preference for imports. We assume that the increase in import demand is not a function of increased income in this case, simply a change in tastes. The additional leakage out of the circular flow shifts the withdrawals function upwards from W^1 to W^2 in the diagram. The reduction in aggregate demand lowers income through a multiplier effect from Ye^1 to Ye^2.

So an absence of balance-of-payments data will not mean that the problem does not exist. It will appear in a different form. Since a correction cannot be made by an exchange rate adjustment, the problem will surface as a regional problem. National income will be too low in such areas. This is well recognised in Europe. As we saw in Chapter 5 there is much concentration on regional issues because of closer European integration. This is likely to increase significantly if the advent of monetary union becomes a reality.

See pp 103–6

d Potential cost one: loss of monetary sovereignty

The most obvious cost of monetary union is that each country which joins it must concede its sovereignty over monetary policy to a central monetary authority. One cannot have each county in England issuing its own money supply! In a European monetary union each country would be like a county in England. We have seen that one way of exercising monetary control is through exchange rate policy. That possibility will also disappear. There are no separate exchange rates to adjust.

The loss of monetary control will also imply considerable constraints on fiscal policy too. As we saw in Chapter 18, fiscal deficits have implications for the money supply or interest rates or both.

Clearly the extent of this loss is a highly contentious one. We argued in Chapter 18 that some would prefer an authority independent of political influence to be responsible for monetary policy. An independent central bank for Britain would need control over domestic monetary policy and the conduct of exchange rate policy. But in a monetary union there cannot be a British central bank at all. It must be a European one.

See pp 363–4

So loss of monetary sovereignty is a real cost. As we saw in Chapter 18, it depends upon one's views with respect to macro-economic policy-making as to whether it matters very much.

e Potential cost two: short-term adjustment costs

If a strong economy is to form a monetary union with a weaker one, there will be difficulties for the weaker one. If the weaker country's budgetary position is weak, in that there is a high PSBR or large national debt, its monetary growth is likely to be excessive. On the other hand, if interest rates are much higher, currency flows will be high, as we saw earlier in the chapter. This, too, will have implications for

Table 20.7 Convergence indicators for EU countries, January 1993

Interest rates	Inflation	PSBR	National debt	Exchange rates (Aug. 1993)
France	UK	Luxembourg	Luxembourg	Germany
Belgium	France	Ireland	France	Netherlands
Netherlands	Belgium	Denmark	Germany	
Ireland	Denmark	France	Spain	
Germany	Netherlands		UK	
Denmark	Luxembourg			
Luxembourg	Germany			
	Ireland			

the money supply. But if its monetary growth is excessive, it is likely to have a problem with inflation. If there are inflationary pressures in the weaker economy, it cannot adjust inside the monetary union via exchange rate depreciation. Therefore countries who wish to achieve monetary union will need to see their economies converging in terms of the key macro-economic variables.

In the light of these factors the only countries who will be qualified for entry into full monetary union are those who, European heads of government are agreed, meet the following convergence criteria.

1 *Inflation performance.* Inflation should be not more than 1.5 per cent above the average of the 'best' three countries' performance.
2 *Government debt.* The national debt should not be more than 60 per cent of GDP.[3]
3 *Government borrowing.* The PSBR should not be more than 3 per cent of GDP.
4 *Exchange rates.* A country should have been in the ERM and its exchange rate should have stayed within the narrow band of the ERM for a minimum of two years.
5 *Interest rates.* Interest rates, the rate on long-term government debt should be not more than 2 per cent above the 'best' three countries' performance.

These conditions were formally agreed in the Maastricht Treaty of February 1992. Some idea of how far away from these criteria the EU was by the end of that year is given in Table 20.7. We have seen in earlier chapters the pain that can be involved in adjusting macro-economic performance in these areas. France succeeded in meeting all the Maastricht conditions, although the tight monetary policy it used inflicted high costs in terms of unemployment. However, by the summer of 1993 the worsening recession in Europe meant that no country met all the conditions and many met none. By August of that year only the German mark and the Dutch guilder were left in the narrow band of the exchange rate mechanism.

5 Conclusion

It is impossible for a country such as Britain to isolate itself from international trade. The Law of Comparative Advantage leaves us in no doubt that Britain would be far poorer without such trade. However, there is great debate about how it conducts policy towards trade in general and its exchange rate in particular. In this chapter we have concentrated on exchange rate policy. What are the major options available to Britain?

At present Britain is not part of an exchange rate mechanism, although it is committed to free trade in Europe as part of the Single European Market. It could remain so, either allowing its exchange rate to float or attempting to tie it informally to what has been the strongest EU country, the Deutschmark.

Alternatively, it could rejoin the ERM which it left in October 1992. As part of a fixed exchange system it may be able to obtain some benefit, although there is less fixity in the system than there was. Inflation rates fell considerably during the period of UK membership, but there were substantial costs that became too high to pay.

If Britain rejoins the ERM it might have to face, at some stage, the decision to abandon sterling altogether for a monetary union, although this seems a long way off at present. It is extremely difficult to compare the costs and benefits of such a decision, although it has enormous implications, social, political and economic.

6 Questions for discussion

1 In Figure 20.3 we showed how the British government might use reserves as an anti-speculative device. We did it by describing a market for sterling in Deutschmark terms and assumed that the speculative pressure came from the sale of sterling. Sketch the same process by constructing a diagram showing the market for Deutschmarks in sterling terms.
2 We considered in Chapter 14 the Bank of England model's figures for the effect of an interest rate increase of 1% on the economy. The figures quoted were assuming that exchange rates were fixed. Table 20.8 below

See pp 281–2

Table 20.8 Bank model simulation: All interest rates + 1% point

	Exchange rate, fixed				Exchange rate, free
	1	4	8	12	12
Retail price index	0.4	0.3	0.2	—	-0.7
Current account (£ billions)	—	0.6	1.5	2.0	1.9

Note: Percentage differences from base, except where stated, after specified quarter
Source: Bank of England Quarterly Bulletin, (1990), Vol. 30, No. 2, May.

reproduces some data from the model but also estimates interest rate effects assuming exchange rates are free to float. Comment on the different predicted effects under floating exchange rates.

3 As we saw in the chapter, the nature of the ERM altered in the summer of 1993. To relieve speculative pressure on European currencies there was a substantial widening of the bands within which currencies were permitted to fluctuate. Was this decision in the interests of the ERM?

4 Table 20.2 showed how much of the EU's trade is with its European partners. Much the same thing can be said of other trading blocs. To what extent is this a good thing?

5 Should sterling float, be in the ERM or be abandoned for a European currency union?

7 Further reading

Exchange rate determination
Sloman, pp. 965–92; pp. 998–1016; Begg, pp. 595–606; Parkin and King, pp. 746–68

The European exchange rate mechanism
Sloman, pp. 1017–33; Begg, pp. 607–10, pp. 616–21; Parkin and King, pp. 768–71

Giving up sterling: too high a price to pay?
K. Habermeier and H. Ungerer (1992) 'A single currency for the European Community', *Finance and Development*, September.
G. Pugh and D. Carr (1993) 'The monetary consequences of German reunification', *Economics and Business Education*, Autumn.

8 End notes

1 As we have seen before, the assumption is that markets adjust easily, quickly and correctly to eliminate disequilibrium.

2 Of course, a fixed exchange rate without a fixed money supply can be inflationary. Suppose sterling is tending to appreciate. The government prevents the rise of the pound by selling sterling. This, in and of itself, increases the money supply. There are more pounds in circulation. To prevent the effects of increased money supply, this will have to be 'sterilised'. The government will have to sell government debt to the value of its foreign exchange dealings, thereby preventing an increase in the supply of money.

3 National Debt and the PSBR are not the same thing. The PSBR is a flow. It represents the difference between government expenditure and government income in a given year. The national Debt is a stock. It represents the stock of all government debt accumulated over many years.

APPENDIX 1: A GUIDE TO SOURCES OF INFORMATION

Many students of economics spend so much of their study time reading the course textbooks, that they do not find time to consult other sources of information. This is understandable. It is also unfortunate. Data in textbooks inevitably becomes dated, so it is good to supplement the texts with information which is being constantly updated. There is a vast amount of such material.

The purpose of this appendix is to provide a list of the major sources of data and information which you will find useful at an introductory level. The list is not comprehensive. It simply points you to those sources which are most widely used and most readily available. These publications will be available at university and college libraries and at larger public libraries also. You can buy your own copies of some titles fairly cheaply. Some publications are free; others are quite expensive.

Annual Abstract of Statistics
This publication covers a wide range of social and economic variables. The data is generally annual observations. It is published once a year.

Bank of England Quarterly Bulletin
The data in this quarterly publication covers mainly financial and monetary topics. It also contains some good articles, not all of which are strictly limited to money and banking matters.

British Economy Survey
Published twice a year by Longmans, this small journal is excellent for keeping abreast of developments in all parts of the economy. Each edition contains fifteen to 20 short, four-page articles, some of which are referred to in the reading material at the end of some of the chapters in this book.

Economic Briefing
Available at four-monthly intervals from the Central Office of Information, this publication is designed and written with students in mind. The coverage of material is limited.

Economic Review

Published five times per year, this publication is aimed at students of economics. Less comprehensive than *British Economy Survey*, it has fewer but longer articles on topics of current economic interest.

Economic Trends

This is very valuable publication by the Central Statistical Office. It is published monthly and is therefore very up to date. A good range of data is published as well as some excellent articles on current economic issues.

Economics and Business Education

Formerly published under the title *Economics*, this is published by the Economics Association. Each of the four editions in the year contains just a few, but quite substantial articles, some of which are on economic topics, some on the teaching of economics and business.

The Economist

A weekly publication, *The Economist* is widely read in the business world. You will see it frequently appearing on news stands. It covers a wide range of stories on economics and political matters. A comprehensive source of economic news and analysis from all parts of the world.

Finance and Development

This is published quarterly by the International Monetary Fund and the World Bank, each contains about 10 articles on international issues. Particularly valuable for third world issues.

Lloyds Bank Economic Bulletin

This is published, free, monthly. It takes one topic of current economic interest and examines it in a way which is usually comprehensible for a first-year student. There is also a brief update on the international financial outlook.

National Income and Expenditure

This is known as the 'Blue Book'. It is published in September of each year, giving data on a wide range of economic topics, not only for the previous year, but for the last ten. It is very useful.

OECD Economic Outlook

This is published twice yearly. It provides data on a range of basic topics across all OECD countries.

Social Trends

This is an annual publication. As its name suggests, it covers much social data. If you are interested in wealth, income and its distribution, or in household spending patterns, it is very useful.

If you require data which you cannot find, the Government Statistical Service may well be able to help. It produces annually a publication called *Government Statistics: A brief guide to sources*. This will probably enable you to find any government published statistics you need. Failing that, consult the more comprehensive, but less frequently published, *Guide to Official Statistics*, which any reference library will hold.

APPENDIX 2: SOURCES OF INFORMATION ON SHARE PRICES

Markets work best in the presence of adequate information. If you are thinking of investing in some equities, what information is available for you so that you can make a rational decision? One source of information is company accounts. In order to have a full listing on the Stock Exchange, a company must produce fully audited accounts twice a year. This can be a valuable source of information about a company's prospects but an analysis of company accounts is beyond the scope of this appendix.

Another valuable source is the financial pages of the *Financial Times* which, among many other things, gives information about each company's shares at the close of share trading the previous day. It would be worth buying a copy so that you can see the information in print for yourself. Turn to the section of the *FT* called 'Companies and Markets'. Near the back you will find 'London Share Service'. Pick a company, perhaps one you know well like Marks and Spencer. You will need to know what general sector it is under, Electricity, Water, Engineering, or whatever. ICI, for example, is listed under 'Chemicals', Marks and Spencer under 'Retailers, general'. Once you have found the sector your choice will be listed with the others in that sector in alphabetical order. Provided you have not picked a Monday edition, you will find the following information.

Column 1

This gives the name of the company and sometimes a technical note about anything to which the *Financial Times* wishes to draw your attention.

Column 2 and 3

Column 2 gives the price at the end of trading on the previous day. This is the mid-price. We saw earlier that there is a spread of prices between what one can buy the stock for and a lower price at which one can sell. So a closing mid-price of, say, 210 pence might represent a closing 'bid' price of 213 pence and an 'offer' price of 207 pence. Column 3 gives the change in the mid-price on the previous day's close. The change can be quite substantial even in that short time. Demand may have shifted in response to some news which significantly affects the prospects of the stock. Possibly, it is simply that shares have gone 'ex dividend' that is, the people buying have just missed this year's dividend and will have to wait a long time for the next one. Hence demand will have fallen suddenly.

Columns 4 and 5
These tell you the highest and the lowest price at which your chosen share has traded in the last year or so. You can now look at the current price to see if this is near the top of its traded range, indicating that the market thinks the company is doing well, or may be its near the bottom, an indicator that market expectations for the company are not good. You can also see how volatile the market has been in the last year or so. You may be surprised at how much the value of your shares can rise and fall in a year.

Column 6
Column 6 is the column headed 'Market Cap £M'. This shows the stock market's valuation of the whole company at the close of dealings on that day. It is simply the number of shares issued multiplied by the market price of each share. It therefore shows the value placed by the market on the value of the whole company. This value is often substantially different from the valuation of the company's assets as shown in the company balance sheet.

Column 7
This is the gross 'yield' of the share. We take the dividend before tax paid multiplied by 100 and divided by the share price. Thus, if your chosen share had a 5 pence gross dividend payment and the share price was £1, the gross yield is (5p × 100)/100 pence = 5.

Remember what we said about risk. If the company is thought to be secure and relatively risk-free, the share price will be higher and the gross yield lower. Higher yields usually indicate riskier shares.

Column 8
This is the P/E, or price/earnings, ratio. It is worked out in the following way. The earnings of the company in the last year, net of taxation, are taken and expressed as a proportion of the share price. So if the company above had a net earnings per share of 25 pence and its share price was still 100 pence then 100/25 = a P/E ratio of 4. Clearly, therefore, all other things being equal, a high P/E ratio indicates a share highly valued by financial investors.

In the Monday edition of the *FT*, some of the above information is missing but several additional pieces are provided, the most important of which are as follows:

Column 3
The column headed WK %/ch'nge' gives the change in the mid-price of the share not in pence but in percentage terms which has taken place in the previous week's trading. Political or economic events can make these changes substantial.

Column 4
This column headed 'div net' gives the dividend paid in pence per share during the last year assuming tax deducted at the standard rate. Some companies may not

have been in a position to pay a dividend at all if their profits have been low or non-existent! Sometimes a company will pay a dividend out of reserves if it is confident that trading has been difficult but will pick up again soon.

Column 5

The proportion of net (after-tax) profits paid out in dividends can vary greatly between companies. So one might like to know how comfortably the company can afford to pay that level of dividend. The cover tells us how many times the dividend is covered by its net profits. So a cover of 2.7 says that its net profits would have paid out a dividend of 2.7 times as much if it had distributed all its net profits. All other things being equal, it is clearly good if a company's dividend is well covered. The company is then giving a return to shareholders and still retaining funds for future profitable use.

The other Monday columns refer to the timing of dividend pay-out by each company, the amount of dividend paid and a 'City Line' number. If you ring 0891 43 followed by the city line number, up-to-the-minute information can be provided on that particular share, although the cost of the call is not cheap.

The *Financial Times* also provides indications of the 'average' level of prices of shares. There are several different averages. The most commonly quoted one is the *Financial Times* Stock Exchange index of the leading 100 companies called the 'Footsie'. It is a 'weighted average' value of all the leading 100 companies' share prices. Unlike most indices, it is based on the number of 1000 – the base at the end of 1983. It now stands at well over 3000. On most days, the Footsie will only change by a small number, but unexpected changes in economic conditions might cause it to rise or fall by 30 or 40 points, or even more. For example, in August 1991 the Footsie fell over 100 points in one day. This occurred following the news of a coup against Mr Gorbachev in the Soviet Union. He had been the architect of the move towards a market economy, which we discussed in Chapter 1. The coup was intended to restore the country to a planned system. The Footsie recovered all of its losses within days when the coup was seen to have failed.

If you have a television with Cefax or Oracle, you can find what is happening to the Footsie every minute! Share prices for many companies are adjusted and given every hour or two. For fuller up-to-the-minute information you can go into a 'share shop' and see current prices of all companies changing even more rapidly.

What we have now looked at is only some of the main features of the British equity market. Information is available in the *Financial Times* and, indeed, on Cefax and Oracle, on the change in other indices for other countries, the best known of which are the 'Dow Jones' index in New York, the Nikkei in Tokyo and the Hang Seng in Hong Kong. There are also measures now of movements in the average of leading European stocks as the British equities market is seen more and more in the context of Europe as a whole.

APPENDIX 3: MEASURING THE DISTRIBUTION OF INCOME: THE GINI COEFFICIENT

It is possible to measure the unevenness of any distribution of income by the use of a *Gini* coefficient. The simplest formula for this is:

$$G = \frac{1}{N} \sum_{i=1}^{N} a(N - 2i + 1)$$

where N = number of income groups
a = proportion of total income received by a given group.

We shall illustrate its use by an example. Let us divide the population into five equal-sized groups (quintile groups). This is the form in which UK data is usually presented. Let us assume that income is perfectly evenly distributed. Here, $N = 5$, $a = 20$ (*for every group*) and i takes values from 1 to 5.

$$G = \frac{1}{N} \sum_{i=1}^{N} a(N - 2i + 1)$$

$$G = \frac{1}{5} \{20(5 - 2 + 1) +$$

$$20(5 - 4 + 1) +$$

$$20(5 - 6 + 1) +$$

$$20(5 - 8 + 1) +$$

$$20(5 - 10 + 1)\}$$

$$G = \frac{1}{5}(80 + 40 + 0 - 40 - 80) = 0$$

See pp 77–9

So $G = 0$. That is, income distribution is completely even across the groups. G is the area bounded by the line of absolute equality and the Lorenz Curve as a proportion of the triangle under the line of absolute equality. The line for the above figures follows the line of absolute equality. For any income data the value of G must, of course, be between 0 and 100. Those values closer to 0 indicate a more even spread of income; those nearer to 100 more uneven. A value of 0 indicates absolute equality. A value of 100 indicates absolute inequality. The Gini coefficient enables us to compare different income distributions even if two Lorenz curves cross as in Figure A.3.1, in that we are comparing the appropriate areas in each case.

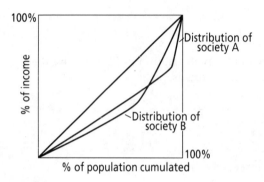

Figure A.3.1   Using a Gini coefficient to compare income distributions

The simple formula given above assumes that all households within a given group have the same (equivalised) income. The January 1994 edition of Economic Trends uses a rather more sophisticated form of calculation in which this assumption is dropped. The values for the Gini coefficient are then given as follows. For 1979, equivalised original income has a value of 44. Disposable income is 27. For 1992 the respective values are 52 and 34. Income is more usually distributed in 1992 than in 1979.

APPENDIX 4: THE DERIVATION OF THE DEMAND CURVE FOR LABOUR

Why do employers hire labour at all? The obvious answer is that labour services are required to produce an output which can be sold in the product market. If we assume that the aim of the employer is to maximise profits, the labour will only be demanded if the output can be sold at a profit. We often say that labour is a 'derived' demand. The demand for labour is derived from the demand for the output which that labour produces.

Let us now consider the relationship between costs and revenue in order to determine the quantity of labour which a firm will demand. The concept of profit maximisation focuses the analysis on marginal revenue and marginal cost, as we first saw in Chapter 6.

See pp 113–18

Recall that marginal revenue is the change in total revenue due to the sale of one more unit of output. In the context of labour demand the relevant concept is marginal revenue product. This is the amount of output produced by the last (marginal) employee multiplied by the marginal revenue received when that output is sold. In other words, we are discovering the value to the employer of the output which the additional worker produces. So the employer's decision about labour employment is determined partly in the product market, where the price of the output is set. However, it is also determined partly by the productivity of the marginal employee, and as more employees are taken on, the less will be produced by the marginal unit of labour. You may remember why this is so from Chapter 5.

In the short run, the law of diminishing returns will set in as the employer expands his workforce. That is, beyond some point, if an additional person is employed, he/she raises output, but by a smaller amount than the previously employed person. We showed that to be the case in Chapter 5 also.

See pp 94–7

Now let us assume for simplicity that the price of the output is fixed as far as the employer is concerned (that is, there is perfect competition in the product market, so that price equals marginal revenue). Then, beyond some point, as the firm employs additional labour, and the amount of additional output declines, what is happening to the value of that additional output? With marginal revenue constant, marginal revenue product must decrease as more labour is taken on.

The marginal cost we will assume to be equal to the wage that the employer must pay. So the employer will take on labour up to the point where the declining marginal product equals the wage rate. This is the amount of employment where the marginal cost to the employer is equal to the value of the marginal output. It therefore represents his profit maximising level of employment. Should the wage rate alter, the employer will alter the quantity of labour demanded. The marginal revenue product curve becomes the demand curve for labour, sloping from top left to bottom right as for most demand curves.

This derivation is based on simplifying assumptions. However, the conclusion about the shape of the demand curve for labour holds when the main assumptions are relaxed. For a more detailed treatment see, for example, Begg, pages 177–82.

APPENDIX 5: THE DETERMINATION OF THE MULTIPLIER

The purpose of this appendix is to demonstrate formally the determination of the multiplier introduced in Chapter 12.

See pp 261–3

Assume a closed economy (no international trade and no government sector). Thus in equilibrium $Y = C + I$ where

Y = aggregate output/income/expenditure
C = planned consumption
I = planned investment

i.e., output must be sufficient to meet demands from consumers and firms' plans to invest.

Assume further that planned investment is autonomous, that is independent of the level of income and consumption is some proportion of income, c.

Then

$$C = cY$$

Hence

$$Y = cY + I$$

$$Y(1 - c) = I$$

$$\frac{Y}{I} = \frac{1}{1 - c}$$

If this is true for levels of national income it will be true for changes also

$$\frac{\Delta Y}{\Delta I} = \frac{1}{1 - c}$$

Now $c + s = 1$ where s – proportion of incomes consumers wish to save – all income is by definition saved or spent.

Hence

$$\frac{\Delta Y}{\Delta I} = \frac{1}{s}$$

In an economy saving is not the only withdrawal from the circular flow of income. People pay a proportion of their additional income in taxes, t, and spend a proportion of their additional income on imports m. Then:

$$\frac{\Delta Y}{\Delta I} = \frac{1}{s+t+m} \quad \text{or} \quad \frac{1}{w}$$

where w = propensity to withdraw from the circular flow.

This is the multiplier. In terms of our example in Table 13.2

$$\frac{40}{20} = \frac{1}{0.5} = 2$$

Index

Note: references to figures and tables are given only when they appear separately from the relevant text and are indicated by italic page numbers

GDP, *104, 299*, 300
health, *82, 83, 84*
inflation, *290, 295, 298, 299, 307*, 348,
    349, 407
motorways, 50
unemployment, *104, 249, 307*
speculation
    and exchange rates, 400–2
    in stock market, 35–6
speculative demand for money, 353–4
sticky prices, 155
stock market, 23–41
    as perfect market, 39–41
    speculation, 35–6
    supply and demand, 24, 25–9, 37–9
stocks, 253–4
strikes, 219–20, 294, *295*
subsidies, 140–2
    for training, 123
substitutes, 30, 34, 39
substitution effect, 102–3, 319
sulphur dioxide emissions, 130–1, 134,
    137, 240, *241*
supply
    aggregate, 300–4
    and allocative efficiency, 196
    changes in, 32–3
    of coal, 131–2
    determinants of, 27
    effect of taxation, 135–7
    of foreign exchange, 391–2
    of health care, 67–70
    of labour, 216, *217*, 218–19, 319–20,
        322–3
    of loanable funds, 271–3
    of money, 352–3, 360–1, *363*, 364
    of road space, 44–5, 53–6
    of shares, 26–7, 32–3
    in stock market, 24, 25–9, 37–9
Sweden
    central bank, *367*
    GDP, 17, *299*
    health, *83, 84*
    inflation, *290, 295, 298, 299, 307*
    savings, *259*
    unemployment, *249, 307*
Switzerland
    central bank, *367*
    foreign exchange turnover, *399, 400*
    growth, *16, 299*, 300
    health, *83, 84*
    inflation, *290, 295, 298, 299, 307*
    unemployment, *249, 307*

takeovers, 29, 156–7
taxation, 311–17
    and externalities, 133, 135–7
    Gutmann effect, 326–7
    and incentives, 320–3
    international comparisons, 317
    Laffer Curve, 325–7
    progressive, 312–13
    and PSBR, 325–7, 361
    regressive, 313–14
    and small firms, 123
    and supply and demand, 135–7, 261,
        314–17
    and unemployment, 327–8
    see also corporation tax; income tax;
        value added tax
terms of trade, 380–1
Thatcher, Margaret, 280
thrift paradox, 255–60
time lags (demand management), 264–5
total variable cost, 97–8, 114
trade unions, 209–24
    as cartels, 213, 215–16, 218, 219
    effect on labour market, 221–4
    and inflation, 294
    and wage determination, 215–18,
        221–3
traffic jams *see* road congestion
training
    and short-termism, 285
    as social benefit, 133, 140, 286
    subsidies, 123
transaction costs, 40, 54, 58, 205, 392–3,
    406
transactions demand for money, 353, 357
transport
    safety records, *159*
    see also airline industry; road congestion
Turkey, *290*
TWA-Trans World Airlines, *152*, 163

uncertainty, 276–7, 280–1, 297–300,
    396–400
underwriting, 24
unemployment, 248–67
    classical approach, 251–2, 302–3,
        304–6, 315
    costs, 139, 147, 286
    demand-deficient, 251, 260–7
    in Eastern Europe, *8*
    effect of increased savings, 258–60
    in EU, 104
    frictional, 251, 327

Self-Testing Disk Available!

It is very important that you check whether you have properly understood the key concepts of Economics. To that end a self-testing disk is available from the address below. The disk has twenty 'chapters' corresponding to the twenty chapters of *Modern Applied Economics*. Each 'chapter' contains fifteen multiple choice questions covering the main ideas of the chapter you have studied.

This disk, already tested by introductory economics students, will serve a number of purposes. First, it will test your understanding of all the major concepts you have already met. Second, it will teach you things you have not grasped. If you get any wrong answers, the program will explain why you are wrong and give you an opportunity to correct your mistake. Third, it will familiarise you with this form of testing. This will be an invaluable asset since more and more examinations are using multiple choice techniques. It will probably give you a lot of fun too. Many students enjoy this kind of activity.

In order to run the disk you will need a computer. It must be an IBM PC compatible running DOS 2.0 or higher. A printer would be useful but not essential. You will not need any computing skills. Once you have loaded the disk, instructions as to how to use it are contained on the disk itself. If you have never used such a disk before you have nothing to fear and much to gain. A copy of the disk is available for your own use after July 1st, 1994 from the address below for *only £9.95*. A copy of the disk plus a site licence is also available to institutions for just £300. Your disk will normally be dispatched within ten days of receipt.

- -

Please fill in this form, tear off the slip and send with a cheque or postal order for £9.95 (or £300 for a disk plus site licence) to James A. Heather, Narnia, 2 Airlie Road, Winchester, Hants, SO22 4NQ. PLEASE PRINT CLEARLY.

Name   ....

Address   ....

....

....

Postcode   ....